CHARLES I

John Bowle

CHARLES I

Published by Sapere Books.

20 Windermere Drive, Leeds, England, LS17 7UZ, United Kingdom

saperebooks.com

Copyright © The Estate of John Bowle, 1975.
First published by Purnell Book Services Limited, 1975.
The Estate of John Bowle has asserted its right to be identified as the author of this work.
All rights reserved.

No part of this publication may be reproduced, stored in any retrieval system, or transmitted, in any form, or by any means, electronic, mechanical, photocopying, recording, or otherwise, without the prior written permission of the publishers.

ISBN: 978-1-80055-405-4.

IN MEMORIAM
RICARDI BOWLE

CHILIARCHI IN EXERCITU
REGIS CHAROLI PRIMI

TABLE OF CONTENTS

PREFACE	9
INTRODUCTION	12
BOOK I: THE PRINCE	24
1: DUKE OF ALBANY	25
2: DUKE OF YORK	41
3: HEIR APPARENT	57
4: PRINCE OF WALES	79
5: SPANISH ADVENTURE	98
6: THE FATAL LEGACY	116
BOOK II: THE MONARCH	129
7: THE ASCENDANCY OF BUCKINGHAM	130
8: CIVIL AND RELIGIOUS CONFRONTATION	155
9: PERSONAL RULE	181
10: INDIAN SUMMER	202
11: BELLUM EPISCOPALE	223
12: THE COLLAPSE OF AUTHORITY	246
BOOK III: THE POLITICIAN AND SOLDIER	270
13: THE DISMANTLING OF PREROGATIVE GOVERNMENT	271
14: PRELUDE TO WAR	292
15: THE STRATEGIC FAILURE	313
16: THE CAVALIER SUCCESS	334
17: THE SCOTS INTERVENE	352
18: THE DEFEAT OF THE ROYALISTS	369
BOOK IV: THE PRISONER	394
19: SCOTS, PARLIAMENT AND ARMY	395
20: CLOSING IN	418
21: THE FRAME-UP	439

22: THE KILL	457
AUTHOR'S NOTE	469
A NOTE TO THE READER	470

PREFACE

IN MY BIOGRAPHY of Henry VIII, to which this book is a sequel, I quoted G. M. Young's precept: 'Read until you can hear them talking.' This advice I have again tried to follow, and very different they now seem to be. For the seventeenth century saw the fulfilment of Tudor promise in a creativeness of English literature and language, decisive for the whole English-speaking world.

While the Tudor English are still in part medieval, the civilization of Jacobean and Caroline England is already part of our own, and one is startled by the modernity of insight and phrase — often superior to much of our contemporary idiom. There are dark areas of superstition and fear — astrological and religious — at a time when medicine was still, in spite of Harvey's then little-appreciated discoveries, primitive and misguided, hygiene rudimentary, plague a constant dread; but in spite of an intellectual climate more pessimistic and medieval than is generally realized, a new confidence is coming through, expressed with uninhibited vigour by a people still predominantly rural who drew their metaphors from nature and the seasons.

Charles I, an alien in his three realms, was not, like Henry VIII, representative of his people. His character is more elusive and complex, introvert and self-regarding, without the bull-headed Tudor force, cold realism and well-timed ruthless action. But, like Henry VIII, Charles was obstinate; if where Henry was an opportunist obstinate for his own interest, Charles was mournfully consistent under the eddy of often futile manoeuvre and deception that made him so inept a politician; and he proved himself in battle in a way Henry VIII never did. He was a highly educated connoisseur and pietist and, unlike Henry VIII, a good family man, chaste and uxorious to one consort. I have therefore tried to see his life in the proportion that he may himself have seen it, and I have not, as do many historians, allotted much extra space to the campaigns of the civil wars, which occupied only five years of it, but have allocated my chapters in due proportion of time.

I have also endeavoured not so much to analyse his setting as to recreate the mood and preoccupations of the time by juxtaposing representative episodes of contrasting colour and significance, sometimes of merely local concern in places that I happen to know best, and depicting them in detail; often a minor episode in a familiar setting will light up whole vistas with a flash. This method has its penalties; and in a book of this size peripheral subjects have had to be sacrificed. I have also devoted relatively little space to the present controversies that dominate historical research and are being argued out in depth, but I have tried to take account of their conclusions, sometimes hard to elicit. Impelled by the evidence as so interpreted, I have had to discard many still popular *idée reçues* of the great nineteenth-century Whig and Liberal historians from Macaulay to Firth and Gardiner, even to Trevelyan, while respecting their narrative power, and to revise the later but now obsolescent view of the mid-seventeenth-century crisis as a conflict between a 'feudal' order (which no longer exists) and a Protestant 'rising bourgeoisie'. These people now appear economically nothing new, but rather to have practised on a wider scale with wider horizons, but without breach of continuity, mercantilist policies long apparent in medieval times, in which many of the greatest supposedly 'feudal' magnates were still involved.

I hope therefore that this portrait of an unusual monarch and his age, based mainly on contemporary evidence as seen in the light of modern research, will bring these people and their setting alive. The narrative historian is not and cannot be a social scientist, but writes out of a sympathetic and justifiable spirit of enquiry, seeking from his time-travel to retrieve impressions so as to share them with others who may be impelled by a similar if less laborious curiosity, and to recall events and personalities fast receding into the past. These impressions must be framed by analysis, but predominantly I have endeavoured to recreate as best I can people as they were and events as they actually happened.

In writing this biography I have consulted many friends whose help I would like generally to acknowledge. I am particularly grateful to Mr Keith Thomas, Fellow of St John's College, Oxford for his advice, to Mr Quentin Davies for his criticism of the economic aspects of the book, and to Mr Kenneth Garlick of the Ashmolean Museum at Oxford for his help over the illustrations. My publisher, Mr Andrew Wheatcroft, has given wise counsel in the design, and Miss Jenny Ashby has taken much trouble in seeing the work through the press. I wish also to thank Mr E.V. Quinn, Librarian of Balliol College, and Mr Britton and Miss Auberton-Potter of the Codrington Library at All Souls. I have also to acknowledge various permissions kindly accorded for quotations cited in this book, and once more to thank Mrs Barbara Phillips for typing the script.

JOHN BOWLE

INTRODUCTION

THE ROYAL AESTHETES of England, and there have not been many, have none of them achieved political success. Henry III, who laid the foundation stone of Salisbury Cathedral and rebuilt Westminster Abbey, complained, 'It is dreadful to think of the debts in which I am involved... I am a mutilated and diminished king', and cried out in battle, 'I am Henry of Winchester, your King. Do not harm me!' He was in effect displaced by his able son, afterwards Edward I. Edward II, the first Prince of Wales, laughed at the Welsh, got bored with state business, coined disparaging nicknames for his magnates, 'made riot' with Piers Gaveston and paid for the velvets and jewels he had lavished on him out of the confiscated revenues of the Templars. He was done to death.

Richard II, who restored Westminster Hall and kept the most lavish Court in Europe, declared that the laws were in his own breast and struck down the Earl of Arundel with a stick when he was late for the Queen's funeral, had his uncle Gloucester garrotted and opened the coffin of his friend Robert de Vere to adorn the cold fingers with rings before reburial. He was pole-axed or starved. Henry VI, an amiable *dévot*, founded Eton and King's College, Cambridge, 'took no grete Rejoyce in pride', hopefully exhorted his scholars at Eton to 'be good boys, meek and docile' and 'preferred the Lyfe Contemplative'. He was driven insane, wounded in the neck at St Albans, captured at Barnet and murdered in the Tower.

George IV, who restored and refurbished Windsor, could be excellent company; he had an ear for music and an eye for architecture and pictures, but he was politically wrong-headed, addicted to gourmandizing, mistresses and cherry brandy, and died convinced that he had ridden a winner at Goodwood and commanded a division at Waterloo. If Westminster Abbey, Westminster Hall, Eton, King's and Windsor are all something for these monarchs to be remembered by, none of them had the resolution, political nous and sense of public image demanded by their position. They all lacked a sense of political reality; their lives have all become cautionary tales. But by far the most famous and the most tragic of the royal aesthetes is Charles I. He, too, lacked a sense of political reality, but he was much more reputable and distinguished than the others: high-minded, well-meaning, industrious for a seventeenth-century royalty, fond of his family, brave, dignified, deeply religious. Moreover he had the luck to be painted by Rubens and Van Dyck.

Yet Charles I's political incompetence led to major civil war, then to his public execution, an event that resounded through Europe. It was one thing, and nothing new, for a ruler to perish in the dynastic feuds of the Royal House, to be put down in Berkeley Castle or Pontefract or the Tower; but it was quite another for a king to be formally arraigned as a traitor and judicially murdered by his own subjects. A precedent had been set; followed when Louis XVI, the grandest monarch in Europe, went to the guillotine. For the 'trial' of Charles I coincided not just with a change of dynasty but with a brief republican revolution, which formally abolished monarchy itself. In fact the republican interregnum, which lasted only eleven years, proved to be an aberration in English history: the lasting revolution had already taken place in 1641-2 before the unnecessary and ruinous war and was in essentials maintained at the Restoration and completed in 1688.

Yet the execution of the King and the overthrow of the monarchy marked the most spectacular revolution of early modern times. Beginning when a Parliamentarian oligarchy in the Commons, in alliance with a minority of great peers, dismantled the Tudor conciliar government and thwarted the King's attempt at continental-style absolutism, the original moderate revolution as usual got out of hand. The army that won the war for Parliament then turned on its masters and established a military regime; at first under the Commonwealth in conjunction with the subservient 'Rump' of a purged House of Commons, then in 1653 under the Protectorate by the plain rule of the sword. It proved an efficient though detested regime, with a neo-Elizabethan foreign and colonial policy; and by abolishing feudal tenures and passing the Navigation Acts in the long run it promoted the agricultural and commercial wealth behind the even more momentous British Industrial Revolution, while it put down the radical attack on property and privilege that the rift in the ruling classes during the Civil Wars had occasioned.

But though it set precedents for America, France and Russia, the republican revolution failed. The Royalists came back and that they did so was considerably due to the steadfast dedication of the King, who to the end refused even to recognize the illegal tribunal who condemned him, considering them as 'rogues' with whom he would make no compromise, even to save his life.

The personality of Charles I dramatized this memorable event. Fastidious and remote in his private world of aesthetic sensibility and religious dedication, too much aloof to play the game of 'winning men by places' in the idiom of the day, or to take anyone save his wife fully into his confidence after the assassination of Buckingham, his only male intimate, he was devious and untrustworthy even to his own supporters. But Charles always retained his sense of divinely ordained mission as a royalty set apart by God, his Scots flair for legal argument and his sense of theatre. He had indulged the last for years over the court masques of Inigo Jones, and it combined with his high ability and courage at his 'trial' to create the legend of the royal martyr that made him politically more powerful dead than alive.

Moreover his sense of design extended to politics. He was not, as is often believed, a 'reactionary' clinging to outworn 'feudal' forms of government. Far from it: it was Charles I and his advisers during the 1630s, not Essex or Pym later on, who were the innovators, politically in tune with the new trends on the Continent. For Charles I, Strafford and Laud were attempting in their insular setting to realize a version of that grand design that Richelieu and Mazarin brought off in France for a centralized and more fully sovereign state.

Over most of Europe, from Spain to Sweden, the future appeared to be with a more rational and bureaucratic pattern of government, with the old medieval institutions and regionalism fading out. But in England Charles I could build only on the ramshackle structure of Jacobean administration. It is true that 'there was a coherent philosophy emerging in the policies of the early 1630s, and a genuine attempt to tackle and cope with the malaise of the Church', and that 'his personal rule was a genuine attempt at paternalism and effective government rather than a scramble for solvency';[1] but Charles's government was only precariously viable and solvent, depending for local order and taxation on the concurrence of the county magnates and gentry, the very people whose fortunes had often been founded when Henry VIII, instead of keeping the vast Church lands he had nationalized, had sold them off, and upon the rich oligarchies of the City of London and the other major towns. The King had not the regular taxation and army which it took Pym to design and Cromwell to impose. Charles I and his ministers were attempting the impossible; it was only during the Commonwealth and Protectorate that there emerged a more systematic and permanent bureaucracy, a regular standing army and an efficient fleet — in a word, the *Leviathan* of Thomas Hobbes.

Nineteenth-century historians believed that the opposition magnates in the Lords and the Parliament men in the Commons were forerunners of modern democratic government and so 'progressive'. In fact the great magnates in the Lords — Essex, Pembroke, Warwick and Bedford, for example — were the conservative 'reactionaries'; they wanted to break Tudor conciliar power and get back to the days of the *Magnum Concilium* when they and their kind had the preponderant and often disastrous voice. Pym and his followers in the Commons were also conservative, if in a different way; but they wanted to control the system not destroy it, and most of them were trained in the common law. Many civil lawyers supported the King, but the common lawyers harked back to medieval precedents and pedantically raked up medieval legislation in incongruous contexts. They cited the thirteenth-century lawyer, Bracton, to prove that the King ought to be under the law, and invoked a medieval commonwealth with no place for Bodin's newfangled sixteenth-century idea of *maiestas*, the absolute *sovereignty* of a ruler responsible only to God. It was the King who had a modern, if quite impracticable, grand design, and his inefficient attempts at centralization provoked conservative regional opposition.

For Charles I had a high and clear concept of kingship. It was to be the apex and regulator of hierarchy, itself part of the chain of being of a divinely ordered world. The monarch alone could command this equilibrium, giving every man his place and his rights; it was the monarch's duty to do so. So with complete sincerity he asserted at his trial, 'I know that I am pleading for the liberties of the people of England more than any of you... It is the liberties of the people of England that I stand for.'

In Great Britain this kind of centralized and would-be absolute monarchy never won through. Cromwell came near to it; but his usurped power rested on the sword, and when the reaction in 1660 brought back the old if diluted elites to greater influence, the key decisions of 1641-2 were conceded, the Crown was adapted first to a 'mixed' and then a 'constitutional' monarchy, reflecting the realities of political and economic power, part of an establishment that lasted into modern times.

This compromise, slowly arrived at or muddled through, then lay far in the future. Charles I himself remained entirely convinced that the king could never be a mere estate of the realm, but must be its head and sovereign; at most he conceded a poised hierarchy so that when, in 1642, he and his advisers (probably Falkland and Culpepper) drafted *His Majestie's answer to the XIX Propositions of Both Houses of Parliament* and cited what they termed 'the Ancient, happy, well-poised and never-enough-to-be-commended constitution of this Kingdom', the King himself certainly assumed that it must be dominated by the Crown.[2] His view of society, as that of most of his contemporaries, was hierarchical: for the Levellers and Diggers were peripheral and, save for the brief influence of the former in the army, then far less important than modern historians have retrospectively imagined. The Crown was the apex of a conservative and time-honoured order, and the more representative clubmen of Wiltshire, Dorset and Somerset who in 1645 tried to stop the war in their neighbourhoods, though they wanted to get rid of the armies of both combatants, were more on the side of the King than of Parliament. Naturally Charles and his advisers — or for that matter Oliver Cromwell — did not believe in a 'democratic experiment'; following Aristotle, in whose writings many of them were grounded, they thought that 'democracy' — then a pejorative word — would end in tyranny. The King's objective was to make the existing order more efficient: only in this was he an innovator.

The most lasting of Charles I's innovations were those then most resented. The Elizabethan Church was austerely Calvinistic; more akin to the official Dutch Church today; with the pulpit, not the altar, the centre of attention; the ministers wearing black gowns, not surplices; and the old Catholic ritual and colour discountenanced. Moreover after the Reformation the wealth and prestige of the clergy had been greatly set back and the status of their wives had long remained anomalous; as when Elizabeth I (who retained the old ritual in her private chapel) remarked to the helpmeet of Dr Parker of Canterbury, 'Madam I may not call you, and Mistress I am ashamed to call you, so I know not what to call you, but yet I do thank you.'[3] The dilapidation of most of the cathedrals and churches and the drabness of the ritual would now appear deplorable, and the overall poverty of the Church was such that to maintain any sort of position the leading clergy had to hold several livings at once, then and since earning some misplaced disapproval.

Charles I and Laud changed most of this: they altered the face of the Church of England; and, although the restored Anglican Church was not Laudian, but rather Erasmian, it is much due to them that it has since been distinguished by its own particular ambience, combining some of the colour of the Catholic ritual with much homely, insular feeling, as in the choirs of its great cathedrals and the cheerful cadence of its bells, while managing in the universities to blend with the changing development of secular thought and even pragmatically to evade the anti-clericalism provoked by more dogmatic and awesome versions of Christianity. And if after the Restoration the Church became more worldly and Latitudinarian, the eighteenth-century Church led by reaction to the ritualistic revival in the nineteenth. Charles I and Laud made this future possible and they died for it.

Charles was also an innovator in the arts. He was a connoisseur of pictures and architecture and of the northern Renaissance culture of which his Court was then the most elaborate expression; he was the patron of Rubens and Van Dyck and the greatest art collector in Europe. The gaudy rough and tumble of the Jacobean Court was superseded by more dignified conventions, its ornate building by the neo-classical Italianate style then becoming prevalent on the Continent, and its florid fashions by an elegance and understatement in dress that was the reverse of Elizabethan bravura. Certain great magnates, such as Pembroke and Arundel, giving up what Aubrey called the 'Old Mastif' way of the Tudor milords, might share the King's cosmopolitan artistic taste and collector's flair and employ fashionable foreign artists; but most of the nobility and gentry, if now more polite, were still content with the flat likenesses of Tudor times and far more interested in hunting, to which Charles like his father was also passionately addicted. For Charles I was no hot-house aesthete: he was a hardy outdoor man, an excellent shot, good at tennis, a fine horseman who could manage the 'great horse', who loved Newmarket and conscientiously practised the Scottish game of golf. Moreover in his early years as king his foreign policy was aggressively martial and he showed bravery, physical endurance and considerable generalship during the first Civil War.

The exotic Court culture was considered by many of the articulate English and Scots to be precious, alien and expensive. The philistine puritanical strain, so strong in both nations and already strident in England with the Lollards under Richard II, had been greatly encouraged by Calvinism, and when the King married a Catholic daughter of France the deep-rooted fear and distrust of Catholic foreigners was naturally exacerbated. The English were now confronted with a monarch who was not merely politically aloof and unapproachable, without that common touch and magnetism that had endeared Henry VIII and Elizabeth I to their subjects, but with one whose interests were in art and, what was worse, in the drama and masques, long the target of Puritan denunciation.

Charles I was a small man; 5 foot, 4 inches in height, who always retained a trace of the Scots accent so apparent in his father; and he stammered — a particularly severe affliction for a king. His personality was an elaborate artifact, deliberately built to meet the demands of his position. In the blaze of publicity in which he had to live, he schooled himself to an aloof dignity. 'He had a quicker perception and did sooner understand a case than any of the Privy Council',[4] and he would have made a good lawyer; at his 'trial' his conduct of his own defence was masterly, for 'he stammered nothing at all but spoke very distinctly with much courage and magnanimity'. In 1631 the Spanish envoy Carlos Coloma, instructing his successor, wrote of him that he gave audience easily, though he disliked business, listened with attention and answered to the point. He understood Spanish and 'it would be a very good thing if you could get him to admit this, so as to avoid the tedium and lack of secrecy of interpretations'.[5]

Charles was neither a wise statesman nor a clever politician, so that he was baffled by men of meaner capacities; but in his dedicated way he had a redoubtably obstinate will as well as a surprising streak of optimism. '*Dum Spiro, Spero* (while I live I hope)' he wrote in his clear Renaissance hand in his copy of the works of Shakespeare, now in the Royal Library at Windsor. This optimism led him to overestimate his power; yet his self-confidence was not the extrovert tenacity of a Henry VIII nor the conscious brilliance of Elizabeth I; it was contrived and fortified by a steadfast personal religion, which made him think of himself as set apart and called by his God to the high duty of kingship by divine right. He took himself and his great office with high seriousness and without humour; unlike his florid old father, he was 'sober in apparel, clean and neat' — not 'gaudy and riotous' and 'never obscene in speech'.

Charles was also by descent almost entirely foreign, for the Scots were then foreigners. Through his grandparents, Mary Queen of Scots and the Earl of Darnley, he had a very distant Beaufort lineage through the Lady Margaret, sister of Henry VIII; but the Tudors were Welsh and on her mother's side Mary had been French. And through his mother, Anne of Denmark, whom he physically resembled, Charles was a Dane, descended from the Oldenburgh dukes of Schleswig-Holstein through Frederick II of Denmark and Norway, whose Queen, Sophia of Mecklenburgh-Schwerin, had been the highly intelligent patron of the astronomer Tycho-Brahe. Her eldest son, Charles I's uncle, was the famous Christian IV, one of the great warrior kings of Denmark and Norway whose tomb at Roskilde is surmounted by a sword. This martial background, with its tradition of fierce campaigns in Scandinavia and the Baltic and North Germany, and of the hard drinking celebrated in *Hamlet*, is often forgotten in the popular estimate of Charles I.

By descent therefore mainly foreign to his English subjects, un-English in mind or temperament and with artistic interests of European range, the King became further alienated from his own realm by the influence of his Bourbon-Medici Queen. Henriette Marie was a daughter of Henry IV — that model Frenchman, brave, gallant, shrewd and amorous — and of Marie de' Medici, whose nuptials had been so lavishly celebrated by Rubens. She was thus half Italian and her son, Charles II, would combine the insatiable Bourbon temperament with a striking resemblance to Lorenzo de' Medici, 'the Magnificent', swarthy and sardonic — even more of a foreigner to the English than his father. Brought up in the grand tradition of the French Court, a cosmopolitan European royalty, Catholic as a matter of breeding as much as faith, and extremely brave in war, Henriette Marie displayed an extravagance, frivolity, wit and high spirits that deeply shocked the more puritanical English, while the Scots, remembering the escapades and disasters of the King's grandmother, had already had more than enough of Frenchified queens.

With the inevitability of fate all these aspects of Charles I's descent, character, upbringing and entourage combined to make the most distinguished of the royal aesthetes of England tragically unsuited to his inherited role. Ironically his elder brother, Prince Henry, seems to have had just the personality and talent for it; but when he died aged eighteen the younger brother was thrust forward. Within his limitations he rose to the occasion and in the last weeks of his life he achieved a touch of greatness. But he was always miscast; conscientious, dedicated, aloof, Charles I could neither understand the realities of power nor manage men in their incalculable and sometimes repellent diversity. He insisted on that risky move in politics, standing on his principles, regardless of the risk to his own life, and defended himself with ability and eloquence against a tribunal quite unrepresentative of the nation, with no standing in law. He paid the foreseen penalty under the axe, but with his death the days of the English republic were numbered and the restoration of the monarchy secured.

BOOK I: THE PRINCE

1: DUKE OF ALBANY

ON 19 NOVEMBER 1600 at Dunfermline Palace, 'the fort on the crooked Linn', where in the *Ballad of Sir Patrick Spens* the King had sat 'drinking the blude-red wine' and where the prospect opens south to Rosyth and south-east across the Firth of Forth to Edinburgh, a second son was born to James VI, King of Scots, and his Queen, Anne of Denmark. Originally a crude royal stronghold, Dunfermline had become a Benedictine House founded in 1072 by St Margaret, the Cerdinga Queen of Malcolm Canmore, and the burial place of all but the heart of Robert the Bruce. It had now been adapted as a royal residence, but it was still gaunt, massive and medieval. In the murk of a Scottish November it was a grim place.

The child, not expected to live, had been at once baptized; then on 23 December, in the depth of winter, he was formally christened Charles and created Duke of Albany and Earl of Ross, the titles of his grandfather, the Earl of Darnley, whose younger brother had been Charles, Earl of Lennox. He was physically frail (two of the Queen's daughters and a son, Duke Robert, died in infancy) and 'so weak in his joints, and especially his ankles' that when he was four he still could not walk or speak. And, indeed, on the Stuart side his heredity was unpromising. They already had a long tale of tragedy behind them; his grandmother, Mary Queen of Scots, had perished on the scaffold of Fotheringay; her passionate, wayward and tragic career and fate and the courage with which she died are still famous. Mary's father, James V, had died in the misery of defeat after Solway Moss, exclaiming of the Scottish Crown, in grief at the news that his only legitimate heir was a girl, 'The De'il go with it; it will end as it began. It came with a lass and it will pass with a lass.' Her grandfather, James IV, had perished in battle at Flodden; and her mother, James V's Queen, Mary of Guise, daughter of Claude, Duc de Guise and Antoinette de Bourbon, had found it hard to adapt herself to the Scots way of life, being accustomed to the amenities of the French Court.

Charles's grandfather, Henry, Earl of Darnley, had been a tall and athletic youth. Like his wife he was descended from Princess Margaret, sister of Henry VIII; but by her second marriage to Archibald Douglas, Earl of Angus. Their daughter, the Lady Margaret Douglas, had married Matthew Stuart, Earl of Lennox, 'a strong man of personage, well proportioned and very streat up in his passage. Quheirfore he appeared verrie pleasant in the sight of gentlewomen.' So their son, named Henry after his formidable great uncle, also had a claim on the English throne and the temperament of the turbulent Douglas family.

When Mary, now Dowager of France, had returned to Scotland, Elizabeth had summoned the young Earl to England, where he had been in effect detained. But 'yonder long lad', as she had termed him, had acquired accomplishments in France and had ingratiated himself as a lute player. Elizabeth may have preferred that Mary should marry a subject rather than a powerful foreign prince, so Darnley had been allowed to return to Scotland. He was now nineteen and his apparently epicene beauty had attracted the susceptible Queen of Scots, still only twenty-two. For the Earl was charming: 'a dextrous horseman, prompt and ready at all games and sports, and much given to hunting, horse racing, dancing and music.' Though a reckless character, he was not the brainless lout generally depicted;

indeed this ancestor of Stuarts and Hanoverians could 'speak and write very well'.⁶

According to Camden's *Annals*, the Queen of Scots had at once been taken with 'the properest and best proportioned long man that ever she had seen', and when she had nursed him through an attack of measles and 'ague' in Stirling Castle, 'under the influence of proximity of the sick room and the tenderness brought forth by the cure of the weak, the suffering — and the handsome — Mary had fallen violently, recklessly and totally in love'.⁷ She had at once sought a dispensation from the Pope to marry her cousin. The marriage was also the obvious dynastic move. Soon the 'rycht noble and illuster Earl Henry' had been created Duke of Albany and Earl of Ross, and on 28 July 1565 the 'lusty young Prince' had married the Queen in the Chapel of Holyrood House by Catholic rites, though he had refused to attend Mass after the ceremony. He had also been proclaimed, without the Scots Estates being consulted, King of Scotland. Next year, in June, the Queen had given birth to James VI. Such on his Stuart side had been the grandparents of Prince Charles.

Unlike Elizabeth, Mary had liked to be dominated; and the English ambassador, Randolph, had reported that she had 'given over unto hym her whole wyll'; but the marriage had been a disaster. The young King's head had been turned; though popular for his youth and looks, he was plainly 'too much addicted to drinking',⁸ though hardly at his age to be blamed for 'rambling up and down' hunting and hawking — a taste inherited by his son and grandson. And no Scot could object to his one known diplomatic success, when he had put the French ambassador — a M. de la Roc Paussey — under the table after plying him with *Aqua Composita*, apparently 'the distilled ardent spirit known as whisky' — a liquor strange to one accustomed to the wines of France.

But Henry had also held 'a scandalous drinking carousel on the island of Inchkeith in the Firth of Forth', and now impatiently demanded the crown matrimonial; not unreasonably refusing to wait for it until he was twenty-one, for it would have made him king in his own right should Mary die. He was now thought 'wilful and haughty' and, like most royalties at the time, 'much given to Venus's chamber'. When the Queen had tried to stop him drinking, he had abused her in public; he had even tried to sign official letters above her signature. By February 1566 Randolph had reported, 'I know now for certain that the queen repenteth her marriage and that she hateth him and his kin.'

Henry, too, had his grievance. For though there is absolutely no evidence that the Italian musician Rizzio had been the Queen's lover and that, as alleged by Henry IV of France and repeated even as late as the dissolution of Parliament of 1621, James VI and I had been Rizzio's son, the Queen had created an appalling scandal by her intimacy with her Italian secretary. Certainly Darnley himself had got it into his head that he had 'a partaker in play and game with him'. He had therefore lent himself to the Italian's murder, in circumstances hideous to his own pregnant wife; then, after trying to escape from Scotland, he had been stricken with smallpox, or perhaps by symptoms of syphilis,[9] and brought back convalescent to Kirk o'Field, a house supposedly more healthy, as it was in a 'suburb' standing on higher ground than Holyrood. Here, at the instigation of James Bothwell, who soon became Mary's third husband, and probably before the house had gone up in a 'great crack' which stunned Edinburgh and reduced Kirk o'Field to rubble, he had been strangled when trying to get away. He had been found dead in a field, half naked in his nightshirt, along with a chair and some rope that had served him in his escape, but without overt marks of violence. 'The King's Grace's Majestie's umquiell bodie' had been promptly embalmed and interred in the Chapel Royal where he had been married the year before. He had still been only twenty.

The young father of James I and grandfather of Prince Henry, Prince Charles and their sister had thus not been a model king; but he hardly deserves the savage strictures of most historians.[10] He had clearly been a fool; but he had looks and vigour, and at an age when many people commit egregious follies, he had to face the murderous nobles and pedantic religious fanatics of sixteenth-century Scotland. Neither James I nor Prince Charles took after him much; but biologically they could have had a worse progenitor.

On the Oldenburgh side Prince Charles's heredity was much better. Instead of the poverty, faction and violence of much of the Scottish kingdom, the Danish monarchs controlled a prosperous realm with an advanced agriculture and sea-borne commerce. The Oldenburghs of Schleswig-Holstein, first established in 1448, had survived the civil wars following the Lutheran Reformation and profited, like the landowners, from the price rise of the later sixteenth century which favoured the export of cereals and cattle. Frederick II, Charles's maternal grandfather, had held his own with the Swedes and reigned over Norway, Iceland and the Faroes, as well as commanding the vital entrance to the Baltic, dominated by the great fortress he had built at Elsinore, which still stands. He had died of drink at fifty-three, but he had been a vigorous warrior and a great builder.

Christian IV, Charles's uncle, who had succeeded as a child in the year of the Armada and would die in 1648, a year before his nephew, was the greatest of the Danish kings — *Dominus Christianus Quartus, Norvegiae Vandalorum Gothorumque Rex, Dux Slesvici Holsatiae, Stormariae et Dithmariae Comis in Oldenburg et Delmenhurst... in Wufterwitz et Bechkow Dominus hereditatus.* He ordered the reconstruction of the palace of Fredericksborg and the creation of many of the copper-sheathed roofs and spires of Copenhagen. Though Anna of Denmark — as she always called herself — was hardly a distinguished character, she came of vigorous and determined stock; her eldest son, Henry Frederick, born in 1594, physically took after her and grew up a versatile and intelligent prince, though cut off by typhoid at eighteen. Charles's sister Elizabeth was also charming, popular and talented. Though she made a politically disastrous marriage with the Elector Palatine of the Rhine and so was looked down on by her mother, who called her 'goody Palsgrave' as a lesser royalty, it was through her that the Stuart blood descended to the present royal family of England.

The Scotland in which Charles's father had survived a precarious and lonely childhood, and which he had come to rule with considerable success, had become more prosperous since the peace with England in 1560; but it was still a poor and primitive country where the laird's retainers were still 'riding and ganging on horss and on futt in Heland and Lowland', though, unlike the Welsh or the Irish, the Scots had preserved their independence. Their traditions were alien to those of the English, who regarded them as rapacious and uncouth foreigners, and their social and economic ties were with the Continent — with France and the Low Countries, where the Scots merchants' house at Veere on Walcheren survives, and with Scandinavia. They had a considerable export trade in fish, wool, hides, linen and livestock, while the younger sons carved out careers abroad, even in Poland and Muscovy. Though the life of the people was often barbarous and Calvinist fanaticism unbridled — for their God was the 'terrible revenging judge of the world' — and the Gaelic-speaking Highland clans untamed — those in the islands, in James's own words, 'Utterly barbares' — the originally Norman aristocracy and even the lesser lairds often had wider horizons.

The country, then as now, was full of vigour. In a society far less stratified than in England the people had great tenacity, power of endurance and respect for learning; the cold climate was redeemed by the brisk air coming off the sea and the mountains under the northern light and by the benign influence of the gulf stream on the south-west. In this turbulent realm James VI had suffered severe vicissitudes, and the most disreputable of them had appropriately preceded Prince Charles's birth. On 5 August 1600 James VI had been rescued from what he claimed was imminent assassination by the young Earl of Gowrie and his brother, the Master of Ruthven, in a tower at Gowrie House near Perth, in circumstances that created much scandal and intense bitterness. The day of Charles's birth had coincided with the hideous sequel when the carcasses of Gowrie and his brother were dismembered.

Such was the atmosphere of violence and hereditary feuds into which the delicate and backward Prince Charles was born. It was odd that anyone with his aesthetic and high-minded temperament should emerge from such a setting where, as an early Victorian historian puts it, 'the deeds of blood were so bold and daring and extraordinary, that were it not for their undoubted authenticity, we are almost induced to view them as a terrible fiction or exaggerated delineation of human depravity'.

But Charles's dynastic prospects were grander than they looked. For all the penury and danger that beset him, James VI was not simply a King of Scots. He was the most likely heir to England and Ireland; potentially one of the most important royalties in Europe. For much as Elizabeth I detested the 'false Scotch urchin' — what could be 'expected from the double-dealing of such an urchin as this?' — she knew that legitimately he was the next in line. In the interests of the state he ought to succeed her: the alternative would have been civil war and the collapse of her main achievement. Moreover James had played his cards pretty well. He had connived at his mother's execution and supported Elizabeth against 'yon stranger', Philip II of Spain. Though he detested Elizabeth I as much as she disliked him, refused to attend her funeral and went hunting that day instead, and was careful to put up a tomb to Mary Queen of Scots in Westminster Abbey as splendid as Elizabeth's, he had never identified himself with his mother's cause, sought revenge for her execution, or indeed, it would seem, felt any affection for a mother he could not remember. He was a seasoned diplomatist who knew how to play Elizabeth's game; and though his prospects of the succession were not certain, they were realized. When on 24 March 1603 the great Queen died at Richmond, a new and splendid prospect opened up, not least for the young Charles, Duke of Albany. 'Saint George,' James VI had observed, 'surely rides upon a towardly riding horse, when I am daily bursten in daunting a wild unruly cobb.'

When the old Queen died in the small hours of a Thursday morning, one of her courtiers was well prepared. Sir Robert

Carey (or Carew), her kinsman whom she had promoted, and who with Lady Carey was to play an important part in Prince Charles's childhood, had witnessed her last hours and how by signs she had called for her Council; by putting her hand to her head when the King of Scots was named to succeed her 'they all knew he was the man she desired to reign after her'.[11] He had evaded the order that no one was to leave the palace, and at nine o'clock in the morning had ridden hard for Doncaster and the north. He had 'got a great fall by the way', he wrote, 'and my horse with one of his heels gave me a great blow on the head that made me shed blood. It made me so weak that [I] was forced to ride a soft pace after.'[12] But he had reached Holyrood House by Saturday evening and kneeling by the King's bedside had saluted him as King of England (France), Scotland and Ireland.

Carey had long ago ingratiated himself with James on Walsingham's mission in 1583. Moreover he now produced a decisive credential. The King had confided a sapphire ring to Lady Scroop, Carey's sister, to be sent to him by special messenger as soon as Elizabeth was dead. This she had thrown to her brother out of a window at Richmond. It had confirmed Carey's tidings and James at once acceded to his request to be made a Gentleman of the Bedchamber. And when the new Queen Consort came south, his wife, Lady Carey, daughter of Sir Hugh Trevannion of Cornwall, had been appointed to her household and made Mistress of the Sweet Coffers. And although at first in August 1604, when the three-year-old Prince Charles came to England, 'there were many great ladies suitors for the Keeping of the Duke,... when they did see how weak a child he was, and not likely to live, their hearts were down and none of them desired to take charge of him'. Fortunately Lady Carey took the responsibility; and by 1605 her husband was given charge of Prince Charles's household. Under her care 'God so blest the Prince that he grew stronger and stronger. Many a battle,' writes Carey, 'my wife had with the King but she still prevailed. The King was desirous that the string under his tongue should be cut, for he was so long beginning to speak as he thought he would never have spoke. Then he would have put him in iron boots, to strengthen the sinews and joints, but my wife protested so much against them that she got the victory.'[13] The Careys kept charge of Charles till he was eleven, and so well that he 'astonished people' by his progress in body and mind.

The wealthy and ostentatious Court on the fringe of which Charles was brought up was dominated by the eccentric and pervasive personality of his father; but his mother's influence was also important for him. Since directly and by reaction they deeply affected their son's development, both parents demand attention.

James I has had a bad press from historians. His concepts of divine right monarchy have been generally denounced or ridiculed; his morals considered deplorable and the addiction of 'old Jemmie' to hunting, dogs and drink, his slovenly appearance and maudlin behaviour widely reprobated, not only by high-minded Victorian liberals but by dedicated Marxists, on principle and by temperament unsympathetic to court life. Yet if an historian accepts the assumptions of the time, James's political ideas made sense in their context, and though his character became eroded by vanity, self-indulgence and the unremitting strain of his position since childhood, he had a shrewd political judgement at least in home affairs. 'He needs no spectacles,' wrote a Venetian ambassador as late as 1621 (by which time some modern historians have called him senile), 'and when he wishes, he can see like Argus.' He was an intellectual, the only king in English history who has written massive and learned books — in one aspect a very clever, strictly trained, Scots dominie. 'They gar me speik Latin,' he wrote, 'ar I could speik Scotis'; and though Prince Charles grew up to react strongly against his father's way of life into a rather cold austerity, he never got away from the intellectual influence of his *Basilikon Doron, The Duty of a Monarch*, written for the elder son Henry: 'God gives not Kings,' James wrote, 'the style of Gods in vain.'[14]

On the other hand James was a most unkingly king. Starved of affection as a solitary orphan, supervised by grim Calvinistic pedants alert for sin, he had grown up boorish, slovenly and ill-mannered, and in maturity became quite careless of regal dignity. His emotional life was homosexual. As a youth he had shown no interest in girls, but preferred a masculine world of horses, dogs and bawdy conversation, not incompatible with the semi-scholastic scholarship that fascinated the clever boy, though he had little interest in music and the arts. In adolescence, when his relative Esme Stuart, Seigneur d'Aubigny, arrived from France, his admirable biographer writes primly, 'he had loved [him] with a passionate affection scarcely normal in a boy',[15] and though he married and raised a family and called his Queen Consort 'My Annie', he remained emotionally obsessed with a series of young men on whom he lavished a deep romantic affection.

Going his own way, with the entire self-confidence of royalty in that age, James I and VI had a bizarre appearance. Restless, badly proportioned, with thin legs and an erratic gait, 'his clothes ever being made large and easy, the Doublets quilted for stiletto proofe... and his breeches in plates and full stuffed',[16] foul-mouthed and unwashed, this queer intellectual had his own force. With a heavy royal humour, touched with contempt, he treated even Robert Cecil, the principal architect of the succession, as his 'Little Beagle'. Gregarious after a lonely childhood, learned, loquacious, in spite of a tongue oddly too large for his mouth, 'which made him very uncomely in eating', so that he was apt to dribble when, often slightly tipsy, he sipped his ale or canary.[17] When the mood took him he would argue familiarly with scholars and courtiers: indeed 'he was very witty and had as many witty jests as any man living, at which he would not smile himselfe, but deliver them in a grave and severe manner'.[18] And when another mood took him, with royal disregard for appearance he would openly fondle the handsome youth who was the current favourite. Whether such gestures, as many contemporaries believed, led to more intimate familiarities (preachers would boldly denounce the King's 'catamites') they shocked conventional opinion and for long most historians. In a more permissive neo-pagan age we may observe that at least the monarch had a disarming capacity for often misplaced affection.

Under the influence of such a king the atmosphere of the Court in which Prince Charles grew up was thus genial, extravagant and *nouveau riche*; reeking of the stable and the hunting field, yet engaged in elaborate florid festivities and not without learning and wit. It reflected the extremely odd but pervasive and original character of his father.

Charles's mother, Anna, whom James had married by proxy at Copenhagen in August 1589, and then, with unwonted dash, when she had been stormbound in Norway in person at Oslo in November of that year, before spending a festive winter in Denmark, was an unreliable though gay and amiable parent. She had been only fifteen when she had come to Scotland, with fresh colouring, brown eyes, fair hair and an obstinate will of her own; with her relatively liberal Lutheran upbringing she could not abide the Calvinist ministers who bullied the Court and who denounced her for 'not repairing to the sacrament but night walking, balling, etc.'.

When she became Queen Consort of Great Britain and Ireland this natural frivolity had greater scope, and she spent her immense income with gusto. It was due to her that the cult of fantastically elaborate and expensive masques came in, and she became a great patron of those who wrote, composed and produced them — such as Campion and Inigo Jones, the latter's first masque, *The Masque of Blackness*, being performed under her auspices as early as 1604. She also set the fashion of daring and flamboyant clothes, and initiated the building by Inigo Jones of the Queen's House at Greenwich. She brought the standards of the northern Renaissance current in Denmark to England, where its form became more Italianate, and she greatly influenced the artistic and aesthetic tastes of Prince Charles, one of his salient and more attractive characteristics. Often dismissed by historians as a lightweight, superficial and even deleterious character, Queen Anna in fact had a salutary and affectionate influence on her son, as well as being a major patron of the arts and the theatre. Unlike her husband, who detested the publicity of his position and avoided the ordinary people, she thoroughly enjoyed her royal progresses. But in another aspect her example was less happy. In spite of a colossal income she was always in debt: she died thoroughly insolvent, though she left a 'world of brave jewels behind' (after all, a form of investment), though most of them were embezzled by her servants. Her Court, it was reckoned at her death in 1619, had been costing £60,000 a year. It is not perhaps surprising, since his father had been equally feckless, that Prince Charles grew up with very little sense of money.

But Charles had one advantage. As far as they could in the stress of publicity, entertainment and business, his parents tolerated each other's eccentricities. The Queen accepted her husband's predilection for handsome young men and tried to steer him towards those who were the least unsuitable; indeed, to get rid of the deplorable Robert Carr, Earl of Somerset, whose iniquities she had helped to ferret out, she contrived in conjunction with Archbishop Abbot to bring George Villiers, afterwards Duke of Buckingham, to the notice of the King. James was quite fond of her, and when she had shot his favourite dog Jowler with a crossbow by mistake, said that the accident might have happened to anyone and sent her £2,000 as Jowler's legacy.

Politically she can have had little influence on her husband. But the King was 'ever best when furthest from her', and she 'carried no sway in state matters and *praeter rem uxoriam* [outside matrimony] [had] no great reach in other affairs'. She admired Sir Walter Ralegh and tried to help him, an admiration shared by her adored Prince Henry, her eldest son, but not by Prince Charles, who at sixteen prevented his mother from visiting Ralegh on his ship before he sailed on his disastrous venture to Guiana. Yet her political sympathies, very strongly royal, were with the august monarchy of Spain; she was vaguely attracted to Catholicism and intrigued to marry Prince Henry to a daughter of the Catholic Cosmo II de' Medici of Florence, but her flirtations with Rome, much canvassed at the time, do not appear to have been very serious — rather, being a Lutheran, she thought little of the Calvinistic Church of England as represented by Abbot, though she died reconciled to it. In general her influence on her family was casual but benign, and her high spirits, love of sport and festivity and general benevolence may have encouraged the more easy-going side of the Prince's nature. It was not her fault that as he grew up there was not much of it to encourage.

Such were the flamboyant and colourful parents who dominated the childhood and adolescence of Prince Charles and by descent and upbringing influenced his character. The tides of history, to contemporaries always largely unpredictable, that drift, surge and eddy beneath the surface of chronicled events and in hindsight often make the relatively well-documented personalities at the summit of affairs seem irrelevant, may appear to swamp the heredity and upbringing that determined Prince Charles's personality. But anyone at all familiar with high public affairs knows quite well that the chances of personality greatly determine events, and that, particularly in the seventeenth century when monarchs possessed enormous powers, their characters were generally decisive. Personalities develop by interaction with the forces and changes of their time, but Prince Charles had to confront them with the cards he had been dealt.

Among them as he grew up appeared a considerable, if entirely unoriginal, power of mind. He was elaborately educated in the learning and languages of the day, and to the end of his life found solace in good literature and translating from the Latin; he was also, following the Renaissance culture in which he was brought up, trained in the accomplishments of a courtier, taught to ride, to hunt and to be proficient in the martial exercises then obligatory on any royalty or young nobleman. Like his father he was always passionately fond of hunting and of an open-air life; he was brought up hardy and versatile. But like his mother he also became a patron of poets, artists and architects in a tradition of princely largesse, whether he could afford it or not. In a word, he became a fine example of a well-educated and versatile northern Renaissance prince. All this he derived from the rich and indeed brilliant society of Jacobean England, of which the Court was the centre and apex. In spite of his limitations and handicaps, Charles became intellectually and even physically as well equipped as he could.

But if his parental background gave him all this, his own limitations were also increased by a reaction against it. The very virtues that the conscientious child would develop — rectitude, piety, aloofness, good manners, aesthetic perception, austerity, tenacity of purpose and principle — proved tragically unsuited for the unprecedented social, political and economic situation he was fated to confront.

2: DUKE OF YORK

IN LATE JULY 1604 young Prince Charles had been brought south, after Dr Atkins, *Medicus Regius*, had certified that he was recovering and 'beginning to walk alone, which he never did before';[19] £500 had been provided for the cortege, and early in August the Queen had ridden up into Northamptonshire from Theobalds, Lord Cecil's great house in Essex, to meet him. (Sir Robert Cecil had been created Lord Cecil of Essendine in May 1603; in August 1604 he would become Viscount Cranborne and in May 1605, Earl of Salisbury.) For £20 a year the Master of the Mint had given up his lodgings in Whitehall for the Prince's accommodation and early in 1605, when already Duke of Albany, Marquess of Ormonde and Earl of Ross, Charles had been created Duke of York and had to preside over a great banquet at Whitehall, dressed in glittering, bejewelled finery for the occasion.

But Charles was brought up mainly in the country. That spring of 1605 he was conveyed to Greenwich with its great sweep of river and air off the sea, the woods rising to the south behind it, and he later moved about to other royal residences, such as Oatlands, Kew and Richmond. Three years after, Holdenby House — the scene of his captivity during his tragic later years — was rented from Sir Christopher Hatton for his accommodation.

Under Lady Carey's general charge a congenial Scots tutor was soon appointed. Thomas Murray, afterwards briefly provost of Eton (1621-2), was a scholar particularly accomplished in Latin verse on whom his contemporaries bestowed encomia. But he was no pedant; rather a member of the King's Erasmian circle of learned wits than a typical divine of the Kirk, whose ministers thought him disaffected and managed to postpone his appointment to Eton for four years. He got on well with his pupil, for in 1617, after Charles had become Prince of Wales, he promoted him to be his secretary, and Murray's nephew William, much the same age as Charles, early became the Prince's playmate, remained his intimate and was afterwards created Earl of Dysart. Under the tutor's humane influence the Prince was attracted rather than compelled to learning, then rather a rare occurrence. The standards set for princes had been extremely exacting since Tudor times — as with Edward VI, Lady Jane Grey, and indeed Charles's own father — and the boy early became proficient in Latin and Greek, learnt French and Italian and achieved some Spanish. He became well grounded in Renaissance learning and well read.

His earliest extant letter, addressed to Prince Henry, is spontaneous, naively affectionate and extrovert:

> Sweet Sweet Brother I thank you for your letter. I will keep it better than all my graith [equipment] and I will send my pistolles by Maister Hinton. I will give anie thing that I have to yow; both my horses, and my books, and my pieces, and my cross bowes, or anie thing that you would haive. Good brother loove me and I shall ever loove and serve you. Your looving brother to be commanded,
>
> York.[20]

And:

> Good brother, I hope you are in good helth and merry, as I am, God be thanked. In your absence I visit sometimes your stable, and ride your great horses.

And again:

> Sir. Please your H. I doe keepe your haires [hares] in breath (and I have very good sport) I doe wish the King and you might see it. I so long to see you, I kisse your hands...

To his father the Prince writes in the same vein:

> To acquaint yor Matie that Monsr le Grand hath sent me a horse by a French gentleman, wherewith I hope yor Matie will be well pleased. The nexte Weeke I meane to use the benefit of yor Marie's gratious favour of hunting in Waltham forrest, the place appointed as fittest for the sport being Wansted. In the mean whyle, and after, I will employ my tyme at my booke the best I can to your Marie's satisfaction.[21]

These are not the letters of a boy strongly addicted to book learning; but by 1609, when he was eight, Charles could write to his brother in quite adequate Latin, expressing affection, as before, and writing: 'I am now reading the Colloquies of Erasmus from which I trust to learn both the purity of the Latin language and elegance of manners. Your most loving, brother Charles. Duke of York and Albany.'[22]

In the following year, when Charles was ten, the Earl of Northampton wrote to Cecil, now Earl of Salisbury, that he awaited the Duke of York in his progress, 'during which they will make war on the King's deer';[23] and in January 1612, when Charles was granted the reversion of the great office of Lord High Admiral of England for life, James ordered that he was not to be burdened with jurisdiction over pirated goods, as he would 'not have him burdened with things of so litigious a nature'.

Charles's household was always well provided: in the summer of 1608 Lady Carey was granted £600 for his linen and apparel, £100 for gifts and rewards already dispensed, and £50 a year for his general largesse. Two years later £60 was paid out for books for Charles's use, as certified by Murray, and an additional £200 a month assigned for the general expenses of the household. Nor were his sports neglected. Early in November 1610, when he was nine, John Webb, Master of the Tennis Play, received £20 'for teaching the Duke of York to play [royal] tennis', and in the same year another was paid for the Prince's apparel.

Under the amiable control of Sir Robert Carey, whose ride had well paid off, Charles's own household shared the lavish style of his parents' Courts. Large sums were disbursed on jewellery and clothes. In 1606 Abraham Jan de Kendor was paid £3,000 for the jewels worn by the Queen, the Lady Elizabeth and Prince Charles at Christmas; the bill for linen worn by the King, Prince Henry and Prince Charles came to £4,776; with £5,597 paid in advance for the Great Wardrobe. This when the Yeoman Pricker of the Privy Buckhounds earned only 20d a day; the Groom of the Otter Hounds 13d, with 20s a year for livery; and the Keeper of the King's Hawks, a highly skilled office, 2s a day or £36 0s 5d a year.

Jacobean Court life, much more expensive than that of the 'late glorious and invincible Queen Elizabeth, soon cost more than that of the Courts of France or Spain, and it was peripatetic, wasteful and confused. The endemic plague that had prevented James passing through the City of London even for his coronation, so that the ritual procession was performed between Westminster Bridge and the Abbey, combined with the King's inordinate passion for hunting to keep royalty and courtiers on the move.

Indeed, the new monarch, as Cecil put it, was 'a great and extreme ryder', liable to fall from his horse 'at least once a month', and he had entered his kingdom often 'hunting all the way as he rode'.²⁴ 'On account of the injury done the game by the inordinate crowding of persons since his Majesty's arrival there', James was expected to forbid anyone but nobles and gentry to enter the Little Park at Windsor; but when at Thetford 'wondering that any churl should kill anything that affords the King his only recreation', he placarded the whole area 'as though he claimed all the game', the country people strongly resented it. James would often cut Council meetings for this 'necessary kind of recreation', or tell the councillors to assemble at the Queen's separate Court at Denmark House. What he liked best was to kill a stag with his own hands; but he was also great on hawking and coursing hares. This horsy, leathery, open-air life alternated with the sumptuous, if often chaotic, ceremonial of the Court at the royal palaces and hunting lodges, and when the King descended on the great house of some rich and loyal subject, often nearly ruined by the colossal expense. On the ceremonial side, when Charles came to the throne his way of life at once became deliberately formal.

This restless, splendid and exciting world in which he grew up can at first have meant little to Charles, who was kept well out of harm's way. He can hardly have remembered directly the monstrous design of the Gunpowder Plot in 1605 — a crime on a scale more for the twentieth century than the seventeenth — when the plotters had 'known not how to seize Prince Charles, and resolved', should the design come off, 'to surprise the Princess Elizabeth' who was living near Coventry, one of the main scenes of the conspiracy, 'and make her Queen'.²⁵ But the memory of this conspiracy to blow up King, Lords and Commons in a holocaust more lurid than anything on even the

Jacobean stage, created a hysteria of popular prejudice that misinterpreted the Erasmian learning and moderate ritualism which he would grow up to admire. Further, the year before, his father had alienated the English Calvinists by rejecting the Millenary Petition, confusing them with the Scots Puritans, 'very pestes of the Church and Commonwealth', of whom he had written: 'Yee shall never finde with any hieland or border theevis greater ingratitude and more lies and vile perjuries than with their phenatick spirit.' The petitioners had, after all, demanded the abolition of the cross in baptism and the ring in marriage, but James's decision had been impolitic, and laid up trouble for his successor.[26]

Charles's father had also early claimed to override the common law. On his first progress into England he had shown his incomprehension of it. When 'at Newark in his Court was taken a cut purse doing the deed, and being a base pilfering thief, though all gentlemanly on the outside, this fellow had good store of coin found about him, and on examination confessed that he had from Berwick to that place played cut purse to the Court, the King hearing this gallant, directed a warrant to his Recorder at Newark to have him hanged, which was accordingly executed' — a sentence that in an English Court could be passed only after due trial. Then in 1607, when Charles was six, claiming to override the common law as supreme judge, James had set off a controversy over principles with the redoubtable Sir Edward Coke, chief justice of the common pleas, over whether or not the king was under the law. And by 1610, when Charles was nine and writing stylish Latin, his father was at odds with his Parliament, a situation the boy early understood, so that he grew up 'with the name of Parliament a bugbear to him'.

So, round the young prince, the clouds that were to close in on his reign were early gathering on the horizon — they arose from the bitter popular hatred of Catholicism and anything that could be akin to it; the detestation felt by the Puritan extremists for the established Church-a dislike fully returned; from stubborn resistance of the common lawyers to the claims of the monarchy and from the impasse with Parliament over supply.

Along with those fateful decisions went the day-to-day state business of minor petitions and outrages that came up to the Council for consideration. As when Lord Howard of Bindon in Dorset desired to impark a thousand acres at East Lulworth; or the Thames watermen, half of whom under Elizabeth had been in the 'marine service', were now in peacetime far too many, so that they begged that at least one waterman should be retained at sea in each ship of a hundred tons; or when David ap Griffith was granted pardon, but for life only, for killing his compatriot John Thomas; or when pardon was accorded to Mary Allen, widow, for killing Edward Chaplin, her apprentice boy, by 'unreasonable correction'; or when the woodwards of the New Forest were ordered to grant a hundred timber trees to repair houses in Blandford, as usual 'injured by fire'. And of course the Dutch were still fishing off the east coast where they should not have been, for the Hollanders were 'increasing in shipping in contrast to our decay thereof', and it was thought that government ought to encourage the English fishing fleets.

Contending thus at once with major problems and matters of trivial import, the Jacobean Council that Charles inherited was already creaking at its multifarious tasks. Over religion, law, taxation, politics and administration, all the great problems that would confront and baffle Charles as king had already been worsened by his father when the Prince was still a child.

Further, when Charles was eleven, the current royal habit prevalent on the Continent of governing through a favourite or *privado* (one way of circumventing bureaucracy) was rousing opposition in England. As early as 1607, when Charles was only six, young Robert Carr's 'bold disposition, comely visage and proportionate personage' had caught the royal eye.[27] By 1611 he had been created Viscount Rochester and by 1612 he was on the verge of obtaining immense power. For Salisbury had been ill for months and was not expected to live, and James thought that he and his own protégé, working as what would now be called Principal Private Secretary, would manage very nicely to conduct the government between them. He had thus set another precedent to contribute to the troubles of Charles's reign, for Charles, inheriting in the Duke of Buckingham another even more powerful favourite from his father, would also attempt to govern in a similar way through him.

On 4 June 1610 the nine-year-old prince was brought to the very centre of Court life at the elaborate ceremonies and masques arranged when his brother was created Prince of Wales — an investiture that had not occurred since that of the future Henry VIII. He stood in the Privy Gallery with his parents in the old palace of Whitehall as Henry, who five days earlier had come down river from Richmond accompanied by the full civic pageantry of London, was presented in state to the Lords and Commons. In the sequel, a most elaborate and beautiful masque designed by Inigo Jones with the libretto by Samuel Daniel, Charles appeared as Zephyr, attended by twelve little girls of his own age.

> [He was] dressed up in a short robe of green satin, embroidered with gold flowers. Behind his shoulders were two silver wings and a fine lawn auriole... on his head was a garland of all colours; his right arm was bare, on which the queen had clasped one of her bracelets of inestimable diamonds. His little naiads were dressed in satin tunics of palest water blue... and their heads garlanded with water flowers. The ballet was so contrived that Charles always danced encircled by four of these fair children, against an elaborate setting of waterfalls and cataracts.[28]

The ballet won vast applause. Charles, now a self-possessed and well-drilled little boy, had shown grace and sensibility.

But behind these Court festivities the scene had long been darkening. Salisbury had long been the lynch pin of the administration, and since his appointment as Lord Treasurer in 1607 he had striven hard to make the government solvent. He had himself accumulated immense wealth, often by dubious means — indeed, he had an unusual grasp of finance — and in 1610 had put forward a design for a Great Contract whereby the King would exchange all his ancient and unpopular feudal rights for a regular revenue. All had seemed to go well, and James himself proved a good bargainer. For he had refused 'nine score thousand' (£180,000) as referring to the Nine Muses, whose followers are always beggars, but said that 'though he wanted eleven score, as relating to the Eleven Apostles' (not counting Judas), he would settle for ten score, that being the number of God's Commandments. So Parliament in return had offered a supply of £200,000 a year. 'The little Beagle,' it was recorded, 'doth run about and bringes the rest of the great hounds to a perfect tune, the King gives up in return the wards, tenures, purveyances and compositions.'

Had the Grand Contract gone through, the Crown would have been better off and fiscally less unpopular and Charles I would probably not have had to fall back on the exasperating claims to feudal rights that made his government so detested during the 1630s.

But the design had failed, swamped in controversies over constitutional principle and 'impositions' in a deteriorating economy in which the merchants, those 'legs of the commonwealth', had been doing badly, in particular in the cloth trade, so that 'God had not blessed the trade of the realm'. There was no money for a regular subsidy.[29] In spite of Salisbury's protests, and at the instigation of Rochester, in February 1611 James had dissolved his first Parliament. The event marked the end of the relatively satisfactory if increasingly difficult collaboration between the Tudors and their Parliaments and the momentous failure of the Jacobean regime to keep control of the House of Commons. On this question of revenue, that would come to a climax when Charles was king, there was right on both sides: the old doctrine that the King should live of his own died hard; the Commons did not understand the rising expense of central government in an age of inflation. As the great French historian Braudel puts it, 'The modern State had just been born, both fully armed and unarmed, for it was not yet sufficient for its task.'[30] Here was a grave political menace already brewing up in Prince Charles's youth, a European and not merely an English fact. For the massive rise in population and a quadruple inflation, along with the increased circulation of money, had benefited agile entrepreneurs and increased the contrast between rich and poor, as well as increasing the difficulties of the decentralized kind of government that James had inherited. The silver from Spanish America continued to come in and be dispersed all over Europe to increase the supply of bullion, so that a contemporary wrote, 'Before the voyages to Peru, one could keep much wealth in a little place, but now that gold and silver have been cheapened by abundance, great chests are required to transport what before could be carried... in a piece of drugget.[31]' The inflation was mainly due to the increasing population of Europe and England since the mid-sixteenth century — rents and food prices led the way. Private wealth was increasing, not that of the government. Add to this the excessive English dependence on the cloth exports, which the merchants had been trying to extend to Muscovy, Iran, India and the Far East, and the general European recession beginning to set in, and the government's position was deteriorating. Nor did the most important external event of the time, the settlement of Virginia, then appear much of an asset.

Though only forty-eight, Salisbury had long been failing; in the spring of 1612 he set out for Bath to take the waters. Returning by Lacock and the Downs through the spring weather, he died at Marlborough on 23 May. So departed the mediator of the succession, the architect of the peace with Spain, the last of the great statesmen of the Elizabethan age. During the eight years since Prince Charles had come to England the prospects of the monarchy had deteriorated — over religion, the common law, the relationship with Parliament, the management of the economy and the personnel of government.

Regardless of his doom, the little Prince was now thriving. He was now eleven and astonished people by his mental and physical improvement. Lady Carey had been pensioned off with £400 a year for life, but Sir Robert had been kept on as

Master of the Robes. He had after all owed his original success at Elizabeth I's Court to spending far more than he could afford on clothes; and he had pointed out to Prince Henry that no one was better qualified than himself to show Prince Charles how to dress. It was not long before he also became Lord Chamberlain to the Prince's household.

Through the hot summer of 1612 Prince Charles's routine went on undisturbed by the frenetic intrigues of the Court that followed Salisbury's demise. Though better at his books, Charles would ride and play tennis and imitate his brother, and not without cause. Henry, Prince of Wales, was now a fine youth: about five foot eight, strong, straight and well made, with broad shoulders and slim waist. His high forehead and rather long face were set off by auburn hair, and he had a 'piercing grave eye'; an attractive smile and a severe frown.[32] He was apparently impervious to the temptations of his position, with a great household of five hundred persons; and 'unlike many a young gent, born to great fortune, in the prime of his years, when impressions and appetite are most strong, his grave and Princely demeanour gave temper [control] to them all'. He was interested in books, as witness his letter written at fourteen to Lord Harington of Exton.

> My good fellow, I have here sent you certain matters of ancient sorte, which I gained by my research in a musty vellum booke in my father's closet, and as it hathe great mention of your ancestry, I hope it will not meet your displeasure. It gave me some paines to read, and some to write also; but I have a pleasure in over-reaching difficult matters. When I see you, and let that be shortly, you will find me your better at tennis and pike. Good Fellow, I reste your friend, Henry.

The Prince of Wales was many-sided, interested in ships and farming and the management of his household — and he died solvent. But he shared one defect with his younger brother: he stammered — 'his speech slow and impedimented' — and he had to practise speaking. Whether heredity or upbringing accounts for this shared defect, psychologically, one would think, being a son of James I can have been no joke.

And it is revealing, in view of his father's lurid and obscene vocabulary, that Henry, like Charles, disliked swearing, as a revealing anecdote attests. For one day, when he was hunting, the exhausted stag was pulled down and killed by a butcher's dog as it crossed a road, 'whereat when the Company came up with them, they fell at odds with the butcher'. But the Prince would have none of it. 'What,' he said, 'if the butcher's dog killed the stag? It was not its master's fault.' Had his father been so served, someone remarked, he would have 'sworn so as no man could have endured it'. 'Away,' said Henry. 'All the pleasure in the world is not worth an oath.'[33]

Obviously, like his brother, Prince Henry had reacted against his parents' way of life. Where the old King was expansive and careless of dignity, taking all in his stride, Henry was 'against disorder at feasts'; 'methodical!', and 'to inable his knowledge of government civill, he read histories'. He was a vigorous extrovert who, 'in the times of year fitt for it', would swim and go for long walks and play tennis for hours 'in his shirt, more becoming an artisan than a prince'. He played golf with the necessary perseverance, and when he played at 'biliors' (billiards) he did so 'nobly' and 'like himself, as for recreation, not appetite for the game'.[34] Which meant that he never lost his temper.

But he did lose his temper with Carr, whom he 'menaced to strike with a tennis racket'. And no wonder, for his father would send the favourite to transmit instructions to him on important business, for instance about Prince Henry's own projected marriage. Henry was a militant Protestant, already concerned with the continental wars. 'Hating Popery to the death', he was inclined to the Puritans, and like his brother he was naturally chaste — a rare attribute of princes. He loved his sister, who tried in vain to come to him in his last illness in disguise, and he was fond of Charles, though on occasion he would chaff him. Once, it is alleged, seeing the archbishop's cap on the table after he had gone in for an audience, he put it on Charles's head and said he would make him an archbishop. Whereat the boy, in a revealing access of temper, is said to have snatched it off and trampled on it. And no wonder: for the prince in this brotherly joke and 'plaie and dalliance with Charles', had also said 'he should be a bishop that his long dress might hide his legs'. But Charles greatly admired this splendid brother, who was also a collector of 'medals and curious coins of gold', and whose many pictures would form part of his own collection; indeed, his main effort was to keep up with him, all the more intense because of his own inferior physique.

With fateful effect on Charles and the country, all this promise shown by the heir to Great Britain and Ireland was written off. In October 1612, as Coke writes, the year 'was wounded up in mournful catastrophe'. Aged little more than eighteen and a half, Prince Henry died of typhoid within a month. His symptoms, as then described and since analysed, are conclusive.[35] And the more so since in the conditions of the time the Prince's diet exposed him to just that risk. His appetite, as described by Sir Theodore Mayerne, Principal Physician to the King, was overwrought and ravenous,[36] for he 'ate strangely to excess of fruit, and especially of melon and half ripe grapes, and often eating his full of fish and of raw and cooked oysters beyond rule or measure at each meal, three or four days in the week'. He would, moreover, finish his day, 'in order to cool the burning heat... during the summer by plunging into the river after supper, his stomach full...'.[37]

After these irregularities he fell ill at Richmond on 10 October 1612. Determined to fulfil his obligations in entertaining his prospective brother-in-law, the Elector Palatine of the Rhine, who had arrived on the sixteenth and had come up river, 'passing before the Tower' when 'four score pieces of ordnance had given him a loud welcome',[38] the Prince insisted on moving to St James's; but the disease followed its usual course. It was gradual, insidious and inexorable, with mounting fever, headache, thirst and buzzing in the ears; once the Prince rallied and played 'a great match of tennis with the Palsgraf', and at cards with Prince Charles, but since he already had a 'distorted countenance and dryness of mouth' and 'ghastly rowling uncouth looks',[39] the experience must have been macabre for the boy.

James I himself, regardless of possible infection, constantly visited his son. The doctors plied the Prince with 'juleps' in which 'unicorns horn', pearls and 'bone of stag's heart' had been dissolved. They tried 'cupping glasses, with scarification' applied to his shoulders, and put an opened pigeon on his shaven head; finally, in desperation, 'a cock split by the back' to 'draw off the putrid humours'. But 'all went from bad to worse'. Then they bled him, 'and his Highness bore bravely the blood letting'. Finally he became actively delirious, calling for his clothes and his rapier, and died of exhaustion. His last words were, 'Where is my dear sister?', while the Archbishop 'with streames of teares poured out at his bedside a most exceeding powerfull passionate prayer'.[40] The post mortem, as recorded, confirms that he died of typhoid, suggesting no alternative cause of the fever. 'The whole character of the onset,' Dr Moore concluded, 'is that of typhoid fever, and the same is true of the active form which the disease takes.'[41]

Whether it was the raw fruit, the raw oysters, or just Jacobean sanitation, the disease finished one of the more promising, if potentially tyrannical, of British princes, who might one way or another have averted the civil wars. And that fruit, that oyster or that sanitation sealed the long-term fate of Prince Charles.

3: HEIR APPARENT

HARD ON THIS bereavement, Charles, his prospects transformed as heir apparent, had to part with his sister, whom he never saw again. He fell ill, perhaps from shock and grief, and with precocious determination refused the medicines prescribed; defying not only the doctors but his old Scots nurse, who said he would die if he was so mulish; whereat the Queen, in momentary exasperation, for she loved him, is said to have remarked, 'No, he will live to plague three Kingdoms with his wilfulness.' The Prince, it would seem, was already obstinate.

The marriage and departure of Princess Elizabeth were due to the ambitious foreign policy of her father. The changing politics on the Continent had given the first monarch of Great Britain and Ireland a considerable if still ill-founded prestige, and James had embarked on a well-meant but unrealistic plan of appeasement and mediation. He now tried to get a foot in both camps, Protestant and Catholic, by marrying Princess Elizabeth to the young Calvinist Elector Palatine of the Rhine (known to the English as the 'Palsgrave'), the nephew of Prince Maurice of Orange-Nassau, Stadthouder of the Netherlands, while also negotiating to marry Charles to an Infanta of Spain.

James had some reason to overestimate his immediate influence, for the prospects of his realms had in fact been transformed. Already the East India Company, attempting to exploit Indonesia but forestalled by the Dutch, had won a foothold in India, and the first plantations — in Virginia as early as 1607 — were being made in North America. When

Charles was still a boy he would name the main river of 'Massachesits' after himself and transmogrify Amerindian Amoughcawgau into Cambridge, Mass. Further, James's more immediate ambitions had been encouraged by the relative political eclipse of France. Here, after the murder of Henry IV, his son Louis XIII was still a child, and the politically irresponsible Queen Mother, Marie de Medici, was dominated by an upstart Italian favourite Concini, created Marechai d'Ancre. In fact Henry IV and his able minister Maximilien de Bethune, Duc de Sully, had laid the political and economic foundations of the absolute monarchy later built up by Cardinal Richelieu, assuaged religious conflict and established the potential of a centralized great state; but the most powerful country in Europe was then incapable of initiative.

In Spain, when in 1598 the bigoted and mediocre Philip III had succeeded the bigoted and formidable Philip II, the government was in the hands of another corrupt and incapable favourite or *privado*, Sandoval de Rojas, Marquis of Dernia, since 1599 Duke of Lerma. Embezzlement, sale of offices, an idle aristocracy and a parasitic Church weighed heavily on metropolitan Spain, and the impolitic expulsion of the Moriscos in 1609-14 had combined with the results of Philip II's crusades against the northern European heretics to bring the government to bankruptcy in 1596 and 1607. The vast Spanish empire was not yet in decline and the treasure fleets were getting through, but the Amerindian population of Mexico had been reduced directly and indirectly by the Spaniards from eleven to two million, with a similar genocide in Peru, while the American colonies had never much supplemented the economy of Spain. Though not yet in full decadence, the huge Spanish empire was now precarious, and the English and the Dutch had successfully challenged it at sea.

In spite of the union with Portugal, the poverty of metropolitan Spain was ineradicable; even Philip II in the last year of his life had been forced to hand over the Spanish Netherlands to the Austrian Habsburgs; in 1604 Philip III had to make peace with England, and in 1609-21 to make a truce with the Dutch, now a great maritime and colonial power. In 1596 the United Provinces of Gelderland, Holland, Zeeland, Utrecht, Friesland, Overijssel and Groningen had obtained official recognition from England and France, and in 1604 had reached out across the Scheldt to capture Sluis, thus dominating both sides of the great waterway, though the English kept Vlissingen and Brill, given them as security under Elizabeth, until 1616.

In the Germanies, also, the Counter Reformation appeared to be an ebbing tide. The Habsburg Emperor Rudolf II had been an eccentric and childless recluse, in effect ousted by 1605 by his brother Mathias, who had formally succeeded to the empire in 1612, but who himself had no male heir. And although his fanatical Habsburg cousin Ferdinand, who was elected to the empire in 1619, launched into the Thirty Years' War and made Austria the greatest Catholic power in the Germanies, under Rudolf II and Mathias the empire had been further undermined by religious and racial conflict, while the quiescence of the Turks had removed the main cause of loyalty. The Union of German Protestant Princes, made in 1608, thus appeared powerful, though some were Lutheran and others Calvinist; by reverting to the traditional English policy, followed by Henry VIII and Thomas Cromwell, of alliance with the German Protestants, James, not then without reason, hoped to increase his influence on the Continent. For on the face of it he was the most influential monarch among the Protestant powers, and his ambitious project of a Spanish marriage for Charles seemed likely to raise the power and standing of his dynasty.

In fact, of course, James was hamstrung by the poverty of the Crown, an inefficient administration, conflict with Parliament and the lack of any standing army. In 1612, after preliminary difficulties, one of the finest ships of its time ever built for the Royal Navy had been launched, designed by the able naval architect Phineas Pett. Standing on the poop, Prince Henry had drained part of a 'great gilt cup', named the ship *Prince* and presented the cup to the designer; but so primitive was the administration and supply behind the navy that although the Spaniards feared that a fleet could be sent to the Mediterranean in conjunction with the Dutch, permanent British sea power was still more potential than actual. It was thus not, as superficially apparent, from a position of strength that the King set about moving his attractive and spirited daughter as a piece in the dynastic chess board; the resulting entanglement in the Germanies was to prove disastrous for himself and for Charles, even if out of the dynastically momentous move the Protestant Hanoverian succession to the British throne was eventually secured.

In February 1613 Prince Charles, walking on his sister's right hand as her royal brother, led the Princess Elizabeth into the Chapel Royal at Whitehall for her marriage to the young Frederick V, Elector Palatine of the Rhine. The bridegroom, who was sixteen, had made an excellent impression: 'his approach, gesture, and countenance seasoned with a well-becoming confidence'. He had hardly seemed put out when the Queen, who at first disliked the match, 'entertained him with a fixed countenance'; he had talked Latin with the Archbishop; appeared straight and well-shaped for his growing years,[42] and when lavishly entertained at Guildhall he had behaved himself in a 'very good fashion at the feast'. On 27 December 1612 the pair had been formally affianced and contracted in the old Banqueting Hall at Whitehall in the presence of the King sitting in state. Charles had conducted the young Palsgrave to the large Turkey carpet on which they both had to stand, Frederick in a black velvet cloak 'coped' with gold lace, the Princess in black velvet — for they were both mourning for Prince Henry — with 'crosletts and quartre foils' in silver and a little white feather on her head. The Prince Palatine, now so entitled as one of the royal family, had proved 'very royal in his presents that New Year's tide': appropriately he had given the King 'a bottle of one entire agate containing two quarts', a diamond tiara and necklace to Elizabeth, said to be worth about £35,000, and for Charles a rapier and a pair of spurs set with diamonds.

This Protestant alliance was very popular in the country 'as being a firm foundation of religion'; but shrewd observers foresaw trouble and thought the Elector Palatine 'much too young and small timbered to undertake such a task'.

The wedding was elaborate, and followed by the traditional feasting, jousting, masques and 'fireworks and fights upon the Thames', the last described with fervour by John Taylor the 'water poet' in *Heavens Blessing and Earth's joy, or A True Relation of the supposed Sea Fights and Fireworks*. Following Tudor custom, the sixteen-year-old Elizabeth wore a gown of richly embroidered white satin for the ceremony, with her hair down in token of virginity under a crown blazing with gems, which were 'so thick that they stood like shining pinnacles upon her amber coloured hair, dependently hanging playted down over her shoulders to her waiste'. Her train was carried by twelve girls, also in white, and so adorned with jewels that her passage 'looked like a milky way'. When she had first met Frederick Elizabeth had 'turned not so much as a corner of an eye towards him,' but she was now in love with him and in this typically Jacobean scene she looked vivaciously cheerful — 'an ordinary smile being elated to laughter... but it could not clear the air of her fate, which shows how slippery nature is, to tole us along to those things that bring danger, nay sometimes destruction with them'.[43]

After the wedding Charles presided in state at a great dinner to the Prince and Princess in the Banqueting Hall, an occasion that ended in 'revels', and next day acquitted himself well before the populace when the 'King and his brave spirited son Prince Charles' rode at the ring. James managed to take the ring on his spear three times, and the Prince — 'the flower and hope of England, mounted as it were upon a Spanish Jennet, with much agility... took the ring clearly four times in five courses'. Thomas Campion had written a masque,

> Now in thy revels frolicke, faire delight
> To heap joy on this ever honoured night

and the spectacles of the Thames would have pleased Henry VIII, when 'all the ships and galleys met in friendly opposition and imaginary hurly burly battalions'. There were 'six and thirty sail of great pinnaces, galleons, galleasses, carricks, etc.' which attacked a 'floating castle of fireworks', as the Lady Lucinda, Queen of the Feminine Territories of the Man Hating Amazonians, fought off the 'black souled hell-commanding Magician Mango who had tried to compel her to love'. The spectacle had been organized by the King's gunners: there was a great deal of noise and the cost came to £2,880 for the fireworks and £4,800 for the ships.

James had been at Newmarket during most of January with Rochester, now acting Secretary of State and in 1614 acting Keeper of the Privy Seal, who was 'very slow in dispatch of business and had many irons in the fire as well for himself as his friends'. The King had only reluctantly come to London for the wedding, and at once took himself off to his hunting lodge at Newmarket, which collapsed when he got back there and as it 'began to sink on the one side with great cracks, so that the doors and windows flew open ... they were driven to carry him out of his bed with all possible expedition'. He had to move up to Thetford. The sequel was probably the commissioning of the hunting lodge designed, but never executed, by Inigo Jones.

The Elector Palatine and his bride now prepared to leave England, Frederick conciliating Queen Anne by giving her a 'carosse' (carriage) made in France; and in April 1613, at a time arranged, it was said, so that they would have moonlight on the sea, Charles accompanied them down to Margate. After an easy voyage the Elector and his wife were acclaimed in the United Provinces when the truce of 1609 with Spain was still giving the Dutch 'a better relish to their banquetting'. The whole affair had cost the English £40,000.[44]

Being devoted to his sister, Charles now became more concerned with events in the Germanies and with the Protestant interests there; but that year a new and influential personage arrived in England who would attain an extraordinary influence over the King and draw him further into the morass of the other aspect of his ambitious foreign policy, the balancing alliance with Spain. The Spaniards never took this seriously, but they used it to hold the English at play — nothing less than the marriage of Charles to the Infanta Donna Maria. For such was the objective of the new Spanish ambassador, Don Diego Sarmiento de Acuna, Count of Gondomar. Set on a general pacification of Europe by an Anglo-Spanish alliance, James was deluded into becoming a pawn of a Spanish policy concerned merely to neutralize Great Britain.

By the winter of 1613 the debts of the Crown amounted to nearly £500,000, with a deficit of about £160,000 on the year. Officials were unpaid and the 'very guard that attend[ed] the King's person at Roiston and the poore posts that trot up and down [were] far behind, and besides clamouring and murmuring, ha[d] made many fruitless petitions to the King himself'. It was essential to call a new Parliament, and against pressure from the pro-Spanish Howards and from Gondomar, the King had to acquiesce.

On 5 April 1614 thirteen-year-old Prince Charles, wearing a long and sumptuous robe, rode in the procession from Whitehall Palace to the Abbey. It was a blustery spring day and riding behind the Lord Chancellor in the procession of knights, officials, judges, bishops, peers and great officers of state, he witnessed a comic scene. The cavalcade was restive and a bishop was thrown; the contagion spread and soon a Puritan peer who had mocked the bishop was himself unhorsed. The Catholics present were much edified.

Opening the Parliament in the Lords, the King told them that its first business was to naturalize the Elector Palatine and place his descendants by the Princess Elizabeth in line of succession to the throne. And since they at once passed the Act and became legally responsible for the Hanoverian succession, in this, if in nothing else, the Addled Parliament belied its name.

Otherwise it was a momentous and utter failure. It began badly and ended worse. In the Lords Charles watched a typical Jacobean muddle reflecting the inability of the government to manage a Parliament that controlled supply. Taking his cue from Sir Francis Bacon, now Attorney General, the King assumed blandly that the Commons would grant supply. 'The affection of his subjects', he declared, was their greatest gift, and he wanted nothing but what they would grant 'out of love'. But the effect, for what it was worth, was spoilt. Summoned to the Lords, the Commons found the space assigned them occupied by 'strangers'; unable even to hear the speech from the throne, they sat about outside the Chamber considerably annoyed. The business before them was much of it practical and useful, and it was a pity they never got it through: for example, an Act for restraint of building in London or next to it, and one for 'beautifying' the city; for the planting and breeding of timber; for 'the increase of the wealth of the realm by fishing with busses'; for 'the better planting of Virginia and the supply thereof'; for enforcing 'good standards of bricks and tiles'. And if an Act 'against the consumption of Gold and Silver in unnecessary vanities' was obviously impracticable, one for reviewing the obsolete penal laws was already urgent. And furthermore, since 'Old Sarum had [already] achieved the state of decay which was the wonder of later generations and was representative, and there were others little better',[45] a Bill to adapt the boroughs of Parliament according to the present state of the towns of the realm, could have made for a redistribution (proposed again in the crisis of the revolution, but not achieved until the 1830s).

The first Parliament that Prince Charles attended as heir apparent probably shocked him in its disorder. Out of 464 members, 160 were officials and courtiers, and of the 252 with a university or Inns of Court background, 135 came from Oxford, the stronghold of the established Church; in spite of this the political leadership for government in the Commons proved singularly incompetent. Sir Ralph Winwood, the new Secretary of State, had never sat in Parliament before and said that the first voice he had heard there had been his own; and though in the Lords (of the eighty-five peers twenty-four were bishops and two were archbishops) the government had a solid majority, there were only four privy councillors in the Commons.

Nor had the members of Parliament any effective leadership in opposition. The elections had often been bitter — and rigged — and the Crown, as Moir puts it, had encouraged its supporters to 'undertake' to return committed members as a 'nucleus around which a heterogeneous group of rural gentleman could be stabilised so that government could be conducted'. But this early attempt at management had roused frenetic opposition: it threatened the patronage of the magnates and the independence of the local gentry; and indeed, had it succeeded, the Commons might have been reduced to a political cypher. Sensing that danger, many of the gentry arrived at Westminster with a new grievance. So fierce indeed had been local resentment that the King's government would not again interfere in the shire elections: it had failed to manage the local magnates and gentry, the latter often socially hostile to the Court. 'The middle way of an absolutist government disguised behind a Parliamentary facade disappeared in 1614... two courses remained, either the King must suppress Parliament entirely or he must be prepared to share his power.' Neither James nor Charles could or would do either.

And the Commons soon proved singularly irresponsible. They accused Sir Thomas Parry, Chancellor of the Duchy of Lancaster, of unlawful interference with an election and expelled him, leaving only three privy councillors in the House; they tried to expel Bacon, saying that the Attorney General ought not to sit in the Commons; and they refused supply before their grievances about 'impositions' were met. And when a blundering bishop — Neile of Lincoln — accused them of sedition and of striking at the rights of the imperial Crown and said they should 'hear the judges touching the King's right', one member said that the bishop's head should be set on Tower Hill and another that he should be 'disabled ether to be aboute the King or to be a busshop or to be amongest reasonable men, but to runne awaye... in the woodes amongest wilde beastes'.[46] The Commons then in effect went on strike — in what they called a 'fore-bearance of all business'. The egregious and terrified bishop climbed down; but the Commons was now like a bear garden and the remaining privy councillors were 'impotent spokesmen of the Crown in an assembly that had escaped from their control'.[47] So the King gave the Commons a week's notice that unless they gave him supply he would dissolve them. The Speaker then got mumps and James dissolved his second or Addled Parliament in rage. Four members were charged with sedition and sent to the Tower.

After two months of turmoil the government was still left almost without ready cash, and fell back on the gifts of the nobility — the bishops each gave their best piece of plate, the City of London £10,000. A general 'benevolence' was exacted from the country of £66,100, and 2d a barrel was imposed on beer; but the King was now financially in worse case than before. The impact of these crucial events, so fateful to his future, on the adolescent Prince Charles can only have confirmed his distrust and dislike of Parliaments as such. Moreover James now set a precedent of doing without one for seven years.

Charles was now also confronted with a scandal that brought his father's Court into further disrepute. In the most dashing picture of Henry Prince of Wales, in which he is about to finish off a stag, a dark youth is kneeling on his left with a look of loyalty and admiration on his face. He was to become one of Prince Charles's most formidable political and military opponents in the closing years of his reign. Robert Devereux, third Earl of Essex, born in 1591 and so nine years older than Prince Charles, came of very grand lineage and was immensely rich; but his father, the brilliant and wayward second Earl, had married Frances Walsingham, widow of Sir Philip Sidney, to the bitter chagrin of Queen Elizabeth and had ended his life on the scaffold after flagrant rebellion. The boy had thus grown up under a cloud, though with the accession of James I he had been 'restored in blood and honour' and become the intimate of Prince Henry and of Lord Cranborne, Salisbury's heir. But while still a boy he had made a disastrous marriage to Frances Howard, daughter of the Earl of Suffolk, whose Catholic family's various adventures in treason had for generations been a danger to the Tudors and a bane for themselves.[48]

By 1611, when Essex had returned from the Continent to live with his Countess, she had fallen madly in love with Robert Carr, declaring that 'of all men she loathed' her husband and bringing an action for nullity against him. There ensued an appalling scandal, which coming after the deaths of Prince Henry and Salisbury, degraded the King and Court, for James himself became involved in an imbroglio that turned out to include witchcraft and murder. The lurid affairs of the Essex divorce and the sequel, the Overbury 'Mystery', cleared up in 1615, were complete with all the facets of Jacobean melodrama; its details are widely familiar; but the Countess, 'articling against the frigidity and impotence of her Lord' to prove her marriage with Essex null, set off a grave political sequel. For this rather dull and conscientious magnate, full of pride in his ancestry and position, was dragged through disgusting humiliations that he did not forget.[49] Naturally, following his father's fate, there were 'not more eyes upon the Earl's father losing his head than upon the Earl losing his wife'. And during these proceedings Sir Thomas Overbury, Carr's erstwhile mentor, died mysteriously in the Tower.

The rather priggish young Prince Charles cannot have avoided the scandal and gossip, for the affair now became political: the Earls of Pembroke and Southampton and Archbishop Abbot backed Essex; the King and the Catholic 'Hispaniolizing' Howards, hot for the marriage to Carr, packed the Court and overruled Abbot: by a majority vote the nullity suit succeeded and Essex had to repay his wife's dowry. He had called out Lord Henry Howard, his brother-in-law, to a duel to be fought at Sluis in the Low Countries, but, frustrated, had retired in disgust and disgrace to his great estate at Chartley, determined on revenge. Ridiculed at Court, the Earl was thought by the populace to have been deeply wronged. During the Civil War he long commanded the Parliamentarian armies.

On 26 December 1613 the liberated ex-countess was married 'in her hair' — that is with it loose in token of virginity — to Robert Carr, who was now created Earl of Somerset. Prince Charles witnessed a masque by Ben Jonson, *The Irish Masque at Court*, with comic Irishmen, Patrick and Dounch, mouthing their dialect — 'For Cheeshe's sayk phair is te King', etc. — and performers dancing 'in their Irish mantles to a solemn music of harps'.⁵⁰ Campion, too, wrote a masque performed in the Banqueting House with elaborate scenery: 'On the upper part [of the stage] a skye with clouds, very artificially shadowed' with ships, some 'curiously painted, others artificially sailing', as a background to 'a great a beautiful garden'.

> Power, triumph, private pleasure, publique Peace,
> Sweet springs and autumns filled with due increase,
> All these — and what good else can thought supply
> Ever attend your Triple Majestie.

There were 'five Scots called High Dancers', and a show in which Silenus representing wine, contested with *Kawasha* representing tobacco.

> Silenus taps the Barrell
> Tobacco topps the braine.

The King was delighted, having made a good match for Carr, the Howards and Gondomar reckoned to have clinched their hold, and Frances Howard, now Countess of Somerset, had got her man. Unfortunately in the course of the affair she had also poisoned Sir Thomas Overbury who had opposed the match. In 1615 a land mine, set off by the confession of an apprentice, would go up and bring the Court into unparalleled disrepute.

Meanwhile early in the spring of 1615 Charles, 'Fair Carolus' as a university poet called him, accompanied his father in the Court's peripatetic life on a visit to Cambridge.⁵¹ That March they rode down from Newmarket through extremely 'foul ways' and in hard weather:

> For now the King's past Trumpington
> And rides upon his brave grey dapple
> Seeing the top of King's College Chapel.

Cambridge, town and gown, was *en fete* and the already hoary joke of rivalry with Oxford was widely current — 'alas poor Oxford thou'rt undone'. Tactfully the Oxonian wit Richard Corbet, who was to ascend by way of the deanery of Christ Church, Oxford, to the bishoprics of Oxford and of Norwich, and who was already a royal chaplain, remarked when asked his opinion of the Cambridge *Comedy of Ignoramus* which had delighted the King, that 'he had left his malice and his judgement at home'. Another versifier made the best of the theme when he wrote:

> But leave it, scholar, leave it,
> For all the world must grant
> If Oxford be thy mother,
> Then Cambridge is thy Aunt.[52]

Accompanied by the Prince, the King visited nearly all the colleges and 'commended them beyond Oxford'; all were decorated and painted up, save the Puritan Emmanuel which

> Would not be like proud Jezebel
> Nor show herself before the King,
> An hypocrite or painted thing
> And Images she would have none
> For fear of Superstition.

James had been so pleased with his visit, when dons and undergraduates had been seen at their best,[53] that he again visited the university in May, coming to Trinity by coach with Charles, to whom the Mayor presented perfumed gloves. But this time James got bored with the sermon, which lasted an hour and a half, and 'showed distaste of the preacher who had no care to prevent tediosity'.

Another and far more attractive personality than Robert Carr now came to dominate the life of the Court and influence the character of Prince Charles. On 24 April 1615 the King had knighted a new favourite 'with the Rapier that the Prince did wear'. George Villiers was the most dazzling of the young men on whom James lavished his affection; and for Charles, as for this brilliant and irresponsible careerist, the event was decisive. The Prince's initial jealousy would turn to admiring affection, and the opening years of his reign would be entirely and disastrously dominated by the only male intimate to whom he gave his entire confidence.

James's habit of putting personal affection before public duty now came to its most damaging climax and his new favourite's rise was meteoric. Born in 1592, and so eight years older than Charles, George Villiers was a younger son of Sir George Villiers of an ancient family of Brooksby in Leicestershire and of Mary Beaumont, daughter of Anthony Beaumont, who came of lesser gentry in that county. His father had died when he was thirteen, leaving an impoverished family, and five years later Lady Villiers had dispatched her son for three years to France. Returning at twenty-one, George had been introduced at Court, and such was his lively charm and sparkle that by August 1614 he had been appointed to the appropriate office of Cupbearer, and by the spring of 1615 it was 'observed that the King began to cast his eye on George Villiers' who, in contrast to Somerset of whom the King was tiring, 'seemed a modest and courteous youth'. In 'the dark vivacious Villiers', then a 'good-natured high-spirited boy',[54] the enemies of

Somerset and the Howards had seen their chance; and Archbishop Abbot, according to his own account, had himself approached the Queen. For James was shrewd and ironical enough to accept familiars recommended only by her; so that 'if after she should complain of the dear one, he might make the answer, "It is long of yourself"'. 'Our old Master,' adds Abbot, 'took delight in things of this nature.'[55] But Queen Anne had been wary: 'I know your master,' she had replied, 'better than you all: if this young man be once brought in, the first persons he will plague will be you who labour for him.'

The Archbishop had replied that 'George was of a good nature which the other was not', and that even if he should prove dangerous, it would be long before he could be able to attain 'that height of evil which the other had'. The Queen had agreed with this rueful argument, and in spite of Somerset's opposition on 24 April George was appointed Gentleman (not Groom as Somerset had wanted) of the Bedchamber, with the large salary of £1,000 a year, a promotion marked by a knighthood. And George appeared grateful: '[He] went in with the King, but no sooner had he got loose,' records Abbot, 'but he came to me in the Privy Gallery and there embraced me.'

But the Queen's suspicion had been correct; as with many a professional charmer 'his countenance of thankfulness did not long continue'; for all his charm, George, if with some reason, was deeply interested only in one person — himself. His ascent now proved meteoric: by 1616 he was Master of the Horse, in control of all the royal stables; that April, a Knight of the Garter; and that August, Viscount Villiers and Baron Waddon, with estates worth the colossal income of £80,000 a year (in such circumstances James did not do things by halves); and by January 1617 the formerly penurious younger son would be Earl of Buckingham and a year later Marquess and the successor to Northampton as Lord High Admiral of England under Prince Charles.

Such was the shift of power — for George Villiers soon made himself the main channel of all important business and patronage; and in contrast with the rising sun of Buckingham, the shades were closing in on the corrupt and murderous couple who had been married with such festivities in December 1613. Early in 1615 James was accusing Somerset of insolent pride and 'a settled kind of induced obstinacy' — he had even refused to sleep in the King's bedchamber. Politically, too, James had long been weary of the triumvirate of Somerset and the Howard Earls of Northampton and Suffolk, who had successively in 1612 and 1614 been Lord High Treasurers.

The King spent the high summer on progress to the west, having obtained credit of £300,000; but what was that among so many that 'gaped and stared after it'? The itinerant Court was not much welcome to his subjects, who petitioned against a visit in the counties concerned 'in respect of the hard winter and hitherto extreme hot and dry summer, whereby cattle are exceeding poor and like to perish everywhere'. But early in August the King and Prince arrived at Salisbury, then went down to Dorset to Lulworth Castle, new-built by 1609, in part out of the stones of Bindon Abbey. The King was intent on hunting in the park and in the Isle of Purbeck.

That autumn of 1615 they came back to Windsor, to be confronted with the retrospective evidence of the Somersets' crimes. What had been 'muttered in corners' was now common talk in the streets, for the apothecary's boy who had given Sir Thomas Overbury the glister that had killed him, falling sick at Vlissingen, had revealed the whole matter, 'which Sir Ralf Winwood [now joint Secretary of State] by his correspondence had full relation of'. Somerset had taken the precaution of drawing up a pardon, modelled on one given to Wolsey by Henry VIII, that the King 'of his meer motion and special favour, pardoned all manner of treason, misprision of treason, murders, felonies and outrages, whatsoever by the said Sir Robert Carr, Earl of Somerset', and this comprehensive exculpation he had induced the King to sign.[56] But it was too much for Lord Chancellor Ellesmere, who refused to pass the seal, 'being stung with feare to be touched with Overbury's death'. Somerset also tried to call in incriminating documents, hoarded money, and put a good face on it by still 'leaning on the King's cushion' in public.

Then that September the Lieutenant of the Tower, Sir Gervase Helwys, made a devastating confession: he had known, he said, that two attempts had been made to poison Overbury before the fatal ministrations of the apothecary's boy. Overbury was now four years dead; but plainly the matter had now to be officially investigated. For his own reputation the King had to appoint a commission with orders that the 'foulness of the fault be sounded to the depth'.[57] Hence the notorious parting with Somerset at Royston in mid-October, when the King 'hung about his neck, slabbering his cheeks, saying "For God's sake when shall I see thee again?"... the Earl was not in his coach, when the King used these very words (in the hearing of four servants of whom one was Somerset's great creature, and of the Bedchamber, who reported it secretly to the Author of this history) "I shall never see thy face more"',[58] an expression of self-pity, not, as sometimes construed, of malice, when perhaps he recalled the boy to whom he had once tried to teach Latin.

By 18 October Somerset was in custody, and by May 1616 he and his Countess were on trial, with the King down at Greenwich on tenterhooks — 'On my soul, I know not what to do… in this great straight' — about what his favourite might reveal. The Countess pleaded guilty; Somerset had 'absolutely refused to be tried', said that they should 'carry him in his bed' to Court, and created such scenes that he made the Lieutenant of the Tower 'quiver and shake'. Both the accused were condemned to death; but the King pardoned them. 'It had been thought,' records James Howell, 'that Cook [the Lord Chief Justice]… would have made white *Broth* of them, but the *Prerogative* kept them from the *Pot*.'[59] Not surprisingly the 'common people did not take it to be good payment', when, as often in public scandals, the lesser criminals were not of course pardoned. The notorious Mistress Turner, of whom her apothecary had testified that she had bought poison from him and tried the effect on a cat,[60] and who had been the 'first inventor of yellow starch' was executed in a cobweb lawn ruff of that colour, and since she wore one at Tyburn at her execution the colour went out of fashion. After six years' imprisonment in the Tower, the Somersets were rusticated to their diminished estates; and by January 1617 Viscount Villiers was Earl of Buckingham.

Charles had not at first taken the rise of the new favourite in good part; just as Villiers's charm had failed to win over Somerset, who had told him: 'I will none of your service, and you shall none of my favour; I will if I can, break your neck and of that be confident.'[61] The King, 'more impatient than any woman to enjoy Villiers love', even insulted his own heir. For when in March 1616 Charles took a ring from the favourite, put it on his own finger and 'forgot' it, and Villiers complained, James 'chided the Prince so severely as to bring him to tears, and forbade him his presence till the ring was restored'. There was also a quarrel at Greenwich 'before an infinite concourse of people', when Villiers 'bade the Prince in plain terms kiss his arse... a second time offering to strike him, saying in most undutiful terms, "By God it shall not be so... you shall not have it."'

The Prince, characteristically, was more shocked at the breach of etiquette than provoked to physical counterattack. 'My lord,' he said, with mild dignity, 'I think you intend to strike me!' In the event Charles was completely won over and combined with Buckingham to bully the King, for the favourite 'so wrought himself into his affections that Damon and Pythias were not more dear to each other'. But the courtiers thought that the Prince showed a poor spirit to be so much dominated, 'more than his father was in the prime of his affection'.

Since 1612 Charles had already had much to endure during his formative adolescence. Following the death of his admired brother and the departure of the Princess Elizabeth for the Palatinate, he had borne a heavy burden as the heir, witnessed the serious breakdown of the Crown's attempt to work with and control the Addled Parliament, and the un-regal behaviour of his father, first to Somerset and then to Villiers; while he had himself played a shy and dutiful role in the disorderly and peripatetic Court.

Not that his life had been melancholy: gone were the days of his physical weakness. He was now at home in the tilt yard and in all 'the manly exercises necessary for a Prince'. He had his own residence at St James's, whence he would regularly run in the park in the mornings, and he enjoyed constant riding and varied sport, the masques and festivities that entertained the royalties on their progresses. Like his father he loved Newmarket and Royston, the open air, the days in the saddle.

He was also now a good scholar with beautiful italic handwriting, and a considerable linguist; his interests ranged from 'models of war engines' imported for him from Holland, to the books, coins and pictures that he had inherited from his brother and was himself beginning to collect. Disgusted as he evidently was with the conditions of the Court, he did not, like Prince Henry, stand up to his father. He was withdrawn and discreet, his stammer persisted, though he tried hard to overcome it; when assailed by bawdy language, he would sometimes blush. His portraits at the time show a serious, obstinate, rather glum face, not yet romanticized by the Van Dyck curled moustache and pointed beard. Saddled with the prospect of unexpected and immense responsibilities, perceptive, fastidious and controlled, his reaction to these trying years came out when immediately on his accession he determined to transform the disreputable, casual, corrupt, jolly and insolvent Jacobean entourage into the most formal, distinguished and aloof Court in northern Renaissance Europe.

4: PRINCE OF WALES

ON 4 NOVEMBER 1616 Charles, 'showing rare proof of promising heroicall virtues', was created Prince of Wales. The ceremony was less grand than it had been at the creation of his elder brother; and the Queen 'would not be present... lest she should renew her grief by the memory of the last Prince — who runs still so much in men's minds that on Thursday I heard the Bishop of Ely, preaching at Court, pray solemnly for Prince Henry without recalling himself'.[62] Charles himself had been unwell; the weather was cold and the ceremony took place indoors without any major public show. But there had been a great procession of boats on the Thames as the Prince came down river from Richmond to Whitehall in state, and he was met off Chelsea by the Lord Mayor and aldermen in their barges to fanfares of drums and trumpets and a 'variety of excellent music'; when a 'Personage figuring London' appeared 'sitting upon a sea unicorne with Tritons sounding before her':

> Sound Tritons, lift our loves up with his fame,
> Proclaimed as far as honour has a name.
> Neptune, sound on...[63]

At Whitehall steps there was a 'triumph' by the dramatist Thomas Middleton, erstwhile satirist of *The Black Book* and *Father Hubbard's Tales*, but now commissioned for official occasions. It was called *The Citie's Love* and Hope and Peace attended the Prince's landing, the latter sitting on a dolphin, although it was late autumn, to the banal lines

> Welcome, oh welcome. All faire joyes attend thee,
> Glorie of Life, to safety we commend thee!

On the following day, in a heraldic procession, Charles entered William Rufus's great hall at Westminster uncovered, bowed deeply three times and knelt before the King, enthroned in state. His Letters Patent were read; then James himself put on the mantle, girded him with the sword, placed the ring on his finger and the cap and coronet on his head. Drums beat, trumpets shrilled and the bells of St Margaret's pealed over all.[64] The ceremony concluded with a state banquet. The following day, being the anniversary of the Gunpowder Plot, was one of needed rest, and James as usual was soon off to Royston and Newmarket. After the usual festivities, celebrated by *Christmas, his Masque* by Ben Jonson (*Christmas, old Christmas, Christmas of London*), in January 1617 George Villiers was created Earl of Buckingham. Charles was now Prince of Wales but Buckingham was now 'sole monarch of the King's affections'.

In the public view, by comparison with Prince Henry, Charles seemed dull — still 'not much enlightened with the people's love, being less alive and splendid (and that I may not call it sullenness) more reserved'.[65] Now the brilliant Buckingham entirely dominated the Court: the King, it was said, 'is not well without him' — he was his 'solace' and 'the Court Grandees could not be well but by him'. He had soon created a vast, ramified empire of patronage, not least for the benefit of his needy relatives. Buckingham was a particularly graceful and agile dancer, so that dancing became all the rage: but his provincial family, whom Prince Henry had detested for their 'general laziness', could not learn the French dances, so country dances became fashionable. The atmosphere of the Court changed:

> King James that naturally in former times had hated women, [now] had his lodgings replenished with them and all of that

kindred... Little Children did run up and down the King's lodgings like litters of rabbit starters about their boroughs [and] above all the miracles of those times, old Sir Anthony Ashley, who never loved any but boyes, yet he was snatched up for a kinswoman.[66]

Even the 'old midwives' of Buckingham's kindred flocked up for preferment. It was thus Buckingham, not the King nor Sir Francis Bacon — far the ablest statesman of the day — still less Prince Charles, who now ruled England. And both Sir Walter Ralegh and Bacon, two men of genius, were sacrificed to his shifting policies.

The fall of the Somersets had briefly crippled the Catholic Howard interest. In 1618 Abbot would succeed Suffolk as Lord Treasurer and in 1617 Sir Francis Bacon, no friend to their interests, had become Lord Keeper and in 1618 Lord Chancellor, being created Lord Verulam in this year and in 1621 Viscount St Albans. Buckingham therefore at first, as again later, favoured a neo-Elizabethan 'Protestant' policy against Spain. So in 1617 Sir Walter Ralegh, who had been imprisoned in the Tower and there, under a suspended death sentence passed in 1603, had written his *History of the World, from the Creation until 130 BC*, begun for Prince Henry and published in 1614,[67] was now loosed upon the Spanish Main on a desperate adventure with which he had long been obsessed. It was designed to find a 'mountain covered with Gold and Silver Ore' on the Orinoco in what is now Venezuela. Secretary Winwood and Villiers had backed the scheme, and in March 1616 Ralegh had been released to make what preparation he could for an enterprise that probably included an attack on the Spanish treasure fleet from Mexico and the seizure of strategically placed Trinidad.

The expedition sailed in June 1617 and proved to be a disaster; San Tomas on the Orinoco was stormed, but Ralegh's eldest son was killed and the second-in-command committed suicide. The men refused to enter the matted forests of the interior to find the mine; the ships dispersed, some to Newfoundland, and since his crews refused to turn pirate Ralegh returned to England in June 1618.

But by now Buckingham had been 'Hispaniolized' and backed Gondomar's demand for Ralegh's head. Prince Henry would have saved him, but Charles, with little influence, made no move. Indeed he ignored an intervention by the Queen herself — significantly to the all-powerful favourite, not to her husband.

> My kind Dog [she wrote] if I have any power or credit with you I pray you let me have a trial of it at this time, in dealing sincerely and earnestly with the King that Sir Walter Raleigh's life may not be called in question. If you do it so that the success answer my expectations, assure yourself that I will take it extraordinary kindly at your hands and as one that wisheth you well, and desires you to continue still (as you have been) a true servant to your master.
>
> Anna R.

But the golden mine had proved 'a meer Chymera', James had never believed in it — 'who would not promise mountains of gold for liberty?' — and Gondomar told the King that he had only one word to say about Ralegh. Asked what it was, he replied, 'Pirates, Pirates, Pirates!' and so departed.[68] Lord Chancellor Bacon, presiding at a Commission of Enquiry, soon found Ralegh guilty of high treason, and on 29 October 1618 he was executed under the sentence of 1603, dying with Elizabethan panache. His fate made him a martyr in the eyes of those critical of a Court that, as he had well said, 'glowed like rotten wood', and the memory of this tremendous, versatile and dangerous Elizabethan, poet, scholar, seaman and adventurer, continued to show up the corrupt lightweights who dominated the King.

That winter of 1617-18, while Ralegh had been sweltering on the Orinoco, James, who had spent the summer in Scotland (without Prince Charles) for the first time since his accession, had been gratified to receive sumptuous furs from the Muscovite ambassador — 'his present the greatest that ever came from thence, the furs worth at least £6,000 as well as coats of crimson satin and other colours, a rich Persian dagger and Persian cloth of Gold'; he was the more pleased to hear that 'Queen Elizabeth had never had such a present hence'.

In January 1618, on twelfth night, the usual festivities were arranged; Prince Charles was now a principal actor, as opposed to simply a dancer — 'his first exercise of that kind' — in Ben Jonson's *Vision of Delight*. The masque was so dull that critics said its author 'should go back to his old trade of brick laying',[69] but the Prince was much applauded.

Christmas had been overshadowed by the illness of the Queen. Since the return of James from Scotland in the previous autumn, she had been ailing with the dropsy that had set in three years before, and by the summer of 1618 she was seriously ill at Oatlands and Hampton Court. By December she was not expected to live, and James feared that the jewels in which she had heavily invested might be dispersed; some to Elizabeth of Bohemia and most to her grasping attendants. It was now understood that she had made no will, and though her estate would fall to the King if she died intestate, he was determined that her hoard should be inventoried and secured. So he pressed Prince Charles to the harrowing duty of urging his mother to make a will, leaving the jewels to himself; then he characteristically shifted his ground and accused the Prince of self-seeking. So entire was Buckingham's influence over the King, which he was careful to use to make the heir dependent on him, that Charles himself had to beg him to intervene. In an agitated, even abject, way he wrote to 'Steenie' (so called from his supposed resemblance to St Stephen as depicted in a stained-glass window), defending himself to the King for having urged his own mother to leave him her jewels. Since James had commanded him to use all the means he could 'to make the Queen make a Will', he had thought his father would have approved his action:

> ... my meaning was never to claime anie thing as of right but to submit my selfe as wel in this as in all other things to the King's pleasure. It doth greeve me much that the King should be so much mouved with it as you say he is... To conclude, I pray you to commend my most humble service to his Matie and tel him that I am verri sorri that I have done anie thing that may offend him, and that I will be content to have anie pennance inflicted upon me so he may forgive me... so hoping never to have occasion to wryte to you of so ill a subject againe, but of manie better, I rest, Your treu constant loving frend, Charles P.[70]

It was an odd letter for a Prince of Wales to write to a subject.

Meanwhile the Queen's immediate attendants had encouraged her in her indecision, and the situation inferred from the Prince's letter is typical of the sort of muddle usual at the Jacobean Court. *In extremis*, she now sent for her son, and keeping to the last a pretence of lighthearted good manners she asked, 'How he did?' He replied in their private banter that he was her (chivalric) *servant*, a point on which all her attendants had to be careful as James intensely resented the idea of anyone but himself having 'subjects'. She then begged him to leave and he refused, whereat his mother remarked, 'I am a pretty piece to wait on, *servant*.' Finally Charles withdrew, leaving the Archbishop and the Bishop of London to attend her, while her two rapacious attendants, 'Danish Anna and French Pierre', tried to keep everyone else out. But the Queen still refused to sign a will; by the evening, locked in with the two servants, she was obviously dying. At last at one in the morning, thoroughly alarmed, they allowed doctors Mayerne and Atkins to enter. They briefly revived the Queen and sent for the Prince, but she could no longer see. And as Charles knelt by the bed, her hand was guided first to his head then to the paper to mark her will, leaving him all her property apart from bequests to her servants. She was now speechless, and died peacefully.

James was too ill with gout to attend either her deathbed or her funeral in Westminster Abbey, so after his harrowing experience Charles attended his mother's funeral alone, walking behind the Archbishop in a procession that included the royal banners of Denmark. But a comet had appeared and James did his best with a poem:

> Thee to invite the great God sent a star,
> His nearest friends and kin good Princes are.

The jewels, about which so much concern had been felt, for they had cost £36,000, were found to have disappeared, and though Danish Anna and French Pierre were 'clapt up' for embezzling them, they were never recovered.

In May 1618, just before the remnant of Ralegh's expedition had returned to Plymouth, a mounting religious and racial crisis had broken in central Europe when the Czechs of Bohemia had set off the Thirty Years' War by the notorious 'defenestration' of two Catholic councillors and their secretary from the Hradshin Castle in Prague. Not since the reign of Richard II, whose first wife had been a princess of Bohemia, and when Wycliffe's followers had fostered heresies there, had the English been concerned in the affairs of the Czechs. Bohemia — presented by Shakespeare with a sea coast — had long been a far-away country of which they knew nothing. But now, through the marriage of the Princess Elizabeth to the Elector Palatine, they became deeply involved. Prince Charles, who was devoted to his sister, became extremely belligerent; but his father, with no army and no money, was more realistic, even if his attempt at 'mediation' was a fiasco. As Howell wrote from the Hague:

> There are great stirs like to arise among the Bohemians, and the elected King [by 1620 the Emperor Ferdinand II], and they are come already to that height that they consult of deposing him, and to chuse some Protestant Prince to be their King, some talk of the Duke of Saxony, some of the Palsgrave: I beliefe the states here, would rather the latter, in regard of conformity of Religion, the other being a Lutheran.[71]

And again from Antwerp:

> The Tumults in Bohemia now grow hotter and hotter, they write now that the Great Council at Prague fell into such a hurly burly, that some of the senators that adher'd to the Emperour, were thrown out of the windows, when some were maimed, some broke their necks.[72]

Feelings had run so high that the Czechs had committed their premeditated outrage as an act symbolic of the widespread Protestant resistance in central Europe, not only in North Germany but in Hungary and Moravia. Religious and nascent nationalist feeling had combined and the Princes of the Empire saw prospects of aggrandizement.

Among them was the inexperienced Elector Palatine, Frederick V, and the spirited Princess Elizabeth, who had declared that she would rather eat *sauerkraut* as the wife of a king than dine off gold plate as the wife of an elector; she at once, against her father's advice, threw herself into the adventure. So when in 1619 the Bohemian estates, partly in a deluded belief that James I was a powerful ally, elected Frederick King of Bohemia, he felt that as a Calvinist he had heard a call; furthermore Elizabeth said she would sell her jewels for the cause.[73] When in early November the Elector and his wife were crowned in Prague, James was in a quandary. He had not the army nor the revenue to make war on the Continent; the alternative, long envisaged, but now more difficult, seemed to be to defend his son-in-law's and daughter's interests by promoting the marriage of Prince Charles to an Infanta of Spain, and to encourage the alliance by indicating the potential threat of English sea power in the Atlantic and Mediterranean. He therefore pressed more vigorously for the Prince's marriage, in the unrealistic hope that the Habsburgs in Vienna might be influenced by the Habsburgs in Madrid. He became an easier prey to the wiles of Gondomar, who achieved an extraordinary influence over him.

Prince Charles on the other hand still favoured an impracticable Protestant crusade to help his sister and her husband directly. Though the appellation 'The Winter King', coined by the Jesuits, proved inaccurate, for Frederick's reign lasted until the autumn of 1620, the comment of the Pope was just: 'that the [Palsgrave] has thrown himself into a fine labyrinth'. In December 1619 Prince Rupert, the third of Elizabeth's twelve children, had been born in Prague and the

Czechs had presented his mother with a golden cradle; but by November 1620 Frederick had been defeated at the brief battle of the 'White Mountain' — or better 'Hill' — outside Prague by Duke Maximilian of Bavaria and fled that night with the Electress to Breslau. From there she wrote to her father:

> I do not wish to importune your majesty with too long a letter. The Baron Dona will not fail to inform your Majesty of the misfortune which has befallen us, and which has forced us to leave Prague and come to this place, where God knows how we shall be able to stay. I most humbly entreat your Majesty to take care of the King and myself by sending us help, otherwise we shall be entirely ruined... There is no one, after God, except your Majesty from whom we can expect assistance.[74]

This heart-rending and embarrassing appeal struck just the note of beauty in distress that appealed to Prince Charles, to the younger courtiers and, indeed, to the broad Protestant mass of the people. Bohemia might be written off, but the Palatinate, long a Protestant stronghold and power base, on the main line of Spanish communication with the Netherlands, ought to be held. Something had to be done — and it had to be paid for; James, who would gladly have passed the rest of his reign without another Parliament, was forced to summon another one.

When on 3 February 1621 James's third Parliament assembled, the political conflict that in Charles's reign was to break down into civil war and that had been foreshadowed even before the Crown had lost control of the Commons in 1614, now became more clearly defined. As heir apparent and Prince of Wales, Charles was now regularly attending debates in the Lords, where 'as a constant member [he] did cast an awe among many of them'.⁷⁵ But there was now a better organized opposition among the magnates, united by a hatred of the upstart Buckingham: Essex, for example, Warwick, Southampton and the first Lord Spencer, with his fields and flocks reputedly now the wealthiest man in England, who had maintained that all peers had equal status and to Arundel's insult, 'My lord, when these things you speak of were doing, your ancestors were keeping sheep', had replied correctly that Arundel's ancestors had then been plotting treason. The opposition groups in the Commons were now also politically more coherent, including such 'pilots of the Commonwealth' as John Pym, later Charles's most redoubtable Parliamentary adversary, and Sir Edwin Sandys, now treasurer of the Virginia Company, who in the previous Parliament had maintained that monarchy had been originally elective.

And while the opposition, though still fluid and changing, was stronger, the government was even weaker. The King had long habitually gone behind the Council, as in his confabulations with Gondomar⁷⁶ and with Buckingham; the small but efficient Elizabethan Council of fifteen had been extended to more than thirty and attendance had been increasingly casual. The King was generally away at Theobalds, Newmarket or Royston, and Charles, though more conscientious, was hardly popular with the Commons, 'disaffected' as the Venetian ambassador reported, 'by hearing that the Prince daily utters opinions contrary to the authority of the Parliament, and seeing him, praiseworthy though it is, follow all the movements of his father like a shadow and take his cue and advice from those ministers who are most hated'.⁷⁷

When James opened Parliament, his speech from the throne disappointed them. He made no proclamation of the Protestant crusade to recover the Palatinate, which the hotheads, including Prince Charles, had desired; he asked for money to prepare for a campaign, but made it clear that he was still intent on influencing Spain and thereby the Catholic powers, by a pro-Spanish diplomacy that implied favours to English Catholics. It says much for the loyalty of the Commons, obsessed by the kind of grievances raised in 1614, that they voted two subsidies.

They then turned to find scapegoats. Since neither the King nor Buckingham could be directly attacked, they went first for minor monopolists, then for the ablest man in the King's government — the Lord Chancellor Bacon, Lord Keeper of the Great Seal, Viscount St Albans. Bacon was now at the height of his career, but he had consented to the issue of patents of monopoly on various essentials of the economy and his transcendent abilities and splendid if slightly shady way of life had long roused jealousy, 'Since what he raked in, he scattered and threw abroad, for his servants, being young, prodigal and expensive which he kept about him, his treasure was the common store. His indulgence and familiarity with them opened a gap to infamouse reports.'[78]

Hot on the scent of monopolists the House of Commons now refurbished a rusty old weapon forged in the fourteenth century but out of use since 1459; it was soon to be used on much more eminent victims, long to be employed in England and to be incorporated to this day in the constitutional practice of the United States. Impeachment had first been recognizably employed in 1376 against William Lord Latimer, a minister in the failing Edward III's unpopular regime. It meant that the Commons, by their own will or under the coercion of the Crown or of disaffected magnates, started criminal proceedings against the accused before the Lords. Richard II himself had used the weapon against his uncle Gloucester, and in 1450 the

Earl of Suffolk had been impeached because, it had been alleged, 'he had sold the realm of England to the King's adversaries of France'. The weapon had last been used against Thomas, second Baron Stanley, impeached as a traitor for failing to support the Lancastrians at Blore Heath. He had been acquitted and had gone on to do the same thing against the Yorkists at Bosworth Field — with excellent results for himself, for he became the first Earl of Derby.

The first and minor victim was a Wiltshireman, Sir Giles Mompesson,[79] who had thought up and obtained a commissionership for enquiry into and renewal of the licensing of inns and who had been knighted by the King, so that 'he could the better fight with the Bulls and Bears, and the Saracen's Heads and such fearful creatures'. Mompesson had charged excruciating fees, imposed heavy fines for offences against obsolescent laws, and, at a price, renewed the licences of inns already closed for very good reasons. He had then obtained a patent for licensing the goldsmiths and the silk mercers, who were to work their gold and silver thread out of imported material and so save exporting bullion; he had also got the monopoly of converting coal to charcoal to save wood.

For the House of Commons this enterprising character — still MP for Great Bedwyn — was an obvious target. The indefatigable Sir Edward Coke, Lord Chief Justice, soon discovered that in all he had prosecuted 3,320 publicans and re-licensed 16 disreputable inns in Hampshire alone. Briskly condemned by the House, Sir Giles's prospects looked bleak; so he escaped to France. The Commons then expelled him from Parliament and brought out against him the ancient engine of impeachment before the Lords. They degraded him from his knighthood, fined him £10,000 (though the money, under Buckingham's influence, was assigned to his father-in-law at Lydiard Tregooze) and imprisoned him, if he could be caught, for life. Still strong in the protection of Buckingham, Mompesson returned to England — at first tentatively, then for good — and went to ground among his numerous and collectively influential relatives in Wiltshire, where he had property at Wylye.

This first impeachment, if not very effective, had set a precedent: clearly an accusation could be brought before the Lords by the Commons. And soon the Commons went for a much more important victim, none less than the Lord Chancellor Bacon, Viscount St Albans. For Bacon's abilities, careerism and way of life had alienated Sir Edward Coke and Sir Lionel Cranfield, who was Master of the Great Wardrobe, the Court of Wards and Chief Commissioner for the Navy. Bacon had even worsted the redoubtable Coke, when as Lord Chief Justice he had overridden him, sanctioning the King's right to dominate the judges by prerogative royal. They were 'lions' indeed, but 'lions under the throne being circumspect that they do not check or oppose any point of sovereignty'. Coke had been dismissed. He was also doubly Bacon's enemy, for Bacon had supported Lady Coke in defending her daughter from a marriage arranged by Sir Edward with Buckingham's entirely unprepossessing brother. Already the Lord Chancellor's standing with the favourite had been undermined.

The case against Bacon was first for sanctioning Mompesson's and other patents; but he was soon also accused of taking bribes: 'If this be to be a Chancellor,' he lamented, 'I think that if the Great Seal lay upon Hounslow Heath nobody would pick it up.' All soon came out: by the standard of the time his offence was hardly grave, but he had taken presents while suits were still pending. One woman, from whom he had accepted such a present and then decided against her, was particularly venomous. 'Greatness is the mark,' he said, 'accusation is the game.' By 1 May 1621, on the impeachment, Bacon made submission in the Lords and surrendered the Great Seal. He was fined £40,000 (which was handed over at the King's command to trustees for his maintenance) and disabled from sitting in Parliament; indeed, from all public life. Though the wind had been tempered, the last man of genius of the Elizabethan vintage had been destroyed — to the great impoverishment of the government. When he petitioned for the congenial appointment of provost of Eton, saying 'he could do as much good as another, be it square cap or round', the position was denied him.[80]

Accepting Bacon's guilt, Prince Charles intervened in another case. Lords and Commons had combined to show their Protestant zeal when the Commons attacked Edward Floyd, a Catholic barrister, who had remarked, 'I have heard that Prague is taken; and Goodman Palsgrave and Goodwife Palsgrave have taken to their heels; and, as I have heard Goodwife Palsgrave is taken prisoner.' The Commons, quite unconstitutionally, fined him £1,000, sentenced him to the pillory in three places, and to be carried there on a horse without a saddle, facing — and grasping — the horse's tail. And when the King, thinking of his pro-Spanish policy, asked them by what right they had condemned him, Floyd was impeached before the Lords, who went one better: they sentenced him to be branded, whipped at the cart's tail, fined £5,000 and to be imprisoned for life. But the Prince intervened, persuaded them to omit the whipping and saw to it that Floyd was set free in a general amnesty in July. The Prince, if dynastically motivated, had at least proved more humane than the Parliament.

That summer (1621) there were promotions in the Church that were momentous for Prince Charles's future. William Laud, one of the royal chaplains, whom James had thought too much of a firebrand for promotion, though he was already an intimate of Charles and Buckingham, Dean of Gloucester and President of St John's College, Oxford, at last got his bishopric. He had hoped for the deanery of Westminster, but it was obtained by John Williams, another royal chaplain, who had won high favour with Buckingham by promoting his marriage to the Catholic Lady Catherine Manners by briefly converting her to the Anglican Church;[81] he continued to hold the deanery when in 1621 he became Lord Keeper in place of Bacon and when elevated to the see of Lincoln.

Laud was compensated by the bishopric of St David's, the poorest see but an important step in the hierarchy — momentous to the High Church party with which the Prince was already identified. At the same time the anti-Spanish Calvinistic interest was weakened by the eclipse of Archbishop Abbot. Out hunting in Hampshire, the Archbishop had his 'sport spoiled by his accidentally shooting Peter Hawkins', the keeper on Lord Zouch's estate at Bramshill, 'who had thrust himself behind a buck at which his grace was shooting'.[82] The local coroner, obedient to the great, decided that it was all the keeper's fault *'per infortunium suae propriae culpae;'* alternatively, the accident was considered all the fault of the deer, which 'leaping up, the arrow [a crossbow bolt] struck the keeper who was hidden behind him'. James remarked that no one but a fool or a knave would think the worse of the Archbishop for such an accident, the like of which — as might be expected — 'had happened to himself'.[83] But the incident disturbed the Archbishop's conscience and gave a welcome handle to his enemies. Abbot said that it had been a bitter potion 'on account of the conflict in his conscience, for what sin he [was] permitted to be the taker of men, to the rejoicing of the Papist and the insulting of the Puritan'. He was now thought 'irregular by casual homicide', and both Williams and Laud, both Buckingham's creations, refused to be consecrated by him. He never lived the episode down. And though he remained in office until 1633, the affair contributed to cripple his influence against the more ritualistic Laud, already his personal enemy, since Abbot had tried to prevent his obtaining the presidency of St John's.

While the influence of Buckingham and Charles, now his devoted admirer, had increased in the Church, the House of Commons had been trespassing on ground that the King and Prince considered entirely reserved for the prerogative. As the Elector Palatine's disasters accumulated, many of the Commons became increasingly concerned with foreign policy and more bitterly opposed to the pro-Spanish manoeuvres of the King. Early in December James, always glad of an argument about principles, however politically undesirable, denounced them roundly.

> Mr. Speaker [he wrote from Newmarket] we have heard divers reports to our great grief, that our distance from the Houses of Parliament caused by our indisposition of health, hath emboldened some fiery and popular spirits of some of the House of Commons to argue and debate publicly of matters far above their reach and capacity, tending to our high dishonour and breach of prerogative royal. These are, therefore, to command you to make known in our name, to the House, that none therein shall presume henceforth to meddle with anything concerning our Government or deep matters of State, and namely not to deal with our dearest son's match with the daughter of Spain.[84]

Continuing the high tone natural to him, and indeed to all monarchs at that time, he infuriated them by calling in question the whole medieval concept of the community of the realm, of which the King was a part, not the master, and declared, as 'an old and experienced King needing no such lessons', that their privileges were not by 'ancient and undoubted right and inheritance', but 'derived from the grace and permission of Our Ancestors and Us'.

On 18 December the infuriated critics in the Commons, to whom argument about principles was equally irresistible, countered by an eloquent and forthright 'Protestation' that

> ... the liberties, franchises, privileges and jurisdiction of Parliament are the ancient and undoubted birthright and inheritance of the subjects of England, and that the arduous and urgent affairs concerning King, State and the Defence of the Realm, and the Church of England, and the maintenance and making of laws, and the redress of mischiefs and grievances which daily happen within this realm, are proper subjects and matter of counsel and debate in Parliament, and that in the handling and proceedings of those businesses every member of the House of Parliament, hath, and of right ought to have, freedom of speech to propound, treat, reason and bring to conclusion the same.[85]

Here, in confident style, is an authentic and formidable note to be heard again with increasing force on both sides of the Atlantic.

But the conflict of principle had been all too plainly declared. It would continue into the reign of Prince Charles, exacerbated by the failure to devise means whereby the King's Council could work with Parliament. Add to this that the Prince was now wholly under the influence of Buckingham; that he had committed himself to giving Laud his start, and above all to the pro-Spanish policy of his father. It was not a stance that would attract loyalty.

Early in January 1622, in petulant anger, the King ended his third Parliament, which 'having bin full ten days in suspense whether to hold or not, on Wednesday was cleane dissolved by Proclamation'. And James afterwards in solemn session of the Council formally tore the record of the Protestation from the records of the House with his own hands. Then:

> The same day his Matie rode by coach to Theobalds to dinner, not intending, as the speech is, to return till towards Easter. After dinner, ryding on horseback abroad, his horse stumbled and cast his Majestie into the New River, when the Ice brake; he fell in so that nothing but his boots were seene. Sir Richard Yong was next, who alighted, went into the water and lifted him out. There came much water out of his mouth and body — His Matie rid back to Theobalds, went into a warme bed, and, as we heare, is well, which God continue.[86]

5: SPANISH ADVENTURE

ON 13 MARCH 1621, although the relics of St Isidore of Seville had been brought to the sick room, Philip III of Spain died at the age of forty-three. His son, now Philip IV, was only sixteen, younger than Prince Charles; he was cultivated, intelligent, long the patron of Velasquez; but politically he was a lightweight and his government was in effect conducted by Don Gaspar de Guzman, Conde d'Olivares, whose showy horsemanship is depicted in the great Velasquez room in the Prado.

Like Richelieu and Strafford, he tried to build a modern great state, and he dominated Spain until 1643. In Madrid he devised a needed *Junta de Reformation*; abroad he tried to destroy the growing Dutch colonial empire by attacking its base — the United Provinces with whom the truce of 1609 had expired. The Thirty Years' War was his opportunity, and Spinola, the Genoese expert in siege craft, with his Spanish *Tercios*, the most formidable troops in Europe, quickly occupied most of the strategically placed Palatinate on the road to the Low Countries, in the campaign that culminated in 1625 in the Dutch surrender of Breda, memorably recorded. Gondomar meanwhile, by his ascendancy over James I and the 'penetrating faculty of the yellow demon' (gold), had been neutralizing the English with negotiations for a Spanish match for Prince Charles 'in which business he had waded very deep', while the Spanish Atlantic fleet was being reinforced. As usual the government of Spain was nearly bankrupt; but the combined Spanish and Portuguese empires were gigantic, and the Court had the greatest dynastic and social prestige in

Europe, setting the sombre, rich and elegant fashions that in Caroline England superseded the clumsy and ornate Jacobean style. The affairs of the Elector and the Lady Elizabeth were now catastrophic: since her despairing letter from Breslau their own palace at Heidelberg — to this day a ruin — had been blown up by the imperialists, and now the Palatinate as well as Bohemia had been lost. The Danes, the Dutch and the English had all failed them.[87]

Prince Charles, told of the fall of Prague, had shut himself up in his room at Royston and would speak to no one; he was now wild to rescue his sister, and in London, as 'Tom Tell Truth' told the King in *A Free Discourse on the Manners of the Time*, in 'your own tavernes for one healthe that is begun to yourself, there are ten drunk for your forraygne children', and people mocked his 'word Great Brittain and offered to prove it a great deal less than little England was wont to be'.[88] Convinced that his 'children in Bohemia' could only be restored by a war that would 'set all Europe by the ears' or else by his own diplomacy, James pressed on with the negotiations already begun in 1616 for the marriage between Prince Charles and the Infanta Donna Maria, sister of Philip IV.

Early in 1621 the King had sent Lord Digby to Brussels and Vienna on behalf of the Elector Palatine;[89] but the ambassador had reported that once in the Upper Palatinate the Emperor would never give it up. So in 1622 James again dispatched Digby to Madrid, in the sanguine hope that Philip IV would send the Infanta to England with a dowry of two million crowns, arrange the restoration of the Palatinate and conclude a close alliance at the expense of the 'Hollanders'. But by the autumn Digby, now Earl of Bristol, had to complain of delays and James commanded him to 'insist' on the restoration of Heidelberg — a *démarche* he secretly admitted would be useful only to conciliate English opinion. Charles himself had already signed articles submitted by Bristol, promising full toleration for the English Catholics, and Secretary Calvert had thought it time for him to write love letters to the Infanta. James, with greater realism, had merely promised not to enforce existing laws or enact new ones save in circumstances vital for the safety of the state.

So began the one rash and romantic adventure of Charles's life, and his only experience of the Continent. It lasted from mid-February 1623 to early October — over seven months: he had a glimpse of France and of the French Court and experienced the austerity and the scale of Spain; in winter the cold uplands of Castile, in summer the scents of thyme and cistus, the olive groves and the cicadas of the hot Madrileno countryside, the stately formalities and sombre colours of a great Catholic Court. Not least, at an age when such impressions are most vivid, he observed a range of architecture and art that made his own realm seem provincial. Though the expedition was a political fiasco, this liberation must have deepened the sensibilities of a born aesthete, and probably made him more aloof towards his own people. For in spite of the stark poverty of the country, the Spanish Court was very grand and imperturbable, and made its elaborate best of the unrehearsed intrusion of these northern heretics on the slow conduct of its tenacious diplomacy.

'Carlo Estuardo soy', wrote a popular versifier with a romantic touch:

> Charles Stuart am I
> Love has guided me far
> To this fair Spanish sky
> To see Maria my Star.

It was a new and exciting role for a still rather inhibited Prince. Buckingham had probably encouraged him in self assertion, and in the curious intimacy of baby talk and sentiment created by their 'Old Dad' and sometimes with the Prince's connivance, he was now bullying the King.[90] James had always feared that on such a visit the heir of Great Britain might become virtually a hostage to Spain and that the visit would be extremely unpopular in the country and throw away most of the diplomatic cards he had. He was terrified at the risk and exclaimed: 'I am undone, I shall lose Baby Charles.'

Albeit, on 18 February 1623 Charles and 'Steenie' set out from Newhall in Essex disguised with false beards — Charles was still clean-shaven — and with the excitement of a cloak and dagger adventure. They called themselves, without much originality, Jack and Tom Smith, and accompanied only by Sir Richard Graham, Buckingham's Master of the Horse, made their way to Tilbury and so to Gravesend. Here, having no small change, they grossly overpaid the ferryman, 'which struck the poor fellow into such a melting tenderness that so good gentlemen' should be duellists intent on a suicidal quarrel beyond the seas that he alerted the authorities to stop them going abroad.[91] The Prince and Buckingham were now riding up the hill beyond Rochester, and meeting the French ambassador, of all people, attended by the King's coach, they had to 'baulk the beaten road and teach post hackneys to leap hedges'. As they were changing horses at Canterbury, the Mayor tried to seize them in a 'blunt manner' under the authority of the Lieutenant of Dover Castle, so Buckingham 'dismasked his beard': as Lord Admiral, he explained, he had come to take a secret view of the fleet. Then the baggage post boy, who had been at Court, 'got a glimmering of who they were; but his mouth was easily shut' — presumably by a substantial tip. So on a dark stormy evening they got to Dover, where the Prince's Secretary, Sir Francis Cottington, and his Groom of the Bedchamber, Endymion Porter, awaited them. A skilled interpreter, in part of Spanish descent, Porter had already been negotiating the Prince's visit in Madrid — though not one in this sudden and informal manner.[92] Next day the party had a rough and nauseating crossing to Boulogne and Charles stood for the first time on foreign soil. In Paris, their disguise deepened by periwigs, they visited the French Court *incognito*, the Prince 'having a great tickling to do so'.

> That we might not leave you in pain [wrote Charles to his father on 22 February] we assure you that we have not been knowen... We saw the young queene, littel Monsieur, and Madame, with... nineteen faire dancing ladies, among which the queene is the handsomest which hath wrought in me a great desier to see her sister [the Infanta], so in haste going to bed... your Majestie's most humble and obedient sone and servant. Charles, and [in Buckingham's hand] Your humble slave and doge Steenie.

The nineteen ladies included the young daughter of France, Henriette Marie and afterwards during their courtship Charles would tell her of the occasion.

In the late evening of 8 March 1623 a certain Tom Smith arrived at Lord Bristol's embassy in Madrid with a portmanteau under his arm; then he called in Jack Smith from the darkness on the other side of the street, and soon the ambassador was horrified to recognize not only the all-powerful Marquess of Buckingham, in fact Ambassador Extraordinary to his own Ambassador Resident, but the heir to the throne. After hard and even dangerous going over the Spanish uplands through Vittoria and Burgos in that cold season, they had left the rest of their small party half a day's journey behind and arrived with only one postillion. Told at once of their arrival, Gondomar hastened to Olivares, who asked, 'What brings you here so late? One would have thought you had got the King of England in Madrid.' To which Gondomar replied, 'If I have not got the King, at least I have got the Prince.' Back in England two ships had been hastily fitted out to convey the Prince's provisions and servants, who were adjured to carry themselves civilly and religiously and not go to Mass, and an expensive relay of posts was set up through France. Soon Buckingham paid his respects to the King, and Olivares to Charles.

Elaborate convolutions of etiquette now began: the Prince was 'very earnest that Olivares should put on his hat, but the Conde would by no means do it, although he bee a grandee of Spain and may therefore be covered before his own King'.[93] Then Philip IV and the royal family drove out in the royal park while, thinly disguised, the Prince also took the air. As soon as the Infanta saw him, her 'colour rose very high' — though officially there was no recognition. The next day the King took Charles into his own coach and remarked, rather ambiguously, that he was much pleased that the King of England 'had put into his hands such a treasure as Charles was'; other meetings followed: the royalties, on horseback, watched a great battue of game — 'hares started, partridges sprung and other fowl put up to wing'.

By now the Spaniards had recovered sufficiently to stage a proper *joyeuse entrée* — windows and balconies festooned with rich hangings, scaffolding set up for the populace, music and dancing and a grand procession. King and Prince, after 'much pressing for the hindmost place', entered the palace hand in hand. Charles was given a great basin of massive gold, a curious embroidered nightgown, two great trunks 'stucke with nails of gold' and a 'faire riche deske full of rarities'. There were fireworks and torchlight processions and Philip suspended the Act for restraint of apparel then in force.[94] What was more, he commanded that all the English serving life sentences in the Spanish galleys for alleged 'piracy and other mortal crimes' were to be released without delay. So something positive had been achieved.

Behind the scenes tortuous and tedious diplomacy was now going on, and by the spring Charles, impatient to meet the Infanta informally, upset the Spaniards very much. Donna Maria used to walk in a walled garden or orchard behind locked doors, so the Prince gallantly climbed the wall and, jumping down 'from a great height, made towards her'. Whereat the strictly secluded girl shrieked and fled, and the old Marquess her guard fell on his knees before the intruder 'conjuring' him to retire, for 'he hazarded his head if he admitted any company'. The garden door was unlocked, and the presumptuous Prince 'went out under the wall over which he had come in'.[95] This escapade, so out of character though suitable for an amateur Don Juan, had hardly been in the best tradition of the Spanish Court, but Charles seems to have persuaded himself that he was deeply enamoured of the blonde Infanta, with her blue eyes, fair complexion and Habsburg underlip;[96] indeed he would watch her in a speculative posture on public occasions, said Olivares, 'as a cat does a mouse'. He never got a chance to talk to her alone.

Back at Theobalds King James had assured his 'sweete boyes' on 1 April that he would keep any secrets in their letters from the Council, that the news of their glorious reception made him afraid that they would 'miskenne your olde Dade hereafter', and had continued, in his Scots spelling, that they must be as 'spairing as ye can in youre spending thaire, for your officers are already... providing the fyve thousand poundis by exchainge, and now your tilting stuffe quhiche thaye know not how to provide will come to three more: and God knowis how my coffers are already drained'. He advised that they should 'keep themselves in use by dawncing privat-lie, though ye showlde quhissell and sing one to another like Jakke and Tom for faulte of better musike'. More seriously, he urged them to conclude the business by 'putting that King bravely to it'.[97]

Economy was the last thing in the heads of the emancipated Prince Charles and Buckingham. In the magnificent Spanish Court they felt sadly outclassed:

> Sir [wrote Charles to his father on the 22 April], I confess that ye have sent [at my departure] more jewells than I thought to have had use of; but since my cumming, seeing manie jewels wome heere, and that my braverie can consist of nothing else, besydes that sume of them which ye have appointed me to give to the Infanta, in Steenie's oppinion and myne, are nott fitt to be given to her; therefore I have the bouldness to intreate your Majesty to send more for my owen wearing, and for giving to my Mistress: in which I think your Majesty shall not doe amiss to take Carlile's advyce.[98] So humblie craving your blessing I rest, Your Majesty's humble and obedient sone and servant, Charles.

Buckingham's postscript was more urgent and familiar:

> I Your Doge, sayes you have manie jewels neyther fitt for your owne, your sones, nor your daughter's wering, but verie fitt to bestow of those here who must necessarilie have presents; and this way will be least chargeable to your Majesty in my poure opinion.

And three days later Buckingham wrote peremptorily:

> Sir, he [Charles] hath neyther chaine nor hatband; and I beseeche you consider first how rich they are in jewels here, and what a poure equipage he came in, how he hath no other means to appere like a King's sonne... These reasons, I hope, since you have ventured allredie your cheefest jewell of your sonne, will serve to perswade you to lett loose these more after him; first your best hatband; the Portugal diamond; the rest of the pendant diamonds, to make up a Neeles to give his mistris; and the best rope of perle; with a rich chaine or two for himself [Buckingham] to waire; or else your Doge must want a coller; which is the redie way [punning on 'choler'] to put him into it.

Finally, his tone to his sovereign became hectoring:

> Sir, Foure asses you have I sent, tow hees and tow shees. Five camels, tow hees and tow shees, with a young one; and one Ellefant, which is worth your seeing. Theese I have impudentlie begged for you... My Lord Bristow sayeth he will send you more camells. When wee come oure selves we will bringe you horses and asses enouf... and I will lay waite for all the rare color burds that can be hard of. But if you do not send your babie jewels enough I'le stope all other presents. Therefore looke to it.[99]

In mid-May it was rumoured in London that immensely valuable jewels from the Tower had gone to Spain — 'so many jewells given away to one Don or another as would make a man's heart ake to read the catalogue'; but the shortage of jewels was less maddening than the devious negotiations in which Spanish demands were now pitched higher. In Madrid tension had mounted. Buckingham, it was reported, had 'so far forgott himself as to intimate a dislike for the slowness of the dispatch, whereupon Olivares had sent to Charles to tell him that my Lord Marquess must consider better how great a

Prince the King of Spain was'.[100] And in fact 'Steenie' was up to no good, for a Spanish official had given him a map of the sites of the gold and jewel' mines of the Spanish Central American empire, including Jamaica, Hispaniola and Florida; a plan for intercepting the Spanish treasure fleet, and also for obtaining indigo from Portobello, a transaction apparently discovered, since the official was said to have been poisoned at once by order of Olivares.[101] But the information probably contributed to the subsequent attack on Spain and anticipated the Cromwellian attack on Hispaniola and the capture of Jamaica.

On a lower level, 'Archie', the King's fool, upset the ladies of honour and the *meninas* — the Court dwarfs depicted by Valasquez — by 'going in with his fool's coat among them and blowing, blasting and blurting out what he listed'. (His Scottish humour was little appreciated.) And by now some of the English were jeering' at the Spanish food.

The essential point was of course the difference in religion: and on that neither side would yield. In June Charles declared if he could bring the Infanta to England, for he 'engaged himself in honour' that all would be done, and the Spaniards inferred that he would not have so far committed himself without intending to renounce his heresy. So when the Prince wrote to the Pope politely but firmly refusing to do so, a dispensation became needed; and it was offered on stiff conditions. Apart from the Infanta's obvious rights to her own chapel, all English Catholics were to be entitled to use the same formula as that devised for the Infanta's household; the education of any children of the marriage would be supervised by their mother until they were twelve, and Charles had to promise that the penal laws against Catholics would in time be rescinded. All these conditions would have been anathema to the vast majority of the English and the Scots, and it is extraordinary that by the end of July Charles had signed a marriage treaty conceding them, especially as no reciprocal agreement had been reached helpful to the Elector Palatine and Princess Elizabeth. In return for consideration of the 'great clemency' to be shown to the English Catholics, the Spaniards had promised to pay the dowry of 2,000,000 crowns in instalments, 300,000 ducats in specie, the equivalent of about £600,000 in English money — then a colossal sum — and £300,000 worth of jewels, the remainder to be placed as a fund in Antwerp to pay an annuity. But they had also suggested that Charles should stay on in Spain over the winter and complete the marriage in the spring of 1624.

Charles was now thoroughly entangled. Having committed himself too far, he characteristically began to evade the commitment. For back in England the King had been 'in great streygth and distress', shocked at the prospect of a permanent toleration for Catholics, a measure so derogatory to his sovereign power that he knew well he could not impose it — still less dictate it to Parliament. In consultation with the Council at Theobalds he had made a 'manly stout speech' pointing out that there must now be no disputing, 'the Prince being in their [Spanish] hands', but insisting that Charles must 'marry and bring the Lady away with him' within the current year. But in August, at Charles's request, Philip IV made a proclamation deferring the *Desposorios* (betrothal) of the Infanta till Christmas.[102]

All concerned now had to put the best face they could on the affair, though in fact neither now meant to carry it out. The Prince's visit ended in a round of gaiety, lavish presents and fulsome politeness. Charles himself had been liked for his dignity and good manners, indeed, outside Court circles 'the romantic character of the Spaniards' had been 'captivated by an exploit which showed such *ardor* and confidence in their own honour'.[103] But Buckingham — whom James had created a duke that May — was detested and the Spanish courtiers were shocked at his familiarity with the Prince. At the conclusion of the visit in the blaze of August in Madrid, the authorities laid on a 'Bull Feast' and a '*Jeugo de cannas*, a tournament of darting with Reedes after the manner of Spain'.[104] Scaffolds were set up in the Plaza Mayor with canopies of green and gold, and the Infanta appeared in white, 'like an unspoiled dove'. The royalties had dined in public and Charles, arriving in a coach with the King, also wore white. There were musicians in carnation satin and silver lace, black hats with carnation plumes riding under royal pennants with the arms of Spain — all of which appeared, falsely, to 'give assurances of what had been treated on'. There were sixty horses with cloths of crimson velvet, fringed with gold, led in by youngsters of the stables after the Turkish fashion. The great magnates came with their splendid entourages, wearing black capes embroidered with silver, 'cassocks' of tawny or 'seawater green' satin, some wearing black plumes striped with white. The cavalcade included over five hundred horses and over all floated the orange and red civic banners and emblems of Madrid.

But the main spectacle was the *Jeugo de Cannas* itself. After a few bulls had been baited, twelve mules had brought in bundles of the 'reeds' and the royalties began the tournament, the King himself riding against the Conde d'Olivares — 'a deserved honour' — with great dexterity and force. Connoisseurs observed that he had left exactly the right track in the sand. The day ended in 'vehement heat' with a grand *fiesta*, masking the basic and obvious poverty of the country from whose empire in the Americas the huge dowry would have to come.

Charles was now loaded with gifts — a pistol, sword and dagger inset with diamonds; crossbows and swords; delicate leather goods and scents; rare flowers and plants. Olivares presented him with pictures and the King with eighteen Spanish genets, six barbary horses, six breeding mares, two stallions and twenty foals, all caparisoned in crimson velvet with gold trimmings. Buckingham was given twelve genets, four barbary horses and a girdle of diamonds. The jewels sent from England were lavished on the Spaniards in return. The Infanta was grieved and angry at the Prince's departure, and Philip put on black for sorrow at his going. Charles had indeed appeared to be tractable and affable enough, as so often afterwards, though inwardly resolved to go back on his protestations.

In September an elaborate cavalcade that included Spanish royalties wound its way along the road that leads up from Madrid across a plain of huge horizons to the Escorial. Here, dismounting in a little field, the King and his guest parted, with 'wondrous great endearments and embraces, held for a long time'. Charles then proceeded north-west and north by coach through the Guadarramas to Segovia, making for Valladolid and Santander on the Bay of Biscay.

Segovia particularly impressed him; he went all over the cathedral and palace restored by Philip II and remarked upon the English arms quartered by descendants of Dom Henriques of Portugal, the grandson of Edward in. At Valladolid he was 'much delighted' by the pictures of Raphael de Urbino and Michelangelo[105] — direct evidence of his artistic appreciation in Spain — as well as with the elaborate fountain that the Grand Duke of Tuscany had given to the former *privado* (favourite), the Duke of Lerma. Here also Charles 'took great contentment in the rich shops of the city'. Then after a long haul through the high Cordillera Cantabrica, he came down on Santander and saw an English fleet off the harbour ready to take him home. He must have seen it with relief for his defensive remark, that 'though he had stole into Spain for love, he would not steal away from fear', shows an underlying anxiety.

The English squadron, *Prince Royal*, *St Andrew*, *Swiftsure*, *Defiance*, *Rainbow*, with three transports and two pinnaces, long and with difficulty assembled, had cost over £8,000 to provision, of which only £2,200 could be paid down; for 'want of mariners' it had been reinforced by a press of seamen conducted from Hampshire to Plymouth, bringing the crews to nearly two thousand men. It had then been held up by westerlies, which the Puritans said were a Protestant wind preventing communication with Spain, and now, just as the Prince was to go aboard, the seas were running so high that his barge was caught between them and the tidal ebb; the rowers were hard put to it to keep way on the boat and 'taught another manner of practice than were put to on the Thames'. Darkness came on; they lost direction for the *Prince Royal*, made for a light that turned out to be *Defiance* and Charles managed to catch a rope and be hauled up. On 13 September he had to be rowed back ashore and transferred to the flagship *Prince Royal* before the squadron stood out to sea. Here Charles and Buckingham were nearly drowned for, going ashore at St Mary's at one in the morning after supper, they 'entered the ketch disorderly' in a somewhat high sea, which prevented the flagship from coming in. They were six hours in an overburdened craft before reaching the harbour. Next day in the early afternoon the flagship ventured in, the Prince and his entourage welcomed her and she passed into the harbour 'with much expression of joy and heaving up of hats'. In nine days they made the Channel approaches, but were forced back to the Scilly Isles in foul weather. While they were at St Mary's some 'Dunkerkers' and Hollanders were heard fighting — 'at it pell mell'. Whereat Charles spiritedly took command and had them 'brought to heel', dealing tactfully with the stubborn Dutch captain to 'win him to peace'. Then, wisely, 'for the prevention of their returning to the quarrel, His Highness set them one from another a good distance off and so let them go'.[106]

While the Prince had been extricating himself from Spain under colour of a commitment that could obviously not be kept, King James had been conciliating the Spanish envoys, who had ostensibly arrived to clinch the treaty. He had met the ambassador, who had thirty attendants, at Salisbury, where a brace of bucks out of Lord Southampton's woods at Beaulieu had to be delivered, 'more Venison being required than the last condition of the game in the New Forest could well spare'. A warrant had already had to be issued for the Spaniards to take venison themselves, to the annoyance of the King's own subjects, who probably not understanding that they merely preferred it matured, said that the foreigners had more venison than they could eat and buried the rest rather than give it to heretics. The people threw stones at them and were 'unruly and rude'. On their side the Spaniards, one of whom had already 'killed a baker in the Strand', had disputed the reckoning of £20 a day for going to Salisbury from Reading.

James had gone down to Cranborne, the Cecils' house in Dorset, and on 20 August he dined on board the flagship at Portsmouth and then proceeded to Beaulieu and out to

Calshot to observe the squadron as it passed down the Solent. 'Haste,' he commanded, 'haste away the ships!'

The full consequences of the treaty were now coming home to the government, but still the Infanta, it was reported, would follow the Prince to England in the spring. The Chancellor of the Exchequer was concerned at the loss of the fines on Catholic recusants — and were they no longer to be informed against? Were they to be exempted from appearing before the Court of High Commission and ought their offspring to be admitted to Anglican schools? The Spanish ambassadors promised to 'labour to prevent all mischiefs following favours to them' (the Catholics) and to urge them to meekness and humility, but were annoyed at not being given the English version of the formula for pardoning them.

Pending these problems being solved, more representative routine business went on: down in Dorset for example, the authorities at Weymouth had petitioned for the right privately to suppress the pirates then abounding along the coast; but it was argued that if they did so it might injure the interests of the Lord Admiral — now Buckingham — who had a grant of the profits of suppressing them. Then the most experienced mariners in the town, which had to pay £20 towards the upkeep of a light at the Lizard, insisted that the light was needless: in hazy weather it could not be seen; in clear weather it was unnecessary and anyway it would only guide the pirates to the coast. The ravages of the Sallee pirates on the west coast and the Dunkerkers in the east continued. Then, inland, the people of Brill near Oxford had also been poaching the Prince's deer; the gentry in Shropshire thought themselves disgraced because a certain Harris had been made a baronet; the King's elephant was costing £275 a year, besides a gallon of wine daily in the cold weather from September to April when its keeper alleged that it must drink no water, and a butcher's mastiff had killed two men who were swimming in the Avon near Ringwood.

It was high time that the Prince returned, and when on 5 October, in foul weather, he arrived in Portsmouth, the people all shouted, 'The Prince is come! Our Charles is come!' They lit bonfires and rang the bells. 'The Brave Prince is returned home,' it was reported, 'bettered in his judgement and in knowledge of Spanish ways.' And he could now show his feelings. In London he refused the Spanish ambassador's request for an audience. On 11 October the Londoners were so mad with joy that if they met a woodcart they took out the horse and made a bonfire of wood and cart, and when Charles happened to meet some condemned prisoners on their way to be hanged at Tyburn, he reprieved the lot. 'Welcome home', it was said, 'is the only business of the Court.' And the old King recovered from his various and partly psycho-physical complaints in the 'ecstasy' of the reunion.

Soon it was put about that 'talk of the Spanish match cooled daily'; the courtiers who had been in Spain, sensing the turn of the wind, complained of coarse entertainment — 'nothing but penurie and proud beggarie' — and when, while the King stayed at Hinchingbroke immobilized by the November floods, Charles again came back to London, he took a leaf out of his hosts' book and received the Spanish ambassador at Whitehall 'with Spanish gravitie, no more capping or courtesie'. At a great feast in Whitehall on 21 November for the King and the Prince and the ambassadors it was observed that they had only six 'carrion' mules, not horses. It was the Prince's return, not the supposed marriage treaty, that was the theme of rejoicing, sustained by 'a superabundant plenty; when twelve pheasants were piled on a dish and there were forty dozen of partridges and as many quails, *et sic de caeteris* in all kinds of provisions'.[107]

That month James had written to Lord Bristol that the 'fine flower' of the Elector Palatine's revenues was still in Spanish hands and that the marriage must be deferred until the Spaniards guaranteed that it would be restored.[108] It was also reported that the Condessa d'Olivares thought the marriage probably a 'dead business'. By December it was plain to all that 'the Papists were hanging down their heads'. In London rejoicing was still unbridled at the Prince's return — John Taylor, the 'water poet', had written *Prince Charles his Welcome from out of Spain* — but nowhere had the rejoicings been more heartfelt than at strictly Protestant Cambridge.

> I shall not need tell you [wrote Meade to Stuteville] the Prince is come to Royston. The news came to our Vicechancellor Monday forenoone: our Belles rang all that day, and the towne made bonefires at night. Tuesday the belles continued ringing. Every college had a speech and one dish more at supper; and bonefires and squibbes in their courts... Wednesday the University assembled; in the forenoone to a gratulatorie sermon at St. Marie's: in the afternoon to a public oration. The close, at night was with bonefires, drummes, gunnes, fireworks, till past midnight all the towne about... the Prince has got a beard and is chearfull.[109]

The Vandyck beard and curled moustachios that would do so much for his legend with posterity had transformed the hitherto rather glum appearance of Prince Charles.

6: THE FATAL LEGACY

ON 10 FEBRUARY 1624 against his will James I opened his fourth Parliament with unwonted pomp and unwonted popularity; it contained most of the old opponents of the Crown, reinforced by the formidable lawyer John Selden and by Sir John Eliot, one of the best orators of the day. With his more dashing appearance Charles was now thought to have 'grown a fine gentleman and never looked nor became himself better in all his life'. Indeed, it was soon considered that he was 'a little too popular' and that 'there was not that harmony between His Majesty and the Prince that could be wished'.

Charles and Buckingham, the latter Lord High Admiral since 1619, now quite irresponsibly determined on war with Spain, had insisted on Parliament being summoned to grant supply. They both made a full relation to both Houses of the 'delays and artifices' they had suffered there, and Parliament promptly petitioned that since the Spaniards could not be trusted the King should break off the treaty: the Upper House, indeed, 'cried out for war, especially the Bishops'.[110] Among those determined to 'take him down' there was still much 'pique' against the Duke for entirely engrossing the Prince's favour, but his *volte face* to the popular anti-Spanish line had made him briefly better liked.

The French, glad of the English rift with Spain, had now followed up their hints at a dynastic alliance, and already at Christmas jealousies of the French and Spanish ambassadors over precedence had led to the masque for twelfth night being postponed. A French nobleman — 'a great falconer' — had brought the King ten casts of hawks on behalf of Louis XIII, with horses and setting dogs. He made a splendid entry by torchlight and promised to stay until he had 'instructed our folk in his kind of falconry'. He was an expensive envoy, whose entertainment cost £20 a day, but the King had been delighted and in one of the coldest winters in living memory had gone down to Theobalds to see the 'new hawks fly'.[111]

James was now increasingly disregarded; tormented by kidney disease and arthritis, he was even more dependent on Charles and Buckingham, both impatient to take control, and 'too blinded', wrote a Venetian observer unkindly, 'by disordered self-love'. He was also blinded by his own 'wish for quiet and pleasure, too agitated by constant mistrust of everyone, tyrannized over by perpetual fear for his life, tenacious of his authority against the Parliament and jealous of his son's obedience, all accidents and causes of his almost desperate infirmity of mind'.[112] Charles was thus now much more influential.

> He never missed a day at the Parliament [wrote Chamberlain] and is so careful to have all things go well that, if any good follow, we shall owe it to his care and solicitation, and to the genuine good will and approbation of his virtuous disposition, as being noted free of any vicious or scandalous inclination, which makes him every day more gracious and his actions seem more graceful than it was at first expected; and in truth his journey into Spain hath improved him so much that it is a received opinion that he concealed himself before.[113]

At Court he was already perhaps behind one notable reform, for the Chapel Royal was now better conducted: all were now to keep their ranks going and coming; no boots or spurs were allowed on Sundays or festival days or in the King's presence; none but noblemen and privy councillors were to come to the inner closet or stalls or put their hats on during the sermon if the King or the Prince were present. The chapel was to be kept the year through with solemn music like a collegiate church, whether the King was present or not, and noblemen and others had to use great respect for His Majesty and civility towards one another.

Politically Charles's influence was less happy. Like Buckingham he had taken a grudge against Bristol, whom they accused of being too favourable to the Spaniards. He was recalled, and though the King had nothing against him and he had conducted difficult negotiations with skill, he was interrogated in Parliament and rusticated to his property at Sherborne; hardly, one would think, a penalty after his experience in Spain. In this episode Charles's rancour as well as his devotion to Buckingham are apparent.

> Steenie [he wrote], Bristo stands upon his justification and will by no means accept of my councells; the King does hait to have him cum to his tryall, and I am affeared that if you be not with us to help charge him and to set the King right, he may escape with too slight a sensure; therefore I would have you send to the King to put off Bristoe's tryall untill you might waite on him: but for God's sake doe not venter to cum suner than you may with the saftie of your health; and with that condition, the suner the better... Take care of yourselfe for my sake and ever shall be your treu loving, constant frend, Charles P.[114]

But Bristol was not to be put down; he became an obstinate critic of the regime in Charles's earlier Parliaments, though, when the crunch came, he proved a staunch Royalist and died in exile.

The goodwill of Parliament was soon eroded by the continuing vacillations of the King, who clung to the Spanish alliance. Friar Diego de Lazuente, formerly confessor to Gondomar, arrived with the dispensation for the Spanish marriage from the Pope; the Spanish ambassadors still made great public parade, and the Commons cut the large supply demanded of six subsidies and twelve fifteenths (over three quarters of a million) by half. Moreover they added an unheard of detailed proviso that they should decide how it would be spent; not directly, as the Prince wanted, on an expedition to the Palatinate, but in preparation for war with Spain — on the fleet, on coastal ports and on subsidizing the Dutch. They also petitioned the Lords that if the Prince married anyone of 'contrary religion', there should be 'no manner of connivance but for herself and her servant strangers', a petition that Charles had to recommend to the Lords. Then at the instigation of the Prince and the Duke, Parliament turned to 'sifting' the Lord Treasurer Cranfield, the one able financier since Salisbury.

Sir Lionel Cranfield, Bacon's enemy, created Earl of Middlesex in 1622, had been one of Buckingham's few good appointments.[115] Lord Treasurer in the previous year, he had already by drastic reforms of the household and wardrobe saved £17,000 a year. 'Until your lordship see it,' he had written to Buckingham of the administration, 'you would not believe any men should be so careless and unfaithful'; but now, when Charles and Buckingham were overriding the King, Middlesex supported James's pro-Spanish policy. He was attacked both by the all-powerful favourite and by the Commons. Even the astute Lord Keeper Williams was hard put to it to keep in office and only did so by an entire submission to Buckingham.[116] But Middlesex stood by the King. So Charles in the Lords 'employed to the full his position as future sovereign and his youthful appeal to the loyalty of the peers', and most of them decided to 'warm themselves in the light of the Rising sun'. The King was reduced to 'courting many to take the side of his Treasurer', but in vain: Middlesex was now attacked by the double-edged weapon of impeachment. Instructed by the King to save him, Lord Keeper Williams had to confess that he could obtain almost no support. Indeed Williams had to tell his master that the Prince was 'the main champion that encounters the Treasury', for Middlesex had personally offended Charles by arguing that even if he had taken a dislike to the Infanta, he ought to submit his private distaste to the good and honour of the kingdom.

Charles's first important intervention in politics had thus been singularly unfortunate and dictatorial. He was set headlong on the ruin of his father's most useful — if tactless — minister: James had either to betray his able Treasurer or oppose his heir. Further, some of those who were to form the nucleus of opposition to Charles's own government — the 'popular' (in the pejorative sense) 'men of the state' — were also encouraged by the Duke. James knew well that he was losing control and complained that he was 'less informed at this Parliament than at any other'. Early in April, aware that the Commons were preparing their charges, Middlesex warned the Lords that if such an attack were suffered, 'no man would be in safety in his place'. Then the still implacably pugnacious Sir Edward Coke and Sir Edwin Sandys, whom the King had tried to send to Ireland but who had been spared going there through the influence of the Prince and the Duke, led the attack on Middlesex. It was based on evidence from officials in the Court of Wards and Treasury, 'corrupted', thought Chamberlain, 'to do him a mischief'. He was accused, like

Bacon, of taking bribes and of manipulating the Court of Wards in his own interest.

James now intervened. 'By God, Steenie,' he said, 'you are a fool and will shortly repent this folly, and will find that in this fit of popularity you are making a rod with which you will shortly be scourged yourself.' Indeed, 'impeachment,' as Feiling puts it, 'was a deliberate step by the opposition, which would link the two Houses together and assert the Lords' superiority over any court outside the Common law.'[117] As for Parliaments, the King told Charles, he would shortly have his bellyful of them. In May the King actually came and spoke at length in the Lords, and though he left the Treasurer to their judgement, he indicated that he thought him not guilty.

From 7 to 12 May 1624 Middlesex was subjected to the full rigour of this medieval procedure; made to stand eight hours at the bar of the House 'till some of the Lords might see him ready to fall down' — a proceeding, he declared, though he had himself helped to hound down Bacon, 'unheard of unChristianlike and without example'. Obedient to the Prince and Buckingham, the Lords censured him for mismanagement of the Wardrobe he had in fact reformed, and for mismanagement of his other duties. He was sentenced to be dismissed from all his offices: 'Thou, Lionel, Earle of Middlesex, shalt never sit or have voyce more in this House of Peers.' He was fined the immense sum of £50,000 and sent to the Tower, though the bishops prevented him being stripped of his titles and honours. Through the King's influence he was in fact soon released and pardoned in the following year, and in 1626 he tried to get his own back when Buckingham himself was threatened with impeachment.[118]

So, in the brief popularity won by Charles and Buckingham after the failure of the Spanish match and before ever Charles came to the throne, the Prince had shown bad political judgement and a dangerous precedent had been set. An able minister had been sacrificed; the monarch's wishes defied. And in principle impeachment might come to imply that ministers were responsible to Parliament, not to the King. James had indeed remarked of the Commons: 'I am surprised that my ancestors should ever have permitted such an institution to come into existence. I am a stranger, and found it here when I arrived, so that I am obliged to put up with what I cannot get rid of.' But he had done his best not to call one. Charles and Buckingham on the other hand, childishly set on war with Spain, had insisted on a Parliament being summoned and so made the Crown more dependent on it, a fact of which the zealous Protestant politicians who clamoured for war were not unmindful. On the home front the Parliament had done good work, passing an important statute against monopolies, but in foreign affairs their provincialism was dangerous, their illusions crystalized in Eliot's neo-Elizabethan phrase: 'Are we poor? Spain is rich. There are our Indies.'

That winter of 1624-5 an even. more impracticable project than a war with Spain was launched. Determined to rescue his sister, Charles backed an utterly incompetent and ill-found expedition against the Palatinate, to which the English were encouraged by the French, anxious to embroil them with Spain. Peter Ernst, Graf von Mansfeld, was a seasoned mercenary captain,[119] who had fought for the Elector Palatine until pay had run out, whereupon he had taken service with the Dutch. Having relieved Bergen-op-Zoom, he had now arrived, a rather dilapidated Protestant hero, in London. And out of the limited supply promised by the Commons, £15,000 was soon raised to scrape some soldiers together and £40,000 to pay them for two months. So that by Christmas 1624 a miserable army of 12,000, including pressed men, was concentrated round Dover to the detriment of the countryside. By late January 1625 they were transported to Vlissingen, not at its best at that season, in the hope of relieving Breda; and on the isle of Walcheren, through starvation and disease, one of many ill-found English expeditions met its usual fate.

But Charles and Buckingham were after bigger game. Already in June 1624 James had made a treaty for two years with the Dutch; now it was extended to an alliance: Christian IV of Denmark, Charles's uncle, offered to raise troops if the English would pay them, and Gustav Adolf of Sweden was eager to invade Germany on the same conditions. The North German princes were sounded out; even the Duke of Savoy and the Venetians. But the most fatal mistake was dynastic. Charles and Buckingham were determined on a French alliance; having evaded one Catholic marriage, Charles rushed into another.

By February 1624 negotiations had been begun for the hand of the Princess Henriette Marie, daughter of Henry IV and Marie de Medici and sister of Louis XIII. Henry Rich, younger son of the Earl of Warwick, was a handsome youth who had attracted the King. Gentleman of the Bedchamber to the Prince, Captain of the Yeomen of the Guard and created Lord Kensington in the previous year, he had been sent as ambassador to Paris, where, as the Prince's representative, he had enthralled the Princess, though his colleague, another former favourite, the Earl of Carlisle, who had arrived earlier, was the more weighty diplomat. For Richelieu the alliance was simply a move in the old European conflict between the French monarchs and the Habsburgs, but he was nearly as exacting as the Spaniards in demanding favours for the

Catholics in England. The English were willing to concede them, but only if expressed in a secret letter concurrent with the treaty. This face-saving device was accepted and the marriage treaty, concluded on 10 November, was ratified in December 1624. The King had prorogued Parliament until February 1625 in the hope that when the Princess arrived they would be in better mind, 'out of respect', as Buckingham wrote, 'for the Princess of France when she shall be here for the virtues and graces that shine in her, as like as for the love and duty borne to the Prince being all joyned in her'. This would not only stay 'exorbitant or ungentle motions... but facilitate those passages, favors, grace and goodness which his Majesty hath promised for the ease of the Romaine Catholickes'.[120] So the 'incomparable lady', Henriette Marie, was now officially the object of the Prince's passion, now switched from the Infanta. His love letters laboriously composed — as witness the corrected drafts in a still relatively unformed hand — contrast with the Princess's more illegible but sloping and forceful script. Though supposed to indicate love, the letters are stilted exchanges about minor illness. The 'least illness she has', for example, gives him 'extreme *dolleur*'; and the Princess replies that 'she cannot worthily praise the present he had been pleased to send her and cherishes the honour of his friendship which will always be agreeable'. Whereat Charles replies acknowledging the constancy of her good will, and announcing '*L'Heureux nouvelle du final accord du Treite.*'[121]

James's decline had long set in, probably as much a psychological as a physical collapse. In March of the previous year he had been well enough to instruct Secretary Conway to inform a local landowner, 'The King is anxious about impaling a place for preservation of the fowl which are his chief pleasure about Newmarket and desires his lordship to require his tenants to suffer the pales to be put up on sufficient payment.' But now he was finally stricken. He was only fifty-nine, but life had been too much for him. His will had been broken; though he still had flashes of his old earthy shrewdness — something never achieved by his son. After his grim childhood in Scotland, his terror of assassination had always remained an obsession: fate had put him where the buck stops, and he was not good at stopping it. Now utterly dependent on other people, he had clung to Steenie and baby Charles — a maddening appellation, one might think, for the Prince.

> God bless you both, my sweete boyes [he had written to them in Spain], and send you a joyfull and happy return to the arms of your dear Dad... I wear Steenie's picture on a blue ribbon under my wash coat next my heart...[122] Alas, now I repent me sore that ever I suffered you to go away. I care not for the match, nor nothing, so I may once have got you in my arms again. God grant, God grant it, Amen, Amen, Amen!... And God bless you both, my only sweet son, and my only best sweet servant, and let me hear from you quickly with all speed, as ye love my my life.[123]

But by the spring of 1624 Buckingham, after a tiff, had been writing to him even more phonetically than usual, and with little respect.

> Dere Dad and Gossope. Notwithstanding of the unfavoured interpretation I find made of a thankful and loyal hart in cauling my words crewell Catonike words... I will tell the Hows of Parlement that you having been upon the afternoune taken with such a fieres rewme and coghe as you are not yet able to appoint them the daye of hereing, but I will forbere to

tell that not withstanding your could, you were able to speke with the King of Spayn's instruments though not with your own subjects.

Proceeding by the autumn of that year to Windsor past St James's, when the Prince and the Duke came out to pay their respects, the old King had cried out that they, too, had deserted him; then, in December, in a passion of reconciliation with the Duke, he had declared that 'he would rather live banished in any part of the world with him', and concluded: 'And so God bless you my sweet child and wife and grant that ye may ever be a comfort to your dear Dad and Husband.'

They had judged it necessary to exclude him from major decisions. 'The Prince [was] now entering into command of affairs by reason of the King's absence and sickness, and all men addressed themselves unto him.' In March 1625 James came to Theobalds where he was to die. He had arthritis, stone in the kidney and recurrent fever — 'tertian ague' they called it and tormented him with 'plaisters' so that he grew 'worse and worse'. And on 27 March 1625 he died. The remedies were supplied by the old Countess of Buckingham and the Duke, and a julep' was concocted by the Duke's servant. When afterwards the doctors were asked to sign a paper testifying that the ingredients of these remedies had been safe, they refused to do so; but probably Buckingham's prescriptions were no more harmful than their own.[124] According to Bishop Williams, who let himself go in a characteristically high-flown artificial sermon at the King's funeral, though the dying James had 'called much after Andrews of Winchester', whose ministrations he would have preferred, his death was edifying. On completing the creed, he testified: 'There is no other belief, no other hope!' And accepting absolution under the Anglican rites, he exclaimed: 'But in the dark way of the Church of

Rome, I do defy it.' According to one account he also then had three hours' private talk with Charles, 'all being commanded from him, a two or three rooms off to be out of hearing'.[125]

But less edifyingly, in another version of his end, his tongue had long been too swollen for him to speak, and according to his modern biographer, whose opinion carries the most weight: '... in fact his death was a horrible one. A day or two before he died he appears to have suffered a stroke which loosened the muscles of his face and caused his jaw to drop. This, with his swollen tongue and with great quantities of phlegm, almost killed him through suffocation. In the end a terrible dysentery carried him away and he died in filth and misery.'[126] But when they came to embalm him: 'The semyture of his head [was] so stronge that they could hardly breake it open with a chesill and a sawe; and soe full of braynes that they could not upon the openinge keep them from spilling, *a great marke of his infinite judgement.*'[127]

That restless, intricate and didactic mind had left a fatal legacy to his son. At first handicapped, shy and retiring, Charles with intense effort now made himself almost the kind of prince he was expected to be: a gentleman of fine manners, fine culture, all-round capacity in Court and hunting field with high chivalric ambitions in pursuit of honour. And he showed a genuinely deep piety unusual in a northern Renaissance prince. He had indeed already shown ominous weakness in diplomacy and in his brashness in foreign affairs; in Spain he had promised what he could not fulfil and extricated himself by deceit, and he had advocated war on the Continent to restore his sister and her consort to the Palatinate when the country almost entirely lacked ships or men to conduct it. But these miscalculations might be put down to youthful inexperience.

But his dogmatic and inflexible cast of mind was politically far more serious. Charles was not in the least original; but he was tenacious and obstinate, and the fixed and then widely believed ideas of regality and its duties that he had absorbed from his father remained with him for life. Like James I he saw himself as a link in the great chain of being that held together the hierarchy of heaven and earth: kings were God's lieutenants upon it, and a monarch inevitably '*Parens Patriae*, the politique Father of his People'. As the head to the body, King James had written in a well-worn medieval simile, so a wise king could sustain the whole 'body politic' in health, a bad one 'poyson and phlebotomyze' it. Laws derived originally not from the people but from God through kings, though the pious king — *lex loquens*, a speaking law — observes his kingdom's laws which derive from him, thus proving himself *princeps* not *tyrannus*. But although James had declared that a just ruler would always explain his actions, 'I will not', he had written, 'be content that my power be disputed upon.'[128] The monarchy of James I, as handed down and accepted by Charles, was a benevolent but in principle an absolute paternalism. That it was benevolent — designed, James had written, 'to beate downe... proud oppressors and protect the poor' and to 'teach the nobility to keep the lawes as precisely as the meanest' — made it in the surge of seventeenth-century social and economic change all the more tragically impracticable. In addition to being naturally rather devious and aloof, Prince Charles had inherited, and would retain and die for, ideas that gave him a touch of Don Quixote.

BOOK II: THE MONARCH

7: THE ASCENDANCY OF BUCKINGHAM

'ACTIVE AND RESOLUTE', as the Catholic convert and wit Sir Tobie Matthew wrote to Sir Dudley Carleton,[129] as one courtier to another, 'and a friend of state and order in the Court', King Charles was impatient to take control; but the Duke, added Matthew, 'stands hugely high in the substantial part of the King's favour'.[130] Charles shared the restless habits of his father and, besides following the hunt, the Court moved about to avoid the plague, already in the spring of 1625 virulent in London. Charles was also impatient for his marriage, ratified in the previous December. But first the funeral of the old King had to be accomplished.

His father had died owing the City a debt that with interest amounted to over £200,000; but with royal disregard for money Charles borrowed another £60,000 and on 7 May staged the greatest funeral ever known in England. Mourning ('blacks') was provided to nine thousand persons, though all recusant Papists were excluded; Inigo Jones designed a magnificent baroque hearse; Orlando Gibbons composed the music, and the cost was £50,000. Then the new coinage, issued only after the funeral, had to be considered: meticulous in detail and in taste, Charles 'misliked the effigy', and ordered Abraham van Doort to provide a new pattern for the engravers.[131] Ironically the inscriptions chosen were: for gold, *Amor civium Regis praesidium* (The King's defence is the love of the people) and *Florent Concordia Regna* (May the concord of the realm flourish); and for silver, *Justitia Thronum firmat* (Justice strengthens the throne).

In May Charles had sent his first letter to Henriette Marie, writing as King in a more confident hand and in a more human way:

> I feel myself so infinitely obliged for your favours that when I desire to express it I find that the happiness of my spirit cannot be in words... [or] the joy and contentment that I feel in your affection, and the impatience that I have and shall have until I can kiss your hands as your must humble, loving and faithfull. Charles R.

Early in June the King went down to Dover, eager to meet his bride, whose progress had been delayed through the Queen Mother's illness at Amiens; he even had to be dissuaded from crossing to Boulogne. The precedent, it was explained, would abase the King of England, besides the danger of putting him in the hands of a foreign power. But he remained on the 'leads' of Dover Castle, where he spent 'two very cold hours'.

The marriage of King Charles and the 'Madam of France' had been conducted in Paris by proxy at Notre Dame, Charles being represented by the Duc de Chevreuse. Then, unexpectedly and very expensively, Buckingham had arrived to conduct the Queen Consort to England. He had taken over a fantastic entourage to fetch her — fifteen lords, twenty-four 'knights of great worth', and far too many pages. For himself he had twenty gentlemen, seven grooms of the chamber, thirty chief yeomen, two master cooks and twenty-five second ones. He had three rich coaches, velvet inside with 'gold and lace all over', with six coachmen and eight horses to each coach. He also brought musicians and watermen — the last in sky-coloured taffeta. And the Duke himself had twenty-seven rich suits laced with silk, besides a cloak with diamonds 'said to be worth four score thousand pounds', a feather made with great diamonds, with sword, girdle, hat band and spurs with diamonds, 'with which suit his grace intends to enter Paris with'.[132]

This kind of show, much enjoyed by all, was part of the protocol of the day, and the Queen Consort brought a dowry of 800,000 crowns of three livre coins of French money, one half to be paid in the City of London on the day before the marriage and the other on its anniversary in the following year, to be refunded to her if Charles died before she did. She had £18,000 a year jointure, and 50,000 crowns for rings and jewels; she had renounced all rights of succession on the crown lands of France, but was allowed to bring up her children until they were thirteen — a considerable concession, for although Sir George Goring had sent her Anglican common prayer books in French, which 'some supposed would give hopes of conversion; others much doubt[ed] it, she having a Bishop and twenty-eight priests, resolute Papists, as are all her servants'.[133]

On 24 June Charles again rode fast down from Canterbury to meet Henriette Marie at Dover, where she had landed after a stormy crossing the evening before. He arrived earlier than expected and she hastened down two flights of stairs to kneel and kiss his hand; but he 'rapt her up in his arms and kissed her with many kisses'.[134] Her first words were submissive: '*Sire, je suis venue en ce pais de vostre Matie pour estre usée et commandée de vous.*'

After an elaborate picnic on Barham Down they came to Canterbury, where Charles himself carved her pheasant and venison, which she evidently enjoyed, in spite of her confessor's warning that on the eve of St John the Baptist, a fast day, she was setting a bad example. And when after supper she went to bed and, after a proper interval, Charles followed, he would have none of the roistering customary under Henry

VIII. The 'first thing he did, he bolted all the doors round about (being seven) with his own hands, letting in but two of the bedchamber to undress him, which being done he bolted them out also.'

Having thus avoided the attendant lords, and after a long lie in in the morning, he was 'pleasaant with them that he had beguiled them' and 'appeared very jocund'. His wife, who he insisted was to be called Queen Mary, was only fifteen and tiny, so that short as he was himself her head reached only to his shoulder. Petite, vivacious and agile, with slightly protruding upper teeth, she had style; 'nimble and quiet', it was reported, 'black-eyed, brown haired and in a word a brave Lady, though perhaps a little touched by the green sickness'.[135] It was also soon observed that she was of 'more than ordinary resolution', and with 'one frown cleared an over-crowded room. She was not for nothing a daughter of Henri IV.

In spite of the plague in London, the usual Tudor-style spectacle was laid on. Under vehement summer rain the King and Queen came up river in the royal barge through London to Whitehall; fifty ships discharged their guns, and when they passed the Tower the royal ordnance thundered in salute. Through the barge windows, open in spite of the rain, the royalties, in green suits, acknowledged the applause of the roaring crowds along the banks. There was a great wedding dinner after the Queen had been formally proclaimed.

Charles had now achieved his two ambitions: accession to full power and marriage. But already there was one cloud. The Queen's foreign Catholic household, who were watching the young Queen like hawks, were already complaining that the chapel at St James's, originally designed by Inigo Jones for the Spanish Infanta, was not yet finished. It was rumoured that King Charles had been firm with them: if the Queen's closet, he had said, was not large enough, let them say Mass in the Great Chamber; if that was not enough, let them use the garden; and if that was insufficient there was always the park.

In the rush of affairs at the King's accession, neither Charles nor Buckingham had taken much trouble about the new Parliament — Charles had even suggested to the Lord Keeper that the old Parliament should be reconvened. But when this proved legally impossible, the writs for the elections had been hurried through. Then, summoned for 17 May, the members of the first Parliament of Charles I were kept hanging about in London in spite of the plague; and it did not meet until 18 June, after the Queen had arrived.

The Duke's brief popularity in 1624 was soon dissipated; the fiasco of Mansfeld's expedition and increasing piracy in the Channel had convinced the Commons that their supply had been ill-spent, while the grandiose foreign policy that Buckingham now had in mind, mustering a whole continental alliance to help the Elector Palatine, was a very different prospect from a traditional war with Spain. Moreover the liaison between Council and Parliament was now even more unsatisfactory.

Charles's first speech to his first Parliament had indeed an engaging lack of pretension. 'I thank God,' he began, 'that the business to be treated on this time is of such a nature that it needs no eloquence to set it forth, for I am neither able to do it, neither doth it stand with my nature to spend much time in words.' He referred to the 'assistance of those in Germany', the Fleet that was ready, and to the rest of 'the preparations which I have followed my father in, so sufficiently had he entered into this action'; he stressed that if he had come to the business like a young man and in consequence 'rashly', it had been only to carryout their 'own intent and engagement'. It would be a great dishonour if that purpose was not now prosecuted and he pointed out that (because of the plague) 'he must adventure their lives if they made it a long session', and so urged them to 'expedite what they had to do'. He concluded 'because some Malicious men... have given out that I am not so true a keeper and maintainer of the true religion that I profess, I assure you I have been trained up at Gamaliel's feet'. No one was more zealous to maintain the Anglican Church. 'Now,' he ended, referring to his stammer, evidently then severe, 'because I am unfit for more speaking, I mean to bring on that fashion of my predecessor to have my Lord Keeper speak for me in other things. Therefore I have commanded him to speak something to you at this time, which is more for formality than for any other matter that he has to say to you.'[136] The King's own mind was entirely on the war.

On other affairs no lead was given by King, Duke or Council, and the speech of Sir Benjamin Rudyard — who was not even a councillor, but tried to speak for the government in the Commons — was thought by Eliot to be as 'languid as the conclusion was inept'.[137] So casual were the courtiers in attending the House that by a snap vote the opponents of the regime got away with an absurdly small supply of two subsidies without fifteenths. But what was much worse and without precedent, they confined the grant of the customs revenue, known as tunnage and poundage and granted to the Crown for life since the reign of Edward iv, only to one year. This was most unhelpful, particularly since the Lord Treasurer had reported that there was 'neither money in the Exchequer left nor any credit at all', and entreated the King to give warrant for payment for victuals for the navy of £8,500, for £11,800 for ordnance, for the £46,000 subsidy to the King of Denmark, and for payment of the soldiers assembled at Plymouth and serving in the Low Countries. Payment of £136,000 had already been made in anticipation of income.

Apart from the lawyers, of whom Sir Edward Coke was still the most implacable, the two most hostile leaders of the Commons who had thus put government in jeopardy were men of great wealth. Sir Robert Phillips, whose father had been Speaker of the House and Master of the Robes, owned Montacute House in Somerset and had represented Looe, Saltash and Bath and then his own county. He had been with Digby in Spain and shared his opinions, and had been foremost in attacking Mompesson, Bacon and Cranfield; indeed he was thought to be the 'Bell wether' of his faction. Sir John Eliot, who had sat in the Parliament of 1621, owned Port Eliot near St Germans in Cornwall; he had studied at Exeter College, Oxford, and at the Inns of Court, and had made a close friend of young George Villiers on the Continent. He now sat for Newport in Cornwall, and reluctantly turning against Buckingham became the most eloquent of his enemies. Both these leaders were rich men of high social standing, representing a formidable but in modern terms far from popular interest.

Meanwhile Buckingham was planning to lead a naval expedition against Spain, ostensibly commissioned by the Elector Palatine, and again himself went to Paris to sound out how substantial Richelieu's help would be. But that shrewd realist would not commit himself to an alliance, and the Duke showed what he thought of the French by openly and insolently making love to their Spanish Queen, to the fury of the French Court.

The plague was now so virulent in London that all who could tried to leave; by August four to five thousand people would die a week, and those infected would be parked out in tents 'in the fields'; one refugee from London died 'in the fields' outside Southampton 'with great store of money on him'. At Westminster School one of the King's Scholars had died of it, and Lord Keeper Williams, who often used to dine and sup in the same room as the Scholars, had broken up his household.

At last, on 11 July 1625, Parliament went into recess; but to the anger of members anxious to get home, it was summoned to reassemble at Oxford on 1 August, the dons having been 'commanded away for better accommodation'. The King and Queen had gone down to Windsor, but they had brought the plague with them, and the Queen had retired to Nonesuch Palace. Charles and Buckingham now came to Oxford, but got no change out of a thin House of Commons. They refused further supply and insisted, as the Venetian ambassador put it, 'on enquiring into the state of affairs and how to advise [the King] on a better way to manage things'.[138] The Commons, he reported, personally appealed to Charles that money voted should be better administered, and not as in the past; and insisted that the government should not be in the hands of one man, though they declared that they would willingly supply money 'provided that the spoiling of the people does not serve private ends'.[139] Of course nothing came of it. The Commons again declared that the conduct of the coming war with Spain should not be left in Buckingham's hands alone, and though he himself addressed them in Christ Church Hall he carried no conviction. So to save Buckingham from further attack, Charles dissolved his first Parliament without recall and retired to Woodstock. And there he uncompromisingly declared his position to the Council: 'Parliament,' he said, 'had wished to touch his sovereignty. But his condition would be too miserable if he could not command and be obeyed. He would employ one or many or nobody in his Councils.'[140]

Regardless of insolvency King and Duke pressed on with their grandiose designs. The navy had long lost command even of the Channel; a Sallee pirate, for example, had recently taken a Dartmouth ship and two Cornish fisher boats — not for the boats but for slaves. The Mayor of Weymouth reported that the pirates so swarmed off the Scilly Isles and Land's End that shipping could not pass; worse still, Turkish pirates had caused terror in the countryside near Plymouth, and at Looe in Cornwall had carried off sixty men, women and children. Further up Channel the French themselves could not control a 'kennel of rank pirating rogues' from Dieppe, while the Dunkerkers were a constant menace. Yet the government were far less concerned to defend the coasts than to press men into the navy for a war against Spain, part of an entirely unrealistic policy on the Continent.

For, in part under Buckingham's influence, Charles, at twenty-four, was far from being the peaceful and artistic monarch he sometimes later appeared; he was aggressively martial. He was also, perhaps under the influence of the Queen, wearing better clothes; in August he signed a warrant to pay £1,000 to his tailors to be spent in France to buy materials, gloves and the like.[141] But he was as intent as ever on the war. 'By the grace of God,' he said, 'I will carry on the war if I risk my crown.' During the summer, in the face of endless difficulties, the government went on pressing men for the expedition; in Norfolk it was impossible to obtain the number of seamen required, so all who were found ashore were rounded up to Cromer and there pressed. In the Cinque Ports the authorities were hard put to it to see that only experienced mariners were taken, not 'loose and unskilled poor men'. And the problem of raising any army was even worse. In Dorset the authorities, masters of delay, explained in October that they had hoped to raise a hundred men; but that after Buckingham himself had passed through Blandford and they had heard the fleet was at sea, they had felt that they had been too late. At Marlborough John Franklin and William Inglis were accused of taking bribes to let men off the press, and in Oxfordshire and Buckinghamshire money had been too short to pay the men enrolled. The men of Essex had mutinied against their 'conductor' within a week, and in Suffolk those responsible were reduced to pressing a couple of rogues convicted of small felonies who had escaped death by pleading benefit of clergy and so were in prison.

It had been planned to concentrate fifteen thousand soldiers at Plymouth, where the Mayor was using his best endeavours to billet ten thousand; but since they got paid only 2s 6d a week they were not popular in the neighbourhood. The poor countrymen, it was reported, were 'no longer able to entertain the soldier and in some places thrust him out of doors'. And there were far too few experienced officers.

Somehow the expedition was mobilized; on 8 October, under a commander nominated by Buckingham, it made for Spain. Sir Edward Cecil was a grandson of the great Burghley through his marriage to Mary Cheke; he had a good fighting record in the Low Countries, but had held no independent command and was inexperienced at sea. The young Earl of Essex, presumably included out of compliment to his father's memory, was even more inexperienced, while many of the ships were conscripted merchantmen, with reluctant captains and crews. There was no coherent plan of combined operations and the decision to attack Cadiz was taken only after the expedition had rounded Cape St Vincent.

The resulting fiasco was total. First Puerto Santa Maria in the low and sandy mainland coast opposite Cadiz was attacked, but without effect; when Essex wanted to go for the ships in Cadiz outer harbour he was not backed up; and when a landing was made at Fort Puntales, which commanded the harbour mouth, the soldiers were left without provisions. When therefore they made an arduous march, south and west, round the bay to San Fernando and there came upon immense stores of wine for the Spanish American fleet, they were soon quite overcome and failed even to cross the bridge on to the island of which Cadiz formed the apex. It was lucky for them that they did, for the town had been heavily refortified in the latest fashion — the functional-looking fort at the end of the causeway by the Phoenician harbour, still extant, quite outclassing Calshot or St Mawes. By 28 October the expedition had to be re-embarked and after hanging about in the hope of intercepting two Spanish treasure ships that easily eluded capture, it returned to England, with sickness aboard and leaking hulls and in even worse shape.

Charles and Buckingham stifled all attempts at serious enquiry, and Cecil was created Lord Cecil of Putney and Viscount Wimbledon; but the facts got about. The first and lesser fiasco of Buckingham's regime had been achieved. By December Charles was pawning plate and jewels in Amsterdam: he hoped to raise £300,000. During the Cadiz fiasco he had been at Salisbury, a city he liked, and now, since the plague still infected Windsor, Christmas was kept at Hampton Court where French pastorals were performed for the pleasure of the Queen.

By 2 February 1626 the 'pestilence had assuaged' in London and Charles's coronation took place. It was in a relatively minor key and not much more efficiently conducted than other operations of his government. Charles himself had sent for the regalia, discovered that the wing of the dove on the sceptre had been broken off, and when his goldsmith advised that he could not make an exact replica, had exclaimed petulantly, 'If you will not do it, another shall!'; whereat the goldsmith 'so skillfully set on an entire new dove' that the King thought it was the old one repaired and was pleased with himself for his perceptiveness.

Another minor problem, the tension between Bishop Williams of Lincoln and Laud of St Davids, had to be solved. In the previous October Williams had been forced to resign as Lord Keeper[142] for he had told Buckingham at Oxford that he was engaged with William, Earl of Pembroke, 'to labour the redress of the people's grievances and to stand upon his own legs'. He had opposed the Spanish war, thus, as he put it, committing the sin against the Holy Ghost and becoming a martyr forced to live off 1,000 marks a year. Yet as Dean of Westminster he had to perform important functions at the coronation and, failing his own participation, had the right to appoint one of the prebendaries of the Abbey instead. One of them was Laud; tension was eased and Williams defeated when he submitted the entire list of them to the King, who appointed Laud.

On coronation day the royal barge missed the prepared flight of steps and went aground at Parliament stairs, so that King and Lords had to use neighbouring boats for landing. On the dais at Westminster Hall Buckingham brought Charles the regalia, which he distributed to the appropriate magnates — as Lord Chamberlain, William, third Earl of Pembroke,[143] had the crown, Essex the long sceptre, and Pembroke's brother Philip, Earl of Montgomery, who succeeded him in 1630 as fourth earl and proved an enemy of the King, carried the spurs — and then moved in procession to the Abbey.[144] But when the Archbishop, still under a cloud for casual homicide, and the Earl Marshal presented the King, bareheaded, to the people, again there was a hitch. For when the Archbishop desired the people by general acclamation to testify their consent, there was silence. Some had expected a longer speech, others had not well heard it, others perhaps were awed by the greatness of the occasion, or else 'those which were nearest doubted what to do' — so that no word followed till Lord Arundel told them they should cry out 'God Save King Charles', at which, ashamed at their first oversight, they managed a little shouting. It was an appropriate prelude to the King's reign.

The elaborate ceremony itself took place behind a 'traverse' or curtain, since the King's naked shoulders and arms had to be anointed, the ancient robes of Edward the Confessor draped round him, and the crown of King Edward set upon his head. He then received communion, ascended the stage and throne, the earls and viscounts having put on their coronets and caps and the bishops their caps, the barons remaining bare, and took the homage of all the peers. Finally, in black robes lined with ermine, Charles returned to Westminster Hall and resumed the regalia from the great lords.

The Queen, advised by her confessors, had refused to be crowned by Anglican rites or even to attend the Abbey, though she had watched the procession from a window, while her ladies with tiresome Gallic gaiety were 'frisking and dancing' in the rooms on the solemn occasion.

After the coronation the second Parliament of the reign had assembled. In the Upper House, reported the Venetian ambassador, Charles had again spoken very briefly, leaving the rest, owing to the impediment of his tongue, to the Lord Keeper, Sir Thomas Coventry, created Lord Coventry in 1628.[145] Hot on the scent of the culprits responsible for the fiasco against Spain, the Commons, when asked to vote supply, at once attacked Buckingham; he was like 'a blazing comet in the firmament whose glare kept the sun of the King's countenance from them'. They set the procedure of impeachment going against him and chose a committee of eight members, each with two assistants, to prepare fourteen articles of accusation. But the King acted swiftly. Sir Dudley Digges and Sir John Eliot, called out of the House as if Charles had summoned them, were hustled into a barge and carried down to the Tower, whereat the House, crying out 'Rise! Rise!', refused to sit and transact further business that day. It was rumoured that troops were being brought in from the fleet to reinforce the Tower — 'a very violent innovation and one very ill adapted to the humour of the country'.

In April Bristol came up from Sherborne to vindicate himself and attack the Duke, and on 8 May Buckingham was formally impeached. He was charged as Lord Admiral with neglecting to put down the pirates on the Channel, with appointing incompetent officers to the Cadiz expedition, with 'selling places' and engrossing great offices to himself and with harbouring Catholics — was not his own mother a recusant? The Duke was now detested by the populace, who took it out on his unfortunate astrologer, 'Dr' Lambe, as he was returning through the City after the theatre, 'being a person very notorious, the Boys gathered thick about him which increased the access of the ordinary people and the Rabble'. He took sanctuary in the Windmill Tavern, but was hounded out by a mob that fell on him crying 'Witch!' and 'Devil!' and left him for dead. Rescued by the Lord Mayor's guard, he died within hours. Civilization was a thin veneer in seventeenth-century London and the King's furious instruction to the Lord Mayor to find the culprits was in vain. People went about singing:

> Let Charles and George do what they can,
> The Duke shall die like Dr. Lambe.[146]

'The populace here,' the Venetian envoy had reported, 'is practically frantic,'[147] and relations with the French were now deteriorating. The wine trade was being ruined, English ships detained in Bordeaux and 'the natural antipathy between the two nations inflamed'; by the spring of 1627, the envoy concluded, 'such is the violence of internal private passions that they leave no room for the consideration of public ruin'.[148] French goods in England were now confiscated and sold, while it was reported that Richelieu, now Superintendent at Sea, was building a great fleet armed with a new kind of gun and boasting that the French would enter the ports of England itself.

In Parliament the Duke's enemies, pressing the impeachment, now swore they would have justice and 'beseeched audience for the King about serious business concerning all the commons in the land'. Charles was more interested in obtaining supply and told them 'if we did not make provision speedily we shall not be able to put one ship to sea this year, *Verbum sapienti sat sit* [let a word be enough to the wise]'. But they were more interested in hounding down the Duke; they had not before impeached a king's chief minister, and some of the charges were criminal. And they still refused supply, for the good reason, they said, that so long as Buckingham was in office it would be misappropriated or muddled away.

Another widespread grievance of which Buckingham was considered a flagrant example was the 'abuse of honour'. Sir John Suckling, the poet's father, a big landowner, former Secretary of State and a privy councillor, exhorted the Commons to examine the kind of people

> ... raised to honour these twenty-five years past... Recollect... how many poor base and needy companions have been raised to the highest top of honour, yea, how many Wills, Jacks, Jockies, Georges and James's have attained the degree of Viscount and baron, that it will appear whether desert, favour or power advanced them... When they see the revenues consumed on these unworthy persons, the ancient and great nobility of the land cannot choose but fret.

The other abuse of honour was 'the base and mercenary buying of it, so that upstart families grown to wealth by extortion, take precedence of old ones and buy degrees of nobility in Scotland or Ireland only for the name of a Lord'. From 'horsekeeping and other base callings' men had been promoted to the degree of baronets and knights.[149] In defiance Charles heaped more honours on Buckingham and compelled the University of Cambridge to elect him their chancellor.[150]

Then on 12 June 1627 Charles dissolved his second Parliament and, now desperate for money, raised it by arbitrary forced loans — the most fatal move he had so far made. 'What can I do more?' he said to Buckingham. 'I have engaged my own honour to mine Uncle of Denmark and other princes. I have in some manner lost the love of my subjects. What wouldst thou have me to do?' The drift into war with France was not arrested by the King's dynastic marriage, for its early years were not a success, and the Queen had written constantly to France to complain of her grievances. His closest affection had been reserved for Buckingham, and the mercurial, still adolescent Queen had been a handful. Her large foreign household had set her against Charles, and already in the previous November, only six months after his marriage, Charles had written to Buckingham from Hampton Court.

> Steenie, I writt to you by Ned Clark that I thought I would have cause anufe in shorte tyme to put away the Monsers, ether by atempting to steale away my wife, or by making plots with my own subjects... seeing daylie the malitiusness of the Monsers by making and fomenting discontentments in my wife, I could tarie no longer from advertising you, that I meane to seeke for no other grounds to easier [cashier] my Monsers.

He had asked the Duke to warn the French Queen Mother of his intended action so that she might not take it unkindly, assured him that he would put nothing into execution without his advice and concluded:

> ... in the meane tyme, I shall think of the convenient meanes to do this business with the best mind, but I am resolute. It must be done and that shortlie. So, longing to see thee, I rest, Your loving faithfull, constant frend, Charles R.[151]

Henriette Marie now lived much in the beautiful Queen's House at Greenwich and in London at Somerset House, the former residence of Queen Anne. After the coronation the King and Queen had again quarrelled because she insisted on nominating Frenchmen to most of the appointments connected with the properties assigned to her for revenue in England — all in fact in the King's gift. Then in June 1626, a year after the marriage, they had had a major scene when in the Queen's apartments in Whitehall Charles found some

Frenchmen 'unreverently curvetting and dancing in her presence'.[152] He had firmly taken her off to his own rooms and shutting out everyone turned the key, having ordered Secretary Conway to clear the French attendants from her suite. They had made memorable scenes, the women 'howling' as if sent to execution; the Queen, locked in with her husband and observing their exodus from the window, had cried out hysterical farewells, broken the glass and torn her hair in rage, while Charles had begged her to 'be satisfied', as 'it had to be'. She had then been sent down into the country, while the King wrote firmly to the English ambassador in Paris, 'I can no longer suffer those that I know to be fomenting of disturbance about my wife.' But the French entourage had managed to make off with the Queen's clothes as perquisites and to run up £19,000 worth of bills. By August they were nearly all dismissed.

> Steenie [wrote the King],... this is my answer: I command you to send all the Frency away tomorrow out of the towne, — if you can by fay er means, but sticke not long in disputing, otherwise force them away... like so manie wilde beastes, untill you have shipped them, and so the devil goe with them. Let me heare of no answer but of the performance of my command.

Out of 440 only six French attendants were left with the Queen: her nurse, her dresser, her baker, a pantry hand and a tailor and — mercifully — her cook. Those expelled were 'very sullen and dogged at their first setting out... but their kind entertainment on the way made them more tame by that time they come to Dover'.

The French King sent the Duc de Bassompierre to smooth out the affair, which had now worsened when Buckingham had told her to beware how she behaved, for in England 'Queens had had their heads cut off before now'. But characteristically and in contrast to his father, Charles refused to discuss domestic affairs in a public interview, saying he could not help putting himself in a passion about them, 'which would not be decorous in the chair of state'; but Bassompierre proved a good diplomat, both conciliatory and firm. When Charles, half-seriously, asked him if he came to declare war on him, he replied, in the high French tradition: 'I am not a Herald to declare war, but a Marshal of France, to make it when desired.'[153] He wrote an admirable account of his embassy.

By the summer of 1627, 'engaged in honour', King and Duke went to open war with France as well as Spain, taking on both the Atlantic powers at once. Richelieu, coldly determined to build a centralized state, was putting down the Huguenot revolt centred on La Rochelle. Charles had always thought of the European conflict in terms of the baleful religious strife then afflicting Europe. On 16 July Buckingham himself, furious because Richelieu had written to him with a nuance of disrespect, left Plymouth with a considerable fleet and nearly seven thousand soldiers, determined to relieve La Rochelle. On 19 July, through high seas, they landed on the sandy, pine-clad beach of the tie de Re, which lies close in to La Rochelle and which could have served as a base to raid French shipping out of the estuaries of the Loire and Garonne. The English besieged the fort of St Martin on the island but it held out, the Rochellois, half-hearted at the prospect of English troops within their town, giving little help; Buckingham, intent on chivalry, and apparently unaware of the ugly realities of the muddled expedition, presented a released Gascon officer who had lost his sword with his own much better one, asked him to 'kiss the French King's hand on [his] behalf' and say that if he failed to take the fort he would have the satisfaction of being vanquished by the greatest and most courageous king in the world.

The scaling ladders then proved too short; the French counter-attacked and the English expedition was taken off the island, having lost more than half its men. Buckingham was so detested that when it became known in London that he had failed, the people were so delighted that 'to vent their hatred they forgot the honour of the nation, a thing [observed the objective Venetian envoy] really worthy of remark'.

Rejecting French peace feelers the incorrigibly spirited Duke now planned to attack Calais; and worse, to raise a royal standing army, supplemented by some German cavalry. It was thus an even more indignant third Parliament that had to be called on 17 March 1628; the more so as Charles had been raising money by forced loans and putting seventy-six recalcitrant men of substance in prison without trial.

The resulting 'Darnell's case',[154] or the 'Trial of the Five Knights', decided in the autumn of 1627, had already roused intense anger; acting impartially under the law the judges had pronounced for the King, who was using the Tudor prerogative power (originally designed to ferret out treason) for a different purpose to raise money in an extra-parliamentary way. 'If, injustice,' Chief Justice Hyde had pronounced, 'we ought to deliver you, we would do it; but upon these grounds and these records and the precedents and resolutions we cannot deliver you, but you must be [in custody] remanded.'

Of those imprisoned — and prison in plague-stricken London was no joke, particularly if like one of the knights one had sixteen dependent children — seventy-seven were released early in 1628 and twenty-seven, among them Sir Thomas

Wentworth, afterwards Earl of Strafford, who had sat for Yorkshire since 1614 under King James, now became members of the King's third Parliament.

It was felt that the King had been cheating, 'antiquating' the law for purposes for which it had not been designed; and fuel was added to the fires of indignation lit by the monumental incompetence of the government. Moreover the Five Knights' case had given the lawyers on both sides something to bite on; in a House of Commons so full of them and of gentry trained in the law, the result was a formidable spate of argument. Following the lead of the now venerable Sir Edward Coke and of the learned Selden,[155] the Lords and Commons between them now devised a *Petition of Right* in which their grievances were set out in lapidary form. Appealing to 'that good old decrepit law of Magna Charta which hath been kept so long and lien bedrid', they interpreted it to their own needs; in defence of the 'ancient fundamental liberties' of the kingdom, both Lords and Commons petitioned against arbitrary taxation without common consent by Act of Parliament and insisted that 'no free man be detained in prison without cause shown'. Furthermore no man should be 'forced to take soldiers but inns, and those be paid for them, and commissions to proceed by martial law should be revoked'.[156]

Charles protested that such demands would 'dissolve the foundation and frame of our monarchy'; moderates in the Lords tried to insert a clause safeguarding the King's sovereignty, but the Commons would have none of it, saying that such a clause had never been inserted before and would invalidate the petition. 'Take heed what we yield unto,' said Coke, '*Magna Carta* is such a fellow that he will have no "sovereign".' And when the King tried to evade assent by omitting the formula '*Soit droit fait come est desire*' they insisted that he include it. Before the combined Lords and Commons he could do nothing else, and by June 1628 the petition had the Royal Assent. The Commons had thus clinched their financial stranglehold on the King, blocked accepted ways of putting political enemies out of the way and crippled the maintenance of such armed forces as were available.

Fresh from this victory they now granted five subsidies, but went on to attack Buckingham again and tighten their financial grip. They drew up another Remonstrance that the Duke was the 'cause of all their miseries, the grievance of grievances'; 'Let us set down the cause of all our disasters,' said Coke, 'and all will reflect upon him.' In fact constitutionally the Duke had committed no crime: he had merely as a 'privado' carried out the King's policy according to his lights. It was the second Remonstrance that was unconstitutional. Also it again tried to hold up grants of tunnage and poundage, the mainstay of government. This policy was too much for Sir Thomas Wentworth, a born administrator. He went over to the King and in July 1628 was created Viscount Wentworth.

Charles had already saved Buckingham from impeachment in his second Parliament, and that June he hastily prorogued his third. 'It may seem strange,' he said, 'that I am come so suddenly to end this session before I give my assent to the Bills. I will tell you the cause, though I must avowe that I owe the Account of my Actions only to God alone.' The Commons had already given him one Remonstrance — how acceptable every man might judge — and now they were preparing 'to take away the profit of my Tunnage and Poundage, one of the chief maintenances of my Crown'.

> This [he concluded] is so prejudicial unto me that I am forced to end this session some few hours before I meant, being not willing to receive any more Remonstrances to which I must

give a harsh answer. As for Tunnage and Poundage it is a thing that I cannot want... None of the Houses of Parliament either joint or separate (whatever new doctrines soever may be raised) have any power to make or declare law without my consent.[157]

Unable to bring the King's ministers to account because they were not responsible to them, the Commons had tried by their money power to bring government to a standstill. The King had defied them. The central and predominant conflict between the King and his Parliament had become acute.

The besieged Rochellois, meanwhile, had been eating their horses, cats and dogs. King and Duke still felt bound in honour again to relieve them and another incompetent expedition was being mounted. In May the veteran Sir Ferdinando Gorges, governor of Plymouth and one of the main founders of the Massachusetts colony, offered to take charge, saying that the officers assigned were not accustomed to such hazards and that he was ready to forsake his peaceable course and hazard his life in this most difficult action. His service was not accepted. On 6 June Charles wrote:

> Buckingham I commend you to draw my armie together to Porchemouth, to the end I may send them speedli to Rochell. I shall send after you directions how and whaire to billett them, until the tyme that you be able to shipp them; for the doing whairof this shall be your sufficient warrant...

It did not prove warrant enough. On the morning of 23 August at Portsmouth, while the Duke was having breakfast, one John Felton, a disgruntled lieutenant of foot 'stung with denial of a captain's place' and because his pay was £80 in arrears, or crazed with a libellous book written by a Scots doctor against the Duke, or merely worked up by the recent Remonstrance, was lurking in a dark corridor leading from the room. He had bought a tenpenny knife — 'so cheap', says the narrator, 'was the instrument of his great attempt' — in a cutler's on Tower Hill and had sewn it in the lining of his pocket so that he could swiftly draw it out with one hand. He had then made his way, though 'indigent of money', to Portsmouth.

So bad were security arrangements that in the press of suitors thronging to wait on the Duke, Felton had easily placed himself by the door.[158] And when Buckingham came out into the passage, having just been told of false tidings that Rochelle had been relieved and 'in the greatest joy and alacrity' coming from breakfast with lords, colonels, and captains about him, Felton struck upwards into his heart and slew him at one blow. The Duke 'cried out "villain" — and never spake a word more, but presently plucking out the knife for himself... made towards the tray tor, two or three paces, then fell against a table, and blood gush[ed] from his mouth, and wound so fast that life and breath, at once left his begored body'.[159] The bystanders cried out, 'Where is the villain? Where is the Butcher?' and Felton, who might well have escaped, came forward saying, 'I am the Man. Here I am', perhaps confusing the cry 'a Frenchman, a Frenchman' for his own name. Meanwhile the Duchess of Buckingham and the Countess of Anglesey, observing the scene from a gallery, gave vent to 'such screechings, teares and distractions', wrote an eyewitness, that 'I never in my life heard the like before and hope never to hear the like again'. Such was the panic that fear overcome curiosity and within a few minutes there was 'not a living creature in either of the chambers, no more than if had lien in the sands of Ethiopia'.[160] In his premeditated crime and martyrdom Felton had thought of everything; sewn in his hat was found a note: 'If I bee slaine, let no man condemne me, but rather condemn himselfe; if for our sinns that our harts are hardened… or else had he not gone soe long unpunished.'

So great Villiers, the brilliant, versatile charmer who had hypnotized King James, dominated Charles I and virtually ruled England for over four years, and, intoxicated by power, designed a foreign policy of disastrous incompetence in pursuit of unrealistic and romantic ambitions, perished at the hands of an obscure officer crazed with a mixture of personal grievance and political and religious fanaticism.[161]

Four miles away at Southwick Charles was kneeling at household prayers. A messenger interrupted him with the appalling news, but the King, with iron self-control and sense of duty and place, signed that prayers should continue.

8: CIVIL AND RELIGIOUS CONFRONTATION

'THE KING TOOK the Duke's death very heavily, keeping his chamber all day';[162] he refused, as after the news of his sister's disasters, to see anyone. But domestically the tragedy brought some good: no longer dominated by the dazzling Buckingham — extrovert, amusing, with a magnetism that made his wildest project seem feasible — Charles turned for consolation to his wife. And it was soon observed that he was actually in love with her. She was now eighteen: 'bright and graceful', as Gardiner has it, 'with flashing eyes and all the impetuous vehemence of her race'.

Her political influence soon proved disastrous; but their family life, until disrupted by the civil wars, was happy. Their first child, born on 13 May 1628, before Buckingham's assassination, had died an infant. One version says that he was born prematurely because two large dogs fighting in the gallery at Greenwich — doubtless an occurrence taken for granted — had snatched at the Queen's dress, and the local midwife, hastily summoned, had fainted at her responsibility; or, in another, after the Queen had been jolted in one of the clumsy royal coaches with their heavy leather curtains, poorly sprung and stiflingly hot. Her mother now sent her a wheelchair, 'to obviate the danger from coaches'. The King wrote: 'My wife has taken the utmost pleasure in going out in the beautiful chair you sent her'.

The Queen this time bore a lusty dark boy, the tall and indefatigable Charles II, whose stature would dwarf his miniature parents, whose insatiable Bourbon temperament would follow that of his grandfather and whose sardonic features would recall those of Lorenzo de' Medici.[163] The Queen bore seven more children: in 1631 Mary, who married William I of Orange; in 1633 James, Duke of York, afterwards James II; in 1635 Elizabeth, who had 'a rare inclination to the study of books' and helped York to escape from the country, parted from her father on the night before his execution and died at Carisbrooke Castle in September 1650; in 1637 Anne, who died aged three; in 1639 Katherine, who died an infant; in 1640 Henry, Duke of Gloucester, who died soon after the Restoration in 1660; and in 1644 Henrietta, who married Philippe, Duc d'Orleans.

To distract himself from the loss of Buckingham, the King turned to state business, which he could dispatch far more quickly and systematically than the Duke; indeed Gardiner maintains that he was 'eminently capable of... industrious attention to business; countless corrections upon the drafts of dispatches and state papers show how diligent he was in moulding the minutest turns of expression to his taste, and how little latitude he allowed those who served under him', though he concludes comprehensively: 'For Government in the higher sense he had no capacity.'[164] There was indeed much to attend to; of closest personal concern was the better ordering of the touching for the King's Evil — the thaumaturgic ritual whereby, until the time of Queen Anne, monarchs touched those afflicted with scrofula. Charles clearly detested this duty, ordained that it should be confined to Easter and Michaelmas and discontinued at Whitsun, 'in respect of the temperature of that season, and of any contagion to his Majesty'. He then ordered the Privy Council to reprove the lords lieutenant of the counties over the neglect of mustering and equipping the trained bands of the militia, and commanded that beacons be repaired, magazines replenished, competent officers appointed and that a muster master be put in charge of the collections made by the constables of the hundreds. And he ordered that no ship timber be exported from any of his realms.

Obstinate and honourable, Charles felt bound to prosecute the disastrous war, until the capitulation of La Rochelle in October 1628 made it pointless to do so, and peace was negotiated with France; then, in 1630, with Spain. Parliament, recalled in January 1629, remained entirely unhelpful. Indeed in the previous summer the Lords had 'considered of the weak estate of the Kingdom and of our friends and allies abroad, and of the great strength of the House of Austria, and the King of Spain's ambitions aspiring to universal monarchy, and of her present great preparations for war',[165] but the Commons were interested entirely in their own grievances over the customs revenue — and now started new ones about religion. Opening the session, Charles had been conciliatory and complimentary to the Lords; being 'nearest in degree, they were the best witnesses unto Kings'. To the Commons he explained that he did not want tunnage and poundage by prerogative or challenge of right. 'Let us not be jealous,' he concluded, 'of each others actions.'[166] But the learned Selden argued that tunnage and poundage had not been granted 'time out of mind' and that Henry VII and his predecessors had merely been given 'some subsidy for guarding the seas'. There had indeed never been a King 'but had some subsidy in this sense time out of mind', but this had been a matter of free gift and not the equivalent of the customs revenue. Well knowing that government was desperate for money, and in spite of urgent appeals from the King, the Commons again deliberately held up supply. They complained about the treatment of the substantial merchant John Rolle, who had refused to pay the small sum of £100 duty on goods worth £5,000, which had been impounded by the customs officers, who had told him that 'if all Parliament were in you, we would take your goods'.

The critics of the King in the Commons also attacked the ritualistic tendencies now gaining ground in the Church. They had been infuriated when the year before one of the King's chaplains, Dr Montague, author of *A New Gag for an Old Goose* and *Appello Caesarem*, had been promoted to the bishopric of Chichester. He was one of the exponents of the Arminian party who attacked the Calvinist doctrine of predestination and asserted that man was not predestinate but capable of salvation through his own efforts. Though they came of a much older pedigree going back to Pelagius, the Romano-British adversary of St Augustine, who had first enunciated this hopeful doctrine, they were rather misleadingly called after Jacob Harmensen, Latinized Arminius,[167] who had denied that the elect had been predestinate before the Fall of Adam and that there was therefore nothing that those not elected could do to obtain salvation; and had asserted that if salvation were offered, men had enough free will to choose it, not merely because God knew which way they would choose beforehand, but freely through their own love of God. He had thus restored some of *la dignité humaine*. The doctrine, more precisely defined by Jan Uyten Bogaert, had been submitted to the States General, who in 1618 had summoned the Synod of Dort, and it had been supported by Hugo Grotius, the founding father of international law and one of the leaders of the Remonstrant Arminians. This relatively cheerful belief horrified the more rigid Calvinists, haunted by their more than Augustinian sense of sin. Moreover they felt that it struck at their political and social domination as the elect. The Synod of Dort had condemned Arminian beliefs and hounded those who professed them, and the English Calvinist politicians now hounded the 'Arminian' clergy as crypto-Papists, by whom 'new paintings were laid on the old whore of Babylon to make her show more lovely'. Well away on the scent of popery, Rome, they declared, was eating into their own 'orthodox' religion; Arminianism was an 'error that makes the Grace of God lackey it under the wit of man'. Indeed an Arminian was the 'spawn of a Papist which may [might] turn into one of the frogs out of the bottomless pit'. The movement was allied to the Pope and the Catholic powers to destroy England. In fact the Anglican High Churchmen were not much committed to Arminian doctrines — being more often neo-Platonists — but the label, with its political implications in Holland, served its turn, particularly for those who wished to involve the country in the ideological conflicts and perhaps the campaigns of the Thirty Years' War then raging on the Continent.

John Pym, the most cunning of the politicians who wanted to replace the monarchy by a kind of dogeship, at once evoked and exploited Calvinist feeling by denouncing the cult of angels, crucifixes, saints, candles and altars, always a politically useful gambit, and a new member, Oliver Cromwell, who sat for Huntingdon and whose religious convictions were far more genuine and tempestuous than Pym's, informed the House that the Bishop of Winchester 'did countenance persons who preached flat Popery'. So, as an interim measure, they petitioned the King to proclaim a national fast. Charles realistically replied that 'fighting would do more than fasting' in the Protestant cause, although, while not himself wholly satisfied by their arguments, he granted their request, while insisting that it set no precedent for frequent fasts.

He then, not unreasonably, asked for tunnage and poundage again. He again got no further, for the attack on the customs officers was renewed. And so to shield them he commanded the Speaker, Sir John Finch, to adjourn the House for a week; whereupon the House declared that the decision belonged to them — an unprecedented claim. The Speaker then quite properly tried to leave the chair; but two young 'militants', Denzil Holles, the wealthy second son of Earl Clare, Wentworth's brother-in-law and member for Dorchester, and Benjamin Valentine, member for St Germans in Cornwall, held him down by force. 'God's wounds,' said Holles, 'you shall sit till we be pleased to rise.' The Speaker then burst into tears, 'yet notwithstanding [his] extremity of weeping and supplicating oration quaintly eloquent, Sir Peter Heyman [a gentleman of his own country], bitterly inveighed against him, and told him he was sorry that he was a Kentish man, and that he was a disgrace to his country and a blot on a noble family'. In spite of such abuse Finch stuck to his guns and refused to put a 'Protestation' by Eliot to the vote, whereat its author threw it in the fire. Informed of these goings on, the King ordered the serjeant to remove the mace — in vain. Then Black Rod knocked on the door with a message from the King, who had called up the Guards. In the general tumult Holles proclaimed the main points of Eliot's extremist 'Protestation', declaring innovators in religion and even advocates of tunnage and poundage being levied by the King as 'capital enemies of the Kingdom and Commonwealth' — thus threatening them with death — and calling any merchant who paid up 'a betrayer of the liberties of England and an enemy of the same'.[168]

After this, on 10 March 1629, Charles naturally dissolved Parliament — he would later write of Parliaments to Wentworth, in a phrase more characteristic of Charles II, that 'they are of the nature of cats that ever grow cursed with age'. On proclaiming the dissolution the King remarked, in his halting way, 'I have never come here upon so unpleasant an occasion', and declared 'to all the world that it was merely the undutiful and seditious carriage of the Lower House that had forced him to it'. He took much comfort, he said, from the demeanour of the Lords and 'well knew there were many as dutiful in the Commons, save a few vipers', who 'must look to get their reward and punishment'.

In fact they had already got them: warrants had been issued for the arrest of Holles, Valentine, Eliot and three collaborators. Holles, fined a thousand marks and imprisoned, escaped and lived a 'banished man' for eight years before making submission and paying the fine. He afterwards reckoned that overall he lost £10,000, but the thousand marks were refunded along with £5,000 compensation by the Long Parliament. Valentine was fined £500 and imprisoned for eleven years, to emerge again in Parliament in 1640. Eliot refused to acknowledge the right of the judges to examine him on statements made in the Commons protected by the privilege of the House; he was fined £2,000 and in 1632, having refused to acknowledge any fault and consoling himself by writing a work of idealistic political theory, *The Monarchy of Man*, he died of consumption in the Tower. Charles, who considered him Buckingham's bane, refused to release him on grounds of health and even refused him burial at Port Eliot. 'Let Sir John Eliot', he minuted on the petition, 'be buried in the parish in which he died.'

The Parliament of 1628-9 had been the fifth to be dissolved in anger since 1614 and its dissolution marked a mounting crisis of authority. Since the Addled Parliament the stable relationship of Crown and Parliament of Tudor times had been increasingly out of balance, and now the prospect of the kind of centralized government developing on the Continent, which the King and his ministers wished to impose on a deeply provincial and decentralized society, worsened a conflict that was increased by economic, religious and social change. The old 'mixed' form of government was in fact ill-adapted to a modern great state, while the new kind implied a concept of sovereignty that men were groping towards but found hard to accept. They thrashed around the question. Thus in a debate in 1627 a member had actually cited Bodin — who had defined the term — and asked what exactly was this sovereign power and ought the King to have it? 'Bodin saith that it is "free from any condition"; by this we shall call a royal as well as a legal power. Let us give that to the King that the law gives him and no more.' But Pym did not claim sovereignty either: 'I am not able to speak,' he said, 'on the question. I know not what it is. This power seems distinct from the power of the law. I know how to add sovereignty to the person, but not to his power, and we cannot leave him a sovereign power: also *we have never possessed it*.'[169]

But the Commons had now 'emerged from being a medieval estate of the realm into a modern deliberative assembly with the right to submit legislation and [had] achieved a lasting corporate consciousness — no longer merely existing like the Cheshire cat only when the sovereign's eye was upon it'.[170] Demanding a voice in the regiment of England, they were not consciously demanding sovereign power, though in effect they came to do so. Charles was nearer the mark when he complained 'they would have all done by Parliament', for in the words of James I the Commons had been invading the inseparable right and prerogatives of the imperial crown, of which he had found himself actually possessed at his accession; and that, he had stated when dissolving Parliament in 1622, was 'an usurpation that his Majesty the King cannot endure'.[171] Charles continued to take the same stand, though he never attained the unbridled sovereignty ironically and briefly attained by Oliver Cromwell's sword government, which imposed far heavier taxation than ever could the King and whose nature Thomas Hobbes appropriately defined.

The other great cause of friction was again the failure of communication between the conciliar executive, responsible to the King, and the House of Commons, which controlled supply but had no means of bringing down an unpopular minister except impeachment. The major councillors were still not even in the Commons, while instead of coming to terms, in the prevalent English way, with representatives of a new and powerful interest, the King defied them and indeed no one quite knew the bounds of his authority or theirs.

In pursuit of Eliot and his colleagues during the crisis in 1629, Charles had enquired of the lords chief justice, 'Can any privilege of the House warrant a tumultuous proceeding?' But he had received a maddeningly indefinite answer. 'We humbly conceive that... though a disorderly and confused proceeding may in such a multitude be called tumultuous, and yet the privilege of the House may warrant it.' Asked, 'if Parliament men conspired to defame the King's government and deter his subjects from obeying and assisting him, of what nature would be this offense?', the law lords replied that they must know what the nature of the offence is, being fully proved. They could not give a directive answer 'until the particulars of the fact did appear'.[172]

Still intent on more centralized government in Church and State, Charles now had to risk doing without Parliament, which had proved itself consistently obstructive and which now threatened to bring his regime to bankruptcy by denying the customs revenue. He was no tyrant in so doing: his father had dispensed with it for seven years; Parliament had nothing like its modern importance in men's eyes. The prerogative power was legal, and in these circumstances essential to keep conciliar government going. In the event, as is not always realized, Charles actually managed to increase his revenue and the personal rule remained just viable until, following his religious convictions, he gratuitously provoked the Scots to rebellion. Clarendon, after all, would look back on the time of personal rule as one of peaceful if insular felicity, with a flourishing elite civilization, before the raucous and lethal violence of political and religious fanaticism disrupted it and the country blundered into a tragic and unnecessary civil war.

The most daunting problem facing the King in his design was the deep-rooted regionalism of the country. 'England', writes a modern scholar, 'in one sense remained a confederation of overlapping communities, politically united only on unusual occasions, when the representatives of these communities were summoned together in Parliament.'[173] And even these 'parliament men' represented the local hierarchies of their 'countries', as they called their counties. Though intensely patriotic, they were often only intermittently aware of the interests of the kingdom as a whole, and their tradition was against the kind of administration that Charles's policy implied.

Yet the means of greater centralization were to hand. Apart from the main Council, whose prevalent amateurishness and subservience to the King has already been indicated and which in spite of his other preoccupations Charles would quite often attend, the Tudor Councils of the North at York, of Wales and the Marches at Ludlow, and the Court of Castle Chamber at Dublin had extensive powers. Charles therefore attempted more fully to exploit them, and when in 1628 he appointed his former opponent, now Viscount Wentworth,[174] to York and in 1633 concurrently to Dublin as well, he found an outstanding administrator, who had been recommended to him by Lord Weston,[175] the Lord Treasurer, who, as Sir Richard Weston, had been Controller of the Navy since 1618 and Chancellor of the Exchequer since 1621.

For Wentworth was a man of iron; industrious, ruthless, systematic he could write in contempt for the common people of the 'arrogance grown frequent nowadays which he could not endure. Every ordinary man must put himself in balance with the King as it were a measuring cast... silly wretches.'[176] And his famous definition (made as early as December 1628 as President of the Council of the North) of the position of the Crown again demands quotation. 'The authority of a King is the keystone which closeth up the arch and order of government, which contains each part in due relation to the whole, and which once shaken, and infirmed, all the frame falls together into a confused heap of foundation and battlement, of strength and beauty.' In friendly collaboration with Laud, by 1628 bishop of London, Wentworth now lived and died for a monarch, who as the latter put it, 'knew not how to be made great' and was 'too often more willing not to hear than hear'. But both these men, who 'stood out head and shoulders above their corrupt and feeble colleagues and were single-minded in their devotion to the King's ideals',[177] were overbearing, tactless and bitterly unpopular.

Much older and more deeply rooted than this Tudor conciliar power, central and regional, which the King and his ministers were now trying to increase, was the omnipresent, complex and ramified structure of the law. It had its own pervasive and archaic authority, going back to medieval times; but though it served the state, the King could not control it. It had its own life. Charles had early affirmed his authority over the judges who sat in the historic Courts of King's Bench which dealt with cases between the Crown and its subjects, in Common Pleas for litigation between subjects, and in Exchequer and Exchequer Chamber. All met in Westminster Hall, and below them, in a wide delegation of authority, were the local justices of the peace, who administered the law at quarter sessions, and the constables and tithing men and the like who looked after the parishes. It was not an efficient system, but it reflected the realities of social and economic power — and it worked; the better in that most of the gentry had some knowledge of the law through their days at the Inns of Court and through the careers that the common law held out to the abler and more ambitious of their class. This entrenched interest tended to resist the prerogative powers of the King, though 'almost invariably the civil lawyers', who were much concerned with fewer and socially less distinguished cases in the ecclesiastical and admiralty courts, 'supported the monarchy and the Church in the political divisions of the seventeenth century'.[178]

The civil lawyers, fluent in Latin and learned in nascent international law — the *jus gentium* — were mainly Londoners; they backed Court against country and were afraid of the Puritans, who might 'overthrow the most excellent study of the Civil Laws, yea, civility itself'.[179] If they did not achieve the spectacular fortunes of the major common lawyers, they did pretty well.[180] Though the common lawyers, citing *Magna Carta* and Bracton ('The King is subject not to men but to God and the Law, because the Law makes the King'), were far more influential, the civil lawyers backed the King, quoting Justinian's *'Quod principi placuit legis habet vigorem'* ('Let what pleases the Prince have the force of law'), and even from the *Digest*, *'Princeps legibus solutus est'* ('The Prince is free of the laws').

These imperial Byzantine maxims hardly reflected the realities of power in seventeenth-century England, but their existence encouraged the King to think they did. And academic civil lawyers argued that the royal prerogative was a double power — one under law, the other above the ordinary course of the common law — and that the political government of ecclesiastical affairs should be a 'point of regality'. They had assimilated better than the common lawyers and the amateur lawyers among the gentry Bodin's continental doctrine of *majestas*, sovereign power. But against the common lawyers, with their overwhelming influence in Parliament, they proved weak allies, and in general the law proved a major obstacle to the King's designs.

Lack of money was also crucial. The collection of revenue was extremely inefficient: poverty crippled the Crown, and ingenious exactions made it unpopular. The crown lands had been greatly alienated since the days of Henry VIII, who had lost the opportunity of building up a massive economic power by retaining most of the monastic properties. He had in fact sold most of them off to pay for wars in France, and now they brought in only £25,000 a year. Prices had risen roughly four times in the last eighty years, yet the archaic crown revenues had remained static. And when Parliament had cut off the main revenue — tunnage and poundage, customs duties that benefited from an expanding economy — they had threatened to paralyse government. The King now therefore fixed the customs duties at his own estimate, and in spite of protests they were collected. Otherwise the personal rule would have collapsed.

A great asset to the King remained the Court of Wards, an unpopular but lucrative relic of feudal rights, whereby the Crown took over and leased out estates inherited by minors until they came of age, or of the occasional rich lunatic, so that '"to beg a fool" of the Crown was an accepted procedure among grasping courtiers'.[181] This source brought in over £35,000 a year (more than the crown lands). Further, the King could make money by granting monopolies or patents and by exacting ancient feudal rights, as fines for encroaching on royal forests or for not taking up knighthood.

Charles therefore had some good cards to play, but at the cost of mounting protest. Apart from Wentworth and Laud, both widely detested, two extremely unpopular characters now controlled the revenues. Lord Weston, the Lord High Treasurer, was a crypto-Catholic, and pro-Spanish, determined on peace, and he even resisted the extravagance of the Queen. His influence had been behind the peace with France and Spain. Until his death in 1634 he contributed to the solvency and the unpopularity of the regime. Even more disliked was an enterprising Cornishman, the Attorney-General William Noy. Having attended Exeter College, Oxford, and Lincoln's Inn and having been promoted by Bacon, he was one of the sharpest of lawyers, and as representative of Grainpound and Helston in Cornwall (where he had an estate at Carnanton), he had originally opposed the King. But in 1631 he accepted his appointment, and being deeply learned on the law, on which he wrote many books, he thought out until his death in 1634 most of the ingenious new forms of taxation, including the hated ship money.

Such, in brief, were the key men and the methods that kept the personal regime afloat; and afloat is the right word, for the entire Caroline establishment was riding a sea of poverty, illiteracy and popular unrest in a rapidly changing, though still hierarchical and by continental standards still comparatively prosperous, society.

> Between 1500 and 1600 the population of England and Wales seems to have increased by as much as forty per cent; between 1600 and the civil war by perhaps another thirty per cent. Hence another widening of the gap between the growing army of the poor and the rest of society, increasing demand for the basic necessities of life, and opportunities for the entrepreneur ready to take advantage of the abundance of cheap labour.[182]

The poor made up over half the population and were the hardest hit by sporadic bad times. The loss of essential markets for cloth in the Baltic countries through the Thirty Years' War, the general economic recession that had afflicted the Continent, a European social and economic crisis of inflation, of religious wars and resistance to centralized government as such and to a new sort of capitalism first fully apparent in England, all combined with a worsening of the climate with harsher winters to make life harder. So beneath the threatened political and religious rift in the fairly prosperous establishment there was a swirl of popular resentment, often exacerbated by religion. The authorities, great and petty, felt that the people were out of hand. It was not only Wentworth who felt it; gamekeeper John Williams, who had command from the Earl of Suffolk to preserve His Majesty's game within the manor of Fording ton at Dorchester in Dorset, felt it too. He told the Earl how he had apprehended a poacher, one Henry Maber, a mechanic, and taken away his fowling piece; but how Maber had again 'sported himself with his greyhound' and how he (Williams) had taken it and his man had led it back to Dorchester. But Maber, being a constable, had assaulted the man and taken the dog back, whereupon Williams's servant had struck Maber who had put him in prison until bailed out. Williams begged that 'course might be taken to curb the rebellious spirit of these Dorchesterians, who factiously contemn all law and justice that is without their own precincts'. Indeed Maber had behaved 'as if he had no King to command him, or himself been exempted from the obedience of a subject, which *is a damnable opinion of a puritan*'.[183]

Soon after the death of Buckingham it had been observed that the King's most intimate adviser was Laud, since 1627 a privy councillor. As Bishop of London, he had long been in high favour with the King, for he shared the same religious outlook, and had attempted reforms within the originally medieval episcopal framework of the Anglican Church, pitting himself against the revolutionary Calvinists who wanted to abolish the medieval structure and substitute the Presbyterian discipline. Most of the militants in the Commons were Calvinists; now in 1629 the dissolution of Parliament gave Laud a freer hand and he worked in even closer harmony with the King. And Laud's *Articles of Reform*, formulated in 1628, had aimed at preserving the 'settled continuance and the doctrine and discipline of the Church of England as now established', from which, Charles was determined, 'we will not endure any varying or departing in the least degree'.

Religion then intimately pervaded almost all men's lives: the Christian cosmology was taken for granted by all but a few radicals and sceptics, who kept quiet about their beliefs, or lack of them, until during and after the Civil Wars the social lid came off with the rift in the establishment and a babel of all kind of heresies and scepticism broke out. The hope of heaven and the fear of hell fire were urgent: it was extremely dangerous to get one's religion wrong, for the penalty could be an eternity of torment; moreover error could bring the punishment of God upon the community that tolerated it. Success in battle was regarded as signifying God's approval and defeat the reverse, while endemic plague, threat of famine and other accidents of men's precarious lives were thought to derive from the divine anger. The hysterical violence of religious controversy and the merciless conduct it entailed is today best paralleled by the virulent ideological internecine conflicts between the exponents of atheist revolutionary and nationalist doctrines; in both circumstances men will vivisect societies and 'liquidate' opponents for their dogmas, and when power-addicts consciously or unconsciously exploit the resulting popular movements cruelties increase.

Two problems demanded the attention of the King and the Bishop of London: the first, perennial since the advent of Christianity, was how to maintain some traditional decency and order in a population still apt to revert to pre-Christian beliefs and rituals, as witness the increased prevalence of witchcraft and magic after the medieval cult of the Mother of God, the saints and the miracles had been undermined.[184] Add to this the task of imposing Judaeo-Christian notions of asceticism and chastity on a vigorous people and the problem was daunting, particularly if the Court set a bad example.

But Charles and Laud and their following wanted to go further: as the latter said on the scaffold, his life's work had been 'labouring to keep an uniformity in the external service of God according to the doctrines and discipline of the Church'.

To the perennial difficulty of keeping the populace somewhere near the mark they had added innovation.

The Puritan influence had now so much increased that Charles felt a stand had to be taken. Since Queen Elizabeth's day, when there had been plays acted on Sundays at Court, Calvinist notions had taken wide root, and already by 1606 it had been considered 'almost incredible how taking this doctrine was... so that the Lord's day began to be precisely kept... the very ringing of the steeples was judged unlawful'.[185] In 1618 James I had issued *The King's Majesty's declaration concerning lawful sports*, permitting 'piping and lawful recreation' after divine service, while encouraging traditional forms of exercise; and in 1625 the Regius Professor of Divinity at Oxford had authoritatively 'determined that the Sabbath was not instituted in the first Creation of the world, nor ever kept by the Ancient Patriarkes' and declared that 'sanctified recreation refined the spirit'. Charles soon reissued his father's book; and of course in spite of denunciations bull-baiting and bear-baiting continued, as well as rough football, wrestling and the ancient game of prisoner's base.

The Puritans had replied by piling up traditional evidence of God's judgements against sinners, and already in 1597 Thomas Beard, who taught Oliver Cromwell and deeply influenced him, had published his *The Theatre of God's Judgment*, abridged in 1618 as *The Thunder bolt of God's Wrath*. This work was several times reissued and augmented, and it provided a rich fund of material for subsequent preachers and moralists. Others carried on the pious work: in *A Divine Tragedie lately Acted* Henry Burton provided fifty-six examples of judgements that had overtaken Sabbath-breakers in the previous two years; his book was clandestinely disseminated as part of the Puritan campaign against the *Book of Sports*.[186]

This Puritan tide Charles and Laud were determined to stem; but it was with doctrine and with the position of the Church that the King was most concerned. 'For the first time,' writes C.V. Wedgwood, 'the Anglican Church had at its head a Defender of the Faith who had never considered the possibility of defending any other faith';[187] a Defender of the Faith who was determined to press on with an Anglican Counter Reformation. The Church had not recovered from the depredations of Henry VIII and the sales of its rich properties sanctioned by him. The bishops, to the disapproval of Queen Elizabeth, now generally had families to provide for, and like Laud, the son of a Reading clothier, often came of middleclass origins. They had not the prestige of the wealthy prelates of the old august and cosmopolitan Church, and by emphasizing the sacred character of the sacrament and the unbroken pedigree of consecration from the early Church, they perhaps sought to enhance their authority. Abbot remained obstinately Calvinistic in the Elizabethan tradition, but Laud, a small, forceful, efficient and sometimes irascible bureaucrat, set himself, first as Bishop of London in close and friendly collaboration with the King and then in 1633 as Archbishop of Canterbury, to impose a change of heart by new routines and if necessary by compulsion.

Such changes of ritual at once provoked the panic fear of Popery and foreign invasion deep-rooted in the English for generations; in particular fear of the Jesuits, who, 'like Brennus his Gauls came stealing by night through the thickets [to attack the Capitol] so these bats in the twilight of our security creep upon us *defensi tenebris* [protected by the dark]'.[188] Through the Court of High Commission, which wielded much of the medieval Church's authority over morals as well as doctrine, Laud now enforced his standards of ritual, discipline and morality, and he was backed by the secular power of the King. Charles did not shrink from cases that were inconvenient or repugnant. When Buckingham's dependent, John Stamford, a wrestler of extraordinary physique and a prime favourite of the Duke, not knowing his own strength and in sudden passion, had committed murder, not even the Duke's intervention had saved him; and when in 1631 Mervyn Touchet, Lord Audley, second Earl of Castlehaven of Fonthill Giffard in Wiltshire, a property afterwards owned by William Beckford, was accused at Salisbury of rape and sodomy the King himself closely supervised the affair.

It was not nice. The elderly peer, whose Irish earldom had been created for his father George Touchet, who had married the heiress of the Mervyns of Fonthill, an ancient family whose crest was a squirrel sejant cracking a nut, had been 'Bawd to his own [second and youthful] wife', a daughter of Fernando, fifth Earl of Derby, and had induced one of his lusty minions to rape her while he held both her hands and one of her feet in the same bed. Perhaps he had wanted thus to get a child and disinherit James, his then eighteen-year-old heir by his first wife, for it was in fact this boy who had now occasioned the case by an appeal to the King. The Earl had also, it was alleged, committed sodomy with his young footman, Lawrence Fitz-Patrick.[189] Charles was deeply shocked, 'strictly commanded that the truth be searched out' — significantly, so that his people should be 'cleansed of so heavy and heinous sins'. But, always careful of the proprieties, he ordered that Castlehaven should come up at the Assizes at Salisbury in his own county before gentlemen of quality. This jury indicted him on both counts, and the Earl stood his trial before twenty-six of the great peers at Westminster. He was arraigned before Lord Keeper Coventry, Weston, the Lord High Treasurer, Arundel, the Earl Marshal, and Philip, fourth Earl of Pembroke and Montgomery; before Manchester, Bedford, Essex, Salisbury, Wentworth, and the Lord Chief Justices of the King's Bench and the Common Pleas. They sat on each side of a great table covered in green, and he was prosecuted by the Attorney General. Before this formidable tribunal the Earl, after six months' close confinement, declared himself 'ignorant of the law' and 'weak of speech at the best', and elected to be tried 'by God and his peers'. So the solemn conclave deliberated on the case — 'these noble men, your peers, whose hearts are full of integrity justice and truth as their veins of noble blood'. In a rumble of medieval Latin[190] and Old Testament quotations, the indictment was pursued, and the prosecutor's English was also eloquent: 'Never poet invented nor historian wrote of any deed so foul... pestilent crimes that draw punishment from God...' The peers unanimously convicted the Earl on the first count. On the second count Fitz-Patrick swore that his master had not enjoyed any criminal satisfaction, but the judges held that what he had done was legally just as bad, and the peers, though relatively sympathetic to one of their own order, condemned him on that one by fifteen votes to twelve. Castlehaven accused his son, now twenty-one, of conspiring to bring him to his death and appealed to the King for mercy; but perhaps just because of the ambience of the Jacobean court and because James I had pardoned the Earl and Countess of Somerset for premeditated murder, Charles was determined to make an example of the Earl; indeed on the first count his conduct had indeed been criminal. The King graciously permitted him to be decapitated, and even provided him with two deans to fortify his spirit: in May Castlehaven made an edifying end; he apologized to the King for bringing a stain on the nobility and showed a cheerful countenance on the scaffold, though his hands shook a little when undoing the bandstrings of his shirt. The young men, who had only obeyed their master, were hanged; Giles Brodway, who had raped the countess, confessed that he had 'sinned through conceit of his own beauty, and gladly read a psalm'; Fitz-Patrick with Irish bravura making a great scene of it, with drawn-out elaborate prayers and pious ejaculations — and calling on the Virgin Mary and the Saints.[191]

After this exact enforcement of the law and the display of Old Testament righteous indignation, the King and his great peers doubtless felt that justice had been done and the wrath of God had been averted from the land. The last heretics to be burnt in England — a couple of Unitarians — had died in 1612, but towards sexual crimes the government remained as ferocious as that of Henry VIII; nevertheless though Charles had in this affair hunted down those concerned, the inevitable sexual licence and scandal of any Court, if less flagrant than under James I, had become and remained a major political liability.

Despite limited resources the King and Queen continued their selective but not extravagant patronage of the arts. The Queen's House at Greenwich, abandoned in 1619 by James I on the death of his consort, was now taken in hand by Inigo Jones who completed it by 1638. As Surveyor to the Crown and of His Majesty's Works, he was at the height of his influence and now, in striking contrast to the clutter of historic red-brick towers, courtyards, banqueting halls and tilt-yards of Queen Elizabeth's favourite palace, he designed a Palladian pavilion, 'masculine and unaffected', with superb wrought-iron 'tulip' winding stairs and south-facing loggia; the pavilion was the first of its kind in England and the model for fashionable building as elaborated, for example, by Webb at Wilton. The ceiling of the Queen's bedroom is entirely Italianate — save the later centre painting — all dull red, grey and gold, with neo-Roman masks, scrolls and godlings of hearth and home and its motto *Mutua fecunditas, spes Reipublicae*; the chimney pieces were by French designers. In its context the Queen's House was then as functional and revolutionary as a design by Corbusier. The Queen's residence at Somerset House was also embellished with a cabinet room and water-stairs, and a sculpture gallery was built in the garden of St James's. Jones was also commissioned to restore the Gothic part of old St Paul's and impose classical surfaces on its surviving Romanesque pillars. In 1633 the King commissioned a great west portico as his personal gift, a monumental and probably incongruous structure modelled on the temple of Antoninus in Rome. The King also put up a new neo-classical screen blocking the long vista of Winchester, rightly dismantled by the mid-Victorians. But none of his architectural projects was grandiose.

The cult of the masque now became even more elaborate and more political, symbolizing the hoped-for harmony and peace, the neo-Platonic serenity of the regime and the chaste affection of the royalties. The new Banqueting House, completed by 1622 after the old one had been burnt down in 1619, now witnessed scenes of complex romantic allegory and subtle nuance, glorifying *recherché* notions of high-minded autocratic rule. The King and Queen also delighted in the stage, so that the Queen had early shocked conventional opinion by acting in pastorals herself and had broken precedent by visiting public theatres. Charles was clever enough at constructing plots to advise playwrights himself and personally restored some innocuous exclamations, as 'Faith!',

'Death!' in Davenant's *The Wits*. He declared these to be 'asseverations', and Sir Henry Herbert, the censor, under protest restored them: 'I doe humbly submit as to my master's judgement, but under favour conceive these be oaths, and enter them here to declare my opinion and submission.'

In 1631 Daniel Mytens painted a pleasant portrait of the King standing easily and holding a stick, with the crown and sceptre unobtrusively on a table. Ten years earlier Van Dyck 'the picture drawer' had visited England, and in 1632 he returned to settle as painter to the Court where he was made much of; in 1629-30 Rubens had come over as an ambassador and he had been knighted and commissioned to paint the apotheosis of James I as a centrepiece of the ceiling of the Banqueting House; Honthorst also painted the King and his nephews. So Charles was already on the way, as in his patronage of the court masques, to creating the impression of aloof and regal elegance and serenity by which the time of his personal rules has been remembered.

Buckingham had been a great collector, and Charles himself had already, as Prince of Wales, been described by Rubens as '*le prince le plus amateur de la peinture qui soit au monde*'. In 1628 the King's agents had bought up the superb collection of the Gonzagas at Mantua, outbidding Richelieu for paintings by Titian, Raphael and Tintoretto. Charles also went out of his way to secure works by Dürer and Mantegna. He extended the collection he had inherited from Prince Henry and had them catalogued, and with his patronage of Rubens and Van Dyck set new standards in painting in England, where equestrian portraits were a novelty, so that: 'In such pictures we find for the last time for a century, painting done in England fully in line with the most advanced contemporary European tradition.'[192]

Charles, the royal aesthete, had indeed now come fully into his own and created his own elaborate inner world, doubtless more real to him than the often boring routine of administration and politics, and, a proud seventeenth-century monarch, he went his own way with a confidence unwarranted by the underlying realities of political and economic power. Sheltered within an ordered world, by family affection and by flattery, Charles came to believe that a similar order and harmony would prevail in his three kingdoms. But decorous as the Court had now officially become, the more raffish courtiers followed the new style in an extremer way, and set the fashions celebrated and caricatured by posterity in their version of the 'Cavaliers' — of cascading lace, the sweep of feathers in a great tilted hat, the rosetted shoes and tapering languid fingers, apt, all the same, for the sword.

All these things infuriated the more philistine Puritans. Already in 1628 the irrepressible and prurient William Prynne had denounced the courtiers' way of life; and indeed that of any ordinarily jovial characters. Born in the same year as the King, whom he outlived by twenty years, the son of a tenant farmer at Swanswick in Somerset of land belonging to Oriel College, Oxford, Prynne had been educated at Bath and at Oriel and became a barrister of Lincoln's Inn. He was a rabid Calvinist, and in the *Unlovelinesse of Love Lockes*, or a *Summarie discourse prooving the wearing, and nourishing of a Locke or Love-Locke to be altogether unseemly and unlaufull unto Christians*, this feverishly eloquent enemy of life and pleasure had declared long hair for men to be idolatrous, lascivious and unnatural: 'Long haire,' he had written, 'is for women, as a natural covering or vaile or a Badge or Emblem of subjection to their husbands.' He denounced 'English hermaphrodites'; said that they 'frizzled like a Baboone'; and that even if long hair was becoming, they should remember beauty was a 'great impediment to chastity'.

This compulsive writer, of whom Aubrey wrote that he had a 'strange saturnine complection',[193] who was described as having the countenance of a witch and whose sensual mouth in his portrait curls down in disgust, had also written *Healthe's Sickness* or a *Compendious and Brief Discourse proving the Drinking and pledging of Healths to be sinfull and utterly unlawfull unto Christians*. Comprehensively he had denounced 'drinking, carousing and swilling', 'ryot', luxury, 'epicurisme' and 'carnal merriment, pott-learned schollars deboist and roaring soulders, goodfellow serving men, base mechanicks, clownes', as well as peasants who made drinking healths the excuse for every 'ebrious round'. And since the King was the subject of more healths than anyone else — and his name and crown and dignity were made daily the table compliment grace and first salute of every courtier, of every riotous gentleman, and of many a trencher chaplain' — this most eloquent and all too representative Puritan had made bold to consecrate his 'meane and worthless treatise' to His Majesty. Unfortunately for Charles the outlook he expressed was deep-rooted, ancient, widespread and politically powerful. Under all the serene elegance of the Court, the King's own excellent taste and connoisseur ship, the learning and eloquence of the Caroline bishops and the salutary restoration of order and decency in the Anglican cathedrals and churches, the Puritan fanatics, insular, self-righteous and driven by a terrifying and total conviction, were gnawing with the persistence of beavers at the foundations of the regime.

9: PERSONAL RULE

CHARLES HAD NEVER visited his Scottish kingdom, which he had left at the age of three, and his coronation there had been long delayed; he was even less *en rapport* with the outlook and prejudices of most of the Scots than with those of most of the English. He was now determined to recover all the authority and crown lands that he could, and at his accession he had at once revoked all grants made since the accession of Mary Queen of Scots. Tenures eighty years old had been questioned, but the nobility and gentry who had acquired them had put up such a resistance that he had to let them keep their estates and compound for them. Charles had thus early touched the Scots in their pockets: he was now determined to touch them in their religion — and on both counts they were highly sensitive.

The King's failures in war and foreign policy had now perforce concentrated his attention on his own realms, and he now felt that he had time to consolidate his position in Scotland; even, he assumed, to impose his will on it.

For Charles had now been forced to accept the fact that he could do little on the Continent: indeed already in 1630 he had written to his sister, 'First give me leave to tell you that it is impossible in the unfortunate business of your's either to give or to take a counsel absolutely good. If I make peace with Spain, I lay my Arms asleep for doing your service.' He had then advised that France and the United Provinces were her best hope though 'for Sweden I admit he is to be harnessed and used as much as may be... I shall be the better able by a peace with Spain to help and hearten him'. But all he had promised was 'to do what lay within him' to engage their friends in an offensive and defensive league to regain the Palatinate and the liberty of Germany. Then in 1632 the Elector Palatine Frederick had died, to the despair of Princess Elizabeth, who wrote that it was 'the first time that ever she was frighted: for it struck her so cold as ice and she could neither cry nor speak nor eat nor drink nor sleep for three days'.[194]

In April 1633, following the King's decision to pay his long-delayed state visit to Scotland, the worst patches of the roads were repaired. The justices of the peace in Nottinghamshire reported that theirs were in 'deep clay', but hoped soon to have improved them; the great bridge over the Trent at Newark could not be completed in time, but there was a good ford, passable even in winter by coaches as well as horses. Carts were mobilized along the route; loads of gravel and stone laid down over the worst morasses.

Charles was himself much put out by the delay in collecting suitable crown jewels and, strangely hopeful that the full Anglican service would attract the Scots, he had the entire personnel of the Chapel Royal at Whitehall, including the choir boys, transferred in HMS *Dreadnought* to Scotland. In the event the progress was festive, as the King and his entourage moved from one great house to another. On 13 May, by way of contrast, Charles 'stept a little out of the way to view a place at Giddon':[195] an amiable Anglican community at Little Gidding in Huntingdonshire. It had been founded by the widow of a rich London merchant who had done well out of the slaving and piratical ventures of Hawkins and Drake; and their son, who had studied at Clare Hall, Cambridge, and helped to finance the development of Virginia, had also retired to a life of contemplation. The little community had to 'pray regularly, eat by measure and drink by quantity'; they had an elaborate chapel and specialized in instructing children and harmonizing the scriptures in elaborately bound concordances. As a religious bibliophile Charles made a point of visiting them before he moved further north.

The Scots were proud to receive their native King. But on 18 June, in the Chapel Royal at Holyrood, Charles alienated most of his loyal subjects by commanding a coronation with the full Anglican ritual. King James had already imposed bishops upon the Scottish Kirk, a decision confirmed by the Parliament of 1612 by statute, and when in 1617 he had visited Scotland, he had attempted to impose ritualistic articles. But they had only been accepted by the General Assembly of the Church in 1618 and then only by the votes of the bishops and the nobility. Discontent had thus long been seething among the Calvinist majority, the more so since the Presbyterian organization beneath the bishops had been left intact. Now the Archbishop of St Andrews and the four bishops who officiated with him appeared in 'white rochets and white sleeves and copes of gold, having blue silk at their foot';[196] but the Scots bishops who were not involved wore plain black gowns in a marked manner. There was an altar with chandeliers and, what was worse, 'backed by a rich tapestry wherein the crucifix was curiously wrought to which the bishops were seen to bow the knee and beck'. And when Charles attended the Sunday service at St Giles in the royal loft, he sent two English chaplains in surplices, abetted by the attendant bishops who 'acted this English service', to interrupt the Scottish reader and take his place. Further, the Bishop of Moray preached in a 'rochet'. It was not surprising that the Scots congregation 'grieved and grudged' thinking that 'the same smelt of Popery'.

The prospects for imposing the English prayer book on the Scots, 'so that the same service book might be established in all his Majesty's dominions', were evidently bleak. But even the Scots bishops, who knew this, depended too much on the King against the predatory nobles to tell him the truth — nor would he have believed them had they done so. Moreover the facts of the situation were masked by the progress that the King now made deeper into his Scottish kingdom; he was once more widely acclaimed, though in returning to Edinburgh he was very nearly drowned in crossing the Firth of Forth — an event that was widely attributed to witchcraft.[197]

Although Charles had not immediately imposed an English prayer book on leaving Scotland, that October he commanded that all the Scots ministers should wear surplices or 'whites' — an injunction obviously hard to enforce. Laud had preached in elaborate vestments and had been driven to Stirling in a coach so grand that 'it had been a wonder there'; but his example had provoked fury, not respect.

Having alienated many of his loyal Scots, the King rode back so fast that he reached London from Berwick-on-Tweed in four days and was back at Greenwich by 20 July 1633. A fortnight later Archbishop Abbot, long ailing and depressed, haunted to the end by his 'casual homicide' — had not a crowd of women, blocking his coach at Croydon, cried out that he had best shoot them? — came to his end. He left ample benefactions, particularly to his native town of Guildford, and his books now form the nucleus of the great library at Lambeth. But to the King his demise was an immense relief. When, two days later, Laud arrived back at Court, 'My Lord's Grace of Canterbury,' said his master, 'you are very welcome.'

During that summer of 1633, when the King returned from

Scotland, Sir Henry Wotton, long ambassador to Venice and now provost of Eton, who had once inscribed in Latin in the album of a burgermeister of Augsburg the famous phrase that 'an ambassador is an honest man sent to lie abroad for the good of his country',[198] composed a panegyric entitled *Ad Regent e Scotia reducem Henrici Wottonii Plausus et vota* (translated as *A Panegyrick of King Charles, Being observations upon the Inclination, Life and Government of our Sovereign Lord the King* and dedicated to 'Our young Charles, Duke of Cornwall and Earl of Chester, [to be hoped] an hereditary Image of Virtue').

This fulsome tribute presents a rather convincing miniature of the King as he then seemed to an admirer, and since Charles I has incurred so much censure from historians it may not be amiss to cite it. Its flattery also evokes the atmosphere with which the monarch was surrounded, and which, continuing over years, must have clouded his judgement and made him overestimate his popularity and power. 'In you alone, Most Imperial Charles,' it opens, 'is confluent the glory of all nations which in all ages since the Romans have possessed Britannia either by right or by Arms.' Wotton dwells on the King's 'untroubled serenity and virtue', on his learning, on his purity of mind — 'your eyes abhorring not only any sordid but even the least lascivious word which perchance under Edward IV [a monarch sufficiently remote to cite], while vagrant loves did reign, was accounted a piece of country eloquence', and he praises the Queen, the 'most worthy consort of the royal bed'; the congruity of disposition that had graced their union. Moreover Charles had 'provided for the maritime strength' and provided most commodious bases for it; he had made an exact survey of arms and musters and had frequented the Council of State more than any of his predecessors (unless perhaps Edward VI), while 'the learned and faithful sagacity of his secretaries [of state] watched over all accidents'. 'I have many times heard,' wrote Wotton, 'how attentively you resolve things propounded, how patiently you hear, with how sharp a judgement you ponder the particulars, how stiff you are in good resolution.' And Charles, he stressed, was also very good at keeping a secret.

> How elegantly [his panegyrist continues] your Majesty doth dispose your vacant hours, with your joy in chivalry and the use of the *Great Horse*. Musick, both instrumental and vocal, under you grows every day more regular, and in hunting, the image of war, you exercise your vigorous spirits. But the most splendid of all entertainments is your love of excellent artificers, and works of either Art both of pictures and sculptures.

The King had indeed so adorned his palaces 'that Italy (the greatest mother of elegant arts and of the Graces and the principal muses) had been seen by his magnificence to have been transported into England'. So, says Wotton, we may contemplate superb works of art and 'behold the mute eloquence of light and shadows and the silent poesy of lineaments'. And here he dwells accurately on the King's taste:

> Here would the spectator almost swear that the limbs and muscles designed by Tintoret did move: here the birds of Bassano doe chirp, the oxen bellow and the sheep bleat; here the faces of Rafael are breathing and those of Titian are speaking. Here a man would commend in Coreggio sweetnesse, in Parmigiano daintiness of limbs. Neither do the Belgians want the praise; who, if they paint landskips, all kinds of plants seem in their verdure, the flowers doe smell...

Yet discriminating art patron as he was and learned in books, the King for the most part read men, aided by his alluring, pleasing suavity, his quick movements, his composed demeanour. For Charles was 'constant, just, courageous and *knowingly good*'.

This favourable view was not widely shared outside the exclusive circles of the Court. For now the ingenious expedients thought out by Noy the Attorney General were beginning to bite. Distraint of knighthood had been invented under Edward I and had then enacted that anyone with £20 a year should take up the honour at a price; in 1630, and with its obligation still assessed at the now absurdly low income of £40 a year, it had been enforced, and those liable heavily fined for not taking it up at the King's accession. This ingenious device had brought in £115,000: it affected not only the 'quality', but people who had little pretensions even to gentility; technically correct in law, it was now farcical and damaging. Further, in 1634 the King also claimed enormous sums from magnates who, in strictly legal terms, had encroached on the royal forests. The Earls of Salisbury and Southampton were heavily mulcted, and the Earl of Bedford had to compound substantially for his enterprise in developing Covent Garden: all three later joined in opposition to the King. The great sheep farmers were also attacked for turning agricultural land to pasture and so depopulating the countryside — a measure welcomed by many villagers, but alienating just about the richest interest in the country, people who thought themselves, and indeed were, too powerful to be so treated by a paternalistic government.

The method of collecting the fluctuating customs revenue also provoked resentment. It was farmed out to syndicates of business men who paid the proceeds monthly to the

Exchequer, retaining their commissions. These had so accumulated that their holders could become in effect bankers to the Crown, lending back the rake-off from the King's own revenues with added profit; in fact they had become a kind of 'collective banking syndicate, able to lend on a scale that no one individual could any longer face'.[199] As the King's demands increased they tended to anticipate revenue, and their useful, if primitive, banking enterprise became unsound.

Charles, like his predecessors, also raised revenue by the grant of patents and monopolies, often to predatory courtiers, such as Sir Giles Mompesson, the first to provoke impeachment; sometimes to foreigners skilled in making glass or in dyeing textiles; sometimes for new inventions, often impracticable. In theory this policy encouraged trade, but often such 'half baked essays in economic planning' created 'more problems than they solved'.[200] The most notorious and unpopular was the monopoly of soap, devised by Noy and assigned, with Weston's bought connivance, for fourteen years, to amateur and often Catholic courtiers, incorporated in 1632 in the 'London Society of Soap Boilers'. Their soap was made from English vegetable oils and they were authorized, in return for paying £10,000 for their charter and £4 a ton to the government. They were empowered to test their rivals' wares, and, when their competitors (some of whom used whale oil) resisted, to prosecute them in the Star Chamber; a move so unpopular that an 'independent' tribunal was set up, including the Lord Mayor of London and the Lieutenant of the Tower. So 'Before this tribunal two washerwomen, one using company's soap, the other independent soap, washed for all they were worth, and, when they had finished, showed their results to the judges. The judges declared in favour of the company, and their verdict was supported by a testimonial in its favour signed by over eighty persons, including peeresses and laundresses, [though in fact the public preferred the usual product]. The Privy Council then circularized the Justices of the Peace, advertising the excellence of the Company's soap, and recommending its use to all.'[201] In Bristol, on the other hand, it was demonstrated that Bristol soap washed better, but the King ordered more than half the independent firms to close down.

By 1634 there were 'soap riots' (about a commodity not much used personally in the mid-seventeenth century), and the independent companies tried to outbid the monopolists by offering a higher fee and doubling the duty; but until 1637 the Court company retained its monopoly, if for an increased sum, until bought out by the King for £40,000 to which the original soap boilers had to contribute half. This kind of thing made the government detested by the whaling industry and in the City.

But the most notorious and politically explosive device was the levy of 'the rare invention of' ship money, for it raised a question of principle. The 'ship writs' were first sent out in 1634 and provoked growing resentment. The ship money, which the writs were issued to collect, had been sporadically exacted from the coastal towns since medieval times.

In 1632 the King had already asked the judges for their opinion of the legality of ship money — an action unthinkable to a Tudor royalty.

> When [he had asked] the good and safety of the Kingdom in general is concerned, and the whole Kingdom in danger, whether may not the King by writ under the great seal of England command all the subjects in the Kingdom, at their charge, to provide and furnish such numbers of ships, with men victuals and musters, and for such time as he shall think

> fit, for the Defence and Safeguard of the Kingdom... and by Law compel the doing thereof in case of Refusal or Refractories; and whether in such cases is not the King the sole judge both of the danger, and when and how the same is to be prevented and avoided?

The judges had then agreed that 'by the ship writs his Majesty can do no wrong'. Originally obliged to provide a ship, the lesser towns were now expected to compound for the obligation in money, and in spite of the usual protests about the relative assessments made, the government had managed to collect £104,000. But in 1635 Charles, thinking as in 1632 in terms of the whole country, but in a way repugnant to conservative regional interests, 'conceived that there was little reason why the maritime ports should bear the whole charge, and that the whole realm was interested therein', and he had taken the opinion of the Lord Keeper, who had pronounced that the writs involved were legal.

The need for a more powerful fleet had long been apparent. It was urgent to put down piracy, and seapower was the only card that the King could play abroad. Still intent on recovering the Palatinate, Charles had been engaged in characteristically devious and secret diplomatic manoeuvres, veering back towards Spain, now again at war with the Dutch, who in 1635 had concluded an alliance conceding Dunkirk, Ostende and even Bruges in the Spanish Netherlands to France. The King was determined to assert English command of the Channel, symbolized by the great warship now building, the *Sovereign of the Seas*.[202] Whig historians and their followers glorifying John Hampden's resistance to ship money have discounted Charles's strong feeling for the Royal Navy, and played down the fact that, in his own words, it never entered into his heart to make use of the money otherwise than on the Fleet.

When in 1635 the writs were sent out to the sheriffs over the whole country, resistance became formidable. National taxation for a national purpose provoked the usual regional resistance: and what was more, the powerful landowning establishment felt threatened by the extension of an extra-parliamentary taxation. The difficulty of collecting it inland was thus daunting...£218,500 had been demanded, over twice the previous sum, and reluctant sheriffs had to collect it through refractory constables. Assessment appeared arbitrary: the Close at Salisbury was assessed at £240; Marlborough had to pay £100; Wilton £5 and Downton 16s. In Nottinghamshire Gervase Markham,[203] an elderly landowner already fined £70 for not taking up knighthood, with £800 a year and reportedly £40,000 in money, though he 'lived meanly' and had no one to leave it to 'but two bastards that he would not acknowledge', protested to the sheriff at 'the great and intolerable oppression which unjudicially you did assess upon me for the shipping'.[204] He had been hoisted, he complained, to the mark of £50, while richer people had paid £35. He was bedridden, too, and 'not portable to London'. Briefly arrested, he paid up, with abject apologies.

More dangerously, the legal-minded magnates who were the strongest interest in the country became alerted to an attack on property by a prerogative power outside the control of Parliament. They objected to the 'Right whereby ship money [was] claimed': it could be indefinitely extended. Against this the King's government argued that 'what concerns all should be supported to all', and that only an efficient navy 'could keep our posterity sure and safe'.

The financial administration, moreover, was now weaker than ever. Since Portland's death in 1635 the Treasury had been put into commission under the control of Laud, and in March 1636, to the general astonishment, instead of Cottington the King had appointed the Chancellor of the Exchequer, the amiable William Juxon, now Bishop of London, to be Lord High Treasurer, and had also in June made him First Lord of the Admiralty.[205] He was, indeed, the one bishop 'whose reverence was the only thing by all factions agreed on... being by love what another was in pretence, the universal bishop'; he also ran a fine pack of hounds — always a passport to popularity, particularly for anyone in holy orders; he was tactful, hard-working and straight. But like Laud he was not an experienced financier, and since the Treasury had not been held by a cleric since the mid-fifteenth century, and he was inexperienced in naval affairs, his appointment was widely resented.

In October 1636, with Juxon in control, a third collection of ship money was levied and most of it was brought in, though in May of the following spring Blandford Forum, representatively, still owed £25 (allegedly embezzled by the bailiff). In Cardiganshire the sheriff, having failed by 'gentle means', had distrained on oxen, kine, sheep and household goods; though since the neighbours refused to buy them, he had not realized a penny. But in the overall result substantial revenues had come in, and the building of the new ships at Chatham was already well forward. Though the shipmasons complained of the lack of shipwrights and the captains of seamen, a powerful Royal Navy was beginning to take shape. It was far the King's greatest expenditure: his personal expenditure and art patronage were not particularly extravagant — he was 'magnificent only on ships'.[206] The cloud of opposition on the horizon, though already bigger than a man's hand, did not yet seem likely to become a political hurricane.

In late August 1636 Charles and the Queen on their own initiative made a state visit to Oxford that marked the climax of the ascendancy of Laud. Proceeding from Woodstock accompanied by the Palatine princes — the Elector Charles Louis and Rupert — they were met a mile from the city by Archbishop Laud in his capacity as Chancellor of the university; together the Court and the university officials processed to Christ Church where the royalties were to be lodged.[207] Laud had himself arrived in a coach and six with fifty attendants from Cuddesdon, where the King had personally settled the impropriation of the vicarage to the Bishop of Oxford and had the house settled for ever on the bishopric. Laud had closely supervised the arrangements at Oxford and even insisted, through proctors appointed by each college, that all undergraduates should have their hair cut, so that Edmund Verney wrote to his father from Magdalen Hall: 'The chiefest thing they will amend is the wearing of long hair. The Principal protested that after that day he would turn out of his house whomsoever he found with hair longer than the tips of his ears',[208] and the young man requested his father to summon him home for the duration of the King's visit in order to preserve his own hair from such mutilation. The King himself had been concerned at the 'multitude of taverns too much haunted by the young gents and scholars'.

After the usual and often tedious allegorical play at Christ Church and after Convocation had conferred many honorary degrees, Charles presided at a great feast in Laud's new-built library at St John's. It was so gargantuan that it cost the immense sum of £2,266 1s. 7d, with 'baked meats so contrived... that there were first the forms of archbishops, then bishops, doctors, etc. seen in order, wherein the King and the courtiers took much content'.[209] That evening in Christ Church the royalties saw and applauded a play by William Cartwright, a former King's Scholar from Westminster, now a Student of Christ Church, and described by Anthony Wood as 'the most florid and seraphical preacher in the University'. His *The Royal Slave, a tragicomedy* was produced with scenery by Inigo Jones, with Persian costumes and music by Harry Lawes; among the undergraduate actors was Richard Busby, afterwards famous as the redoubtable and apparently perennial headmaster of Westminster. The Queen was so delighted that a command performance was laid on that autumn by the King's Company at Hampton Court, when it was thought that the Oxford undergraduates had acted much better.

Charles left these celebrations, which he attended as a tribute to Archbishop Laud — who had found them a worry and a bore — convinced that all was well with the university, and indeed it was in Oxford that Laud's policy had its best and most lasting success. It had been only part of a far wider design first formulated in 1629, when after the dissolution of the King's third Parliament, Laud, as Bishop of London, had drawn up an important paper, *Considerations for the Better setting on of Church Government.* He had already recommended the King to command the bishops to their several sees unless they had duties at Court; to reside in their 'episcopal houses', and 'not to waste their woods if any were still left'. They were to make triennial visitations of their dioceses, refrain from 'frequent and unworthy' ordinations and keep an eye on lecturers, who 'by reason of their pay are all the people's creatures and blow the bellows of their sedition'. Afternoon sermons were to be turned into catechizing by question and answer, the lecturers, properly garbed in a surplice, were to celebrate divine service before their sermons and, as opportunity served, to be tied down to the responsibility of a living with the cure of souls. Further, only noblemen were to have private chaplains; only men of courage, gravity and experience of administration were to be made bishops, and Emmanuel and Sidney Sussex colleges at Cambridge — those 'nurseries of Puritanism' — should 'be provided of grave and orthodox men in their government'. Finally, some privy councillors were to attend the Court of High Commission, when important cases were being taken, to give it countenance.[210] With this programme the King had entirely agreed and during the 1630s it now determined ecclesiastical policy.

In April 1630 Charles had already been able to reinforce Laud's authority at Oxford. William, Earl of Pembroke, chancellor of the university (whose statue stands proudly in the quadrangle of the Bodleian Library) had died suddenly of a stroke, and within two days of the event Laud had been appointed his successor. Here he had set about his most enduring work and had begun a root and branch reform of the university. Backed by Charles, his objective had again been precise, 'to collect and perfect the broken, crossing and unperfect statutes of the University of Oxford, which have lain in a confused heap some hundred years'. He had also designed to procure a large charter for Oxford 'to confirm their ancient priviledges and obtain liberties for them as large as those of Cambridge, which they had got from Henry VIII and Oxford had not'.[211] With these objectives Charles had been in close accord, and in backing Laud he had become one of the great royal benefactors to the university. For by 1636 Laud's achievements had become decisive and permanent. The Laudian statutes, confirmed in June of that year by the King and by Convocation, gave the university 'the first comprehensive embodiment of its rules'.[212] Most decisively, it changed the medieval system, based mainly on competitive declamations, to a regular examination for degrees, and through the personal command of the King a better code of discipline had been devised. Archbishop Laud had also founded a lectureship in Arabic to which in 1635 he had appointed Edward Pococke (1604-91) of Magdalen Hall and Corpus Christi College, the Orientalist and pupil of William Bedwell, the pioneer of Arabic studies. Pococke had long been chaplain to the Turkey merchants at Aleppo and became expert in many Eastern tongues.[213] The archbishop also attracted several Orientalists from the Continent and the Levant; one, the Cretan Canopius, was a refugee from the household of the murdered orthodox Patriarch Cyril of Constantinople. He was housed in Balliol, and is memorable as the first man to drink coffee in England.

These achievements had been due to the King's support, and the fine new Canterbury quadrangle that Laud built for over £5,000 at his own expense at St John's, with its Italianate colonnades blending with a conventional late Gothic design, had elaborate classical frontispieces at the east and west ends, bearing elegant bronze statues of the King and Queen by the famous Hubert le Sueur. There had been trouble over its construction, for the workmen, it was alleged 'out of sheer improvidence', had run into debt, and Laud had dealt more benignly with their complaints than had the Heads of Houses, who had promptly dismissed them, though recommending charity. For when in November 1633 the workmen had renewed their petition for 'doing the great work in beautifying St. John's College, Oxford, through which they had suffered great loss, so that their wives and children were undone and they would not be able to follow their profession again', and had begged him 'for God's sake to give them £100 to keep them from prison', and a hundred marks more, which would be 'enough to enable them again to follow their vocation', Laud had made a humane and businesslike decision. He was content, he had said, to give them what they desired, provided that the vice-chancellor and his colleagues saw that the money was fairly distributed, so that 'no after-reckoning among themselves bred further clamour'. So the masons had got £170 13 4d, the total sum previously paid being £997 11 10d. Such, Laud had noted, in days before powerful trade unions, was 'the final end with the masons about my building St. John's'.[214]

In London one of Charles's main interests had been in the repair of St Paul's to which he had personally assigned £500 a year for ten years, though the Lord Mayor and aldermen had insulted the King by a derisory gift of £10. He had also commanded the clearing out of the clutter of St Paul's Walk, which over the centuries had become one of the main resorts of the City for business, gossip and assignations, creating a hum of talk and movement that could be heard far outside. Subscriptions had been demanded; fines spent on the good work. Laud was equally zealous: in 1633 on his way to Scotland he had inspected the Close at York and deplored the houses built almost against the cathedral; at Durham, disgusted by the state of the splendid cathedral, he had directed that it be cleaned up. At Rochester the new bishop appointed in 1629 from the deanery of Salisbury had complained — as Laud reported to the King — 'that the Cathedral Church suffers from want of glass in the windows, etc... the Churchyard lay very indecently, the gates were down, etc. that the Dean and Chapter refuse to be visited by him... with some other circumstances with which I will acquaint your majesty more at large'. Backed by Laud the Bishop had taken action, so that by

1635 Laud was able to report that the diocese was 'clean through in good order'.²¹⁵

Concurrently with their admirable work in Oxford and in the dioceses, Charles and Laud had long been savagely punishing their ideological enemies. In 1630 Dr Alexander Leighton, for example, a Scotsman of 'low stature, fair complexion, a yellowish beard and high forehead' between forty and fifty years old, had been arraigned in the Star Chamber. In *An Appeal to the Parliament or A Plea against Prelacy* he had declared 'prelacy in Church' to be 'satanical', called the bishops 'Ravens and Magpies',²¹⁶ advised smiting them under the fifth rib, and 'most audaciously and wickedly' called the Queen the 'daughter of Heth'. He had been thrown into the Fleet prison, fined £10,000 — such huge sums were, in fact, generally modified or even remitted as only the rich could pay them — and sentenced to have his ears cropped, his nose slit and his cheeks branded. And when the defiant Scot had escaped, having changed clothes with two visitors and walked out with one of them, within a fortnight he had again been apprehended, brought back and the full rigour of the horrible punishment exacted. He had first been severely whipped, pilloried 'two hours in frost and snow', one ear clipped, one side of his nose slit, and branded on one cheek: 'SS — Stirrer up of Sedition'. Then a fortnight later 'his sores not yet healed', he was given the same treatment on the other side. He afterwards complained that he had been poisoned in Newgate so that he had lost his hair. The routine atrocity was thought too much: 'Many people pitied him, he being a person well known for learning…'

Charles had been more closely touched by the renewed scurrilities of Prynne, who in 1633 had grossly insulted the

Queen. As Prynne had well known, early in 1633 she was to take part herself in Walter Montague's *Shepherds Paradise*, and by implication he also had compared the King to Nero and other tyrants. In *Histrio Mastix, the Players's Scourge*[217] which runs to over 1,000 pages, Prynne had particularly denounced all actors, male and female, as well as 'effeminate mixed dancing, dicing... lascivious pictures and lascivious eliminate music and excessive laughter'. The *Unloveliness of Lovelocks* had been mild beside this. He had cited St Ambrose, Tertullian, Clemens Alexandrinus, St Basil, Lactantius, St Bernard, as well as many passages from the Old Testament, and dwelt with gusto on the bad effect of plays on women and boys. He had lashed out at 'swaggering lasses' in strange meretrecious lust-inciting apparel', dancing on the stage before swarms of lustful spectators corrupted by ribald and amorous ditties sung to 'itching ears' in 'amourous pastourelles' — 'our play houses resounding always with... voluptuous melody, profane, lascivious laughter and immoderate apparell, pricking men on to flagitious lubricity'. Lust for women furthered the general corruption of men's minds — hence Fury, Anger, Tyranny, Revenge and Rapes. Women actors, he asserted, though well knowing the Queen's tastes, were 'notorious whores'. As for the boys, it was very bad for them to put on women's apparel, and bad for the spectators too; and the boys 'were instigated to self pollution' and to that 'unnatural sodomitical uncleanness to which the reprobate gentiles were given over'.[218] They became *Succubi* and Ganymedes, with unshorn womanish lust-provoking hair, corrupted by 'abominable wickedness... The very putting on of women's apparel on Boyes,' he had concluded, 'to act a play, is ever execrable to all Christian men's hearts'; it led to vices practised by Persians, Italians,

Turks, Greeks, 'Chinoyses', Peruvians, Moors in Barbary and of course by Popish bishops and cardinals.

The stage, in sum, was a sink of corruption, 'drawing young gents from their studies to the dancing schools' and 'young madams' from their needles, and 'as many faces as a man makyth in dancing, so many paces doth he make to Hell'. Two young gents, formerly civil and chaste, had become so 'prodigal incontinent and deboist' that their parents had cut them off. Lascivious picture masters — among whom Prynne had presumably included Rubens and Van Dyck — and their meretricious paintings had further corrupted youth, who wasted time reading players' books, doubtless including Shakespeare. And all this cult of the stage was a sinful expense of money. Consider, too, the cost of getting to the theatre by coach, boat or barge — and all but for the 'fomentation of lechery'.

Prynne, who had been pouring out other pamphlets and books, such as *Lame Giles his Halting*, against bowing to the altar, and defending subversive sectaries in the Court of High Commission, had asked for persecution and he had got it. Early in 1633 he had been sent to the Tower, and the Inns of Court, anxious to disown him, had put on a particularly splendid performance of Shirley's *Triumph of Peace* to appease the King. Then in February 1634 Prynne had been fined £5,000, imprisoned for life and degraded from his academic and legal degrees. He had been made to stand in the pillory and have both his ears cropped, one at Westminster, the other at Cheapside, while his book had been burnt under his nose. But it was found, when in 1637 he again suffered the same penalty, that the executioner — bribed, humane or careless — had left plenty of ear for another time. The victim was too obviously odious to excite much sympathy, though 'most men', wrote Sir

Simonds D'Ewes, 'were affrighted to see that neither his academical nor barrister's gown could free him from the infamous loss of his ears'.[219]

10: INDIAN SUMMER

CHARLES HAD ALWAYS been steadfastly religious, an aspect of his character now sometimes not much appreciated. The other support of this aloof asethete was his wife, to whom he was now devoted. And she was Catholic, part of a European dynastic world where heresy was doctrinally and socially unacceptable. He had even become attracted towards reunion with Rome, and as the Queen's influence increased, the Court became a hothouse centre of Catholic and crypto-Catholic influence. It was in this deep-rooted tradition that the royalties were brought up: so that Charles II, who remarked that Presbyterianism was no religion for a gentleman, died a Catholic, and James II lost his throne for becoming one. Both the austere Wentworth and Laud, who refused a cardinal's hat, remained staunchly insular and Anglican, but the clique who controlled the unreformed administration — Portland, the Lord Treasurer, Cottington, the Chancellor of the Exchequer,[220] and Sir Francis Windebank,[221] who in 1633 had succeeded Sir Dudley Carleton, Lord Dorchester, as joint Secretary of State with Sir John Coke, a former Fellow of Trinity, Cambridge who had made his reputation in the administration of the navy — were crypto-Catholics.

In December 1634 Charles himself instructed his secretary to negotiate with the papal agent, Gregorio Panzani, the first, if unofficial, papal envoy to the English Court since the reign of Philip and Mary, on the reunion of the churches. Windebank, who had called the creator of the Anglican Reformation or Schism 'that pig of a Henry VIII', now arranged that an official papal agent should reside permanently in the Queen's household. So in 1636, to the disgust of Laud, a Scots papal envoy — George Con — also arrived at Court. This suave Italianate diplomat,

> combined the narrow views of the *émigré* with the universal affability of the professional ambassador... and in the dilettante society of the English Court, accustomed to the uneasy presence and brusque manners of the Archbishop, his success was immediate. As long as he continued in England the King dabbled with the idea of reunion, discussing religious topics freely and sympathetically with the supple Agent... He was invited everywhere to dinner, and was made to go hunting with the royal party, and presented with the antlers after the kill.[222]

This fashionable Catholicism at Court, which coincided with the pro-Spanish policy renewed in the vain hope of recovering the Palatinate, compromised further the merely Anglican ritualism of Laud and further evoked the deep-rooted panic fear of Popery and foreign invasion, the strongest emotional force in English politics. The Puritan divines who whipped it up regarded even the Anglican prayer book as 'newly crept out of Popery' and the Laudian ritual as 'cringing and bowing'. In 1635 the Puritan caricaturist, Samuel Ward of Ipswich, who was again in trouble for having proclaimed that any man who practised such ritual was a jackanapes of a baboon', denounced the Church as 'ready to ring the changes and hunt the wild goose chase', and declared that the 'leaders of the Church should be elected of the people'.[223] Over much of the country such sectarian 'market sermons' were popular, indeed doubly welcome in the towns as helping to draw in customers on market days.

Despite this mounting tension the Indian summer of the Caroline Court saw a deceptive calm; and the peak of the apparent success of Charles's personal rule came in 1636, in a brief prosperity before the sharp European-wide economic decline in 1640. Apart from its growing strategic advantage as an Atlantic maritime power with the potential of mercantilist empire, England was at peace and had benefited from the ruin of competitors in warring central Europe. Although with the development of a national market there was widespread distress in the old-fashioned industries, the inflation which had raised the cost of food nearly six-fold since the early 1500s was at last stabilizing, with the renewal of old leases landowners had recouped themselves, while the increased volume of a nationwide and overseas trade, together with improved agricultural and industrial skills, were making the well-to-do more prosperous and the greatest landowners immensely rich.

In this prosperity the archaic royal government did not share. Even Elizabeth I had been forced to sell off a massive amount of Crown property, James I had made grants with extravagant prodigality, and the simultaneous war with France and Spain had further strained the Exchequer. In 1635 the King was £1,730,000 in debt, with his land revenues greatly diminished, and the grants of monopolies, patents and lucrative sinecures were made not out of fecklessness but to appease courtiers and creditors. Yet by now, by withdrawing from adventures abroad, Charles had managed to make his revenues almost cover expenditure, in part by patently unjust 'antiquarian' taxation, but mainly by continuing, in spite of protests, to collect the revenue from tunnage and poundage, unsanctioned by Parliament, for, with a greater volume of trade, they had increased. The Court was of course currently in debt — in 1638 the royal household would owe £1,900 to the poulterers for bills for the royal children and £1,000 to the purveyors of 'sea-fish' — debts doubtless unknown to the monarch; but far more serious than this sort of muddle was the incompetence of a rudimentary, amateurish, yet top-heavy bureaucracy. The ruling elites and political nation were more precarious than they looked.

The luxury of the Jacobean and Stuart Courts and magnates had always been based on a predominantly rural population of whom at least half were desperately poor, plague-stricken and beset by local famine, who were only partially relieved and kept under some control by the authorities who administered the Poor Law. If political and religious conflict disrupted the rulers' solidarity, revolutionary violence might break through. Bad harvests and high prices meant malnutrition when even employed labourers and apprentices might get only tenpence a day, while the King spent £4,000 on a masque and magnates spent £5,000 on entertaining him. The great cities, of which London was far the largest and comparable to the greatest in Europe, were still prosperous regional capitals — as Bristol, Exeter, York, Norwich (with twenty thousand people), Newcastle-upon-Tyne and Hull — but the ancient lesser towns, many dependent on the cloth trade, were in decline. The decay of basic industries, such as cloth-making and leather work, had impoverished flourishing medieval cities, whose civic pomp and impressive buildings had 'made the countryfolk wonder', and the 'putting out' of clothmaking by piecework among cottagers had undercut the urban workers. Since the Reformation the pilgrim trade had entirely fallen off and the Crown and the big landlords now took the rents that the clergy had often put into the treasuries of the cathedral cities, while foreign luxury goods depressed the native manufacture of lace, serges and gold thread. The King himself ordered his gloves and suits in Paris.

The development of a national market — with London its overwhelming centre — was of course salutary in the long run, but it meant that the 'chandlers of London haunted all the markets near unto London and swept the markets of all the corn that comes'. The lesser towns, if now centres of more civilized life for the local gentry and people of education, were no longer self-sustaining. In the ancient and representative cathedral city of Salisbury for example, where, as at Wilton, Charles and his Queen would often stay, the population were now only about 6,500, the corporation supported many 'impotent' poor, and the 'sturdy' unemployed formed a reservoir of misery and disorder — 'vagabonds generally given to horrible uncleanness, they have not particular wives, neither do they range themselves into families but consort together as beasts'; like the Irish vagrant there 'taken drounke, not able to yeld any accompte of his ydle course of lyffe'.[224] In Salisbury, as in other cities dependent on the cloth trade, the slump in cloth exports in 1620 had led to the city being 'much overcharged with poor', for example Goodwife Hoskins, 'who now lyeth in childbed [and] hath four children', whose husband had been 'prest for a soldier'. In 1629 the corporation had taken within its liberties Milford, Fisherton and East Harnham because of the 'disorder in the suburbs'; beggars were 'swarming about the city Close [with] no restraint', and bastardy had much increased 'to the great grief of the inhabitants'. So the authorities here, as often in other cities, did their best; they started a large workhouse and supported thirty poor children to keep them off the streets; but with over a hundred licensed inns and alehouses, one for every sixty-five inhabitants — 'the meanest beggar dare[d] to spend all he hath… for the pore man drinks stifly to drive care away'. The corporation had nonetheless set up a common brewhouse, as at Dorchester, with the profits assigned to poor relief, and 'storehouses' in each parish where the poor could buy bread, butter and cheese with tokens instead of money from the rates; but by the 1640s the brewhouse had to close through a boycott — there were plenty of other places to go to — and the storehouse had been put out of business through the hostility of the bakers, maltsters and brewers. In sum, as in similarly placed cities, though Charles's own purposes were benevolent, with so little help from the central government he had not the drive or the administration to realize them, and there was not much that the authorities at Salisbury could do.

An historic structural shift was now taking place in the economy, with greater capitalist enterprise, the beginnings of oceanic trade with the East and with the new plantations in North America and the West Indies; and the national market encouraged new industries in textiles, coal and iron working,[225] while the traditional centres of national prosperity dependent on the wool trade declined. With this momentous change Charles's government, no more than local authorities — though like them, often with the best intentions — was ill-fitted to cope. Though by continental standards the bureaucracy was small and cheap, local government being based on the unpaid roles of lord lieutenant and justice of the peace, the central administration that Charles and his ministers were trying to extend was cumbrous and often provocative; interfering without being effective. When, for example, Charles himself in Council was informed that tobacco was being mixed with unwholesome ingredients to increase its weight, which altered its colour and flavour, the best he could do was to hand over the problem to the Company of Tobacco Makers of Westminster; and when proprietors of Cornish tin mines asked for an increase in price Charles agreed, with the proviso that 'the poor labourers belonging to the said tin works should receive the benefits'. But he had no means of ensuring that they did. With little understanding of the economic forces at work, acting from mixed motives — concern to aid the poor, to maintain the existing social and economic order, to reward importunate courtiers, to promote a rudimentary mercantilism — government intervened haphazardly to forbid enclosures, maintain franchises and monopolies, challenging in the economic as well as in the religious sphere the jealously guarded independence of the regional squirearchy and town corporations, while impeding rather than promoting the economic opportunities of the time. And when, after Portland's death, with his personal accounts already under investigation, and after a year of supervision by Laud and Commissioners, Juxon had become Lord Treasurer, although the world of expensive fantasy, art collections, art patronage, music, drama, masque and fashion, still apparently flourished in the Caroline Court, the sands were running out. Economic discontent was reinforcing conflict over religion and law. This is not to postulate any fated conflict between economic 'classes' or 'ideologies', often misguidedly extrapolated into the past; on the contrary, when the civil wars came, successful and unsuccessful merchants and industrialists, rising and impoverished gentry and aristocracy, were all found on both sides of the lines. And both sides shared the belief in mercantilism, an *idée reçue* derived from Venice and Genoa in the Middle Ages, and as much an orthodoxy in Catholic as in Protestant countries in the early seventeenth century as the doctrines of Adam Smith in the mid-nineteenth. But Charles's government failed to please anyone. Those who complained of interference were fully justified, while the supporters of royal authority were exasperated by its incoherence. In its economic aspect the personal rule, though it just achieved solvency, was precarious and unpopular.

In the face of this tide of economic and social change Charles's personal limitations became more serious, nor had he the administration or military power to assert the kind of despotism that succeeded in France. Wentworth had done this in Ireland, though his work would not last, and the King never liked him; so when Charles could have appointed him, his ablest minister, Lord Treasurer, he missed his chance. It was anyway probably too late; the turning point had probably arrived long before in 1610 when Salisbury in that office had failed to achieve reform.[226] Insidious and ramified inefficiency and delay — termed by Laud to Strafford the '*Lady Mora*' (delay) to whom Cottington, as Chancellor of the Exchequer, was 'waiting maid' — had worsened. Nor had the King the realist vision to set about administrative reforms that might have won over his opponents, exasperated by the social aloofness and financial irresponsibility of the Court. Nor was he like Louis XIII, merely a cypher who allowed a Richelieu his head. Charles's good qualities, his high-minded sense of duty, his obstinate tenacity, his aesthetic perception, handicapped him as a ruler and *politique*. It was in part because the unreformed regime

> ... remained administratively and economically as well as aesthetically 'the last Renaissance Court in Europe' that it ran into ultimate disaster: that the rational reformers were swept aside, that more radical men came forward and mobilized yet more radical passions than even they could control, and that in the end, amid the sacking of palaces, the shivering of statues and stained glass windows, the screech of saws in ruined organ-lofts, the last of the great Renaissance Courts was mopped up, the royal aesthete was murdered, his splendid

pictures were knocked down and sold, and even the soaring gothic cathedrals were offered up for scrap.[227]

Charles's revenues no longer depended on what he could obtain through Parliament by consent but on what he could exact by an interpretation of the law. The resulting controversies resounded through the political nation and rallied the opposition of some of the ablest men in the realm. Was the King *Lex Loquens*, a speaking law in his own right, or was the ultimate authority in the community of realm expressed through the law to which even the King was subordinate? In 1637 the storm that had threatened in the previous year over the 'ship writs' blew up into fierce legal and political confrontation. Most of those assessed had grumbled but eventually paid up; now a litigious and influential landowner and member of Parliament, a close colleague of Pym and friend of Eliot, a zealous committee man, his talent for such public service now unemployed, brought a test case that became famous. John Hampden,[228] a wealthy Buckinghamshire squire now, as Clarendon put it, 'grew the argument of all tongues, every man enquiring who and what he was that durst at his own charge support the liberty and property of the Kingdom and rescue his country from being made prey of the Court'.[229] In fact Hampden had wide political and business connections and the test case had powerful backing: Hampden himself was one of a syndicate who had purchased large tracts of what became Connecticut from the Earl of Warwick. The case was argued in the Court of Exchequer between 6 November and 18 December 1637; then referred by the Barons of the Exchequer to all the judges of England, who gave their judgements separately over the first and second legal terms of 1638. Finally, on 12 June of that year, Chief Justice Finch[230] gave judgement for the King, for whom seven of the judges had decided, with three giving judgement for Hampden and two supporting them on technical grounds. On such a narrow margin a major source of Charles's revenue had to depend.

The facts were not in dispute.[231] In 1635 Hampden had been assessed on his estate at Stoke Mandeville, Buckinghamshire, at 20s: 'Mark the oppression,' wrote Hobbes retrospectively, 'a Parliament man at £500 a year taxed at 20s.' But though Hampden would have been liable for much more on his many other properties, he took his stand over this estate as a matter of principle. Once the King's right had been admitted to tax by prerogative power and not through Parliament, he felt no one's property would be safe.

Yet Charles's object in imposing the tax was the safety of the state. The contribution of Buckinghamshire was specifically directed towards a ship of 450 tons, with a crew of 180, fitted with ammunition and tackling and maintained at Portsmouth for twenty-six weeks 'to defend the Dominion of the sea' which in 1636 the learned Seldon vindicated. And the quibbles of Hampden's lawyers were not convincing: the realm, they said, was not really in danger; all that was needed was to put down piracy, a task unworthy of a royal navy; and the writ had commanded an inland county 'to find a ship' — a thing impossible and so void because '*lex non cogit ad impossibilem* (the law cannot compel the impossible to be done)'. More realistically, they argued the essential point: 'If His Majesty would have 20/-, why not £20, and so *ad infinitum*? The subject would be left entirely at the mercy and goodness of the King.'[232]

Macaulay's eloquence has so inflated Hampden's reputation that the merits of Finch's rather diffuse judgement, if better in commonsense than in law, have been obscured. He declared that the case was crucial, for it weighed 'the regal power, or rather regality itself' against 'the privileges and liberties of the subject in his person and estate'. 'For us islanders,' he declared, 'it is most necessary to defend ourselves at sea', and *Bellum Piraticum* points at us as much terror as *Hannibal ad Portas*: if the county could not 'find' a ship it could hire one. For the King might charge his subjects for the defence of the kingdom — and of the degree of danger he was the only judge. He concluded that Mr Hampden be charged with the 20s assessed and that the Lord Chief Baron (of the Exchequer) ought to give judgement accordingly.

Charles was entirely satisfied with this decision, which gave him, in his own opinion, his just rights, essential for the defence of the realm, to meet an inevitably recurrent expenditure, but it had been made by a narrow majority and the intensely legal and politically-minded English of that day had been passionately concerned. Wentworth of course thought nothing of Hampden, afterwards such a hero to Whig historians: 'Mr. Hampden,' he wrote to Laud, 'is a great Brother,[233] and the very genius of that nation of people leads them always to oppose civilly as well as ecclesiastically all that ever authority ordains for them; but in good faith, were they right served, they should be whipped home into their right wits.'[234] Yet it was now more widely believed that the King could not be trusted, and to resentment against taxation as such had been added the frustration of prerogative rule without Parliament. The Hampden case had given a focus to all these grievances: in spite of the favourable judgement, ship money, which in 1637 had brought in £178,599, with £17,814 in arrears, in 1638 fell to £55,690 with £14,059 still uncollected.

Yet the building programme for the fleet went on, and in 1639 Charles would go on board the great new-built *Sovereign of the Seas*, equipped with 102 pieces of brass ordnance at the cost of over £24,447. His policy had been realistic and necessary: unhappily he could not, as Elizabeth I might have, so manage the magnates and gentry that all could combine in a common interest to command the sea, and they were so terrified for their large properties that they would jeopardize national defence to protect them. In fact, of the two, Charles's centralizing view of government was more in accord with the needs of the times. The revolutionary governments not only used the King's ships against him, but reimposed ship money in 1642-52, while in general 'there can be no doubt that even under the Protectorate the tax burden was heavier than it had been under the monarchy'.[235]

In 1637, when the ship money storm had blown up and the economy had begun to turn into recession, Charles's serene and unjustified self-confidence had also faced mounting religious as well as political dissent. Impelled by Laud, the Star Chamber and Court of High Commission had been more briskly at work, and that year three victims had won popular acclaim. One was already notorious, the ebullient Prynne, who had this time libelled Bishop Wren of Norwich, one of the most energetic of the Laudian prelates, and in June he had been sentenced to lose what remained of his ears. Lord Chief Justice Finch, having instructed the usher of the court to pull back Prynne's hair, which although he was a Puritan he wore long for very good reasons, had remarked how inefficiently his ears had been clipped under the previous sentence. So this time the hangman had made a point of hewing off his ears 'very seriously', which 'put him in so much pain that after it it was a long time before his head could be got out of the pillory'.

His fellow victim John Bastwick, an Essex man from Emmanuel College, Cambridge, *'Flagellum Pontificis et Episcoporum'* and a doctor of medicine of Padua, had at first written in the relative obscurity of Latin and Greek invective; but he had now excited a wider public with his *Letanie of John Bastwick*, which denounced the bishops as 'the tail of the beast' in terms as gross as anything achieved by Luther. He had been fined £5,000, sentenced to lose his ears and to life imprisonment. With the example of Prynne in mind, he had besought the hangman to cut his ears close 'so that he might come there no more'. The third to suffer had been Henry Burton, a Yorkshireman from the East Riding and St John's College, Cambridge. He had been Clerk of the Closet to Prince Henry and Prince Charles, but in 1618 he had become a clergyman and in 1625 denounced Laud to the King, who had dismissed him. Two years later he had published *The Baiting of the Pope's Bull*, and had gone on in 1636 to call the bishops caterpillars and 'anti-Christian mushrumps'. He had been fined £5,000 and sentenced to lose his ears; but he had made the most of his situation — 'I never had such a pulpit before'.[236] Laud afterwards complained that the offenders ought to have been gagged, for all three pamphleteers had won haloes of martyrdom, though a callous female Papist called three cats Prynne, Bastwick and Burton and cut off their ears.

It seems odd that any monarch of Charles's sensibility still sanctioned such barbaric punishments, devised to deter, which were proving counterproductive when the populace, in medieval times unsympathetic to heretics, were now on their side. But in a true medieval way their admirers treasured 'the bloody sponges and handkerchiefs that did the hangman service in cutting off their ears'. Prynne had been dispatched to Caernarvon Castle, with a monoglot Welshman as his keeper, and what was even worse, deprived of pen and ink; but he was later removed to Mount Orgueil Castle in Jersey, where under a tolerant governor he was allowed to write about the scenery. Bastwick had been relegated to St Mary's Castle in the Scilly Isles, and Burton, likewise deprived of pen and ink, to Lancaster Castle; then, since he still managed to write, to a cell in Castle Cornet in Guernsey. To the mortification of the King and the archbishop, as these martyrs had proceeded to their destinations, they had been feted by their often substantial civic admirers in scenes that had become demonstrations against the government.

In spite of Charles's personal leanings towards reunion with Rome, equally savage but since less celebrated sentences had been imposed on Catholics. William Pickering, for example, accused of being a 'beggarly Papist', had replied, 'I am a Papist, and the Queen a Papist and the King a Papist in heart and conscience.' He had also affirmed that all Protestants were damned heretics and devils, and hired part of a churchyard as a pigsty. In 1638 he too was sentenced to lose both his ears and pay £10,000; to be whipped, branded with the letter L (for Libeller) and 'his tongue bored with an awl'. In this, the highest sentence, Laud concurred.[237] There followed a spate of virulent libels against the Archbishop Laud and his colleagues, countered by further drastic censorship on the printing and import of books and pamphlets.

Another unedifying, and in the eyes of many opponents of the regime unjustified, persecution occurred within the Church, when Laud had prosecuted the former Lord Keeper Williams,[238] Bishop of Lincoln and Dean of Westminster, in disgrace since 1625, for 'scandalizing' the government: and when, in defence, Williams had suborned false witnesses, in 1636 he was fined, suspended and imprisoned in the Tower.

Nor when, in the following year, he was retrospectively charged in Star Chamber with writing of Sir Richard Weston and Laud, 'let them scratch each other to the bones' and encouraging Lambert Osbaldeston,[239] the Head Master of Westminster School, to call Laud 'vermin', 'the little urchin', and 'the little meddling hocus pocus', did the case do the Church or the archbishop any good. And it ended in farce; Williams was fined £8,000, and would remain for three years (in comfort) in the Tower; but the Head Master would escape the penalties of his power of wounding and memorable phrase. In February 1639 he would indeed get short shrift. 'If this pedant,' remarked the Earl of Dorset with fine scorn, 'had kept within the rules, he might have been taught not to disturb government, and Osbaldeston would be sentenced to pay £5,000 to the King, £5,000 to the Archbishop, to be deprived and imprisoned and — a culminating disgrace for any Head Master — to stand in the pillory nailed by the ears before his own boys, some of whom might have relished the spectacle. But they would be deprived of it. Seeing the way things were going, Osbaldeston would escape from the court to his house, then retire to friends in Drury Lane, having scribbled a misleading note, 'If the Archbishop enquire after me, tell him I am gone beyond Canterbury.' This mordant and resourceful man had been a successful schoolmaster, 'very fortunate in breeding up so many wits', but the affair was not altogether unfortunate, for his departure occasioned the appointment of the great Dr Richard Busby. Since Osbaldeston had 'many doctors at both Universities gratefully acknowledging their education under him', the prosecution made Laud many enemies, and Williams would get an indirectly lethal revenge on the Archbishop when, in 1640, he was released and promoted and again able to influence the King. The cumulative effect of these persecutions of Puritans, Catholics, and a rival bishop gravely added to the doctrinal tension long building up.

At Court, meanwhile, the stately routine went on. Charles seemed in the full tide of prosperity and, writes Clarendon, 'he kept state in full which made the Court very orderly': he was punctilious in his devotions so that on hunting days the chaplains had to get up early, and very strict about intemperance. Once, for example, when 'very many of the nobility of the English and Scots were entertained, being told… what vast draughts of wine they drank, and that "there was one Earl, who had drank most of the rest down, and was not himself moved or altered"', the King said that 'he deserved to be hanged'; and that earl coming shortly after into the room where his majesty was, in some gayety, to show how unhurt he was from the battle, the King sent one to bid him withdraw from his majesty's presence…'. On occasions, in fact, the monarch could be a prig.

It was also observed that, to put it mildly, 'he was not in his nature very bountiful'. He could little afford to be, but he had not the knack of giving a little gracefully, and his bounty when it came was apt to seem forced. His own flair for conciliation in legal disputes now had full scope, but plainly though 'he had an excellent understanding; [he] was not confident enough of it'; which, as Clarendon puts it, 'made him sometimes change his own opinion for the worse'. In spite of his industry over detail his long-term policy seemed uncertain and unreliable, and 'had he been of a rougher and more imperious nature he would have found more respect and duty'. With his tidy mind, Charles attended to much detail as well as encouraging learning, developing gardens and architecture, and following up his far-ranging interests as an art collector, the patron of Rubens and Van Dyck.

On Laud's initiative, for example, he again instructed his sea captains to bring back books from the Levant and Persia. 'His Majesty', they were told, had a great desire to increase the knowledge of Eastern languages; but the archbishop had 'only received two'. 'You shall do well,' wrote Windebank to the Master of the Turkey Company, 'to be careful of it that His Majesty may see how willing you are to comply with his princely and just desires.'[240] There were many minor problems for decision: friction at Salisbury for example, where Bishop Davenant had maintained that the citizens should hold their liberties from bishop, dean and chapter, as in old charters, and not as a free city; the parties had to be heard and the charters viewed. At Chichester there had been controversy between the dean and chapter and mayor over whether the mace should be carried before him in the close. In July 1638 the local JPs referred trouble at Milton Abbas, Dorset, direct to the King. Mr Tregonwell, a descendant of one of Thomas Cromwell's officials forward in putting down and taking over the monasteries, had so much exasperated the vicar that the vicar's son, aged twelve, had attacked the Tregonwells' boy in church and the child had not yet recovered: 'We endeavoured,' they insisted, 'to make an accord between the parties, but were not able to effect the same.'[241]

The usual minor domestic problems continued. In June Inigo Jones reported to the Council that 'the water that serves His Majestie's houses of access is of so great importance both for His Majestie's diets and other necessary use', that people 'should be prohibited building or digging pits near the springs, or conduits or breaking up any of the pipes to take away the water'; His Majesty's plumber should be 'strictly charged to give notice of any abuse or nuisance upon pain of punishment'. The royal household was constantly on the move, and a list of carriages was made attendant on the Queen's removals, which included her dwarfs, her monkeys, her dog and 'the billiard bord'. There were the usual complaints. The Master of the King's Music, Clement Lanier, had been given the profits of weighing all hay and straw to be sold within a three-mile circuit of London, but petitioned that though he had spent £300 doing so — and for the public good — he had been interfered with by order of the Lord Mayor and aldermen and now appealed to the King.

Such is a representative cross-section of the business, trivial or more essential, that came in to King and Council, often now forgotten in our retrospective view of political crises, but then demanding — and getting — the King's personal attention.

New appointments also had to be made and the choice of a poet laureate closely concerned the King himself. Ben Jonson had died in 1637 and Charles, who had found his hard-hitting satire and controversies uncongenial to his own fastidious taste, though he had sent him a cask of canary in his illness, now appointed Sir William Davenant, long a popular poet and dramatist.[242] He had, indeed, lately killed an ostler, but the King had pardoned him and now also appointed him governor of the King and Queen's Company acting in the cockpit at Drury Lane, and assigned him a patent to put up his own playhouse. In a rowdier field of entertainment Charles granted the office of the Chief Master of His Majesty's Bulls, Bears and Mastiffs to Thomas Manley and Richard Davis at tenpence a day for themselves and fourpence a day for their deputy — hardly a generous rate of pay for so exacting an occupation, though the Yeoman of the Revels got only a daily sixpence, sums doubtless supplemented by quarters and keep. The

Master of the Harriers and Beagles was better paid: £120 a year for himself and £100 allowance to keep up a footman, four horsemen, and a 'couple of hounds for his Majesty's particular disport'.

But far more congenial to themselves and important for posterity was the continued patronage of the painters and care for architecture of both Charles and his Queen. At its peak in the early 1630s it was now necessarily on a reduced scale. In 1638-9 they paid out relatively small sums for famous pictures by Van Dyck, principally portraits of themselves and the royal children. Charles himself 'rated' the list of fifteen and marked with a cross those for which the Queen had to pay. The whole amount came to no more than £608; and even adding the £1,000 in arrears on Van Dyck's pension of £200 a year, it is not much compared with the thousands habitually lavished on plays and masques. Anxious now to economize, the King even cut down payments from £30 for a half-length portrait to £26; £50 for whole-length to £40, the fee for the celebrated *La Roi à la Ciasse*. Van Dyck, the most fashionable court painter, had been deservedly raking in money from the nobility, but the King and Queen now had to be careful what they paid for his masterpieces,[243] a sad sequel to the days when Charles had bought up the entire collection of the Duke of Mantua, and to the commissioning of Rubens in 1629 to paint the ceiling of the Banqueting Hall, when the painter had been staggered at the range of the royal collections. In 1634 the work had been completed, and in 1639 as a particular mark of personal appreciation a chain of gold weighing 82½ ounces was delivered to Endymion Porter 'on His Majestie's behalf to be conveyed to Sir Peter Paul Rubens as bestowed by his Majesty'.

In March 1638 he showed his benevolent interest in his royal foundation of King's College, Cambridge, by seizing on a chance created by a petition from the neighbouring Clare Hall to improve the setting of King's Chapel.

> Having seriously weighted the several desires of the Master and Fellows of Clare Hall, together with your dutiful answers [he wrote to the Fellows of King's] we have thought good to signify our royal pleasure therein. Although it were easier both for us and you to permit them at their own charge to land a bridge from the middle of Our College and make a sufficient causeway through the close, called the But Close, by which they might directly pass into the fields, yet considering the many benefits that will accrue to our unparalleled Chapel, the beauty whereof we are most desirous to advance, and to our other structures there by the removal of Clare Hall, we are not willing to remit so fair an opportunity, but, attending the mutual good and accommodation of both Colleges, and more especially Ours, bearing Our Own Title, we order that our whole College of Clare Hall, the Chapel and Library excepted, be removed seventy feet lower to the West, and that such portion of ground as shall remain between that College and the South West of King's shall be conveyed to you for the enlarging of our royal Chapel.[244]

Arrangements followed for compensation to Clare and for the mutual leasing in perpetuity of the relevant ground. Though an admirer of the new Palladian style of Inigo Jones, Charles appreciated and fostered the unparalleled 'beauty of King's'.

In a less lasting but more topical and symbolic sphere of art, in January of the same year Inigo Jones put on an elaborate masque: *Britannia Triumphans* with the text by Davenant. It was a political manifesto that celebrated the triumph of the King in the case over ship money. Charles was Britanocles, who had suppressed the pirates and imposed peace, order and civilization on the realm; the sets were highly elaborate, one of the scenes opening on a vista of a restored St Paul's and culminating in a vision of the British fleet sailing into harbour. It has been well remarked that 'the sets epitomise this increasingly unrealistic view of a disintegrating reality'.[245]

11: BELLUM EPISCOPALE

IN OCTOBER 1637 the Venetian envoy, Anzolo Correr, had reported to his masters on the monarch to whom he was accredited. 'Absolute royalty', he had written, was 'definitely the goal that Charles had set himself, forced to it by his subjects attempting to make a limited government by the laws and disorder';[246] and he had added, resignedly, 'The English do not now seem to take an interest in anything but themselves.'

He had gone on to describe the character of the King: 'Charles is just but rather severe and serious than familiar... He handles his arms like a knight and his coursers like a riding master... he is not subject to amours... [but] anyone who he has once detested may be sure that he will never recover his favour.' He was literary and erudite without ostentation; his motives honourable and 'spirited' — probably too spirited. 'It remains to be seen,' the observant diplomat had continued, 'if he can do by royal authority what former kings did by the authority of the realm.' Here, indeed, was the essential point; for the attempt might 'prove a difficult matter and most perilous'; the 'estates' were perturbed about religion and liberty and the King would be 'very fortunate if he did not fall into some great upheaval'.

It was a shrewd prophecy. Financially, Correr had considered, the current regime had so far done well, for he understood that Charles had raised the £500,000 annual revenue at his accession to £800,000; but the Calvinists were 'contumacious' about both King and bishops, 'as if', he added scornfully, 'it was possible to live in civil affairs without a magistrate or in spiritual without a heirarchy'.[247] So Charles was constantly making enemies; some 'seeking a democratic state, which does not exist; others the monarchy, which exists, but is a Spanish one'. Charles therefore risked both 'the hurt of ruling by old forms and the dangers of new ones'; all would depend, Correr concluded, on whether he adopted 'gentle' measures, and could agree with his people — for 'Queen Elizabeth did what she did by cajoling them'. If he had the patience 'to hollow out the stone drop by drop', he could become 'very rich' — the highest compliment a Venetian could pay; but at present Charles ought to realize that he was 'putting the state in a constant fever, and making it turbulent, rebellious and greedy'. It would be best, the wise Venetian reflected, 'not to forsake the old ways', at least in appearance.

Although the Venetian reports are not always factually reliable on information hard to obtain, they are consistently penetrating and objective. Here is an experienced diplomat, who was also serving in France, and one who in the interests of his own commercial state, desired the stability and success of Charles's government, even if his Italian sympathies were naturally with a spirited prince. Yet he foresaw the dangers that the English King seemed determined to provoke and objectively reported them.

Events now amply proved him right. For while the personal rule was still internally viable, and by more diplomatic political tactics might have remained so, the King now risked his position in England itself by imposing his policy on religion in his turbulent and predominantly Calvinistic realm of Scotland. Here, at the extremity of north-western Europe, was a country hardened in centuries of warfare against a more powerful neighbour, and all too highly articulate, with a force and vigour of mind and cult of disputatious learning that in happier circumstances in the eighteenth century would make

Edinburgh the 'Athens of the North'. In so rashly extending his commitments the King was only following what he thought his duty, but he provoked the crisis that brought his personal government to collapse: for following the First Bishops' War of 1639 — *Bellum Episcopate* — he had to call the Short Parliament in the spring of 1640, and in the autumn following the second war in the summer of 1640, to summon the Long Parliament that sealed his fate.

His decision was at least logical. The sketchy grand design of his personal rule implied not merely a more centralized and authoritarian government for England, but for the outlying realms of Scotland and Ireland as well. The first objective was difficult enough; both the others were quite unrealistic: most of the Scots were militant Calvinists and most of the Irish were Catholics who detested the Protestant English, now treating Ireland as a colony. Yet in his amateurish way the King was only following a trend of the times, whereby, as Trevor-Roper writes,

> In response, no doubt, to economic pressures, the Kings of Spain, France, England all sought to impose the bureaucratic system, which had been established in their greater kingdoms upon the different societies of the lesser realms which their ancestors had ruled as independent kingdoms but which were now without resident princely Courts... The revolt of the Netherlands had been such a revolt...[248]

The Scots rebellion was comparable to those in Bearn, Catalonia and Portugal. First the Scottish revolts in 1639 and 1640, when the 'smoake and smother in England concerning ceremonies broke out into fire in Scotland',[249] and then the Irish rising in 1641 were both fatal to the King; the former bringing the regime to bankruptcy and putting him at the mercy of Parliament; the other setting off a panic that made an already tense situation in England uncontrollable and precipitated the Civil War.

The perennial miseries of Ireland, worsened by the Elizabethan wars and exploitation, came to a climax in the seventeenth century when, following the rebellion of 1641, then the Civil War and its sequel, the victorious republican government sent Oliver Cromwell with formidable artillery and a professional army to make a conquest with all the ferocity of religious zeal and racial prejudice. Charles I, determined to bring the country under better control, had tried milder measures: appointed in 1631, his ablest administrator, now Viscount Wentworth, had arrived in 1633 to govern the island. Since 1628 President of the Council of the North at York, and himself a Yorkshire magnate, this baleful yet sensitive man had shown an efficiency in marked contrast to that of the King's other administrators. 'He as much outstript all the rest in favour as he did in abilities, being a man of deepe pollicy, Sterne resolution and ambitious zeale to keep up the glory of his own greatness.'[250] His drive in his secular office is comparable to Laud's in the affairs of the Church. Close friends, they agreed upon Wentworth's policy of 'thorough' or 'going through with it' and desired the same kind of centralized government, driven through if necessary by methods that roused bitter opposition.

 Charles may well have been subconsciously afraid of Wentworth and have felt the distrust of conscientious mediocrity before a domineering careerist with a streak of genius. Yet it was Wentworth who on taking up his appointment at York on 30 December 1628 had made the well-known declaration, already cited, that 'The Authority of a King is the keystone which closeth up the arch of order and government', and which had concluded, 'For whatever he be that ravels forth into questions the right of a King and of a people, shall never be able to wrap them up again into the comeliness and order [wherein] he found them.' Wentworth was one of the few men of action who could formulate his own political theory. Here is the classic conservative case, foreshadowing Burke's 'great contexture' of the whole 'mysterious' society, and by its architectural metaphor expressing in political terms the vision of ordered harmony centring on the monarch that was illustrated in the court masques of Inigo Jones.

'Comeliness and order' had been the last thing that Wentworth had found in Ireland. Appointed Lord Deputy, an office he combined with the Lord Presidency of the North, he had taken on a hard assignment, but one with wide scope for public service and personal profit. Already a great landowner with £6,000 a year, in Ireland Wentworth had made an annual £13,000; he invested £30,000 in the Irish linen trade which his own government was promoting and himself farmed the taxes from the customs and tobacco.[251] But if he amply served his own interests, he well served those of the King. He attacked the vast vested interests of the new Anglo-Irish magnates and converted an annual loss of revenue of £20,000 to a surplus of £50,000. As Lord Deputy he had made Ireland pay.

This unprecedented achievement had been bought at a price of bitter hatred that pursued him till the end. When in July 1633 he had arrived at a dilapidated Dublin Castle, he had found the Council of Ireland corrupt and incompetent, and the place itself depressing — 'no prospect of his favourite sport of hawking, as not a partridge had been seen near Dublin within the memory of man'.[252] He had at once reinforced the prerogative Court of Castle Chambers and made its judgement final, and in 1634-5 he had called a Parliament and temporarily squared the Catholics by promising 'graces' to mitigate the recusancy laws that, if enforced, could mulct them. So he had obtained large subsidies and increased his own power by creating a Commission on Defective Titles whereby he had forced some of the greatest new magnates to disgorge part of their enormous gains, and rescinded the charter of the English Adventurers Company and fined them £70,000 — an action that the City of London did not forget.

The most successful of the parvenu Elizabethan English adventurers, Richard Boyle, Earl of Cork, had bought up Ralegh's vast confiscated estates for £1,000, made a huge fortune developing the linen industry and iron mines, and provoked much ill-feeling among the ancient and often already decayed Anglo-Irish peers. His career had been typical of the basic conflict between the native Catholic Irish and the 'old' Anglo-Irish aristocracy with the 'new' Protestant English which divided the more settled and profitable parts of the country, while in the west the 'wild' Irish raided cattle and fought one another in traditional style. In 1615 the Jacobean Council of Ireland, scraping the barrel, had even been collecting fines for the 'barbarous custom of ploughing with horses drawing by the tails', thus combining profit with a then unusual feeling against cruelty to animals.

As the law stood, the established Protestant Church of Ireland had 104 articles of religion; many more than the Anglican thirty-nine and more Calvinistic. In conjunction with his chaplain, the forceful and choleric John Bramhall, Archdeacon of Meath and Bishop of Derry, a zealous Royalist who in 1661 was consecrated Archbishop of Armagh,[253] Lord Deputy Wentworth had imposed the thirty-nine articles on the

Irish ones and put the confused finances of the Church of Ireland in better order.

But the immense grievance had been the plantation of Ulster. Following the subjugation of Ireland in 1603, 'The Flight of the [Catholic] Earls' — O'Neill and O'Donnell — along with nearly a hundred of the old Irish aristocracy to Italy and Spain — had given the English government occasion to confiscate half a million acres in the north; in Donegal, Tyrone, Cavan, Fermanagh and Armagh. In 1609 this huge area had been 'planted' with Protestant English and Scots. Only about a tenth of the land had been assigned to the native Irish. Further, in the north the Anglican Church of Ireland had obtained fresh endowments; Protestant boroughs had been founded; a Scots Presbyterian interest had dug itself in and doggedly prospered. This experiment had been followed in other areas and Catholic owners had been ousted or had decamped — as around Wexford in the south-east, in O'Rourkes' county, in Offaly and in MacMurrough county around Wicklow. Two-thirds of the original owners had been swamped out by Protestant settlers.

Though sympathetic to the Catholic majority, Charles had now worsened their grievances. Anxious to increase the wealth of Ireland, he had extended the Protestant plantations and even planned one in the Gaelic west in Clare and Connacht, a project that had to be abandoned. He hoped, as have many people since, that Protestants and Catholics would be reconciled in a growing prosperity. So although it was only after the Cromwellian conquest that the Protestant ascendancy came entirely to dominate the country, religious, social and economic tensions had long been mounting up that would further disrupt Ireland. All this Wentworth had to contend with; in the short term he won, but his very success worsened the basic and unappeasable conflicts that erupted in 1641, a prelude to and an immediate cause of the English Civil War.

But for the moment he had succeeded: he had cowed the Irish Parliament, increased the wealth and revenues of the country by promoting Irish industries, putting down piracy and increasing overseas trade; moreover he had raised an army of nine thousand men; capable of overawing the factions in Ireland and available, as he later and for himself fatally suggested, to put down rebellion in Great Britain itself.

If in Ireland Charles had appointed an able administrator, in Scotland he stirred up trouble himself. Following the creation of a more authoritative Scots Court of High Commission, by 1636 a *Book of Canons* had declared that as head of the Scots Church he could dictate its ritual. The aged and experienced Archbishop Spottiswood of St Andrews had warned his master of popular feeling, but Charles had remained obdurate. Not surprisingly on 23 July 1637 there had been a notorious riot in St Giles's Cathedral, Edinburgh. Before a representative hierarchy of Church and State, the dean had begun to read the new Anglican-style service book; whereat the infuriated congregation, 'most of them women', accustomed to John Knox's Presbyterian *Book of Common Order*,[254] 'raised such a barbarous hubbub that none could hear or be heard', and when one of the bishops tried to calm them, a woman hurled a stool at him which nearly hit the dean. After raucous confusion the rioters had been evicted and the service continued with a much diminished congregation, while the dissidents bayed outside. It had soon been apparent that the city was out of control and Spottiswood attempted compromise, referring the question to the King's pleasure. The King's pleasure had been that popular protest must be put down. 'For as much as we,' he had replied, 'out of our princely care of maintenance of the true religion already professed, and the beating down of all opposition, having ordained a book of Common Prayer to be compiled to the general use and edification of our subjects within the Kingdom of Scotland, the same [had been] accordingly done.' He had 'taken great care and pains' over it for the 'safety and quietness of our religion and kirk'; the new prayer book must be imposed.

Safety and quietness had not been achieved. In February 1638 the Scots had responded with the famous National Covenant, subscribed on a tombstone in Greyfriars Church by thousands of all classes. 'It was no sooner framed but it so took that it was presently sworn, first at Edinburgh… then everywhere throughout the country.' This document, more talked about than read, and since suffused with much religious and nationalist sentiment, became a legend in the history of Scotland.

As another Italian realist, Francesco Zonca, Venetian secretary in England, observed, the Scots would 'not be subordinate'; and if they 'chose another King, the whole power of England could not subdue them'. Yet Charles, he wrote, 'clung persistently to his idea', and the members of the government 'washed their hands of any disaster that might ensue'.[255] The Covenant explains why. As Dr Balcanqual, Dean of Durham, the reputed penman of the King's declaration that provoked it, observed, 'The first dung from these stables that was thrown upon the face of authority and government was that lewd Covenant and seditious band annexed into it.'[256] For the Scots in Edinburgh, following their Presbyterian organization, left intact when James VI had superimposed bishops on it, had erected four principal 'tables' or committees of nobility, gentry, burgesses and ministers, with subordinate ones in the shires. They had evoked the confession of faith of the Church of Scotland of 1580. And 'After long and due examination of our consciences in matters of True and False religion,' they had declared, 'we have thoroughly resolved of the truth... received, believed, and defended by many kirks and realms, but chiefly by the Kirk of Scotland, the King's Majesty, the three estates of the realms, as God's eternal truth, the only ground of our salvation.' They had then plunged into a fierce attack on the Pope's opinion on transubstantiation, on praying and speaking in a strange language, on auricular confession, on the 'devilish' Mass, on monuments and such 'dregs of bygone idolatry' as crosses. 'Grounded with God's written word,' they had declared, 'they abhorred and detested' all contrary doctrine, but chiefly all kinds of Papistry in general: 'We detest and abhor the usurped authority of that Antichrist upon [over] the scripture of God, upon the Kirk, the civil magistrate and the consciences of men.' They had further denounced the Pope's corrupted doctrines concerning original sin, and his Five Bastard Sacraments: they had called upon the living God to witness their sincerity as they would answer on the Great Day, under pain of infamy and loss of all honour and respect, and prayed the Lord to strengthen them to the end. They were still, they had insisted, loyal subjects and swore that they did not wish to diminish the King's greatness; Charles was still a 'comfortable instrument of God's mercy'; and one 'granted to the realm for the maintenance of the Kirk'. The Covenanters had repudiated 'the foul aspersion of rebellion'; but they had also covenanted to defend one another against anyone, including the King himself in his personal capacity.

Charles had no intention whatever of maintaining a Presbyterian Kirk. But faced with this roar of protest, in August 1638, he characteristically wrote from Greenwich 'as concerning the explanation of that Damnable Covenant (whether it be with or without explanation) I have no more power in Scotland than a Duke of Venice, which I will rather die than suffer. Yet I command the giving ear to the explanation or anything else to win time.' In July the King had been forced to call a full Council to deal with Scottish affairs, which he normally dealt with himself through the Marquess of Hamilton, the commissioner. He was so worried, reported the Venetian envoy, that he had 'cut down his hunting and his game of Mall', as well as his summer progresses, a decision that greatly relieved the local magnates concerned. For 'they could not,' Charles had told the Council, 'be ignorant of the troubles in Scotland; some wild heads had been the causers of it.' Orders had already been given to repair the defences of the key northern towns, Carlisle, Berwick-on-Tweed and Newcastle-upon-Tyne. But the fleet was under supine leadership, for the Earl of Northumberland, acting Lord High Admiral for the Duke of York, now aged five, was ill and the master gunner 'dared to his great regret' to tell the King that 'there are few gunners in your kingdom at this time who understand the several range of ordnance, or the use of the mortars'.

By the autumn of 1638 Charles also had a tiresome domestic preoccupation. Marie de Medici, Queen Dowager of France and Charles's mother-in-law, was a very grand royalty indeed. But she had now fallen out with her son Louis XIII and his advisers, and for some time Charles had tried to fend off her threatened arrival in England. Why not, he had suggested, retire to Florence? But at the end of October, with an entourage estimated at six hundred, she landed in England and at once took to her bed. Fortified by medicine she came up to London, entering it to the edification of huge crowds, and on

10 November she proceeded to St James's. Always punctilious and polite, the King treated her with the utmost deference: uncovered before her, visited her daily, provided £5,000 cash down and £3,000 a month for expenses. But the relict of Henri Quatre and Dowager of France received the Council seated and maintained a most rigid *hauteur*. Doubtless recalling his experience of the 'Monsers' earlier in his reign, and desperate for money, Charles now endured this added strain.

On the other hand, Prince Charles, now aged seven, was thriving; his governor, the Earl (afterwards Marquess) of Newcastle, was one of the most dependable of the great peers, a model of courtly accomplishments, a connoisseur of poetry and music and of general good manners. Nor was the boy's health neglected: his mother fussed over him and a special order in Council wisely directed that the sewers at his house at Richmond were to be cleared.

The Prince, like his father in childhood, already had a mind of his own:

> Charles [his mother had to write to him] I am sore that I must begin my first letter with chiding because I heere you will not take physike. I hope it was onlei for this day and that tomorrow you will doe it, for yf you will not j must come to you, and make you do it, for it is for your healthe. I have given order to my lord Newcastell to send me word to night whether you will or not, therefore j hope you will not give mi the pains to goe and j rest your affectionat mother, Henriette Marie R.[257]

The Prince presumably obeyed; but, already perhaps with a diplomatic indirectness, wrote to his governor: 'My Lord, I would not have you take too much phisick; for it doth allweies make me worse and I think it will do the like with you. I ride every day.'[258]

In January 1639 the climate was appropriately unpropitious. 'The last great lightning,' wrote Secretary Windebank, 'hath done a world of mischief all over England, and the people are generally so molested with predictions and rumours of supposed visions, as if they were all struck with panic fear. For my part I never regard any such things.'[259] They were in fact symptoms of social and political trouble. For the Covenanters were plainly intransigent. 'The Scots,' as the Venetian envoy observed, 'have learnt his majesty's weakness by experience and utter very high flown ideas.'[260] Both Hamilton's missions of June and August 1638 had failed, and even when Charles had climbed down — with no intention of keeping the bargain — so far as to revoke the canons and service book, the Covenanters remained bent on abolishing bishops and swore that, when deposed, they would be treated as 'men accursed'. With politically unwise loyalty the King now refused to let Laud take the blame for the outcome of a policy, which, Charles insisted, had been his own.

In 1639 Charles now actually prepared for full-scale war. He issued his fourth ship writ and raised an army of sorts from the trained bands of the northern counties, and by the antiquated feudal expedient of summoning his tenants-in-chief to provide men or money. He even tried to hire Spanish soldiers from the Netherlands in return for allowing the Spaniards to recruit in England and Ireland — an initiative that fortunately failed. Concurrently, the Queen urged Catholics to subscribe, and it was hoped that the clergy of England 'would teach the ministers of Scotland duty and obedience'. Indeed the Anglican clergy were the only people enthusiastic for war: the diocese of Canterbury contributed £534, and the dean and prebends of the cathedral £300; the rich dioceses of Norwich and

Winchester raised £1,094 and £1,305; £764, and so on in proportion. But most laymen remained hostile or apathetic, and the King got only a token £5,000 from the City.

In theory the army, raised with much difficulty, amounted to 19,483 men: Yorkshire provided the largest contingent; 6,720 musketeers, 5,521 pikemen, 60 horse; Lincolnshire raised 1,080 musketeers and 750 pikemen. But there were far too few horses, and the southern counties did as little as they could, Wiltshire sending 50 horses and 17 carters; Dorset a mere 20 horses and 7, presumably reluctant, carters.

The King's strategy followed that of Henry VIII in 1544: an attempt by the navy on Leith on the Firth of Forth, combined with an attempt to gain command of southern Scotland by land. Wentworth, writing from Ireland, urged an attack on the west — on Dumbarton on the Clyde — as well as on Leith in the east, both of which he said should be permanently occupied, thus blocking Scotland on both sides. He had an Irish army ready; but he advised caution. 'I must disadvise a rash and sudden declaring of war, and yet I would not sacrifice my will and honour to their mutiny... The first resolution I should pitch upon would be not to fight with them hastily, unless upon all advantages possible, but because I would give them time to come to their wits again,... and that much is to be lost by the King, little unto them, by the mischance of one day.'

Disregarding this advice, Charles, his martial side now ascendant and impatient to assert himself as King of Scotland, advanced on Berwick-on-Tweed, but on 1 May 1639 Hamilton failed even to make a landing near Leith. And by now the Scots, who had seized Edinburgh and most of the King's castles and impounded the regalia, were moving south. Under the command of Alexander Leslie, a veteran in the Swedish service of hard campaigns along the Baltic, they advanced to Kelso in the Tweed, then to Dunse Law on the border itself. And here the discrepant armies confronted one another, the Scots hoping to obtain their demands without battle, since the King lacked the sinews of war, his revenues, it was rumoured, pledged for five years ahead. So on 18 June 1639 the futile first *Bellum Episcopate* was called off by the Pacification of Berwick.

It settled nothing and was meant to settle nothing; only to gain time. Charles was as determined to impose bishops as the Scots were to hound them out.

In August Charles was back at Theobalds, where his nephew Charles Louis of the Palatinate had arrived as a refugee after yet another defeat — this time at Vlotho on the Weser in Lower Saxony in a battle in which his brother Prince Rupert had been captured (to be imprisoned in Linz in Austria until 1641). And the Queen Dowager of France was still in England — at the King's expense.

The fiasco in Scotland had at last brought home to the King the incompetence of his advisers. At last he brought himself to send for the only one of them who had been a success and who had advised him against the Scots war. Wentworth was entirely free of suspicion of having intrigued with the Scots, whom he detested and who had officially denounced him, and he commanded an efficient Irish army, supplied with arms direct from the Netherlands; but he had been uninformed of the King's plans for the campaign and his offers to garrison Dumbarton unheeded. Now, early in August, Wentworth received a summons from his master in his own hand. 'Come when you will, ye shall be welcome to your assured friend Charles R.' The message was his death warrant.

During September the usual pleasures of the chase detained the King, and in October there were the usual Garter ceremonies at Windsor, but there were anxious meetings of the Council and by Christmas the magnates on it had themselves subscribed a loan of £300,000. Wentworth, his ambition belatedly attained, was now in virtual control, a position recognized when, in January 1640, the King created him Earl of Strafford and Lord Lieutenant — no longer Lord Deputy — of Ireland. 'The Viceroy of Ireland,' reported the Venetian envoy, 'whom the King trusts more than anyone else, studies to advance his own fortune amid the troubles and increase of his personal authority. Thus he constantly urges His Majesty to take spirited measures and tells him that the Irish will help his just cause.'[261]

Wentworth was now half crippled by gout and other ailments, but for once he entirely agreed with Charles: the question was who governed Scotland, and for that matter England. His immense ability at last had full scope, but in fact he faced a 'situation that called for the inspired insinuation of a Richelieu, or the cautious and lucid diplomacy of an Oxenstjerna, not the sledge hammer blows of a Wentworth'.[262] He was now, at last, at the inner centre of power, along with Laud, Hamilton, Northumberland (Lord Admiral and President of the Council of War) Secretary Windebank and the newly appointed other Secretary, Sir Henry Vane, who succeeded the aged Sir John Coke as Joint Secretary with Windebank in February 1640. Vane detested Strafford, who when created an earl had insisted on the title of Baron Raby for his son, a title that Vane had coveted, and he would prove an instrument of Strafford's ruin. Given his record, the new Lord Keeper Sir John Finch was naturally unpopular in the Commons.

Strafford, like the King, Portland and Cottington, was ready to make a Spanish alliance against the Dutch, and when in

November van Tromp destroyed a Spanish squadron weatherbound in the Downs on the way to the Netherlands — to the fury of the King at the impotence of his cherished fleet — monarch and minister agreed to turn the occasion to good account by offering to convoy the Spanish army's pay to the Netherlands for a large fee.

It was now obvious to them both that, reluctant as he was to do so, the King would have to call another Parliament: in fact by December 1639 Charles had already decided to call it; told the Lords of Council of the 'disorders in Scotland still continuing' and of the 'huge and insolent carriage and demands of our rebellious subjects there'. And when they had agreed that he must reduce the Scots to obedience by force, he had stressed that the task was a 'public business of great weight and of public charge'. He had then declared 'our own desire to meet our people and to demand their assistance in the ancient and ordinary way of Parliament', and in February a foreign expert, John de Cretz, had been ordered — for £650 — to refurbish the royal barge of state. By February the King had also made his intentions plain to the Council. There was 'no government in the Christian world where the head was left out and had not a negative voice'. They must acknowledge 'the Supreme Magistrate's power to call and dissolve'.

This position seemed reasonable, and it was hoped that Parliament, resenting the apparent treachery of the Scots and aware of the perennial need to help the Elector's cause on the Continent, would grant supply. And in March, to set them an example, Strafford, in spite of severe illness, crossed to Ireland, where he obtained from a subservient Irish Parliament four subsidies of £45,000 and consent to employ 8,000 troops outside Ireland against the Covenanters in Scotland. But in England the government had long lost the initiative; and the

King was in such straits that his own apothecary, Johan Wolfgang Rubier, had not been paid for ten years. Above all, the common ideology between the English and Scots Calvinists had eroded English loyalty towards the Crown: both were united in the panic fear and hatred of Catholicism expressed in the Covenant itself.

When, on 18 April 1640, Strafford dragged himself back to London, Charles had already opened his first Parliament for eleven years. The King's speech had been laconic, even perfunctory. 'My lords and gentlemen, there was never a King that had more weighty cause to call his people together than myself. I will not trouble you with the particulars. I have informed my Lord Keeper and commanded him to speak and desire your attention.' One can imagine the tremendous oration of Henry VIII or Elizabeth I in similar crisis: Charles was incapable of such eloquence. Finch, the former speaker, now the Lord Keeper, who was naturally unpopular, began a rather pompous and platitudinous discourse. 'You are here this day assembled by His Majesty's gracious wish and royal command to hold a Parliament, the general ancient and greatest council of this renowned Kingdom. By you the whole Kingdom is presented to His Majesty's royal view and made happy by the beholding of his excellent and sacred person… even the meanest,' he continued, not very tactfully, 'graciously allowed to participate and share in the honour.' They represented the suffrages of the whole nation and they should be grateful to His Majesty for 'sequestering the memory of all former discontents in preceding assemblies'. He then produced a treasonable letter from the Scots Lords to the King of France.

It fell flat. The Commons had not 'sequestered' their own memories: on the contrary they had harboured them up, and as in previous Parliaments they at once aired all the old grievances, still their main concern, dwarfing even the emergency in Scotland and the devious pro-Spanish foreign policy of the King, long a matter for disillusionment at home and abroad. This was expressed, for example, by one Edmund Rychers, who was said to have declared at an inn in Long Acre that 'the oath of the King was not valid in foreign parts', even though, when arraigned, he had apologized; declared that he could not recall his words; that he had been in drink, and if such words had passed from him in his drink he was heartily sorry, and would ever draw his sword in the service of his prince.[263]

The atmosphere was thus from the first unpromising; the old hands were out of practice and the new ones inexperienced, and, as usual, the government gave no effective leadership in the Commons. The 'Short' Parliament proved, if not 'addled', ephemeral; it sat only from 13 April till 5 May and it proved no help in the crisis.

The King was now living from hand to mouth. Besides the big loan of £300,000, to which Strafford had contributed £20,000 — only a year's income to one, by modern standards, a millionaire — Charles had also managed to raise £25,000 at 8 per cent to redeem his 'Great Jewell' in pawn to the King of Denmark. The Commons well knew the weakness of the regime and they exploited it. For Parliament was set for a showdown, not a reconciliation. The King was insolvent and his regal assumption of authority failed to overawe the newly elected Commons, who continued to raise all the grievances that had been mounting up for over a decade. In doing so they were representative, as was the petition of the freeholders of the county of Northampton.

> We have to represent to your honourable House that of late we have been... insupportably charged, troubled and grieved in our consciences persons and estates by innovations in religion, exactions in spiritual courts, molestation of our most Godly and learned ministry, ship money, monopolies, undue impositions, army money, waggon money, horse money, conduct money and enlarging the Forest beyond its ancient bounds and the like... Not yielding which things, divers of us have been molested, detained and imprisoned.

They also asked that they 'might have a Parliament once a year, as by law we ought — 4 Ed. III Stat. 4. 36 Ed.: III Stat. 10'. And the petition had been presented by the two members for the county, John Crewe Esquire and Sir Gilbert Pickering.

Such and many similar and reasonable demands, reflecting public needs, would be exploited by the clique that now coalesced round Pym in their attempt to transform and then take over the whole structure and authority of the old conciliar government; and Pym was backed by powerful magnates — Essex, Bedford, Hertford, Pembroke — who detested Strafford and the whole grand design of a centralized royal government and who wanted to dismantle the essential apparatus of the Tudor state, which the King had now been attempting to develop on continental lines. The Short Parliament thus witnessed an alliance of opposition gentry in the Commons and magnates in the Lords, the former wanting to go ahead with and control a more modern state, the latter mainly quasi-medieval ultra-conservatives. It would prove extremely formidable.

Ironically, Strafford himself had urged the King to summon the Parliament, paying him the undeserved tribute that he would know how to manage it and gain supply by conciliation of grievances. This, he considered, would be the best defence the King could make against the designs of both Pym and his faction, and against Essex, long Strafford's most bitter enemy, and the recalcitrant great peers. Charles, he had said, should appeal to public loyalty against the 'treachery' of the Scots, who had intrigued with the French King, and for help for his nephew the young Elector Palatine on the Continent.

But Pym, the first master of Parliamentary management in English history, well knew how to play on the old obsession with Popery and foreign invasion, going back to the Marian persecution, the Armada and the Gunpowder Plot.[264] Myths in politics, he knew, were often more powerful than facts, and to move public opinion one had to harp on what was already there. Moreover he stuck to the essential point: no supply before redress of grievances; and when, on 24 April, Charles and Strafford persuaded the Lords to vote supply by a big majority, the Commons said it was trenching on their privileges for the Upper House to 'chalk out a way' to give supplies and only then to demand redress of grievances.

At this, Charles sent a message through the new Secretary Sir Henry Vane urging the dangers of delay, and with unwonted political tact struck out from his original draft the words: 'His Majesty cannot but resent it, as that which... is without any precedent of such behaviour of subjects to their king.' He then, on 4 May, declared that by his grace and favour, if they gave him twelve subsidies to be presently passed and paid within three years, he would 'forebear the last Ship Money', which it will be recalled had amounted to very little, and give way to the utter abolition of the tax by any course that the Commons should think best, consider grievances at Michaelmas next, and not close the session.

Even this olive branch was rejected; the Commons merely stepped up their demands. So on 5 May they were summoned to the Chamber of the Lords, and there, crowned and robed, Charles dissolved the Short Parliament: '[There] could not a greater damp have seized upon the spirits of the whole nation,' Clarendon would write, 'than this dissolution caused.' Speaking afterwards to the Lords, the King declared, 'I know that they have insisted very much on grievances, and I would desire them to know that I was ready if not more willing to hear any just grievances outside Parliament.' But the Commons, he declared, had gone too far: they were about to petition for a reconciliation with the rebel Scots; now, since he knew that his enemies in Parliament, in Lords and Commons, were plotting with the Scots, Charles had dissolved them. He further issued a declaration saying that the malcontents had attempted to direct him and to examine and censure his acts, as if kings were bound to give an account of their regal acts and the manner of good government to their subjects assembled in Parliament.

In contrast to the Commons, the Loyal Convocation of the Church, on the King's order, had continued to sit contrary to practice, and had voted a subsidy of 4s in the £1 for six years. But in the previous autumn Bishop Hall of Exeter had written to Laud complaining of the effects of the Scottish schism among his clergy, one of whom had vented doctrines prejudicial to the divine institution of episcopal government. In the diocese of York the King himself had instructed Laud to proceed rigorously against the non-conformism of Dr Jenison, lecturing in Newcastle, which was 'dangerous to his government, especially considering the ill-symptoms it carries with it of his correspondence with the Scottish faction'.[265] This fear of an alliance between the Calvinists of both countries was well founded, as the Civil War would witness.

In the early summer of 1640 the King had thus again provoked the opposition both of the Commons over money and of Puritan opinion, clerical and lay, about religion. The combination would prove highly combustible.

12: THE COLLAPSE OF AUTHORITY

THE FAILURE OF the Short Parliament in no way deflected the King from his resolve to make war on the Covenanting Scots. Though Strafford had originally thought the attempt to force them to religious conformity 'a senseless freak', now that they were in actual rebellion and 'addressing themselves to foreign states', he encouraged Charles to reckless action.

The Scots had continued 'preaching and praying' and 'drilling to be quit of bishops', and the King had issued a proclamation against their 'public condemning of our Canons and mutinous protesting against them, a course not to be endured in a well ordered Kingdom'. He intended, he said, 'God willing, to be in a short time in Edinburgh to settle this disorderly government'. They had behaved as if he were not their King but 'their sworn enemy'. But the Scots had remained intransigent, saying that there were 'never any bishops in the old time before', and that they 'would not have them now'; they had sworn that 'they should never come in more', and, if they did, that 'the women would beat out their brains with stones'.

On 5 May 1640, the day that the Short Parliament was dissolved, Charles summoned the Council that dealt with Scots affairs. The occasion proved fateful for Strafford, since he used words later distorted to bring him to the block with the forced acquiescence of the King, a decision that tormented Charles until his own judicial murder and 'proved the axe against his own life'.[266] For according to 'some notes of what passed in the Junto or Committee of State' by Secretary Vane[267] (who in 1640 had succeeded Sir John Coke, who had reformed the administration of the navy, but though an able official was now nearly eighty and known as 'Old Noddy'), of which a copy — taken by Sir Harry Vane,[268] his son, when rummaging in his father's papers ostensibly for a document connected with his own marriage settlement to an heiress — had been transcribed by Pym, Strafford now stated that he intended to use the army he had raised in Ireland to deal with the Scots. Misinterpreting his remark with a politician's sleight-of-hand, Pym would allege that he had intended to use it in England, thus setting off another wave of the panic anti-Catholic obsession on which Pym was riding to power.

With an authentic note of a high-level discussion, curiously modern, the hastily written notes speak for themselves:

> *Strafford*: The shipping money to be put vigorously on collection. A few months will make an end of the war.
> *The Lord High Admiral* [Northumberland] If no more money, then what proposed? How make offensive war? Whether to do nothing and let them alone or go on with vigourous war?
> *Strafford*: 'Go vigorously on, or let them alone. Go on with an offensive war as you first designed, loosed and absolved from all rules of government, being reduced to extraordinary necessity, everything to be done as power will admit and that you are to do. They [the Scots] have refused [peace]. You are acquitted towards God and man. You have an army in Ireland you may employ here to reduce this Kingdom' [obviously Scotland was the subject of the Committee's discussion] 'I would venture all I had, I would carry it or lose all.'

Hume is particularly lucid and impartial on this point. 'Even retaining the expression *This Kingdom*, the words may be fairly understood of Scotland, which alone was the Kingdom that the delegate regarded, and which alone had thrown off allegiance…'[269]

Laud: They had 'tried all ways' and [the Commons] 'had refused all ways'. 'By the Law of God you should have subsistence and ought to have it, and may lawfully take it.' All fiscal expedients, it was concluded, were now just, and Strafford also advised that the old-fashioned Commissions of Array be put in execution to raise troops: 'In reason of state you have power.'

The King therefore went ahead with a thoroughly unrealistic campaign. Surrounded with an accustomed deference, it was natural that he should be deluded. But Strafford, though horribly ill, now controlled policy, and Charles sanctioned raising money from Spain in return for protecting Spanish convoys up the Channel, a plan frustrated when the Dutch said they would regard it as an act of war. Charles then tried to borrow the stock of spices held by the East India Company and sell it for the Crown; but the Company refused consent; so he seized the bullion which, in the absence of proper banks, London merchants were in the habit of depositing for safety in the Tower.

Since March 1640 the Scots had been mobilizing, and now on 2 June they convened their Parliament themselves under its own elected president. It was in three estates — nobility, gentry and burgesses — for the higher clergy — 'Kirk or Kirkmen' — were excluded from 'ryding and wotting in Parliament'; with their removal the lower clergy were left to conduct their own Presbyterian assemblies and organization, always independent of the prelates superimposed by James I. Both these departures were revolutionary — to convene the estates without the King's mandate and to remove the bishops — for the existing hierarchy assumed a collaboration of King, Church and State. And the Covenanters now rigged academic appointments — important in Scotland. So Charles faced open defiance. To convene a Parliament without his command set a precedent not lost on his English subjects, and Parliamentarians from both Houses were in correspondence with the Scots. As during the Civil War itself, fear and hatred of Rome and the will for political power cut across national differences and united Scots and English Calvinists against the regime in both realms.

In London, meanwhile, fanaticism and social discontent combined. The apprentices in particular were notoriously and naturally turbulent. And since they appear constantly during the breakdown of Charles's regime and in the Civil Wars, they demand attention. Mainly poor and by origin provincial, they often had dim prospects unless their families could raise the substantial premiums demanded by the major companies, which the apprentices could not join until they were turned twenty-four. Their indentures were necessarily strict: 'The said apprentice his said master shall well and truly serve; keep his secrets close; his commandments, lawful and honest, shall willingly do; hurt nor damage to his said master he shall not do.' In return, the master kept the youth entirely; a patriarchal relationship that for good and ill depended on his temperament and his family — including the women. The clothes provided by the master were sober and the apprentice's hair had to be cut in 'a decent and comely manner' — restrictions often resented. Moreover the youth could be fined even for 'dancing and masquing' and frequenting cock-fights; and he promised during a seven-year bondage, covering the most exciting years of adolescence, not to commit fornication or to marry. One can sympathize with those who committed the conclusive offence of 'running away'.

Some apprentices were virtuous and married into the family; others dishonest and lazy, most probably mediocre and not ill-meaning. A few in desperation would sue their masters — one alleged that he had been beaten with a 'boathook'. All were doubtless rowdy, some loutish and violent, some jolly and spirited. Since their organization was medieval, it was also religious, and services and festivals made for fraternity — Shrove Tuesday was their particular holiday; and there was a sub-culture of apprentice tales and romances with its heroes and anti-heroes. They were not, as liberal historians presented them, hearty young political radicals; but more akin to modern 'protesters', resentful of poverty and discipline, though their 'leftish' ideology of protest was then religious. They could be guaranteed to stoke up a riot and, if disciplined and drilled, could be vigorous in battle.[270]

They were now a formidable element in the mounting crisis. After demonstrating in Southwark, hundreds of them, reinforced by seamen from London docks, marched on Lambeth Palace. Charles had already commanded Archbishop Laud to take oars for Whitehall, where he was guarded by cannon, but the riot lasted three days. Two of the rioters paid for it. The glover who had led the march beating a drum was taken up, racked for information and executed. The other, not an apprentice but 'a poor sailor', a boy of sixteen, one Thomas Bensted, who had been wounded by a pistol shot in the riot, fell an easy victim. He was judged guilty of treason and on 23 May was hanged, drawn and quartered. The Archbishop's enemies rightly did not forget this savagery,[271] nor should we, in considering the high Anglican seventeenth-century beauty of holiness, the contrast between the refinement of these people and their cruelty.

Only the Anglican Convocation, who knew well their fate if international Calvinism won, still supported the second *Bellum Episcopate*. When, through the dissolution of the Short Parliament, the subsidies it had granted had become technically void since they required confirmation by Parliament, Charles had intervened and ordered them, on medieval precedents, to remain in session as a 'Synod' and make the subsidies a straight benevolence. So they sat until the end of May and formulated and published seventeen canons of doctrine, which insisted on the King's divine right and on the errors of Rome, and devised the notorious *etcetera* oath, obligatory on all clergy, masters of arts (the sons of noblemen alone excepted), doctors of divinity, law and medicine and schoolmasters, who had to swear that they would not subvert the established church government 'by Archbishops, bishops, deans and arch-deacons, *etc.*'. This misguided manifesto, sanctioned by the King, proved a target for ridicule and abuse and a cause of dissension in the Church itself.

The Scots were now set to advance into England: not, of course, they insisted, to plunder or to attack a monarch for whom they continued to pray, but in pure self-defence.

> The question is not [they said] whether we shall content ourselves with our own poverty, or enrich ourselves in England... But this is the question, whether it be wisdom and piety to keep ourselves within the Borders till our throats be cut and our Religion, Lawes and country be destroyed; or shall we bestirre ourselves and seeke our safeguard, peace, and liberty in England. Or shall we fold our hands and waite for the perfect slavery of ourselves, our posterity in our Souls, Bodies and Estates... or shall we seek our relief in following the calling of God?[272]

On 20 August a formidable Scots army of at least twenty

thousand men, again commanded by Leslie and including many officers seasoned in the wars in Scandinavia, northern Germany and Poland, crossed the Tweed, by-passing Berwick, and advanced into Northumbria to the Tyne. There was no resistance, but on the twenty-eighth an officer, watering his horse in the river, was shot by an English musketeer from an entrenchment at Newburn on the ford nearest to Newcastle. After a brisk cannonade, in which the Scots artillery commanded the English positions, the demoralized and discontented defenders simply turned and fled. The Scots then crossed the Tyne, advanced on Newcastle and on 28 August routed an ineffectual cavalry counter-attack; soon Newcastle, the key to that part of the north and the main source of London coal, inadequately fortified and worse defended, was in the hands of the invaders. Charles's directive that the suburbs should be razed to give a field of fire had proved impracticable as they were built of solid stone.

The King, who had ridden up from London through the late August countryside, was by then in York. On 25 August he 'wondered that the proclamation declaring the rebels traitors had not been sent' and that 'neither the Clerk of the Council or of the Signet or his messenger could be heard of'. The officials had not even been able to declare war on time, and when the proclamation was at last issued Charles merely referred contemptuously, in medieval style, to 'certain rebels from Our Realm of Scotland'.

Charles had deluded himself into over-confidence. He had reckoned that the Scots incursion would rouse traditional feelings in Yorkshire, and while the defence was already crumbling in the north, Strafford told the Yorkshire gentry that 'they were no better than beasts' if they refused to attend their

King, 'his Majesty in person offering to lead them on'. But privately he had written:

> Pity me, for never came any man to so mighty lost a business. The army altogether unexercised and unprovided of all necessities. That part which I bring now from Durham the worst I ever saw. Our horse all cowardly, the country from Berwick to York in the power of the Scots, an universal affright in all men, a general disaffection to the King's service, now sensible of his dishonour. In one word, left alone to fight with all these evils, without anyone to help. God of his goodness deliver me out of this, the greatest evil of my life...[273]

By now even Charles realized the condition of the army. 'Incredulity and despising of the rebels strength,' he afterwards complained, 'had brought him and his state into great straits', and into danger that 'threatened the safety of all'. For even the levies that had reluctantly come in to York were inefficient and ill-disciplined, and the contingents from the south were even more disaffected and often fanatical. In Devonshire, for example, in Colonel Culpepper's regiment, the men had killed an officer in cold blood for cutting church services, saying that he must be a Papist. In Berkshire to avoid the press the men had left their cottages and taken to the woods, leaving their families on the parish and 'the harvest work undone'. In another incident the Dorset levies, who had got as far north as Faringdon in Berkshire, had broken into the chamber of Captain Lewknor, Lieutenant Mohun and his ensign. All three had scrambled out of the window astride the signpost of the inn, but while Lewknor and the ensign slid off it and escaped, Mohun had clung on; so the levies had beaten him with cudgels, dragged him down, put him in the sewer, dragged him round the town and finally knocked out his brains and hanged him on the pillory. Afterwards the officers ventured to take him down and give him a decent burial. Such were the morale and discipline of the pressed men of Dorset, and such some of the raw material of the subsequently idealized Puritan army.

After these episodes and others like them — and not before — it occurred to the government to issue commissions to the colonels to hold courts martial and impose martial law; but even that was of doubtful authority without consent of Parliament. 'We must use no martial law, though we have it under the broad seal,' one officer had said, 'but such as is Westminster Hall proof.' He had thought it wiser to use the civilian remedy of whipping and dispatching to a house of correction — hardly the way to run an army. The Scots on the other hand were full of zeal and well equipped. They had eleven big cannon, fifty-four field pieces, with ammunition trains, and thirty wagons with a 'thing like a harrow' to impede cavalry. They had 25,000 foot and 4,000 cavalry with a reserve of 5,000. They were well disciplined (to prevent looting no Highlanders, who 'wore uncivill kinds of clothes, such as plaids, mantels, truses and blue bonnets', had been included) and they brought along and lived off their own frugal oatmeal and bannocks. No wonder that the local farmers were said to fear the King's army more than the Scots. And the Scots had already shown their mettle.

Charles now had to face the facts, and having created Strafford a Knight of the Garter at York and still anxious to avoid calling a Parliament, he summoned the Ancient *Magnum Concilium* of his tenants-in-chief-a body not summoned since the reign of Edward in. They promised to guarantee a loan of £200,000 in the City to pay the army, but they had not the power to levy taxation and insisted that negotiation be opened with the Scots who, now in occupation of Northumberland and Durham, were demanding £850 a day for their expenses.

Sixteen peers now proceeded to Ripon, where early in October they haggled with the invaders, whose representatives refused even to come down to York; but they failed to diminish their demands or persuade them to return to Scotland. On 28 October Charles had to sign the treaty of Ripon, and the Scots, well reimbursed, remained in occupation of the north. So, ignominiously, after a brief encounter, the King brought his second *Bellum Episcopale* to a conclusion.

He had no alternative. Back in London, Bedford and Hertford, who were backed by the influential magnates Essex, Pembroke, Warwick and Saye, had petitioned the Council for a Parliament: yet Pym and his colleagues were more sympathetic to the Scots than to their own monarch, both on ideological grounds and because the Scots pressure strengthened their own position. The Lord Mayor and aldermen also petitioned the King to summon a Parliament — it was now being mooted that if the King failed to summon it, the peers concerned would summon one themselves. Finally the Queen, who was at Hampton Court, strongly advised Charles to acquiesce and to return at once to London. Writs were therefore issued for the new and fateful 'Long' Parliament.

On 3 November 1640, robed and crowned in the Lords, Charles opened the most momentous Parliament of his reign.

> The knowledge [he began] I had of the desires of my Scottish subjects, was the cause of my calling the last Parliament; wherein had I been believed, I sincerely think things would not have fallen out as we see. But it is no wonder that men are so slow to believe that so great a sedition should be raised on so little ground. But now, my Lords and Gentlemen, the Honour and safety of this kingdom lying so near at the stake, I am resolved to put myself freely and clearly on the love and

affection of my English subjects as those of my Lords that did wait upon me at York.

Their common and first concern was 'the chastising out of the Rebells'. But he emphasized that he had incurred great charges only for the kingdom's good, and to maintain the army he must request supply; he would then consider redress of grievances. Ironically, in the event, he charged them 'that you on your parts, as I on mine, lay aside all suspicion of one another... It shall not be my fault,' he concluded, 'if this be not a Happy and Good Parliament.'[274]

Two days later Charles further explained himself to the Lords. 'I told you that the rebels must be put out of this kingdom. Its true, I must needs call them so, so long as they have an army that do invade us; and although I am under treaty with them... I do call them my subjects and so they are.' He again indicated the state of his affairs and concluded, 'Had the Lords as much power as affection, I should by this time have brought these distempers to a happy period.'[275]

Seldom was the King's curious optimism more misplaced than in both these speeches. The majority of the Commons and a powerful group in the Lords were determined to shackle the entire Tudor prerogative power as now developed. In the Commons Pym and his following set about their business with zest and method. The House, it was agreed, would go into committee in the afternoons — on Mondays for religion, Tuesdays for trade, Wednesdays for general grievances, and on Fridays for justice. With a novel professionalism they ordained that 'some place for the better preservation of the Records and Books of the House should be considered'; hitherto only the clerk of Parliament had kept them and they had been 'left to the executors' and so 'lost and embezzled'.

The old grievances of the Short Parliament were at once taken up — innovation in religion, abuse of feudal and forest rights, monopolies, ship money. The Commons desired to 'have Parliament more often' and to bring 'insufficient and unmeet' ministers to book. They denounced the pressing of men, the ignorance and indiscipline of the trained bands and — more sinister for the government — they moved to 'enquire after the fomentors of the calamities of this kingdom, that they may be punished'. They would give nothing, they concluded, until their grievances were settled.[276] They had no other course, they claimed, for 'to suffer these burdens were to betray our Duty to the King, who has suffered as much as wee'.

Pym's parliamentary tactics were consistent and masterly. When organized parties were still unheard of and would have appeared 'factions', he kept the House on just the scents they relished. First, that of Popery and of the 'high flying' bishops and their officials. There was a 'design to alter the Kingdom both religion and government... the highest of treason, blown up by peece meales...'. Here again it 'concerned the King as well as wee'. Exploiting the immediate crisis, he said that there was a threat of the present fortification of the Tower' and of 'the planting of ordnance towards London', whereby no good was meant to the City. 'A man would thinke wee lived rather in Turkie than in Christendom!' As Ranke wrote of the English revolution in words too often forgotten, 'persons as much as principles were the great exciting cause of the movement'.[277] The most immediate objective of Pym and his colleagues was personal revenge on the 'Lieutenant of Ireland' and on Archbishop Laud, and by 11 November the former was in the Tower, where the latter joined him on 18 December. On 5 December, in fog, Secretary Windebank fled to France, rowed in an open boat from Queensborough to end his days in Paris, on 21 December Lord Justice Finch fled to Holland, where he remained until the Restoration of 1660, returning to die. The virulence of hatred displayed by the Calvinist politicians admired by Whig historians was natural: the price of failure at the summit of public life was not then a seat in an innocuous House of Lords, well-paid directorships in the City, or thousands from a publisher for one's memoirs; it could be one's head. It was necessary to get in first, and Essex's remark of Strafford — 'stone dead hath no fellow' — could have been said in Hitler's Germany of Rohm, though even then in England judicial murder was embellished by the forms of law. The dismantling of prerogative government was the massive and decisive achievement of the Parliament from which all else followed and which in fact rendered the Civil Wars superfluous, but the hounding down of its two ablest exponents had priority.

And here, inevitably, Charles was deeply involved. Though never an intimate of Strafford, he had confided in the Archbishop, with whom his own legal-mindedness and piety were in accord; in so far as any royalty by divine right took a subject seriously, he respected this 'father in God'.

The sins of the ministers were of course still carefully distinguished from the conduct of the King, but as the attack on Strafford mounted much eloquence was let loose. Lord Falkland,[278] described by Aubrey as 'this great Witt, the greatest master of Reason and Judgement of his time', and the owner of Great Tew near Oxford where many learned men were entertained, spoke of 'removing pernicious cankers who have of late years by their wicked practices provoked aspersions upon the Government of the most gracious and best of Kings'. They had not allowed Charles to appear to the people in his own native goodness, but had eclipsed him. For himself, he concluded of Strafford, in a speech already in a great parliamentary tradition, 'I love no man's ruin; I thank God I neither hate any man's person, nor any man's fortune; only I am zealous for a thorow Reformation in a time that exacts, that extorts it.' Sir Benjamin Rudyard declared that there had been 'a doleful deadly knell over the whole kingdom'; his ministers had made the King's power a 'miserable power' and 'peremptorarily pursued an obstinate and pernicious cause'. As for ship money, he said, 'It cries aloud, it strikes the first born of every family, I mean our inheritance.'

That of course was the point. And as for the monopolists they were 'a nest of wasps and vermin that had overcrept the land'. They were 'pollers of the people. They sup in our cup, they dip in our dish, they sit by our fire, we find them in the wash house [soap] and in the powdering tub; they share with the Butler in his Box.'

Such was the indignation forcefully expressed in the early months of the Long Parliament. Against such a tide not even Strafford's towering abilities had a chance. Some of the most eloquent of his accusers were afterwards Royalists, for example Edward Hyde, afterwards Earl of Clarendon, who declared that 'the Court of the President of the North had so far broken its bounds as to have almost overwhelmed the country under a sea of arbitrary power'. Thus as a critic of the regime the best statesman among the Royalists and the greatest English historian of his age and one of the best of any other, first took a lead. He had represented Wootton Bassett, Wilts, in the Short Parliament and now sat for Saltash in Devon, having made his way by the law from his origins in South Wiltshire, where his father Henry Hyde owned a property at Dinton, which he had inherited. After studying at Magdalen Hall,

Oxford and the Inner Temple, 'Ned' Hyde had been one of a circle of wits and writers though he had made his career as a barrister: always an enemy of arbitrary power he would help to prosecute Strafford; but he parted company with the opposition over the desire to abolish bishops and impose a Presbyterian order, and would support the King and what he held to be the laws of the land against what he came to consider the arbitrary power of a majority in Parliament.

When Charles had left York to open Parliament in London, Strafford was the most hated man in England, accused not only of exercising arbitrary power, but of responsibility for the King's failure in the Second Bishops' War. Hamilton, who had a good sense of self-preservation, had sensibly advised him to leave England; but 'Black Tom' was not one to evade his enemies; moreover Charles had summoned him to London, perhaps in a contrived plan that Strafford should act as a lightning-conductor, suffer impeachment and then be vindicated; protected, anyway, by the King. The King with his usual and fatal optimism, and Strafford out of pride and contempt, may even have thought that they could manage Parliament. 'Did he really know,' writes Strafford's biographer, 'when he agreed to come to London, that he was gambling with his life? He may have done so. Certainly his last request to the King that he might have two or three days to set his affairs in order at Woodhouse suggests that he knew his journey to London might be his last.'[279] 'I am tomorrow,' he wrote on 5 November, 'to London, with more danger beset, I believe, than ever man went without of Yorkshire; yet my heart is good and I find nothing cold within me.'

On 10 November in Whitehall Palace the King was in deep consultation with the Lord Lieutenant who that morning had taken his seat in the Lords, when it was announced that the

Commons intended to impeach Strafford of high treason before the Lords that very afternoon. They had also cunningly resolved that 'the prelates ought to have no vote in this thing'; and with their long, legal memoirs they had cited the precedent of 1388 of the de Vere Duke of Ireland, favourite of Richard II. At once Strafford drove over to the House, but Pym had got there first and the process was already in train. With a 'proud, glooming countenance' the Lord Lieutenant made to take his seat, but it was too late. He had to withdraw; then after a brief interval he was recalled and commanded to kneel at the bar while the charge was read to him. He was refused leave to speak, bundled into the official coach of the Gentleman Usher of the Black Rod and driven to the Tower under arrest, to await trial. And there he stayed until March 1641, while Charles attempted conciliation.

The long-delayed trial, which took seven weeks, was an event comparable to that of Warren Hastings, though it was much sooner over. It was held in Rufus's Great Hall at Westminster and the King and royalties attended, blatantly incognito, in a box, the throne being left vacant though Prince Charles, aged eleven, sat in his robes on the right of it. Fully and accurately reported by the Scots Commissioner, Robert Baillie, who had a sharp eye for detail and a realistic pen, the scene that began on Monday 22 March still comes alive. Those attending had to be there by five o'clock in the morning and the proceedings began at eight; Charles arrived by 7.30 but 'came not to the throne, for that would have marred the action for it is the order in England that when the King appears he speaks what he will, but no other speaks in his presence'.[280] So the King, Queen, Princess Mary and the Prince Elector sat in a room at the side. Charles himself drew back the 'tirlies [curtains] that made them to be secret' with his own hands, so that they sat in the eyes of all, but little more regarded than if they had been absent, for 'the Lords sat all covered and even the lower House only discovered [took their hats off] when the Lords came, not else'.

It was an impressive scene, with a great platform taking up the middle of the hall and banks of seats at either side up to the roof. The judges were in scarlet, and the earls and lords in red robes lined with ermine, differentiated in their dignities by bars of white fur: earls by three, viscounts by two and a half, barons by two. In contrast, the black-gowned clerks of Parliament sat round a little table covered with green frieze. At the green-covered bar were the eight or ten representatives of the Commons making the impeachment, while in the midst was a little desk at which the prisoner could sit or stand, accompanied by his keeper, the Lieutenant of the Tower. Already disconcerted by the informal royal incognito, Baillie was shocked that 'in the most glorious assembly the Isle could afford, the gravity was not such as I expected'. There was great clamour at the doors and in the intervals both the lords and the Commons got up, walked about and 'clattered'. There was much 'public eating' not only 'of confections but of flesh and bread, bottles of beer and wine going thick from mouth to mouth without cups, and all this in the King's eye: yea, manic but turned their back and let water go through the forms they sat on: there was no outgoing to return; and often the sitting was till two, three or four o'clock'.[281]

The high drama of the trial has been frequently described. Strafford, with the fine manners of his kind, entered with two deep 'courtesies', then, having knelt at the bar, rose quickly to salute both sides of the House, whereat 'some few of the Lords lifted hats to him'. The clerk then read the charges, inaudibly, and Strafford's own detailed defence — 'very large, accurate and eloquent' — was counter-attacked by Pym, whereat 'all fell to clattering, walking, eating, toying', while the accused, in the midst of the noise, conferred with his secretaries and diligently read his notes. On 27 March, the anniversary of the coronation, the noise was further diversified by bells ringing all day. Following convention, Strafford gave large daily tips of £10 to his guards, changed every day. By 10 April the impeachment had so obviously failed that in the chaotic adjournment of the proceedings by the Lords — without naming a date for another hearing — Charles and Strafford had exchanged glances and laughed, the more so since the King had been in contact with officers of the army, still mobilized and disgruntled in the north. A plan was afoot with the Queen's connivance to transfer the command from the Earl of Northumberland to the Earl of Newcastle, with the adventurous George Goring (now governor of Portsmouth and a friend of the Queen), as Lieutenant General to be in command of the Tower of London. But for some courtiers, the prospect of this appointment was too much: they had prevented it, and in pique Goring had revealed the plot in confidence to the enemies of the regime, now naturally all the more determined to have Strafford's blood.[282]

But Charles and Strafford were not yet out of the wood; Pym now fell back on a political Bill of Attainder, far apter for judicial murder. And here the minutes transcribed by the younger Vane from his father's account of the proceedings in Council on 5 May the year before became decisive. They were just the kind of garbled evidence whereby a skilled politician can raise a stampede of panic, and the prospect of an army in Ireland reducing 'this kingdom' — here garbled to mean England — set one off. All Strafford's fine eloquence — Heath calls it 'sinewy' — displayed in the final session of 13

April thus became irrelevant, including his able summing up of the crux of the matter: 'I ever did inculcate this: the happiness of a Kingdom consists in the just poise of the subjects' liberty and that things should never be well till these went hand in hand together.' Nor was his warning to the peers heeded, that the prosecution were creating a new and arbitrary definition of treason, which 'raked out of some moth-eaten records might tear them and their posterity to pieces: be not more skillful, more curious than your father's in the art of killing'. And when he broke off weeping and silent when he spoke of his first wife and their children, and concluded with a dramatic and pious elevation of his eyes, even the austere Baillie was moved: 'The matter and expression exceedingly brave... doubtless, if he had grace, and civil goodness, he is a most eloquent man.'

The Bill of Attainder remained before the Commons, where Falkland's hair-splitting arguments supported Pym, as against Selden, too learned in the law to admit of Strafford's treason. The Commons, in a thin house, voted for the Bill by 204 to 59. But Charles remained confident that he could at least save Strafford's life, and on 24 April Strafford was writing to Hamilton: 'It is told me that the Lords are inclinable to preserve my life and family... All that I shall desire from your lordship is that, divested of all public employment, I may be admitted to go home to my own private fortune, there to attend to my own domestic affairs.' Further, Bedford and Hertford, powerful magnates in opposition, sought to gain concessions from the King by sparing Strafford's life. But Essex's humiliations were deeply rooted in his hatred of the Court, and Pym, to whom the King had offered the Chancellorship of the Exchequer vacated by Cottington, refused it, since he knew the City would never pay up with Strafford alive.

Pym would take no part in government until his enemy was finished. For the 'great engines with which they [had] raised the mobile', as the Royalist partisan Nolan puts it, were now in full swing; and howling mobs in the City and at Westminster were demanding Strafford's death. A monster petition — a new technique often to be copied — was signed by twenty thousand in the City and on 27 April, before the Lords, Oliver St John, the Solicitor General, argued on the second reading of the Bill: 'He that would not have had others have a law, why should he have any himself?... It was never accounted either cruelty or foul play to knock wolves and foxes on the head.'

Then on 1 May, while the Bill was being debated, Charles addressed both Houses of Parliament in an attempt to save Strafford's life. In effect he disowned him, saying that he was unfit to serve 'even in the office of constable', but he denied that he had ever advised him to bring in an Irish army or to subvert the fundamental laws. But it was now well known that Charles had already spoken of himself taking command of the army at York and had considered dissolving Parliament and retiring with the Queen to Portsmouth. He did not inspire confidence, even in the magnates anxious to spare Strafford's life.

His politically effective course, as advised by Francis Russell, fourth Earl of Bedford (whose death from smallpox that month removed a wise mediator from the ranks of the Opposition, left his son William, later the first Duke, to vacillate between Parliament and King and then, to concentrate on the more rewarding interest of draining his fenland for his Bedford level), was to refuse to create new precedents for treason as a potential danger to all concerned; in fact, with typical lack of political insight, he declared that on his own personal conscience he could not pass the Bill. And this emphasis on his own conscience proved fatal; it enabled the astute Bishop Williams, now released from the Tower and soon to be Archbishop of York, to advise him, at the agonizing climax of the crisis, to distinguish between himself and his public capacity as monarch.[283] He ought now, the plausible Williams argued, as monarch, to sanction Strafford's death. And the decision was perhaps made easier by the victim's curious letter from prison, setting the King's conscience at liberty to prevent 'evils that may happen by the refusal to pass this Bill' — a petition perhaps designed to sway the Lords in Strafford's favour. In the event, the Lords passed the Bill by 26 to 19 votes.

The ball was now in the King's court and nowhere else. His position was dreadful; mobs of apprentices were bawling 'in loud and hideous voice' for Strafford's execution; a 'sudden bruit' ran in the City that the Papists had set the House of Commons on fire and beset it with arms; the King's English army was said now to be marching on London. To stop the King or Queen joining the army, the royal servants were commanded not to stir without the King's and Parliament's leave. Charles, Baillie reported, 'was now very sad and pensive'.[284] The mob now broke into the purlieus of Whitehall Palace itself and the Queen took refuge in her inner rooms.

Charles took refuge in prayer. He also again summoned his spiritual advisers, and though Juxon and Ussher urged him to stand by his conscience, Williams again took his chance. So inadequate were the guards at Whitehall that Charles now feared for the Queen's and his children's lives, and that Sunday, 9 May 1641, he consented to his minister's execution, with the words 'My Lord of Strafford's condition is happier than mine.' It was his first appalling crisis; it was humiliating, touching himself, touching his family — power politics and fanaticism had struck home into his private world and the royal aesthete acquiesced. Characteristically he tried to have it both ways. On 11 May he sent the unfortunate Prince of Wales to the House of Lords with a last ineffective appeal.

> I did yesterday [he wrote] satisfy the justice of the Kingdom by passing the Bill of Attainder against the Earl of Strafford; but mercy being... inherent and inseparable in a King as Justice, I desire... that unfortunate man to fulfill the natural course of his life in a close imprisonment; if this may be done without the discontentment of any people. It will be an unspeakable contentment to me... but if no less than his life can satisfy my people I must say *Fiat Justitia*. Thus I rest your unalterable and affectionate friend. Charles R. and if Strafford must die, it were charity to reprieve him until Saturday.

The appeal was ignored: Strafford had gained nothing and the King had further lost face. It was not a gambit conceivable for Henry VIII or Elizabeth I; and well might Strafford exclaim, 'Put not your trust in Princes nor in the sons of men, for in them there is no salvation.'

There remained the last elaborate public spectacle. On the scaffold he said, 'I am at the door going out, and my next step must be from time to eternity; to clear myself to you all, I do solemnly protest before God I am not guilty of that crime laid to my charge, nor have ever had the least inclination or intention to damnify or prejudice the King, the State, the laws or religion of the Kingdom, but with the best endeavour to serve all and support all.' Spared at least the full horrors of execution for high treason, on 12 May he was beheaded at one blow, to the edification of enormous crowds, who roared their satisfaction; then as 'the executioner lifted the bleeding head; from the outer edges of the crowd riders galloped out into the country, shouting to all they passed as they clattered through the villages "His head is off. His head is off". Through the jubilant city the Scottish commissioners made their way to the King at Whitehall, wondering how they would find him. The long strain relaxed at last, Charles was cheerful and calm.'[285] On the same day he had made another appalling political mistake; he had given his assent to a Bill that made the Long Parliament perpetual at its own discretion.

Pym and his colleagues had also set about their other victim. Laud had been in detention since 18 December 1640, and at the end of February the Commons had presented articles of impeachment before the Lords against him for 'traitorously endeavouring to subvert the fundamental laws and government of this kingdom of England, and instead thereof to introduce an arbitrary and tyrannical government against Law'. He had, moreover, 'assumed to himself a Papal and tyrannical power both in ecclesiastical and temporal matters, [been] addicted to Romish superstitions and traitorously and wickedly endeavoured to reconcile the Church of England with the Church of Rome' — to these Calvinist Christians a criminal act. He had also started the war against the Scots, and the Scots commissioners provided Pym with further evidence by charges of 'novations'.

Laud had defended himself with spirit, though not with Strafford's eloquence.[286] The worst of his torment, he declared, was to have to do so at all — to appear *Causam dicere*, to plead his cause. And his brief defence concluded with a list of people whom he had 'settled in the true Protestant Religion': for example Mr Benkingstead of Trinity College, Oxford, 'seduced by a Jesuit', yet saved; and the two daughters of Sir Richard Leckford in Surrey, diverted from a nunnery; and two scholars (Toppin and Ashton) of St John's, Cambridge, who had got the French ambassador's pass and were hotfoot for France, but whom Laud had saved at the last minute, obtaining for Toppin a Fellowship at St John's, so that he was 'now as hopeful a young man as any in his time'. And there had been the late Duke of Buckingham himself, 'almost quite gone between his mother and sister', and 'the old Countess too'. And he had diverted the son and heir of Mr Winchcomb to Wadham: nor, he had concluded, 'did any of them lapse again'.

Laud's well-meaning defence had been brushed aside: on 1 March he was conveyed to the Tower. 'All was well,' he recorded in his diary, 'till I passed through Newgate Shambles, and entered into Cheapside, then some one prentice first halloo'd out; more and more followed the coach, the number still increasing as they went along… and so they followed me with clamour and revilings even beyond barbarity itself, not giving over until the coach had entered the Tower gate.'[287] Baillie, his ideological enemy, felt rather sorry for him; for he now seemed 'so contemptible that all cast him by out of their thoughts as a pendicle at the Lieutenant's [of Ireland] ear'.[288]

BOOK III: THE POLITICIAN AND SOLDIER

13: THE DISMANTLING OF PREROGATIVE GOVERNMENT

WHILE THE SPECTACULAR trial of Strafford and the persecution of Laud filled the foreground, more important things were being debated: after Strafford's execution Parliament made decisions crucial for England, indeed, for the English-speaking world. 'Reformation,' wrote one partisan, 'goes on apace, hot as toast.' Significantly, on the day of Strafford's death, the Commons authorized the publication of Sir Edward Coke's *Second Part of the Institution of the Laws of England*, with its tendentious but politically vital misinterpretation of key clauses in *Magna Carta* to apply to all free men.

But for the moderates in Parliament the pace was becoming too hot. After the essential measures had been passed into law that curbed the Tudor-style prerogative and reduced the monarchy to an integral part of a 'mixed' form of Parliamentary government with the Lords and Commons, compromise looked possible; many members, such as Edward Hyde, Culpepper, Falkland, would have been content to settle for it. Unhappily — and in the seventeenth century, predictably — religious fanaticism, exacerbating social and economic tensions, destroyed the prospect of accord, and instead of an effective if muddled compromise, the extremists of both sides took control: two civil wars had to be fought over a question already decided, for even at the Restoration of 1660 the Tudor prerogative courts were not restored.

The extreme Court party centred on the Queen, who saw English politics in French terms; but the Court party now became backed up by representative gentry. Prerogative power had been accepted for eleven years, and loyalty to the throne went deep: 'Prerogative being wound up to that height,' wrote the republican Wiltshireman Ludlow, years after, in exile at Vevey, '"what," said a gentleman at the Inns of Court, "shall we suffer these fellows at Westminster to dominate thus? Let us go to the country and bring up our tenants to put them out."'[289] There were immense reserves of conservative royalism, though their economic power was limited. In contrast the legal-minded Parliamentarians, of whom Pym, the political manager, was the most astute, 'desired', as Hobbes puts it in *Behemoth*, 'the whole and absolute sovereignty and to change the monarchical government into the oligarchic'.[290] And although the richer London merchants were Royalist or neutral — and retired to the country — the lesser men and the artisans and apprentices in London, Birmingham and Manchester supported Parliament. Many towns such as Salisbury — in spite of a Royalist Mayor — tried to stay neutral; but Chichester, Coventry, Southampton, Exeter and St Alban's obeyed the King's summons to arms. The long accepted picture of the towns being predominantly Parliamentarian by choice has to be modified; so much depended on local politics, though since London was so very much the largest and richest city in the country its control by Parliament proved decisive.

The political conflict had always been worsened by religious strife: High Church Anglican against Presbyterian Calvinist, and by a roar of protest from a great number of sects; 'Brownists,' as Hobbes put it, 'Anabaptists, Independents, Fifth Monarchy-men, Quakers, and divers others, all commonly called by the name of fanatics; in so much as there was none so dangerous an enemy to the Presbyterians as that brood of their own hatching.'[291] The sects actually demanded toleration. The resulting rift in the ruling classes briefly broke down the usual solidarity of the establishment both at the centre and in the counties; letting in lower-class radicals and military adventurers, who attacked property and who were quelled only by Oliver Cromwell, a military 'saviour of society'. On Oliver's death the ruling interests restored the monarchy, on terms little different from those that could have been obtained in 1641-2, though not before the English had set the precedent of republican revolution sensationalized by the judicial murder of their own king — an example that, confirmed by the resistance of the American colonies to George III, would contribute to inspire the French revolutionaries to kill their monarch and in due course, the Russians theirs.

The original objective of the moderate reformers — or rather conservatives, for they wanted to restore the supposed liberties of a medieval past — was to assert what they regarded as the ancient rule of law against the arbitrary power of the King. Their main concern was of course to protect property, and by January 1641 they had stated, in their legal language, that 'neither his Majesty nor the Privy Council have or ought to have any jurisdiction, power or authority to dispose of the lands, tenements, hereditaments, good, or chattels of any of the subjects of the Kingdom'. But as usual in revolutions the originators were swamped by the tide of events, opinion hardened and narrowed on both sides, and with the long war military republicans and their civilian supporters took control until in 1653 Cromwell, 'put his foot on the neck' of the remnant of the Long Parliament, already in 1648 purged into a 'Rump', and a 'sword government' briefly commanded far greater revenues and military and naval power than any rulers of England before it.

On 2 May 1641, ten days before Strafford's execution, Charles had married his eldest daughter Mary, now aged nine, to Prince William of Orange, aged twelve, son of Frederick Henry of Orange, Stadthouder of the Netherlands. Intelligent and attractive, the child had originally been destined to marry Baltaser Carlos, son of Philip IV of Spain (he died in 1646), but in spite of the protests of the Queen and of the King's nephew, the refugee Charles Louis of the Palatinate, who had hoped to marry her himself, Charles had now veered away from his pro-Spanish policy to a Dutch alliance, a policy in line with his appeasement of his enemies in Parliament.

On 10 February the King had explained his decision to the Lords. The marriage needed no religious dispensation. 'I have no fear,' he had said, 'that my daughter's conscience will be anyway perverted', while a strict alliance and confederacy with the States would be as useful to the kingdom as that with any of his neighbours. Moreover, 'use may be made of this alliance towards the establishing of my sister and nephews'. So there was an interval of rather muted festivity in the growing crisis, the little girl, sedate in cloth of silver, and the boy with the grave demeanour of a Dutch prince as depicted by Van Dyck.

The marriage was still a formality, and the boy slept that night in the King's own room; nor did the Princess go to Holland until the following year, when her mother took refuge there to raise funds and armaments for the Civil War. But the decision was important for in the long run it brought Mary's son, William of Orange, born in November 1650, a few days after his father's death, to the joint sovereignty of Great Britain and Ireland.[292] Immediately it also brought substantial help to the King's cause, and for Charles II in exile.

Meanwhile since early that year the dismantling of prerogative power had been proceeding rapidly. The four subsidies voted in December had been deliberately inadequate, and in January 1641 Charles had addressed both Houses in the Banqueting Hall at Whitehall. 'My lords,' he had said, 'and you Knights, citizens and burgesses, the principal cause of my coming here at this time is by reason of the slow proceedings in Parliament, touching which is a great inconvenience. First I must remember you that there are two armies in the kingdom, in a manner maintained by you, the running of which doth most clearly show the inconvenience thereof than a better tongue than mine can express.' He then assured them that he would put down 'innovations' and alterations in Church and Commonwealth: 'My intention is clearly to reduce all things to the best and purest times as they were at the time of Queen Elizabeth.' Powers that were 'illegal or heavy' to the subject he would be 'willing to lay down, trusting to their affection'.

But in essentials he still remained firm: for example, referring to the extremist Root and Branch petition against the bishops, he had declared that he would not make them 'to be but ciphers'. 'Now I will tell you, I make a great difference between Reformation and Alteration of government, though I am for the first, I cannot give way in the latter.' He would not be 'content that the voices of bishops in Parliament be taken away, for in all the time of my predecessors since the Conquest and before they have enjoyed it'. He had also refused, on principle, to allow Parliaments to be summoned by anyone but himself, even if no Parliament had been held for three years. 'There is a bill lately put in concerning Parliament. The thing I like well, to have frequent Parliaments [a considerable change of front]; but to give power to sheriffs and constabulary and I know not whom, to use my authority, that I cannot yield unto.'

He had now shown them, he had concluded, 'the state of his affairs, his clear intention and the rocks he would have them eschew'.[293]

But Charles had been in no position to bargain. On 15 February in return for another subsidy he had given way, not without protest, over the Bill for 'triennial' Parliaments.[294]

> This I mention, not to reproach you, but to show you the state of things as they are; you have taken the government all to pieces and I may say it is almost off its hinges. A skilful watchmaker to make clean his watch, he will take it assunder, and when it is put together, it will go better, for that he leave out not one pin of it. Now, as I have done all this on my part, you know what to do on yours. And I hope you shall see clearly that I have performed really what I expressed at the beginning of Parliament.[295]

He had in fact, under duress, performed a good deal more. The future power of Parliament was now secure: it could no longer be an appendage, summoned and dismissed at will, as James I or Charles had conceived it; nor could the monarch prorogue or dissolve it within fifty days without its own consent. It was now indispensable. And this crucial measure had been only the beginning. In the four months following Strafford's death the whole structures of Tudor prerogative courts and of Charles's extra-parliamentary sources of revenue were dismantled. It was now resolved 'that the court commonly called the Star Chamber from the first of August 1641 be absolutely dissolved and taken away and determined and made void'; in July they abolished the prerogative courts of Wales, the northern parts, and the palatine courts of Lancaster and Chester; in August ship money was also declared null and void; the royal forests were limited to their Jacobean boundaries; distraint of knighthood was made illegal. Retrospectively, the officials who had collected tunnage and poundage and other impositions on the King's sole authority, were fined and had to compound for £150,000, and the current proceeds were now voted only for a year. The King also consented to appoint the judges, not during his pleasure, but during good behaviour. These decisions taken together were revolutionary: within less than a year the prerogative power had been shackled, the Crown put financially at the mercy of Parliament, and both the executive and the judicial branches of the government made dependent on the legislature. As Ranke puts it, 'It really seemed as if the King was ready to abandon... the modes of government of his ancestors insofar as they were inconsistent with the restrictions laid upon him. Some of the chief foundations of the royal authority which the Tudors had enjoyed had been removed.'[296]

A more pliable and astute monarch might have accepted these conditions and, like George III, played a formidable political game within the rules; to Charles such compliance was unthinkable. He might appease, he might attempt to win over his opponents as he now tried to win over Pym; but he was always determined to maintain his old power, and ready for any expedients to do so — even to raising troops and money abroad. His immediate instinct was to play off his Scots subjects against the English, and he determined, in spite of their protests, again to visit Scotland.

Yet his deviousness was both amateurish and dangerous. Nor, given his religious and political convictions, held always with invincible tenacity to the end, could he have acted differently. For another great obstacle to a settlement on Parliament's terms, with the monarchy a sort of dogeship as Charles described it, was religion. Here the Commons had been getting their own back. While concentrating the attack on Strafford and Laud, they had early released and rehabilitated

Bastwick, Burton and Prynne. In December 1640 the former had returned in triumph from the Scilly Isles; his fines were now paid.[297] Burton, released from Jersey, had come up to London amid vast popular applause, been voted £6,000 — unpaid — and reappointed as lecturer to his old benefices in London, where he preached regularly against the King's party until his demise in 1648. Prynne triumphantly returned in Burton's company: he was restored to his degree at Lincoln's Inn; but his claim to compensation of £9,000 was still outstanding in 1648. He at once penned *A New discourse on the Prelate's Tyranny* and a pamphlet against Laud — *The Popish Royal Favourite*. But by 1644 he was denouncing the Independent sects — *Independency Unmasked and Refuted*.

The Commons had also attacked representative High Church Anglicans, as the Papistical Dr Cusin, who had spent £2,000 on adorning Durham Cathedral, provided copes with rich images on them and said that the King had no more power in ecclesiastical matters than his horse. It was decided that the Cusin should 'lend his helping hand to the clearing of Durham church'.

But the Commons did not like being criticized themselves: the vicar of Rotherthorpe in Northumberland had said that Parliaments in England never did good — and worse, that his 'hoggs were fitt to make Parliament men of, and their stye a place fitt for them to sitt in', and that enthusiasts who went from sermon to sermon 'were like jack-dawes that lept from twigg to twigg'.[298] They sent him to the Gatehouse during the pleasure of the House.

The other revolution, the supercession of the Anglican Church by a Presbyterian hierarchy, was concurrently pressed forward. In the autumn of 1640 a convenient scandal had occurred in the Irish Church, which was used to cast the kind of aspersions on all the clergy that were traditional since the days of Simon de Montfort, the Lollards and Henry VIII. For Bishop Atherton of Waterford and Lismore, a creature of Strafford's, had just been indicted and convicted of whoredom and unnatural crime:[299] doubtless, declared the Calvinists, other bishops were like him — and a scandalous life the way to preferment. This medieval gambit never failed.

But on the main doctrinal question, as debated on 8-11 February, the Commons were divided. The extreme Calvinists, in league with the Scots, wanted the 'root and branch' abolition of the bishops, a view encouraged if not consistently supported by Pym; others, as Hyde and Falkland, wanted a limited episcopacy — with the prelates' wings clipped, but not to set up a Calvinist 'Pope in every parish'. And Lord Digby touched the heart of the matter when he declared, 'I do not think a King can put down bishops totally without safety to monarchy.' For the whole pattern of royal government had always assumed the collaboration of Church and State, as in the great monarchies on the Continent, if England was the only one of the Protestant countries that had kept the Catholic medieval order of bishops, deans, archdeacons and the rest.

But on 27 May 1641, with an eye on conciliating the Scots Covenanters, a Bill was introduced to abolish them entirely, and carried in the second reading in the Commons — many of the county members, less inclined to Puritanism, being absent — and on 11 June the House discussed it in committee. In the Lords however it never had a chance: it struck at the age-old constitution of the Upper House, of which bishops were an integral part, and where the rehabilitated Williams had on 1 March been appointed chairman of a committee to consider all 'innovations' in religion. The attempt to secularize cathedrals and colleges also roused Oxford and Cambridge universities to vigorous protest. A second bishops' exclusion Bill was held up in the Lords; resentment against the destruction of the time-honoured institutions of the Church and its property, which touched the gentry whose relations generally held the best livings, was widespread. An attempt to abolish the Anglican establishment and secularize its property was blocked by the Lords.

Pym and his supporters also tried to purge the King's household. So Charles had conciliated the discontented great peers by appointing the Earl of Hertford,[300] brother-in-law to Essex, as tutor to the Prince of Wales instead of Newcastle, to whom the Prince was attached. And he replaced his learned, witty, Laudian tutor, Brian Duppa (who was made Bishop of Salisbury, then, at the Restoration, of Winchester, and author of *The Souls Soliloquy and Conference with Conscience*), by John Earle, a Fellow of Merton College, Oxford,[301] rector of Bishopstone in the Ebble valley in Wiltshire, and a member of Falkland's circle at Great Tew. The Prince with his own natural cynical insight into character enjoyed Earle's conversation, and a lifelong friendship came about. So some good came of Pym's move.

But Pym now went further and attempted to ensure that Parliament should control all major appointments to the Queen's household, especially those touching on the education of the royal children. The papal envoy, Rossetti, was expelled and Father Ward and Father Greene of Douai, the latter a chaplain to the Venetian ambassador, were attacked. Greene, protected by his diplomatic immunity, escaped but Ward was hanged, drawn and quartered. Such was the sadistic venom of the time, exploited by ruthless politicians sometimes still regarded as liberal champions of democracy. But the attack on the Anglican Church had been held. Far from abolishing innovations, the Puritans in Parliament had proved innovators themselves, and over both Church and State a strong body of opinion was building up that enough was enough. The making of a King's party was in the offing.

Charles continued his appeasement. Essex, a consistent opponent and personally disliked, replaced the choleric Philip, Earl of Pembroke, as Chamberlain to the Household, after the latter in a fit of temper physically attacked Lord Maltravers at Court. The King also raised money in one of the very few ways left to him, by selling baronetcies: nineteen baronets were created in July, twenty-four in early August, and at a cut price — £350 instead of £400.[302]

Charles was still determined on going to Scotland to open the Scots Parliament, leaving the Queen at Oatlands to deal with the complicated departure of the Dowager of France, who by 2 September 1641 at last sailed for Flushing with a fair southwest wind, where she was met by her granddaughter's husband, the young William of Orange. And when, on 10 August, the King rode down to Westminster to dispatch final business and demonstrators against his departure for Scotland jostled his horse, he remarked, with point and irony, that he was glad he was so much wanted in both his kingdoms. As usual his hopes were unjustified. The quasi-medieval politics of Scotland, with the great magnates manoeuvring against each other and using ideological differences to maintain their followings, were still much as they had been under James VI, and soon an extraordinary 'incident' involved the King himself.

Charles's first objective was to win over the very peculiar commander of the Scots army. The bastard offspring of a minor laird, probably George Leslie of Balgonie and a 'wench in Rannoch', Alexander Leslie was a veteran of many horrible wars on the Continent, 'perhaps the last *Condottiere* on the grand scale,... There may be something in the story related by Lord Hailes that his instruction in reading did not reach beyond the letter g'.[303] Long ago in 1605 he had taken service with the Dutch, but his main service had been in Sweden, where he had been governor of Stralsund. After service in Germany with Hamilton he had bought an estate in Fife: 'there is no doubt that booty was a subject on which the general was well informed'.[304] But the German wars were not what they had been, and Leslie, like many of his countrymen with similar experience scenting trouble in Scotland, had returned. He was a foxy-looking character with close-set eyes, and he did nicely out of the British wars, for he had 'causit send to Germanye, France, Holland, Denmark and other countries, for the most expert and valiant capitanes, levetennantis and wnder officiares', and with such a following and reputation,[305] had become the obvious expert to command the Covenanting armies.

Charles with his domestic background and aesthetic tastes was no match for this hard-bitten soldier; nor was the Marquess of Hamilton, the next claimant to the Scottish throne after the King's branch of the Stuarts, the King's virtual viceroy in Scotland, either competent or reliable. And the ablest and most influential of the Scots magnates, Argyll, with the most compact territorial power, was the most deeply committed to the Presbyterian Kirk. It was not a fair prospect, as the King came north through the harvest weather to his native realm, and he got little good of his visit.

On 17 August 1641, preceded by Hamilton carrying the crown of Scotland and by Argyll bearing the sceptre, Charles formally opened the Scots Parliament, the young Elector

Palatine at his side, for ostensibly it was for him that the King now requested money for arms and men. Charles further appeased the Scots Parliament by accepting limitations on the monarchy as far reaching as those on the English Crown, 'a subtle design of gaining the popular opinion, and weake execution for the upholding of monarkie'. It was not enough: the Covenanting politicians and ministers pressed their advantage. 'There never was King so much insulted,' a Royalist reported. 'It would pity any man's heart to see how he looks, for he is never quiet among them.' And Sir Harry Vane, the principal Secretary of State, wrote to the able and systematic Sir Edward Nicholas,[306] now in succession to Windebank, the other, acting Secretary of State, 'This day hath been solemnized heare as a day of thanksgiving: His Majesty hath heard too sermons, sung many pshalms, according to the manner of the Scottish Kyrke with as great attention as I have seen him.'[307]

Then the Royalist courtiers and soldiers staged the 'incident', an amateur plot to kidnap Hamilton and Argyll, and the King was compromised since his confidential attendant, William Murray, was involved. 'An accident hath happened,' wrote Vane to Nicholas, 'to the Marquise Argyle... I pray God itt make not a great distraction, for the humors are up. I do much apprehend what will be the issue of this distraction; I beseche God itt have not an influence in England and Ireland, but to send His Majestic a safe return whenever itt be.' Montrose, one of the King's loyalist supporters in Scotland, was also compromised, though he was thought so gallant a gentleman and so well beloved that they were fearful to meddle with him. Damaging rumours of the 'incident' or 'accident' went south.

Charles had indeed got little from appeasing his enemies, though he had created Argyll a marquis and 'Felt-Marshal' Leslie, Earl of Leven; but he left under the illusion that he could rely on them, and on 18 November, after feasting the Scots Lords at Holyrood, he rode south with surprising equanimity. He had counted without the ideological ties of international Calvinism, which bound the Covenanters to the opposition in England, and he had counted without the Irish.

On 27 October, when playing golf on the links at Leith, Charles had received shocking news. Four days earlier in Ireland a long-planned rising had flared into massacre and arson. 'Here are today,' wrote Vane, 'expresses come of a revolt in Ireland under one Sir [Phelim] Oneale, the next akin to Tirone, that he hath taken some townes, one called Neerery, wherein is a magazine of armes and ammunition of His Majestie.'[308]

After Strafford's recall the government in Dublin had been conducted by two incompetent lord justices, and the disbanded army had hung around, worked upon by Catholic priests from the Netherlands, Italy and Spain and incited by Irish officers, experienced in central Europe. Lord Leicester, the new Lord Lieutenant, was still in England. But the rising in Dublin itself had misfired: 'One Owen Conelies [Connolly], a servant of Sir John Clotworthy's, made the first discovery of the rebellion, from accidental conversation in a taverne',[309] where one of those involved had been boasting in his cups; and Connolly, also the worse for drink, had promptly alerted the authorities in Dublin Castle. The ringleaders in Dublin had thus at once been taken up on the night before the rising, and the strategic centre of Dublin was held. But the rising in Ulster and the north, led by dispossessed Celtic tribal aristocrats, spread like wildfire. About five thousand English settlers were massacred — the Scots were spared, though no less hated — another ten thousand dispossessed and driven out, refugees who added to the panic in England. 'The Rebells,' reported the Council of Ireland, 'with great multitudes proceeded at their outrages; even to great cruelty against the Protestants in all places when they came... the Irish servants and tenants... rise against them with great malignity.' The rising extended to within the Pale and south into Munster, the Butlers, under Lord Mountgarrett, eager as ever for the fray. The few English troops took refuge in garrison towns, such as Derry and Drogheda or Bandon and Cork. But Dublin held.

Charles had not at first sensed the danger. He thought his English and Scots subjects would sink their differences with him in the emergency. In fact the tidings from Ireland, embellished with lurid and often unjustified tales of rape, arson and slaughter, set off the full panic of anti-Catholic hatred, the strongest force in politics. And the Irish were embarrassingly loyal to the Crown: some of the rebels, trying to come to terms, swore that they were loyal subjects, while complaining of the 'Restraint of Purchase' of lands imposed on the 'meer Irish'; of the 'quids and quiddities of the English law', and of 'the incapacity for Catholics for honour as against strangers and foreigners'. They signed, 'Hugh MacGiller now Ferrell, his Mark, Taghna MacRory Farrell, Carock MacBrau Farrell, etc.'.[310] This loyalty confirmed suspicions in London that the Court was somehow implicated in the rising and with foreign intrigue; the slender prospects of religious compromise in England disappeared; above all the question of who would control the army to put down the rising became urgent. 'The business of Ireland,' wrote Vane, 'grows a deep blight in the north... God send their Majesties' affairs to a better ply and more prosperities But at first the rising seemed at least to have rallied the Scots to the King, and on 30 October Secretary Vane was writing with misplaced confidence, 'The Parliament here [in Scotland] is stiff and resolved; it is high time to give over talking of party, and that King and people [in England] should heartily unite, for this is not a time to contend.' The danger was not just from Ireland: it was feared that a continental coalition would exploit the crisis.

While Charles was in Scotland Pym's supporters in the Commons had gone much further than a conservative return to supposed ancient ways and were reaching out for the supreme power in the state. During August 1641 the plague and smallpox had been severe in London ('The sickness in the tavern next to the Upper House'); but Pym and his colleagues had drawn up a 'Grand Remonstrance' in which all the misdeeds of prerogative government were rehearsed, thus deliberately and retrospectively creating an ill will and fomenting public indignation by propaganda in a new way. This course did not appeal to moderate men; as one of them put it they had 'never imagin[ed] that Parlyament would have took upon them the redressing of things amiss, by a way not traced out unto them by their auncestors',[311] and as another remarked, 'When I first heard of a Remonstance I presently imagined that like faithful councillors we should hold up a glass to his Majesty, I did not dream that we should remonstrate downward and tell stories to the people.'[312] Against the protests of Falkland, Hyde and Culpepper, who argued that such a raking up of old grievances would alienate the Lords and encourage the extremists at Court, Pym was determined on this stroke of political warfare, not least against the Lords who had held up the attack on the bishops. For the Irish rising had pointed up the crisis of authority and the Parliamentarians were determined to control the army necessary to quell it; to check also the reaction that their measures and the babel of religious sects they had unloosed had provoked in favour of the King. For they were now afraid for their own lives. With Scotland apparently appeased, Charles had already dispatched a small force to Ireland; if he could now raise an army and quell the Irish, he might be dangerously strengthened in all three kingdoms.

Hence the *Remonstrance on the State of the Kingdom* in over two hundred clauses, or as Nicholas described it to the King on 8 November, '*A Declaracon on ye state of ye affaires of this kingdome*, which relates all ye misgovernmt and unpleasing things that have been done by Councells (as they call it) since 3 of yo maties raigne to this present.' It reflected, he construed, 'so much to the prejudice of your Matie's government as if your Majestie come not instantly away, I tremble to think what wilbe ye issue of it', and Charles at once minuted 'by all means possible this must be stopped'.[313]

It was urgent that he return to London: letters, which took at best three days, were generally much slower and sometimes intercepted. On 10 November, for example, the Queen wrote, in her still imperfect English:

> Maistre Nicholas, I am vere sory that my lettre did not come time enouf to go. I have reseaved your, and I have writt to the King hasten is coming. [If Will Murray, her confidant, was not well enough to go, Nicholas must provide another messenger] for I would not trustid to the ordinaire poste. I am so ill provided whitt personnes that I dare trust that at this instant I have no living creature that I dare send, prey doe whatt you can to helpe me if little Will Murray can not goe to send this letter, and so I rest your assured true frend Henriette Marie R.

So on 18 November Charles left Edinburgh for London, and on 22-3 November, when he was already at what the Queen called 'Tibols' (Theobalds), Nicholas reported that the

Commons had been 'in debate about the Remonstrance touching the ill effects of bad Councells ever since 12 at noone and are at it still, it being now near twelve at midnight'.

The Remonstrance summed up past evils, reforms accomplished and those still to come, and it culminated in the revolutionary demand that Parliament should have 'the approbation' of all officers, councillors, ambassadors and ministers, and the King merely the 'nomination'. It had, they claimed, 'been so heretofore' and so was 'an ancient right'. They thus struck at the King's essential prerogative, as if they were trying to provide a constitutional alternative to the clumsy method of impeachment by making ministers responsible to themselves. Though emanating from the Commons, the Remonstrance demanded that the King be

> ... humbly petitioned by both houses to employ such councillors, ambassadors and other ministers... as the Parliament may have cause to confide in... It may often fall out that the Commons may have cause to take exceptions at some men for being Councillors, yet not charge these men with crimes... we may have good reason to be earnest with His Majesty not to put his great affairs in such hands, though we may be unwilling to proceed against them in any legal way of charge or impeachment.[314]

Here, in mild language, is a demand; that a predominant but shifting interest in the House of Commons — there were then no party organizations — should in effect appoint the executive.[315] And the Remonstrance also contrived an attack against the Upper House:

> But what can we, the Commons, without the conjunction of the Lords, and what conjunction can we expect there, when the Bishops and recusant Lords are so numerous and

prevalent that they are able to cross and interrupt our best endeavours for reformation, and by that means give advantage to this malignant party to traduce our proceedings?

Here is the authentic flavour with its political terms 'reformation' and 'malignancy'.

The debate itself ended in tumult, the rival members of Parliament banging their scabbarded swords on the ground, pulling each other's hair and brawling in the candlelight, while the Speaker announced a narrow majority of eleven — 159 against 148. And when the large minority tried to register a formal protest at its being printed, shouts and threats escalated among the armed men in the narrow St Stephen's Chapel in the November night. As a landmark in the rise of English liberties the scene has been much written up, but to those who voted against it, the Remonstrance probably seemed lamentable, while Cromwell's notorious remark to Falkland that 'if the Remonstrance had been rejected he would have sold all he had the next morning, and never seen England more; and he knew there were many other honest men of the same resolution',[316] sounds like the retrospective rhetoric of an excited politician. It is doubtful whether England might in fact have had to manage without him.

The scene in the Commons had not much appealed to the Royalist Sir Richard Gurney, Lord Mayor of London, or to the richer merchants of the City who disliked 'King Pym'. And when on 25 November Charles arrived from Theobalds in a great coach with the Queen, the Prince of Wales, the other children and the Elector Palatine, and without a dreaded Scots army at his back, Gurney and his colleagues attended upon the King at the entrance into the City 'with all the lustre and good countenance it could show, and as great profession of duty it could make or the King expect'.[317] In full pomp the civic authorities, attended by five hundred horsemen, 'all advanced in a comely manner' to meet the royalties from Theobalds; they had a great tent pitched — 'the night being rainy and the morning gloomy and cloudy'[318] — in which were 'seats and forms where his lordship and some of the nobility reposed themselves till their Majesties came'. When at ten o'clock Charles and his entourage arrived, the Recorder of London assured him, 'I can truly say this from the representative body of your City, from where I have my warrant: They meet your majesty with as much love and affection as ever citizens of London met with any of your royal progenitors... pardon their failure, if you meet with any.'

The King replied, graciously but pointedly, that he could not express his contentment: 'For now I see that all these former tumults and disorders have only risen from the meaner sort of people, and that the affections of the better and main part of the city have ever been loyal and affectionate to my person and government.' And for good measure he gave back to them that part of Londonderry in Northern Ireland which had been taken from them. 'This I confess,' he said, 'as that Kingdom is now, is no great gift: but I intend to recover it, and then give it you whole and intirely.'

Charles and the Prince of Wales then took horse and rode to London, the procession making a gallant show; they entered London by Moorgate, with the crowds well under control, the conduits on Cornhill and Cheapside running claret and tapestries hanging from the windows, while 'as their majesties passed along the trumpets and city musick were placed in several parts, sounding and playing'. The Lord Mayor was created a baronet, the Recorder knighted, and at the City's request Charles agreed to keep Christmas at Whitehall instead of, as intended, at Hampton Court, an unfortunate decision. In a flurry of good will Charles even unexpectedly drew his sword and knighted seven aldermen as they knelt to kiss his hand. More deservedly at Whitehall he knighted Sir Edward Nicholas, and confirmed him as principal Secretary of State, Vane having been removed from that office. 'Now am I returned,' he said, 'with an hearty and kind affection to the people, and the city in particular', and promised, with an eye on 'King Pym' and the Presbyterians as well as the Catholics, to maintain the Protestant religion in all its purity as it had been established in the reign of Elizabeth and his father King James. 'That I will do, if need be, to the hazard of my life and all that is dear to me'.

The ceremonies culminated in a colossal civic banquet. Such occasions, better suited to Henry VIII, were probably uncongenial to the fastidious monarch, but occasioned a display of confidence and loyalty that could prove misleading. The King's words went down well with Lord Mayor Gurney and the aldermen, but not with the majority of lesser merchants represented on the Common Council and with the populace. Buoyed up by this acclamation, when on 1 December he received the text of the Remonstrance, Charles felt in better heart to defy the narrow majority in the Commons. He declared firmly that he would choose his ministers for himself; that he knew of no 'malignants', and that he would consider only grievances presented by both Lords and Commons in the parliamentary way. Since the Lords had again blocked further attacks on the bishops and the Church establishment, he seemed on safe ground.

14: PRELUDE TO WAR

'TRULY,' WROTE THOMAS HOBBES, with his usual flair for the essential, 'I think if the King had had money, he might have had soldiers enough in England. For there were very few of the common people who cared much for either of the causes, but would have taken any side for pay or plunder. But the King's treasury was very low, and his enemies... had the command of the purses of the city of London...'[319]

Although the rich Lord Mayor Gurney and aldermen had given Charles so flattering a reception and escorted him back to Whitehall in a torchlight procession through the November dusk, most of the Common Council of the City were hostile; while mobs of apprentices and workmen, their traditional hatred of Catholics and the Court increased by reports of the Irish rising and by the incitements of sectarian preachers now free of the censorship of the High Commission Court, were demonstrating in the streets and assaulting the bishops when they tried to attend Parliament. The curious Tudor equilibrium maintained without the standing armies on which the great continental monarchs relied was breaking down. The late medieval resistance to the Crown by landed magnates, 'good lords' to their following, had been suppressed by the Tudors; now the tradition was revived by civilian magnates, many closely related by kinship, working in collaboration with wealthy landowners in the Commons — 'the grandees of the faction' — and with the lawyers, merchants and entrepreneurs who associated with them.

Essex was related to both Northumberland and Warwick, who had married sisters of his father, Elizabeth I's favourite;

many leaders of opposition in the Commons were involved in speculations in North America and the Caribbean; the astute Pym himself was a major patentee for Connecticut and treasurer for the Providence Company, which was developing the strategically placed island of (Old) Providence, between the mainland of Central America and the Antilles. Charles indeed now faced a new form of many pre-Tudor attempts to bring the Crown under the control of an oligarchy; not this time by jostling baronial over-mighty subjects, using private armies, but by politicians in both Lords and Commons working through the laborious and formidable technical proceedings of Parliament, already organized in a labyrinth of committees; manageable, too, by astute leadership and by timing to the shifts of opinion among the politically conscious nation and to the volatile and exploitable passions of the London mob. It was thus an ugly prospect that confronted the high-minded, obstinate and unpractical King, provoked the contemptuous hostility of the Queen for civilian politicians, and confirmed her affinity with the amateur and professional soldiers who now swarmed at the Court.

As the bitter winter of 1641-2 closed in and the City became more turbulent — at Christmas the Londoners even attacked Westminster Abbey and were only just beaten off-the demands of the Commons became more exacting, Charles proceeded with his military plans designed to secure control of Hull and Portsmouth, and on 23 December he appointed one of the more ruffianly soldiers to be Lieutenant of the Tower. Thomas Lunsford was not a prepossessing character;[320] but perhaps because he had served the French in the royalist wars, both King and Queen thought him skilled and reliable. The appointment at once proved entirely inept: that very day the Common Council of the City petitioned against it, the

Commons conferred immediately with the Lords, and when the Lords refused to petition for Lunsford's dismissal, they went ahead with one of their own, backed now even by the Lord Mayor.

So Charles had to climb down. On the day after Christmas Lunsford was replaced — an occasion he celebrated by a free fight in Westminster Hall. He was succeeded by Sir John Byron of the Byrons of Newstead, a more respectable person, who had been High Sheriff of Nottinghamshire and fought in the Low Countries. But he did not last either; he found his position 'vexation and agony', and by 11 February he was released.

On 1 January 1642, having rejected the Grand Remonstrance and having conspicuously failed to buy off Pym by offering him the Chancellorship of the Exchequer. So that eventually it went to John Culpepper, afterwards Lord Culpepper, a Sussex gentleman who had opposed the Remonstrance. He held office until February 1643, when Edward Hyde, who had been recommended by Nicholas and had already refused to be Solicitor-General, succeeded him — to a position soon to be of greater importance since during the war the Lord Treasurership would fall into abeyance.

At Court it was a tense Christmas, the usual festivities overshadowed by the crisis; the winter was so bad that January that many MPS could not come to London because of the floods, and there were rumours of a move to impeach the Queen herself for intriguing with the Pope. 'I never saw the Court so full of gentlemen,' wrote an officer, 'everyone comes hither with his sword... and it is a wonder there is no more blood yet spilt seeing how earnest both sides are.'

On the misguided advice of the young Lord Digby, always a hothead, and without the knowledge of Edward Hyde and the moderates, Charles decided to strike first. His order in his own elegant handwriting of 3 January to the King's Attorney to impeach his principal enemies for high treason was clear.

1. You are to accuse those six [five struck out] jointlie and severallie.
2. You ar to reserve the power of making additionalls.
3. When the comittie for examination is a naming (which you must press to be close and under oathe of secresie) if eather Essex, Warwick, Holland, Say, Wharton, or Brooke be named, you must desyre that they may be spared because you ar to examine them as witnesses for me.

The five members of the Commons designated were Pym, Hampden, Denzil Holles, William Strode and Sir Arthur Haselrig.[321] Among the peers — as an afterthought — Lord Montague of Kimbolton, whose courtesy title was Lord Mandeville, son of the Earl of Manchester.[322]

Both Houses defied the King's order. The Commons refused to deliver the accused; the Lords refused to confirm it. So Charles, on the advice of one of the more dashing and attractive courtiers, the Earl of Bristol's son Lord Digby — now, in spite of his treatment by Charles and Buckingham over his embassy to Madrid, of the King's party — decided to make a coup himself. This ill-conceived attempt was naturally a fiasco. Charles himself had the sense to see its danger, but was pushed into it by the reproaches of the Queen, who told him to 'go and pull those rogues out by the ears'. He was always vulnerable to her contempt; eager to prove himself the man she wanted him to be.

He acted in a setting of roisterous confusion. Early that morning of January 5 there was a 'great confluence' of men about Whitehall and the rumour ran that 'between thirty and forty cannon went yesterday to the Tower at ten of the clock'.[323] *Coups d'état* should be prepared in secret and sprung suddenly; but Charles had neither the will nor the power to achieve surprise. The victims had long been warned by Essex[324] and dispatched by barge down river to the City; the King himself had been preceded by three or four hundred officers and court swordsmen — 'divers of the late army in the North and other desperate Ruffians' and 'loose persons', said their opponents. When at last the King arrived, borne slowly in his clumsy coach and accompanied by his nephew, the Prince Elector Palatine, his followers were already out of hand. They had forced and kept open the door of the House; one of them stood next to it holding his sword upright in the scabbard, another holding up his pistol ready cocked saying, 'I will warrant you I am a good marksman'; another shouting, 'A Pox take the House of Commons.'[325] The King had to order them sharply to keep outside.

Within the House the formalities were of course observed. As the little King advanced with his usual dignity, the members stood up and uncovered, while the Speaker stood by his chair. Charles himself, for most of the way uncovered, bowed right and left, a courtesy that the silent ranks of the Commons returned. Arrived at the Speaker's chair he remarked that 'he must for the moment make bold with' it; whereupon the Speaker came out of his chair and 'His Majesty stept up into it'.[326] There was a pause, then in his high, hesitant voice, the King asked if Pym were there; to be answered by a significant silence. He then asked for Holles and got the same response. 'Well, well,' Charles remarked, having again looked round carefully and satisfied himself that the 'birds had flown', 'tis no matter, I think my eyes are as good as another's.'

As usual the King had tried to have it both ways; having made this unprecedented incursion and ineffective show of force, he declared lamely, 'I do expect from you that you shall send them unto me as soon as they return hither. But I assure you,' he continued 'on the word of a King, I never did intend any force, but shall proceed in a legal and fair way. I never meant any other.' And so he stepped down, turned and walked back out of the House. 'Zounds,' remarked one of the courtiers, 'they are gone, and now we are never the better for our coming.' The honours of the day had gone to Mr Speaker Lenthall, standing below the chair. When the King had asked him whether he saw any of the accused and where they were, falling on his knee he had replied 'May it please your Majesty… I have neither eyes to see nor tongue to speak in this place, but as the House is pleased to direct me, whose servant I am here; and I humbly beg your majesty's pardon, that I cannot give any other answer than this to what your majesty is pleased to demand of me.'[327]

The King's disastrous initiative was of great political profit to Pym. Charles had entered the House of Commons where, they said, 'Never King was but one' — and he had been Henry VIII; the Commons had been physically frighted: all the animosity of civilians for the military had been roused. A Captain Thomas, it was alleged, had been heard to say that he would go twenty miles to see Mr Pym hanged, and would then 'cut off a piece of Mr. Pym's flesh to wear about him in remembrance'. The King, it was said, was going to enter the City with his swordsmen and sack it; people shut up their shops; there was panic, some cried out, 'Arme! Arme!'.

More constructively, it was moved in the Commons that their privileges extended 'to all capital causes, as treason and the like, in which the persons and goods of the members of both Houses involved are free from seizure till the said Houses be first satisfied of their crimes and so do deliver their bodies up'.[328] There was loud acclamation and murmurs of 'well-moved'. They concluded that the proceedings against the five members were illegal and that they ought to demand 'safety for their persons to come and sit among us till their crimes shall be proved before us'.[329] They then voted the attempt a breach of privilege of Parliament and the liberty of the subject, and that 'such persons as should arrest any such member should be declared a public enemy of the Commons'. There is nothing like fear to create solidarity; 'men might not come in safety', it was now felt, 'and give their votes freely'. And always the usual rumour of a Popish Plot haunted their minds. Even the harmless but Papist Lord Herbert, engaged on mechanical experiments at Vauxhall ('exercising his engineering'), was plainly up to no good.

That night the Council proclaimed a watch on all the seaports, and Digby and Lunsford offered to hunt down the accused; but they were well concealed in the City, where the people were in arms and defiant. Undeterred, on the following morning Charles took a coach to the Tower and at three o'clock summoned the Lord Mayor and Aldermen to Guildhall, round which vast and militant crowds were assembled.

'Gentlemen,' he said bluntly, 'I am come to demand such prisoners as I have already attainted of high treason; and doe believe that they are shrouded in the city; I hope no good man will keep them from me; their offences are treason and misdemeanor of a high nature. I desire your loving assistance there in that they may be brought to legal trial.' He then again denied favouring the 'Popish religion' and swore to maintain and defend the Protestant establishment. Not daring to attack the monarch, the crowd took it out on the Lord Mayor, who was most violently assaulted by a multitude of rude citizens, and other uncivill women... his chayne broken which was about his necke, and his gown torn upon his back'.[330] The King himself returned through the winter evening, his coach accompanied by a threatening crowd shouting, 'Privilege, Privilege!' of Parliament.

His bluff called, Charles had again shown his weakness. Scenting his failure, both Commons and populace pressed their advantage. Parliament, on the pretext that at Westminster they were unsafe, appointed a committee of both Houses and met in Guildhall, then in Grocers' Hall, and supported by the Common Council they exploited the grievance offered them by the King's *démarche*. 'A Parliament, Mr. Speaker,' said one of them, 'is the clearest looking glass for a state to see itself in' — and moreover it was medicinal. They were acting to protect the King against 'devilfish designs', but in particular the design against 'this grand privilege of parliament... by his accusing those six worthy members of the same... and upon this accusation to break open their chambers, trunks and studies and seysing on their books and writings; those I conceive are great breaches of this privilege'.

By an extraordinary miscalculation Charles had stirred up a hornets' nest: his protests that he had acted only according to law for the public safety were brushed aside, as was his offer to send two hundred men of the trained bands to guard Parliament. While the Royalist Lord Mayor Gurney complained of 'many thousands in arms without any lawful authority to the great disturbance and fright of the inhabitants', and before the attempt on Kimbolton and the five Members, the King's own guards had to ask for reinforcements from the gentry at the Inns of Court. On the Committee's side the Thames mariners offered to escort and guard their way up the Thames to Westminster, with artillery, and 'so through the bridge at high tide'. They were infuriated by the decay of trade, the laying up of shipping, and because they dared not adventure their ships in foreign parts as 'things were not yet settled' in England and Ireland — 'no man following his trade cheerfully' — a situation mainly attributed to the Papists. They apparently feared a foreign invasion. The Committee of Parliament which included the five members now illegally appointed a Captain Skippon — he was a Norfolk man and a Godly ranker, who would prove, next to Cromwell or Fairfax, the best of their commanders, and who had won promotion in the Palatinate and at the siege of Breda, — to be Sergeant Major General at £300 a year to command eight companies of trained bands. 'Thus in England' writes Ranke, with his detached and Olympian view, 'the King's essential sovereignty was already challenged, even when he claimed to use it for the safety of the state — when every day's experience showed that this power was exercised in the great neighbouring monarchies without any reserve whatever, and powerfully contributed to their strength and stability.'[331]

During these few hectic and decisive days Charles and his family, inadequately protected, were still in the Palace of Whitehall, which was in great confusion and infested, the Queen was sure, with spies, and with no force to defend it against Skippon's companies from the City. The King and Queen had originally planned to keep Christmas at Hampton Court, and on the night of 10 January along with the two princes and the Lady Elizabeth they suddenly left Whitehall, a flight that proved as catastrophic as that of Louis XVI to Varennes.[332] Charles had abandoned his own capital and by doing so lost the Civil War. And the next day a triumphal procession of boats escorted the returning five members and their colleagues up the Thames when, as previously arranged on 11 January, Parliament came back to Westminster; while Skippon and his trained bands with martial mien and music marched down the Strand to Whitehall and Westminster.[333] The Crown had not suffered such a humiliation since the Wars of the Roses, and for seven years Charles would not again set eyes on London until brought back there to his death.

From Hampton Court, which in the winter cold had been quite unprepared for their reception, the royalties moved to Windsor, strategically a better base for the Court and for the Royalist 'Cavaliers' as they were now being called — a term of abuse like 'Roundhead', which had caught on and which now entered the mythology of British history. Originally simply a horseman — a *Caballero* in Spanish or, as Charles I put it, 'a gentleman serving his King on horseback' — the term was now coming to symbolize a brutal and licentious swordsman apt to rape and plunder; swashbuckling, over-dressed and arrogant, a 'Commander about the Court'. Accepted, as such names often are — for example 'Old Contemptibles' — by those against whom it was directed, it would also convey a gallant and picturesque nuance. 'Roundhead', now also current and equally a term of abuse, was more directly physical.

> The name of Roundhead comming so opertunely in [wrote Mrs Lucy Hutchinson] I shall make a little digression to tell how it came up. Among other affected habits, few of the Puritans, what degree soever they were of, wore their hairs long enough to cover their ears... and the ministers and many others cut it close round their heads, with so many little peaks it was something redicklous to behold. From which customes of wearing their haires that name of Roundhead became the

scornful terme given to the whole Parliament, whose army indeed marcht out so, but as if it had been sent out till their hairs were grown, two or three years after, any stranger that had seen them would have enquired the reason for their name.[334]

As the two sides began to line up, Charles and the Queen now came to a hard decision. Henriette Marie was not safe in any of the royal castles, feared the degradation and danger of being captured by people whom she considered plain rebels and socially impossible, and was convinced that war was bound to come. She had valuable jewels, including some that Queen Elizabeth had owned, with which she intended to purchase arms. Officially the King still discountenanced the prospect of war and Prince Rupert was for the time commanded back to the Continent.

Rupert, born in 1619, the third son of the Elector Frederick Henry and Princess Elizabeth, had been campaigning intermittently since he was fifteen, and in 1636 had first visited England where he had been well received by his uncle. He had early been involved in a wild scheme for colonizing Madagascar: Charles had thought it a good idea, but Rupert's mother had written 'Sir Thomas Roe knows the romances some would put into Rupert's head for conquering Madagascar... when he shall, Quixote-like conquer that famous island'; and the ambassador had written, 'his spirit is too active to be wasted in the softness or entangling of pleasure... he will prove a sword to all his friends if his edge be set right'. By 1637, Rupert had been happily employed in the siege of Breda, but in October of the following year he was taken prisoner, after a gallant resistance, by the Imperial troops at Vlotho on the Weser. He was incarcerated for three years at Linz in Austria, when he developed his considerable talents as an artist, and in due course was allowed much freedom. Charles had been mainly instrumental in obtaining his release.

It was obviously urgent to obtain support from the Dutch and the Danes. So that February of 1642 saw the break-up of the royal family, when, by way of Canterbury, Charles accompanied his wife and the Princess Mary of Orange to Dover. Here Captain John Mennes awaited her in HMS *Victory* with four other ships. At once courtier and seaman, he had voyaged to the West Indies and Virginia, in 1629 escorted Rubens to England, and had a reputation for witty and ribald verse. The occasion brought him a knighthood, and after the Restoration he would become an amiable if inefficient colleague to Samuel Pepys at the Admiralty.

Charles, even in the public farewell, was in tears, as the Queen, the Princess and their attendants went aboard HMS *Lion* on 23 February; and he rode along the cliffs as the ships made sail for the Low Countries to keep them in sight — a genuinely tragic occasion, independent of any political myth. Of course their hopes of substantial help from Holland and Denmark proved vain. From Dover Charles and the Prince of Wales rode up to Greenwich, then proceeded to Theobalds and Royston and Newmarket, making for York, their northern capital (where armaments, they hoped, could be supplied to them from the Low Countries through Hull, which already contained munitions).

The political conflict continued: at Greenwich the King had refused Parliament's Militia Bill — a demand to control the armed forces. He could not, he declared, 'consent to divest himself of the power which God and the laws of this Kingdom [had] placed in him for the defence of his people'; and at Theobalds he had reproached the Parliamentary envoys for creating the *impasse*. Parliament then defied him by turning the

Bill into an 'Ordinance' — an illegal measure since it had not the royal consent. And when at Newmarket, a scene of happier memories, the Earl of Pembroke tried to persuade Charles to compromise on a temporary control of the militia by Parliament, he answered, 'By God, not for an hour.' At Cambridge the King and Prince visited Trinity and St John's, and on his way through Huntingdonshire Charles again called at the pietistic retreat at Little Gidding. Though Nicholas Ferrar had died in 1637, his two sons had carried on the community, but its Anglican atmosphere was now provoking hostility, and the Puritans were denouncing it as an 'Arminian Nunnery'. In the stress of the crisis the King found the retreat more than ever congenial: 'Truly,' he remarked, 'this is a worthy sight. I did not think to have seen a thing in this kind which so well pleaseth me. God's blessing be upon the founders of it.' Then he went his way up to York to prepare for civil war. Five years later Little Gidding was sacked by the Roundheads.

Arrived at York, Charles, though without the Queen, tried to reconstitute the normal ceremonial of the Court; but his world was breaking up. His cherished pictures and *objets d'art*, his splendidly bound books, his architectural projects, his elaborate masques and music, the elegant flattery of the courtiers and the pampered yet austerely formal routine of his normal life were being pushed aside by the brutalities of power politics and the bitterness of religious rancour in a game he had not the human insight, coarse-grained business sense, or the *faux bonhomie* to play.

During that summer of 1642, as both sides blundered into the unnecessary war, the first political virtuoso in the management of the House of Commons was now well in his stride. John

Pym was a fixer and manipulator, a forerunner of Walpole and Baldwin; mediocre in mind, but astute in management, as sensitive as litmus paper to the shifting moods of the House, never so far ahead of political opinion as to be distrusted, but flexible enough to express what had not yet been formulated. He is a world away from the great Tudor statesmen, such as Wolsey and Thomas Cromwell, essentially grand viziers of a powerful monarch, and different from Burghley or even Salisbury, who were essentially counsellors and courtiers. He is the first really astute House of Commons man. His speeches are dull but methodical, he lacks power of phrase, but he goes for essentials — he is a minor Somerset landowner trained in the law and experienced in business; he is representative. Already sixty, he is systematic and laborious, with a mastery of boring detail: he knows men's interests and weaknesses, and he is a good committee man; he is the first modern professional politician in English history and his concern is with power and the next move. He is the antithesis of the King. He has not the vision of parliamentary democracy once attributed to him, but he is determined in the interest of his kind to keep the monarch within a mixed frame of government — King, Lords and Commons — and if necessary, on medieval precedents, to resist him, even to war.

As has been well written, 'In all the Parliaments that Coke pontificated to and Eliot electrified, Pym sat. He sat, and he worked with a capacity for work given to few men.[335] He had the dull but useful knack of squeezing the maximum political energy out of the most unpromising raw materials and of applying that energy at the time and place where it would be most effective; somehow or other he kept things going'. Naturally, 'the attempt to ascribe any clear new ideal to Pym involves a fundamental misunderstanding of the man. Not a political theorist like Ireton, and not a religious theorist like Vane, he had nothing in him of the architect of brave new worlds. He was a political tactician, a political engineer.'[336] In a time when there were no organized parties, this prosaic man managed tenaciously to hold together a majority in the Commons, which he could persuade rather than inspire. And he managed to believe, in the English way, that somehow fighting the King was preserving the monarchy, that by promoting illegal ordinances he was vindicating the law, and that by manipulating the House of Commons he was interpreting its will. He thus set lasting political precedents, much admired.

Established in York, Charles became the centre both of local patriotism and of a new Royalist party. The Grand Remonstrance had been a calculated provocation — 'of such a nature that it must create, and having created, sustain, a bitterer partisanship in the House than had existed before — an appalling aggravation of the situation';[337] in March despite the King, Parliament passed the Militia Ordinance, asserting control of the armed forces and empowering their own appointed lords lieutenants to 'lead conduct and employ the militia under the Orders of the Lords and Commons'. During the controversy over who should mobilize it, Charles had written from York, 'I wish my residence near you might be safe and honorable that I had no cause to absent myself from Whitehall. Ask yourselves whether I have not? I shall take that of my son as a cause, which shall justify me unto God as a father and to my Dominions as a King. I assure you upon mine honour I have no thoughts but of peace and justice to my people.'[338] Finally, when Northumberland arranged against the King's will that Warwick should command the fleet, Edward Hyde realized that the 'law of the land and the liberty of the subjects had been resolved with a vote of the two houses... a foundation laid for the anarchy and confusion that followed'.

The King now regarded his opponents as rebels,[339] and in April, following his original design, Charles tried to secure Hull, with its munitions accumulated for the Scots war and its communication with Denmark and Holland. Already, in January 1642, he had appointed Newcastle governor, but Parliament had at once ordered Sir John Hotham, a man of much local influence, to take over the town. Hull wanted to stay neutral, but Captain Hotham, his son, had briskly occupied it with Yorkshire trained bands.

In April James Duke of York had been brought into York by his guardian, the Marquess of Hertford, and been created a Knight of the Garter; Charles chose the occasion to send him on his first political mission. Along with the Elector Palatine, the boy appeared at Hull, ostensibly to inspect the fortifications, and was duly entertained; but when, while they were at dinner, the King himself appeared, Hotham barred him out. After an undignified exchange, the King had Hotham proclaimed a traitor to his face, but he had to turn tail, followed by York and his entourage. It was not an auspicious opening move.

The one thing on which King, Parliament and the Scots were still agreed was to put down the Irish rising. That April the Scots General Munroe landed at Carrickfergus and in collaboration with the Scots settlers in Ulster and with the Irish Protestants launched a major counterattack: Ireland was now in a welter of civil war and the final breach between King and Parliament would prolong it until the victory of Parliament would give Cromwell the chance for a ruthless 'pacification'.

As spring turned into summer, political warfare was stepped up. On 21 May Hyde had come into York and put his eloquent pen directly at the King's disposal — a mixed blessing, thought one contemporary.

> I remember a wise lord, who had great influence on them all, would complain that [the King's propositions] in their wit and elegancy, as it was very delightful so it would not long last useful... and that [it] would beget rather a forwardeness in men to see such things treated with elegancy and irony, than any delight or complacence; and therefore he was wont to say 'our good pen will harm us'. I find Mr. Hobbes hath made a reflection on this in his late book on the Civil Wars.[340]

On 27 March 1642 Charles had issued a royal proclamation forbidding his subjects to obey the Militia Ordinance; on 1 June Parliament replied by an ultimatum prepared by the Grocers' Hall Committee and called *The Grocers Hall Remonstrance of Nineteen Propositions*. From the King's point of view they were outrageous: his Council, his Court officials and the tutors for his children were to be appointed by Parliament; the Militia Ordinance was to become statutory, and so a permanent Act of Parliament, and Parliament was to settle the Church of England to their liking. These propositions were not new; but they were more extreme.

Charles and his advisers at once repudiated them in *His Majesties Answer to the XIX Propositions of Both Houses of Parliament*. Charles called God to witness that he would never subvert (though in a parliamentary way) 'the ancient and equall well poised and never enough commended constitution of the Government of this Kingdom', and he declared for a 'regulated' monarchy. The House of Commons, he argued, 'an excellent conserver of liberty' was 'never intended for any share of Government or the chusing of them that should govern': it was concerned only with supply — 'solely intrusted with the first Proposition concerning the leavies of money'. Having thus put the Commons in their place, the King declared that if the power of preferring (to office) were added to the Commons, 'we shall have nothing left for us but to look on' — exactly what Pym and his oligarchic followers wanted. 'These being passed,' he added of the propositions, 'we may be waited on bare-headed, we may have our hand kissed, the style of Majesty continued to us, and the King's authority declared by both Houses of Parliament may be still the style of your commands; we may have swords and maces carried before us, and please ourself with the sign of a crown and sceptre... but as to true and real power, we shall remain but on the outside, and but the picture, but the sign of a King.'

And what would be the result? The Crown would become despicable and those upstarts vested with unaccustomed power would become intoxicated by it. The Church and the House of Lords would go down, 'till full power being vested in the House of Commons, and their number making them incapable of transacting Affairs of State, with the necessary secrecy and expedition', they would be entrusted to 'some close committee' not responsible to anyone. To this evolution there could be only one end. 'The Common people (who in the mean must be flattered, and to whom license must be given in all their wild humours how contrary soever to... their own real good) will discover this *Arcanum Imperii* [Secret of State] that all was done by them, but not for them.' They will then turn on the Commons itself, and 'by this means this splendid and excellently distinguished form of government [will] end in a dark equall of chaos and confusion and the long line of our noble ancestors in a Jake Cade or a Wat Tyler'. 'To all these demands,' the King concluded, 'our answer is *Nolumus leges angliae mutari* — we will not have the laws of England changed.'[341]

Whoever drafted the answer — King, Hyde, Culpepper — foresaw pretty exactly some of the dangers of the democratic experiment.

In June, while this paper warfare was going on, both sides took action. The Parliamentarians in London were particularly concerned to raise cavalry: seventeen of the Lords subscribed to provide 186 horses and their keep for ten weeks; seventy members of the Commons, some members two horses each, some members one; thirty-three asked for time, and fifty absolutely refused. Others discreetly absented themselves. In York a large roll of Royalist peers pledged themselves to pay for 1,695 horses for three months, counting thirty days to the month at 2s 6d a day. Charles now had a thousand foot and two hundred horse as a small personal guard; and on 8 June the gentry, ministers and freeholders of the City of York met on Howarth Moor in their thousands. The Prince of Wales 'rode at the head of his horse troop consisting of the prime gentry of the county excellently mounted',[342] while the Lords of the Council at York resolved with their lives and estates to defend the King's royal person, prerogative and posterity.

Back in London on 4 July the two Houses appointed a 'Committee of Safety' — thus setting a notable historical precedent — and on the twelfth, equally anxious to 'preserve the safety of the King's person' as well as of themselves and 'the true religion liberty and peace of the Kingdom', they declared that they would live and die with the Earl of Essex, now nominated Lord General in their cause.

Still with a tiny force, Charles decided to move south from York into the Midlands. First he made for Coventry in Warwickshire, already surrounded by Parliamentarian trained bands, but sheered off north-east up to Nottingham where the

Trent was navigable to the mouth of the Humber; and here on 22 August, in an apparently muddled ceremony, he raised the Banner Royal for war.

At six o'clock on a blustery late summer evening the King led a small cavalcade, which included Prince Rupert and his brother Maurice, both newly arrived that month, to the top of the small hill above the town where a dilapidated medieval castle survived; in driving rain Sir Edmund Verney, of Claydon, Buckinghamshire, the Knight Marshal of the King's Palace, who had been with Charles in Spain and was considered by the King 'the model he would propose to gentlemen', set the banner up. He did so with foreboding, telling Hyde that he 'did not like the quarrel, having no reverence for bishops for whom it had come about', but since he had 'eaten the King's bread and served him for nearly thirty years, he would not do so base a thing as to forsake him'.

As the trumpets sounded a fanfare and the great standard flapped in the gale,[343] a herald made to read a proclamation setting out the cause of its being put up. But the fastidious King, called to view it, looked it through and then, in the rain, demanded pen and ink and altered it. The herald found the corrections hard to read and this impeded his delivery. No one present apparently knew the correct way of setting up the Banner Royal, so long a time had elapsed since there had been occasion to do so. They had first hung it out of one of the turrets in the castle, but Charles had insisted on its being set up in the park where it would be easy of access. Unhappily, the ground proved too hard and stony for it to be firmly secured. It may have been deliberately taken down that evening. According to Clarendon the ceremony was even less convincing, for the standard was 'blown down the same evening by a very strong and unruly wind, and could not be fixed again in a day or two till the tempest was allayed'. In either version the occasion had been a melancholy opening of a campaign reluctantly begun.

Outside Coventry some of the Parliamentarians were also getting on with the war. By 26 August the trained bands under Lord Brooke had plundered the local deer park and got great store of venison — 'almost as common with us', one wrote, 'as beef with you'. They had also shown their Puritan moral principles by tormenting a whore who had paid them the compliment of following them from London, only to be 'led about the city, pilloried, and ducked', while 'we officers, wet our halberds with a barrell of strong beer called "Old Hum"'.[344]

15: THE STRATEGIC FAILURE

WELL BEFORE EVER he raised the Banner Royal at Nottingham Charles had sustained a major strategic reverse. Algernon Percy, tenth Earl of Northumberland, Lord High Admiral of England since 1638, with whom the King had long 'conversed as a friend', had defected and with him most of the royal navy, for which the King had done so much. A northern magnate of ancient lineage, the proudest, wrote Clarendon, of all the great peers, he had early become disgusted with 'the daily disorders in the fleet and [with] not having the means to remedy them', in an employment as he wrote to Strafford 'where a man can neither do service to the state, gain honour for himself, nor do courtesies to his friends — a condition that I think nobody would be ambitious of'. Though against the Bishops' Wars, he had been appointed to supreme command in both and during the second one he had conveniently fallen ill. A regional potentate with a medieval distrust of an innovating and centralizing power, he now refused to go along with the King and the Cavaliers and veered towards Parliament in an attempt at mediation.

Early in 1642, again ostensibly unwell, he had refused to take the fleet to sea, whereat Charles had ordered him to appoint Sir John Pennington, a veteran now with him at York, who had served under Ralegh and since 1631 been Admiral for the 'Guard of the Narrow Seas'. Northumberland however, at the behest of Parliament, had appointed Robert Rich, Earl of Warwick. One of the close group of major peers in alliance with Pym and Hampden, Warwick was a cheerful, extrovert neo-Elizabethan with wide experience at sea. Clarendon says that he was 'a man of pleasant and companionable wit and conversation; of an universal jollity; and such a license in his words and in his actions, that a man of less virtue could not be found..., but with all these faults he had great authority and credit'. Long one of the most powerful magnates of the opposition, he had early been concerned with colonizing the Bermudas, Virginia, Old Providence and Massachusetts, and had done much privateering on his own account. He was popular in the fleet; reported as being 'never sick one hour at sea', and would 'as nimbly climb up to the top of a yard as any common mariner in the ship'.

In Northumberland Charles had lost a key man, and that June he had at last dismissed him, whereupon on 1 July Parliament by ordinance had reiterated Northumberland's appointment of Warwick to command the fleet. He had at once taken charge, dispelled opposition, arrested Royalist captains and put sixteen men of war and twenty-four armed merchantmen and their crews at Parliament's disposal; an event quite unexpected by the King, who 'had an opinion of the devotion of the whole body of the common seamen to his service, because he had bountifully so much amended their condition and increased their pay, that he thought they would have thrown the Earl of Warwick overboard';[345] for, Clarendon continues, 'the seamen [were] a nation by themselves, a humorous and fantastic people, fierce and rude in whatever they are inclined to, unsteady and inconstant in pursuing it'. Yet the King had been 'so confident upon the general affection of the seamen, who were a tribe of people more particularly countenanced and obliged by him than other men... that he could believe that no activity of ill officers could have corrupted them, but that, when the Parliament had set out and victualled the fleet, it would upon any occasion declare itself at his devotion'. In fact the men attributed their better conditions not to the King but to their officers, so that 'a greater defection of any order or men was never known'.[346]

Charles therefore entered the Civil War a king of England without a navy; he might dismiss the irresponsible seamen as 'water rats', but he became discredited abroad; what supplies he could raise there could be intercepted, and Parliament would control most of the ports — such as Hull, Dover, Portsmouth, Weymouth, Lyme Regis, Plymouth and at first Bristol, the second city in the kingdom. This handicap and his lack of regular revenues would prove Charles's decisive strategic weakness. It was early said of the Cavaliers that they were 'strong in men and horses, but weak in purse'; Royalist nobility and gentry might sacrifice their plate, and loyal colleges bring their medieval treasure to be melted down (Cromwell characteristically pounced on the plate of the Cambridge colleges early in August 1642 before the war had officially begun), but Parliament's hold on London and in many counties proved far more profitable, in time yielding substantial and regularly collected revenues.

As already observed, contrary to much accepted opinion, most of the towns tried hard to evade committing themselves in the civil wars.

> In an age of developing consciousness and communication in the new world of ideological combat, it is surprising that so few urban centres took anything that might be considered as a constructive role in 1640-1660. London, Gloucester, Coventry and Birmingham are isolated instances of political involvement with the common denomination of vigorous Puritan leadership.[347]

In spite of powerful royalist influence among the rich, London, 'the graveyard of pauper England', was swarming with apprentices and mariners, by far the largest town in the country and the only one comparable to the great cities of the Continent. It became predominantly a centre of political and religious radicalism, which the Parliamentarians could exploit, and already in the winter of 1642 the four Inns of Court would petition Parliament to 'get better order in London, that you will not suffer learning to be defaced by ignorance'. What Baillie called the King's 'extraordinary caressing of the City' had been directed specifically to the greater merchants; but by August the Royalist Lord Mayor, Sir Richard Gurney, whom Charles had knighted, was in prison.

In the autumn of 1642 the Parliamentarians raised £30,000 from the London parishes and — with London the natural and time-honoured centre of government — the Commons had resolved that the King's income remitted to London and arising out of rents, fines and the Courts of Justice, from wards and the like, and 'all other of his Majesty's revenues, brought in paid in the normal way', should be frozen there until their further orders. The Puritan clergy kept up their political and theological warfare from the pulpits,[348] and it was soon reported that the whole city were 'either real or constrained Roundheads'.[349] The confiscated revenues of the Anglican establishment in the areas under Parliamentary control and the systematic fines on Papists and 'malignants' brought in increasing revenues, and by 1643 Pym, in imitation of the Dutch, collected a steady revenue by making a regular general imposition through the Office of Excise or 'New Impost'; he also saw to it that 'malignants and neutrals' who by 'cunning ways had evaded their obligations under the General Burden', might be compelled to pay what would now be called their 'fair share' in rebellion.

Early in September 1642 Sergeant Major General Sir Jacob Astley[350] (the 'sergeant' at this level gradually became dropped in both armies) warned Charles that he could not guarantee that he might not be 'taken in his bed' if the rebels under Essex's command attacked in force. The King had finally broken with Essex when, summoned as Lord Chamberlain to attend Charles at York, he had refused the royal command. 'We are much unsatisfied,' Charles had written, 'with the excuse you made for not obeying our command for your attendance on us here, according to your place in Our Household', and he had at last directed him to surrender his Lord Chamberlain's wand, the ensign of his office. As Parliamentarian Captain General and Commander-in-Chief, this mediocre but dependable magnate, of impeccable lineage and with £8,000 a year, lent needed respectability to the Roundhead Parliament's cause. 'If the Earl of Essex had refused that command,' wrote a supporter, 'our cause would in all likelihood have sunk, we having never a nobleman capable of it.' A veteran of slow-footed campaigns in the Low Countries, when he had 'first trailed a pike' and 'refused no service in the field', as well as of the disastrous campaign against Cadiz, Essex was a stolid commander prepared for all eventualities, for he took along with him not only his own doctor but a coffin and a winding sheet. He had an elite bodyguard, mainly from the Inns of Court, under the command of Sir Philip Stapleton, and a standard of orange tawney and white with the motto, 'God with us'. On 12 August Charles had proclaimed him a traitor, and the Cavaliers, remembering his Jacobean divorce for alleged impotence, called him 'His Oxcellency'.[351]

In view of Astley's warning, the King now moved west to Derby, where he recruited some tough miners, and then on to Shrewsbury; he still had only five hundred horse, five regiments of foot and twelve guns. Here he stayed from 20 September to 12 October: he hoped to recruit Welsh infantry and set about melting down plate into coin to attract them. Many Royalist gentry now came in from Cheshire and Staffordshire, and a sizeable army began to coalesce. It had at least the advantage of a united command, for the King was himself Commander-in-Chief, and in the twenty-three-year-old Prince Rupert — now back from Holland and known to the English as Prince 'Robert' — he had a cavalry commander and siege expert of outstanding ability. For this 'diabolical Cavalier' was not just the romantic and feckless figure of legend, but an experienced campaigner with a passion for war. While in captivity in Austria, he had studied its theory and he had come to England despite the attempts of Elizabeth of Bohemia and his brother the Elector Palatine to stop him. Indeed that October they even sent from the Hague a *'Declaration and Petition of the Prince Palsgrave of the Rhyne and the Queen his Mother* disclaiming and discountenancing Prince "Robert" in all his uncivill Actions in the Kingdom, desiring both Houses of Parliament not to stoppe the annual pensions due to them for his Cause, which they cannot help'. They were 'grieved', they declared, 'to their very soules at the cruelties committed by one whose passion we cannot confine, whose hot spirit we cannot control', and again petitioned that their annual pensions be duly paid — 'which is our chiefest livelihood under God'.

But Rupert went his own way; and had his advice been better regarded, the war could have had a different outcome. Even so, mainly because of his royal blood but also in admiration for his ability, the King put his nephew under his own direct command and not under that of his Lord General, the Earl of Lindsey.[352]

Essex meanwhile, after a rousing and pompous send-off in London, had also made for the west to seek out and destroy the King's army before it became more dangerous; and by 24 September he had arrived by way of Northampton and Coventry at Worcester, which the Cavaliers had tried in vain to capture. For some of his soldiers, as for many others in these wars, to traverse England was like visiting a new country. One who arrived in Worcestershire in late September wrote how every hedge and highway was 'beset with fruit, especially pears, which they sell for 1d. a quart, tho' better than ever you tasted in London',[353] and the Malvern hills were the highest he had ever set eyes on. But the people of Worcester gave the Londoner a shock: they were 'base and papistical' and the place 'like Sodom'; and at Hereford the inhabitants seemed 'totally ignorant in the ways of God and much given to drunkenness and other vices'. Many here, he added, spoke Welsh.[354]

In a proclamation to his army, which by now amounted to over thirteen thousand men, Essex had promised to maintain the Protestant religion, and of course to protect the King against whom he was in arms. He promised not to engage them in any danger in which he would not run an equal hazard himself, declared himself open to receive the complaints of the poorest of his soldiers, and ready to deal impartial justice to all, regardless of rank. 'Your pay,' he had said, 'shall be constantly delivered to your commanders'; if it were withheld, he would make speedy redress. Such, said Essex, was his side of the bargain. Theirs also should be carefully performed: every officer should command the soldiers by love and affable carriage since what is done for fear is done unwillingly. They were not to busy their men in ceremonious forms of military discipline, but instruct them (and they needed it) in the rudiments of war — how to fall on with discretion, retreat with care, maintain their order and make good their ground. All who had voluntarily engaged in his service were expected to obey their officers, take care of their arms, rendezvous to the colours at the sound of the drum or trumpet and not to plunder the local people. They must be vigilant sentries and not profane 'the Saboth either by being drunke or by unlawful games'. If they neglected to feed their horses they risked a month in prison and being cashiered, and no trooper was to suffer his 'Pedee' (his foot attendant) to 'feed his horse on corne or steal men's hay', but was to pay 'everyman for hay 6d a day and night, and for oats 2/- a bushell'. And though at war they were to avoid cruelty. For, he concluded, 'it is my desire rather to save the life of thousands than to kill one, so that may be done without prejudice... These things faithfully performed,... let us advance with a religious courage, and willingly adventure our lives in the defence of King and Parliament.'[355]

Essex had wished to be appointed Grand Constable of England to be able to negotiate in his own right with the King, and he was never wholehearted in the war; but the fervour of the Puritan preachers, who testified for hours in 'heavenly' sermons, did much to inspire militant zeal.

Charles, too, had issued his instructions, along with a more belligerent address.

> Gentlemen, you have heard my orders read: it is your part in your several places to observe them exactly. The time cannot be long before we come to action... and I must tell you I shall be very severe on those who transgress these instructions. You shall meet with no enemies but traitors, most of them Brownists, Anabaptists, and Atheists, such who desire to

destroy both church and state, and who have already condemned you to ruin for being loyal to us.

He had promised 'to live and die with them'. So in the autumn weather, down the line of the Severn, the King at Shrewsbury and Essex at Worcester, the armies prepared for major battle.

Anxious also to secure the north, Charles wrote from Shrewsbury to the Earl of Newcastle:

> NewCastel, This is to tell you that this Rebellion is growen to that height, that I must not looke what opinion men ar who at this tyme ar willing and able to serve me. Therefore I doe not only permitt, but command you, to make use of my loving subjects services without examining their condenses (more than there loyalty to me) as you shall fynde most to conduce to my just Regall Power.[356]

The King's correct strategy was obviously to capture London, dissolve Parliament and finish the war at a blow: Essex's objective was either to destroy his army, before it got stronger, or failing that to get between him and the capital.

Charles's personal life had now been much altered. Once he had left York the normal Court routine had broken down, and though it would be revived at Oxford in miniature, his habits became military. In spite of his withdrawn, pious and aesthetic temperament, he had been a martial young prince, and he now began to show physical endurance and bravery and to prove himself a better soldier than politician. But if the 'excitement and the open air life suited the King's restive nature',[357] he was inexperienced in war and learnt the hard way.

By continental standards both sides in the English Civil War were amateurs, and by modern standards their weapons were primitive, their intelligence faulty, their commissariat inadequate and their medical services almost non-existent. Only with the advent of Fairfax's and Cromwell's 'New Modell'd Army' (a contemporary spelling) is a greater professional expertise apparent, though its since vaunted Independent sectaries were probably outnumbered by pressed men, or men who had changed sides. Over the years severe casualties were inflicted for the numbers engaged, but in a population of about five million, of whom one and a half million were males of military age, the numbers actually under arms were relatively small. At the first big battle at Edgehill the combined numbers of both sides were well under thirty thousand and at Marston Moor, the largest battle of the war, in which the Scots also were engaged, the combined numbers were around forty-six thousand. On the other hand the medical services were so bad that anyone at all seriously wounded was unlikely to survive.

Shorn of the bogus romance which nineteenth-century writers and popular tradition have attributed to them, both Civil Wars, romanticized like the American War between the States, were horrible, though they did not include sack and pillage on a scale comparable to that common in the contemporary Thirty Years' War. Indeed civilities were often exchanged between the members of a divided ruling class, although the common foot soldiers got short shrift and were generally paid rather worse than agricultural labourers'.[358] In proportion to the terrain covered and the numbers involved, the wars were as brutish as such internecine and ideological conflicts normally are, and it is time the complacent belief of liberal historians that, somehow, they were humanely conducted with English good will and sportsmanship was revised. The devastation grew as the war progressed and became more bitter. In 1645 the country people of the Severn valley, in Wessex, Surrey, and Sussex, known as the Clubmen, turned out in their thousands to warn the pillaging armies off their land; and to the human carnage must be added the suffering of the horses.

Though to a continental eye the aspect of both armies must have been unprofessional, it is in fact another 'of the hoariest myths about the civil war... that its soldiers did not wear uniform... records of the issue of uniforms to the armies of both sides abount'; and both cavaliers and roundhead cavalry 'favoured helmets while in action' — so that it is a common error to regard the lobster tailed helmet as a purely Parliamentarian issue'.[359] The popular notion of the Cavaliers charging in stylishly tilted plumed hats, elaborate lace collars and cuffs and streaming cloaks, like the Mamluks at the Battle of the Pyramids, against dour opponents clad in buff coat and steel, must give place to a less picturesque view, and though scarves and sashes distinguished the opposing sides — orange tawney for Parliamentarians and red for Royalists — both armies would have looked much the same.

The most decisive arm were the relatively well-paid cavalry. Following Swedish tactics, they were now beginning to charge home, three or sometimes six deep, holding their fire until among the enemy, in contrast to the old-fashioned custom of caracoling up the enemy in deep formation, discharging pistols and trotting away — thus wasting the momentum of the horse in an inefficient manoeuvre 'as generations of horsemen have found to their discomfort, [since] a horse does not make the steadiest of weapon platforms'.[360] The other offensive arm was the musketeers, working under the protection of the phalanxes of pikemen, whose weapons, eighteen feet long and held in the left hand, presented a bristling hedgehog to the enemy. But the muskets were clumsy, loading them slow and laborious and, being fired by a slow-burning match, they were unreliable in wet weather, while their range and accuracy were poor.

The dragoons — mounted infantry with swords and carbines — were a more serious menace to cavalry. When dismounted, they fought from hedges, ditches and what cover they could find. Artillery was primitive: the heaviest guns drawn by oxen and carthorses fired only ten or twelve rounds an hour, over a range of a thousand yards; the ten-pounder culverins and the lighter Sakers and Drakes, placed between the infantry formations, fired scattering case shot, probably more effective than the iron cannon balls, though the noise and black smoke of the big guns, as in late medieval battles, would have affected morale. Transport was best by river barges or by sea: over the atrocious roads, it was slow and difficult, though cavalry on good horses could move fast. The expensive heavy armour, in which it was the fashion to be painted, was not in fact very much used; a light breast and back piece and leather or 'buff' coat gave more freedom, and no worse protection, against firearms, pikes, or against the thrust of a 'Pappenheimer' rapier or the cut and thrust of a 'Walloon' sword.[361]

Such was the form in both armies as they made a halting race for London through a countryside that was then often more heavily wooded, but was generally unenclosed and often still under medieval strip cultivation and with huge areas of sheep and cattle pasture. It was no picnic: the weather broke in autumnal storms, they had no tents and few wagons, and 'artillery, senior officers, coaches, spurs, saddle horses, pack animals, victuallers and inevitably women clogged the muddy midlands roads as the King moved south'.[362] Essex, generally a sluggish commander, might have sought out and perhaps captured the King in the first few weeks of the campaign before he had secured a following; but aiming not at victory but at a negotiated peace, with one eye on the Committee of Safety at Westminster, and probably believing that once his deleterious advisers had been got rid of Charles would come to an accommodation, he had not pressed his advantage. Though the odds still seemed in his favour, he had in fact lost the initiative. Charles had got a start on him.

The Royalist second-in-command or Marshal-General (Chief of Staff) under their Lord General the Earl of Lindsey was an aged Scot, Patrick Ruthven, Earl of Forth and Graf von Kirchberg bei Ulm, veteran of the Swedish wars, who had been promoted by Gustav Adolf of Sweden for his prowess in battle and for his 'extraordinary power of withstanding the effects of intoxicating liquor'.[363] Charles had made him governor of Edinburgh Castle and although in 1640, after a gallant resistance, he had surrendered it to the Covenanters, he had since created him Earl of Forth. Although, according to Clarendon, he was a very loyal and good officer of great experience, he had now become deaf and slow in the uptake, and 'with the long continued custom of immoderate drinking dozed in his understanding'. Neither Lindsey nor Forth was thus an inspiring commander; and already Lindsey was complaining of Prince Rupert's independent position. The day before the battle of Edgehill he declared that 'he did not look upon himself as a General'; and therefore he was resolved, when the day of battle should come, 'that he would be at the head of his regiment as a private colonel where he would die'. As the King's standard bearer, Sir Edmund Verney, was also convinced (rightly), that he would die too, the King's immediate subordinates had not much will for victory. Only Rupert had plenty of initiative, and it was he who by a night march placed the King's army between Essex and London.

The ridge of the Cotswold escarpment at Edgehill, today covered with woodland, overlooks the Warwickshire plain and commands a wide view away beyond Kineton over fields now intersected by the rails of an army ammunition dump and to the left over the village of Radway. The declivity of the escarpment, here at over seven hundred feet above sea level, faces north-west and descends steeply three hundred feet into the plain, but the country towards Kineton was practicable for cavalry. It was along this exposed ridge that on 23 October, with the surrounding trees turning to autumn colours and the nights turning cold, that the King's army took up its position.

Charles had intended to avoid battle and make straight for London; but though Essex had caught him up the King had won the strategic advantage, and he had himself with his 'prospective glass' viewed the enemy round Kineton; being asked what he thought of them he answered: 'I never saw the Rebels before in a body: I am resolved to fight them: God and good men assist my righteous cause.'[364] The confrontation was indeed dramatic — the first major conflict on southern English soil since the Wars of the Roses — and addressing his soldiers in the field Charles is reported to have declared:

> You are called Cavaliers and royalists, in a disgraceful manner: if I suffer in my fame, needs must you do also. Now express yourselves my friends, and not malignant: fight for your King, the peace of the Kingdom and the Protestant religion... you are called *Cavaliers*, in a reproachful signification, and ye are all designed for the slaughter if you do not manfully behave yourselves in this battell. They call all the king's troopers *Cavaliers*, but let them know that the valour of the *Cavaliers* hath honoured that name, both in France and in other countries, and now let it be known in England as well as horseman or trooper; it signifying no more but a gentleman serving his king on horseback... Hee that made us a King will

protect us. We have marched so long in hope to meet no enemy, we knowing none at whose hands we deserve any opposition; nor can our sunne-shining, through the clouds of malignant envy, suffer such an obscuritie but that some influence of my regall authoritie derived from God whose substitute and supreame governor under Christ I am, hath begotten in you confidence of my intentions…[365]

How far these sentiments were later concocted, and if spoken, how far they may have carried in the autumn air, must remain unknown; but Charles evidently made a speech, and the vindication of 'Cavaliers' and the claim to be God's representative under Christ both ring true.

Essex, meanwhile, having emerged from church at 9.30, for it was a Sunday, was marching out from Kineton. He deployed in the same direction as the modern road to Banbury, where a dull little monument, like a black pillar box, commemorates the battle. Soon he was so far within range that one of his gunners took a shot at the King, conspicuous upon Knowle Hill. Perhaps annoyed at this affront, 'and determined to stop the advance of the guns', Charles on the right ordered an advance down the hill: Rupert, also on the right, descended it in column and deployed into line in the Swedish fashion, poised for the charge with the advantage of the ground and wind.[366] The infantry, too, had taken up positions in the centre in the new-fangled Swedish style, with musketeers in close formation with the pikemen — the decision that had provoked Lindsey to resign on the spot, to be hastily replaced in his command by the elderly Sergeant Major-General Sir Jacob Astley.

To the left of the infantry were four regiments of horse under Henry Wilmot, afterwards first Earl of Rochester, who had served the Dutch in the Low Countries and been Commissary General of Horse in the Second Bishops' War, one of the more dashing and ambitious Royalist commanders. Charles himself, elegant in a black velvet coat lined with ermine, his standard borne by Sir Edmund Verney and accompanied by his red-coated footguards, was determined to fight in person in the battle. 'Come Life or Death,' he had told his officers, 'your king will bear you company.'

Rupert was the first to charge. Riding from wing to wing he had already instructed his cavalry to keep close formation and reserve their fire; then he launched them full tilt against the enemy. The charge swept all before it, like a steeple chase over all obstacles, for the Parliamentarians who had met it halted, broke and fled, and did not stop until they were well beyond Kineton, the Royalist cavalry hunting them like hares. On the right the Royalists had won complete victory. But its completeness had its price: once launched, the cavalry could not be stopped, and only prolonged drill and a habit of discipline they had not had time to acquire could have checked them. They 'fell on the wagons', plundered Kineton, their horses were blown, their formation lost. And worse, the cavalry reserve behind them could not resist joining the hunt.

The right flank of the Royalist infantry in front of Radway and the King himself were therefore exposed in their weakest point, for 'all the distrust was in the Welch Infantry, who at first beginning were somewhat skittish';[367] and although Wilmot with his cavalry on the left had routed his opponents, he had been harassed by musketeers and dragoons on the hedges that had also provided cover for a cunning counter-attack made under Sir William Balfour (a Scot from Fife, who had held Strafford in custody as governor of the Tower) which had been made by part of the Parliamentarian cavalry reserve along the lower slopes of the hill behind the village. This counter-attack now got in among the Royalist artillery, though

Balfour was unable to spike the guns; in a welter of noise and smoke Verney was killed, Lindsey mortally wounded and the King's standard taken. But not for long; Captain John Smith with some of Rupert's horse had now returned and when a boy cried out, 'Captain Smith, Captain Smith, they are taking away the standard', Smith — next day knighted for his exploit — yelling, 'They shall have me with it if they carry it away', had dashed forward and retrieved it. Charles, Prince of Wales, too had been in danger and cocking his pistol cried out before he was hustled away, 'I fear them not!'

Having rescued the standard Smith had rounded on Balfour's horse, now scattered in the melee, and drove them back. The crisis passed: in spite of Balfour's successful counter-attack the Royalists now held the field. 'It was now neer evening... both armies stood at gaze': Charles, by his personal decision, refused to leave the battlefield, 'passed this night with the Prince in his coach'[368] and so outfaced the enemy, 'his army keeping great fires' through the October night. 'Contrary to the general expectation,' reported the Venetian ambassador on the battle of 'Edgiel', 'he gave prrofs of great courage and established the devotion of his troops. For quite three hours he was taking part in the fighting, always with his sword in his hand, and more than once he placed himself without any reservation at the head of his army.'[369]

The price of tactical stalemate and strategic victory had been severe. By modern or even contemporary continental standards a loss of about fifteen hundred dead[370] out of the twenty-six to twenty-seven thousand engaged was not much, but the civilian English were then unaccustomed to slaughter, and for Charles It was his first battle. The proportion of officers killed was high, and these high-spirited gentlemen died hard, Lindsey, for example, bleeding to death 'upon a little straw in a poor house, when they had laid him in his blood... no surgeon having been yet with him', but 'still with great vivacity in his looks' and denouncing 'so foul a rebellion and Balfour's odious intratitude'. The battle had ended in mutual exhaustion with many of the wounded lying out to die in the frost that night.[371] Ruefully both sides drew off: Essex three-quarters of a mile towards Kineton; the Royalists towards the hill. The former, declining the King's implicit offer of a renewed battle, then retired on Warwick, leaving seven guns and many colours in Royalist hands.[372]

Now was, in the opinion of his generals, Charles's opportunity to march on Westminster, even on the City of London itself, and finish the war. Rupert urged this course; cautious and experienced, old Ruthven, Earl of Forth, concurred, begging the King to let him make a forced march on the capital with all available horse and three thousand foot. But Charles, his nerve perhaps shaken by his first battle when his own bodyguard had been badly cut up, listened in Council to the elderly civilian, John Digby, first Earl of Bristol, that 'man of grave respect', who had now rallied to the King. He may well have been hoping for a compromise peace. Indeed the natural reaction of courtiers, politicians and administrators was already to call the war off. In fact, of course, things had gone too far. A more formidable monarch, sensing this and his blood now up, would have put all to the hazard, advanced on Westminster, if not the City itself, dissolved Parliament and probably won the war. Characteristically, in spite of Rupert and Forth, Charles sheered off via Aynhoe and Banbury — an important stronghold — to Oxford, a place he liked and where loyalty was fervent. He still regarded the war simply as a large-scale rebellion and not as a lethal contest for sovereign power.

So what looks like a great opportunity was thrown away, and on 29 October 1642, as Anthony Wood puts it,

> ... being a Saturday, the Kinge's Majestie, towarde the eveninge, came from Edgehill or Keinton battell and from Banbury-side to Oxford, in at the Northgate on horsebacke, with his army of foote men; Prince Robert, and his brother Maurice, allso the younge prince Charles and his brother the duke of Yorke came in allso: they lodged at Christ Church... they came in their full march into this towne, with about 60 or 70 cullours borne before them which they had taken at the saide battell of Edgehill from the Parliament's forces... The ordnance and great guns were driven into Magdalen College grove, about *26* or 27 pieces with all their carriages.

Two days later 'the Kynge's horsemen or troopers and dragoners came through Oxford, a very great many of them, in all about 4,000, and marched toward Abingdon, stayenge not in Oxford at all'.[373]

The university was eager in official welcome. It had in fact, after the King's proclamation for suppressing the rebellion, early bestirred itself on his behalf. 'Dr. Robert Pink [Warden] of New Coll.', writes Wood, 'the deputy Vice Chancellour, had called before him in the public schools all the privileged men's armes, to have a view of them where... many scholars appeared, bringing with them the furniture of armes of every college that then had any.' They had trained in New College Quadrangle — and 'it being a novel matter, there was no holding of the school boyes in the schools in the cloyster...'. So that Wood 'remembered well that some of them were so besotted with the training and activite and gayitie there in that some young scholars... could never be brought to their booke again'.[374]

Though he had missed his chance of entering London before Essex's army had got there, Charles did not linger in Oxford. By 4 November he had occupied Reading, and by the seventh Rupert had summoned Windsor Castle to surrender, to be met with defiance. By the eleventh the Royalists were at Colnbrook, between Datchet and modern Heathrow; and while the King was negotiating with a delegation led by Northumberland and Pembroke, both anxious to compromise, next day Rupert, attacking through the dawn mist, stormed and sacked Brentford in continental style, taking five hundred prisoners and fifteen guns; a victory confirmed when a convoy of Parliamentarian barges was blown up, sunk or captured on the Thames off Sion House.

Charles was now very close to London (Brentford is near Kew and Chiswick); almost within striking distance of Westminster. But he had reckoned without the manpower of London, mustered in the time conceded on interior lines; moreover an unmistakable threat to their property had roused the Londoners. By 9 November Essex had returned, his defeat celebrated by the Westminster politicians as a victory — both sides gave God solemn thanks (on days set apart)[375] — and morale had risen to defy the depredations of the detested Cavaliers. On the outskirts of London, reported the Venetian envoy, concerned because the English were cutting down on imported currants from the Greek islands, there was 'no street however little frequented that was not barricaded by heavy chains'; trenches had been dug, earthworks thrown up. And the preachers excelled themselves; Skippon paraded the trained bands in Chelsea, and by November 13 the very large force of twenty-four thousand men reinforced with armaments and artillery from the Tower confronted the outnumbered Royalists at Turnham Green. All day the two armies glared at one another; but the most decisive battle of the war never physically took place. The Parliamentarians won it without fighting, and Charles withdrew to Hounslow and then to Oxford. He had failed to enter his own capital. The war settled down over the winter to a rueful pause.

16: THE CAVALIER SUCCESS

WHILE THE KING and the Cavaliers settled on Oxford and the routine of the Court was in part revived, opposition against Parliament was growing in London. Alderman Sir Henry Garraway, for example, objected to their domination of the Common Council of the City, where four members of Parliament had intruded and made 'bitter invectives' against the King's proposals for peace. Once the immediate threat had receded, factions were breaking out as the full implications of the conflict for trade and taxation sank in. Complaints were made about the 'countenance' being given to 'Anabaptists and Brownists', and against Parliament's exactions the cry had already gone up: 'No money! Peace, Peace!' Two thousand apprentices, reported Giustinian, 'formerly most seditious', were now demonstrating against the war; although, he concluded wisely, there was even greater 'penury and disorder' among the Royalists.

Down at Oxford in a relatively congenial setting and in the best strategic situation he could find short of London, protected by rivers and meadows and ringed round with fortified strongpoints, Charles's confidence remained unshaken. If the first attack on London had failed, a second more elaborate one on exterior lines must be mounted; in the immediate future he hoped to blockade London in collaboration with the Royalists in Kent by closing the river on either side; in long-term strategy he intended that the 'remote armies' of the north and west, under the magnates Newcastle and William Seymour, who had been created first Marquess of Hertford in 1640, and possessed immense estates in the West

Country, would close in a pincer movement concerted with his own renewed attack along the Thames valley. And the Royalists soon took the initiative to clear communications with the west: in the depth of winter on 5 December Wilmot's cavalry took Marlborough, 'notoriously disaffected',[376] and on 2 February, after a heavy snowfall, Rupert captured Cirencester.[377]

On 1 February 1643 the King received a Parliamentary Commission who came down to Oxford empowered to make a treaty, with nothing more than a touch of 'temperate indignation'; indeed he had appeared polite and co-operative. They often attended on him in his lodgings in Christ Church and were allowed apparently frank discussion, during which Charles, they reported, showed 'great abilities and quickness and would himself sum up the arguments and give a most clear judgement upon them'. But his 'unhappiness was that he had a better opinion of others' judgement than of his own, though they were weaker than his own': he would come to a reasonable conclusion at night, the delegates complained, but go back on it in the morning.[378] He was in fact playing for time; he would not of course abolish the bishops or give up control of the militia.

In London the Committee of Safety were considering 'some speedy way of guarding the river of Thames' to prevent supplies going up river to the Royalists, though they allowed sick children through the blockade to be touched by Charles for the King's Evil — a duty that later earned him the disrespectful name of 'Stroaker' among the more brutish Parliamentarian soldiery. In Oxford the Court made the best of its situation in overcrowded and uncomfortable quarters, but with plenty of company. In the New Year appeared the weekly news sheet, *Mercurius Aulicus*, edited by John Birkenhead, a brisk young Fellow of All Souls, a sadler's son from Cheshire, who kept it going with far more wit and punch than its London equivalent, *Mercurius Britannicus*, until 1645.[379] The courtiers brought a new style of life to Oxford — to Aubrey, then a youth at Trinity, a touch of colour and romance. 'When I was a Freshman at Oxford,' he writes, 'I was wont to go to Christ Church to see the King at supper'; but Trinity Grove was 'the Daphne for the ladies and their gallants to walk in, and many times my Lady Isabella Thynne (who lay at Balliol) would make her entry with a Theorbo or Lute played before her. I have heard her play on it in the grove myself, which she did rarely. With her Mrs Fanshawe was wont, and my Lady Thynne, to come to our Chapell halfe dressed, like Angells',[380] to the fury of that tremendous character, Dr Ralph Kettle, President of the College.

The crotchety Anthony Wood on the other hand saw another side: 'To give a further character to the court, though they were neat and gay in their apparell, yet they were very nasty and beastly, leaving at their departure their excrement in every corner, in chimneys, studies, colehouses, cellars. Rude, rough, whore mongers; vain, empty, careless.' These habits and their overcrowded lodgings gave rise to the 'camp fever' from which many people perished, among them the brilliant young William Cartwright, Student of Christ Church, the 'most seraphical' preacher in the university, whose play had won so much applause when the King and Queen had come to Oxford in the 1630s and for whom Charles himself put on mourning 'for the loss of such a subject'.

In these varied conditions the city became a centre of frenetic political rivalries and intrigue, in which the amateur courtiers often thwarted the soldiers over important decisions. When in the summer of 1643 the Queen returned and set up a separate household and clique at Merton, this situation grew worse. Through it all the conscientious monarch did his best, aided by the Secretaries of State Nicholas and Falkland (though the latter complained in April of his ill-health 'and all my business to boot'). They attended to a stream of routine petitions about local grievances, economic distress, minor promotions for dependents, livings for the clergy and family disputes among the gentry over inheritances. For Charles was still very much the head of state and so regarded by the vast majority of his subjects.

Early in 1643 the King's prospects looked deceptively good. He had great faith in Newcastle and Hertford, the two grandees, the natural leaders of their regions who, though without military experience, had been placed in command in the north and west. And although in the west Sir William Waller[381] who had earned the name of 'William the Conqueror' from his capture of Farnham Castle, Arundel and Chichester, had been put in command of the Parliamentarian Western Association[382] and in March established himself in Bristol, Prince Maurice defeated him at Ripplefield near Tewkesbury, and the Royalists took the initiative to the south-west into Somerset, Devon and Cornwall.

For most of the population the conflict remained inexplicable and lamentable, and even those involved thought mainly in terms of the local rivalries within their own counties; for, indeed, 'The War was being fought by the two minorities struggling in a sea of neutralist apathy'[383] and 'gradually to most people the issues in dispute lost whatever relevance they had, taking second place to the preservation of hearth and home. The real enemy was the plunderer.'[384]

But the Royalists were still relatively superior in horsemanship and morale. Oliver Cromwell's well-known comment, probably after Edgehill, hackneyed though it is, deserves quotation. 'Your troopers are gentlemen's sons, younger sons and persons of quality... You must get men of a spirit that are likely to go on as far as gentlemen will go or else I am sure you will be beaten still.' So in the west the Royalists did well. Sir Ralph, afterwards Lord Hopton, who had fought for the Elector Palatine in the German wars and had been member of Parliament for Somerset and for Wells, and was now serving under Hertford as Lieutenant General of Horse, had early gone into Cornwall. Although in an initial reverse Hertford had crossed to Wales, Hopton had restored the position, and raised a redoubtable force of Cornish infantry, and on 19 January 1643 had routed the Parliamentarians at Braddock Down near Liskeard. Already it had looked to Charles as if he might well clear the entire west.

The news from the north had also been encouraging. Here in November 1642 the other magnate, the Earl of Newcastle, had early taken the field. As Clarendon puts it, the Earl, that model governor of the Prince of Wales, found campaigning 'contrary to his humour, nature and education', though 'a very fine gentleman, active and full of courage, and most accomplished in those qualities of horsemanship, dancing and fencing which accompany good breeding; in which his delight was'. Indeed though 'he loved the pomp and absolute authority of a general... the fatigue of a general he did not in any degree understand [being utterly unacquainted with war], and though he displayed invincible courage in danger', he was apt to retire 'to his softer pleasures' and shut himself away from even the senior officers of his command. But Newcastle's wealth and influence in Yorkshire were immense, and with eight thousand men in the worst of the winter he had forced the Parliamentarian Ferdinand, second Lord Fairfax,[385] to abandon the siege of York and by December 1642 had moved south to Pontefract, thus cutting the Parliamentarians' communication with Hull. In mid-December Charles had written to him from Oxford:

> New Castell,
> The Services I have receaved from you hath beene so eminent, as is likely to have so great an influence upon all my Affaires, that I need not tell you that I shall never forgett it, but alwaies looke upon you as a principall instrument for keeping the Crowne upon my heade. The business of Yorkshire I account almost done, only I put you in mynde to make yourself maister (according as formerly but breefly I have written to you) of all the Armes there... I have no greater want than of Armes, nor meanes I supply myself than from you... My next greatest want is dragooners [mounted infantry] which I want the more, because it is the Rebelle's (indeed only) strength, theire foot having no inclination to winter marches; wherefore if you could spare horse and arme 500, and send them presently to mee, they might be of very great advantage... I have given order for you to command all the countries beyond Trent.

And again, at the end of the month, getting more anxious for arms, he had written:

> I wonder to heare you say that there are few Armes in that country, for when I was there, to my knowledge there was twelve thousand of the trained bands (except some few Hotham got into Hull) compleat, besides those of particular men; therefore in God's name inquyre what is become of them, and make use of them all; for those who are well

affected will willingly give, or lend them, to you; and those who ar not, make no bones to take them from them.

Careful of Newcastle's pride, the King had continued:

I shall not impose anything upon you... (according to my owen rule) and doe not command, but earnestlie desyre you to see if you can comply with my desires... My conclusion is to asseure you that I doe not only trust your fidelity... but lykewise your judgement in my affairs. [With the negotiation with Parliament in the offing, Charles had added a postscript] I promise you to be as wary of a treatie, as you can desyre.

In February, to the King's profound relief, the Queen had landed at Bridlington. Her adventures had been dramatic. Sailing from Holland on 2 February in the *Princess Royal*, with eleven transports with supplies for the war and a Dutch escort, she had been struck by north-easterly gales — no joke in the North Sea at that season. Following the example of William Rufus, she had exclaimed to her entourage that 'Queens of England are never drowned', and though forced to put back she had set out again, escorted by van Tromp himself, and on the twenty-second made Bridlington. But in the small hours of the next morning a Parliamentarian ship coming close in on the tide, on which the larger Dutch vessels could not venture, had bombarded the house in which she lay. Having rescued her dog — an 'old and ugly and beloved' animal called 'Mitte' — under fire, she had taken refuge in a deep but frosty ditch, 'like that at Newmarket', while the cannon balls streaked overhead, where, as the poet Cartwright put it, 'she was shot at for the King's own good'.

She had brought great quantities of arms and much money; her vivacity had heartened the Royalists at York and her diplomacy had won over both the Hothams, who still held

Hull for the Parliament. Charles's devotion to his wife, who did not join him until July, is apparent from the letter he wrote on her arrival:

> I never till now knew the good of ignorance, for I did not know the danger thou went in by the storm, before I had certain assurance of thy happy escape... I think it not the least of my misfortunes that for my sake thou hast run so much hazard; in which thou has expressed so much love. To me that I confess it is impossible to reply, by anything I can do, much less by words; but my heart being full of affection for thee, admiration of thee, and impatient passion of gratitude to thee, I could not but say something, leaving the rest to be read by thee, out of thy own noble heart.[386]

Such was the state of affairs in the early spring of 1643 when negotiations finally broke down: the King well established in Oxford, the Parliamentarians in London, stalemate in the Thames valley, but in west and north the Royalists predominated. It was hard to hold together any regional hegemony, and financially the King was living from hand to mouth, but the overall strategy of a triple-pronged movement on exterior lines against London perhaps still looked feasible, even promising.

This prospect Parliament was determined to prevent, and in April 1643 Essex moved out of London on Reading, which he captured on the twenty-seventh, striking towards the heart of the Royalist position. By June he had captured Thame and his 'Parliamenters' even plundered 'Whatelye' (Wheatley)[387] only six miles north-east of Oxford itself; but the long June days and summer foliage gave Rupert's cavalry their chance. With about a thousand horse Rupert tried to intercept a convoy making for Thame and bringing £21,000 of the army's pay. And on 18 June, cut off from his base at Oxford by Hampden at Chalgrove Field — a broad open terrain good for cavalry — he wheeled and routed his assailants and returned to Oxford. John Hampden was hit by a bullet in the shoulder, so that 'he rode off the field... resting his hands on the neck of his horse'. A few days later he succumbed — an event that Clarendon, though not liberal historians, describes as a 'great deliverance to the nation'.[388] This skirmish, still commemorated by a large and repellent monument on the battlefield, marked the turn of the tide. Essex's army, short of pay and diminished by illness, could not be kept longer in position, and he ordered it back to Aylesbury and so to the outskirts of London. The thrust up the Thames valley from London had failed.

In the west and north that summer the Royalists' 'remote armies' had won success. At Stratton in northern Cornwall, inland from Bude, Hopton and Sir Bevil Grenville routed a large Parliamentary force, mastered Devon and advanced with their thick-set Cornish pikemen to Chard in Somerset, where Charles had ordered Prince Maurice and Hertford to rendezvous. The Cornishmen, far from home, quarrelled with Prince Maurice's Horse, but this formidable western army proceeded to Bath where on 5 July, though they failed to take the city, they held the field against Waller at the hard-fought battle of Lansdown Hill. But Hopton inspected some Parliamentarian prisoners sitting on a cart that contained a lot of gunpowder, who then lit a match for their tobacco. He was blown up — 'miserably burnt, his horse singed like parched leather' — and put out of action, as well as the powder being wasted.

The Royalists now drew off to Wiltshire, and Waller, undaunted, intercepted their march on Oxford and so he 'cooped up Lord Hopton' and three thousand of their foot 'in the Devizes'.[389] But the Royalist horse got away and rode fast to Oxford, then, reinforced by Wilmot's cavalry, regrouped at Marlborough and advanced down the Bath road to relieve Hopton, who had so far recovered that, short of match, he had ordered all the bedcords in Devizes to be seized, softened up and resinated, an 'expedient' that produced '15 cwt. of match'.[390] So on 13 July 1643 at Roundway Down, north of Devizes, Prince Maurice and Wilmot, charging over resilient Wiltshire turf, routed Waller's horse in the most spirited cavalry action of the war, driving them over the escarpment of the high down into a 'steep place where never horse went down or up before', and since known as 'Bloody ditch' under an eminence today commemorated by an obelisk. Waller's failure at Lansdown Hill had been followed by rout at Roundway Down.

The control of the west was then clinched by the King's biggest strategic success of the war — the storming of Bristol on 26 July 1643 by Prince Rupert, when the Royalists mastered far the biggest port in the west. This success, which restored to the King a measure of sea power and prestige abroad, had its local consequences. That summer Prince Maurice cleared most of Dorset, taking Dorchester, Weymouth and Portland, and leaving only Poole and Lyme Regis to hold out for the Parliament. He also relieved Corfe Castle, then massively intact, whose owner Sir John Bankes CJ, who had made a fortune by the law, was in Oxford with the King, but whose wife, Lady Mary, had held out with a tiny garrison against the assaults of six hundred Parliamentarians from 23 June till 4 August.[391]

In the north, too, the King's successes continued. Since March Lord Fairfax had been blockaded in Leeds, and although in a sortie to the south of it the younger Fairfax captured Wakefield, in June Newcastle with ten thousand men moved down from York into the West Riding and defeated both Fairfaxes at Adwalton Moor, near Bradford, west of Leeds. And although the strategic port of Hull was not, as agreed with the Queen, surrendered by the Hothams, whose designs had been penetrated so that they were arrested and later executed, by July Newcastle controlled all the country north of the Humber and was advancing into Lincolnshire, threatening East Anglia itself. Charles created him a marquis.

By 4 July the Queen, in jest calling herself 'Her she-Majesty Generalissima', had been met by Rupert at Stratford-on-Avon where she stayed at New Place, the best house in the town, with Shakespeare's daughter Susanna (widow of the successful physician Dr John Hall). On 14 July the day after the victory at Roundway Down ('Runaway Down' the Royalists called it) Charles and the Queen at last entered Oxford together. She brought with her ample supplies and three thousand men, 'great store of Walloons, French and other foreigners'. The Parliament's thrust at the city had failed, Bristol would soon be stormed, and except for Lyme, the 'sea towns' of Dorset had been cleared for the Royalists and the north had been overrun for the King.

Charles himself now went on campaign. With the assault on Bristol imminent, he set out by Faringdon and Malmesbury for the west and stayed in the captured city for a week; then, having wasted vital time in discussion, but intent on clearing the Severn valley, he proceeded with the army to the siege of Gloucester. It opened on 10 August and it proved, in Aubrey's opinion, 'the protractique cause of his mine'. For the Royalists were faced with the problem that constantly paralysed their major strategy. A pincer movement by the 'remote armies' co-ordinated with a thrust down the Thames valley demanded that the forces in the west and north should be willing to advance out of their own regions on the capital; but this they were often unwilling to do, being much concerned with local conflicts and unwilling to leave their neighbourhoods. They were still more reluctant if Parliamentarian strongholds remained unsubdued behind them. Hence Charles's strategic decision, when he found that he could count neither on adequate co-ordinated attacks from west or the north to mop up Gloucester first rather than advance on London directly.

And here too the King's own humanity proved tactically disastrous: 'a fatal mistake'... for 'there was no opposition in readiness against him nor any place to stay him'.[392] Rupert demanded that Gloucester be taken at once, as it could have been, by storm; and pointed out that the ground was too marshy for digging mines; but Charles, shocked by the carnage at Bristol, vetoed the proposal; he preferred a siege — hardly ever successful with the artillery then available. When therefore in early September a fresh army of fifteen thousand men under Essex advanced across the Cotswolds from London to relieve Gloucester, the Royalists, now bogged down by heavy rains that made the mines useless, were forced to raise a siege that ought long ago to have been over.

There remained one chance: the second major Royalist opportunity of the war. And it was very nearly taken. Aiming to cut off Essex on his march back to London, Charles shadowed his army in its march through Swindon for the Kennet valley; and when at Albourne Chase, over downland perfect for cavalry, Rupert deflected them down to Hungerford, the Royalists just got to Newbury first, evicting the enemy quartermaster who was already in the town surveying billets. Although he was now so short of ammunition that Rupert correctly advised against giving battle until fresh supplies had come from Oxford, Charles had interposed his army between Essex and London: that night, after 'dinner in the field', he slept in Newbury confident of success — 'Supper and bed, Mr. Cox's.'[393]

The terrain of 'first Newbury' (20 September 1643) is easy to observe. To the south of the Kennet and the town there is a ridge, which extends westwards from the monument that commemorates Lord Falkland, the joint Secretary of State (who sought and found death in the battle[394]) to the extremity of Round Hill, so called not because it is separate from the ridge but because, from the fields north of and below it, it appears so. Though much of this ridge has been built over, Round Hill is still clear and very thick hedges and small fields surround and lead up to it. Had the Royalists occupied this tactically decisive point and brought up artillery, while holding Wash Common south of it, which they did, they could have enfiladed the Parliamentarian march along the valley from Enborne, south of the Kennet, and threatened their whole flank.

By singular incompetence they failed to secure it, though they occupied the rest of the ridge and the common. So, in the dawn, Essex with unwonted insight sent Skippon, his most capable senior officer, up through the thickset hedges and closes, still with their summer foliage, to seize Round Hill and place two 'drakes' firing casehot upon it. The battle opened with these light guns playing upon the Royalists. The gruelling day-long battle ended in exhaustion, neither side having given ground. Then the King, told that ammunition was running short, made a fatal decision. During the night he disengaged, though putting a garrison into Donnington Castle, north of the town, and then retreated through the September night over the downs to Oxford leaving Essex master of the field. But Prince Rupert next day beat the retreating Parliamentarians at the

'Heath's End three miles from Newbury' and had Charles decided to hold his ground until the morning and bluff it out next day, it is by no means certain that Essex would have persevered in the fight. Charles's decision was a strategic disaster: if Edgehill was the first lost chance, 'first Newbury' was the second.

That the Parliament had been able to launch an army of fifteen thousand men so rapidly to relieve Gloucester was due, like the effort at Turnham Green, to the Londoners' belated but vigorous response to immediate danger. During the summer the Parliamentarian prospects had looked increasingly black, and the prestige of Essex had fallen low. Waller, a more resilient and popular fighter, had managed to put the blame for Roundway Down on the Lord General, who, he maintained, had failed to draw off the Royalists by a renewed attack upon Oxford; and the republican extremist Henry Martin, whose morals were notoriously such that Charles had once exclaimed of him 'Let that Ugly Rascall be gonne out of the [Hyde] Park, that whore master, or els I will not see the sport'[395] — and so earned Martin's undying hatred — had begun a political intrigue to raise a volunteer army for Waller, independent of Essex's command.

In mid-August Sir Hamon L'Estrange's rising in King's Lynn could have threatened the Parliament's hold on East Anglia, had Newcastle, who had lost Gainsborough following a battle on 28 July (when Lord Charles Cavendish, 'a princely person', says Aubrey, who had travelled in Greece and the Levant and been a favourite courtier of the King, had been unhorsed, stunned and run through after being captured by one of Cromwell's officers[396]), disentangled himself from the siege of Hull and moved south-east. But early in October the King failed to follow up the Royalists' capture of Newport Pagnell from which they could have struck at the Parliamentarian communications with East Anglia ('the mistake about Newport Pagnall that spoiled all'). Newcastle was fully occupied at Hull, where a sortie by the defenders captured his two heaviest guns (known as Gog and Magog or 'The Queen's pocket pistols') and on 11 October Cromwell won the small but decisive cavalry action at Winceby in Lincolnshire, which put paid to any advance by Newcastle on London. Even so and counting the failure at Newbury the long-term prospect still seemed fairly favourable to the King.

In fact Pym's long-term strategic insight had already decided it. On 23 May 1643 he had made reconciliation more unthinkable for his followers by impeaching the Queen — who in law had no peers — an occasion on which his physical debility first became painfully obvious, for he was dying of what Clarendon terms *morbus pediculosus* — literally the 'lousy disease' — apparently a cancer of the lower intestine. For the second time on July 24 he got through the Commons the ordinance for the Excise, now extended to tobacco, beer and ale, which however unpopular would bring in a steady revenue,[397] and in early August an ordinance for compulsory impressment of men for the army, a measure to be fundamental for the raising of the big 'New Modell'd Army' in 1645 and for all its political consequences of sword government. Most important of all, through Pym's decision and the initiative of Sir Harry Vane, negotiation had been opened with the Scots.

The success of the King had greatly worried the Covenanters, further alarmed by Ormonde's success in coming to a truce — hopefully called by the Irish a 'cessation' — with the native Catholic Irish, so that his army might be transported to England to reinforce Newcastle's already dominant army in the north. For the Scots a Royalist victory would be a disaster, and since the two Bishops' Wars ideological ties, despite doctrinal bickering, had united them with the Parliamentarians. Further, that spring when Charles had received Chancellor Loudon as Commissioner from the Scots Council and Alexander Henderson as Commissioner from the Assembly of the Kirk in Oxford, he had treated them coldly and the Court cavaliers had insulted them. For the King had wanted to keep the Scots out of the war and at once cold-shouldered the Scots Commissioners and discouraged attempts at a Royalist rising in Scotland. Now with the growing power of the King's armies and the threat of an Irish army in mind, the Scots had been further alarmed by the defection of Montrose, who had broken with Argyll and Henderson and ridden south to the King's Court at Oxford.

Events had thus played Pym's game, and the initiative for the alliance that was to transform the Parliament's fortunes and win them the war came from the Scots. In reply to their proposals he had at once sent Sir Harry Vane to Edinburgh by sea. By 7 August, while the King was in Bristol, Vane and his colleagues were in Edinburgh, devising with the Scots the terms of a 'Solemn League and Covenant', and this curious religious document was now imposed both on Scotland and on all England under Parliament's control.

> We, noblemen [it ran], Barons, Knights, Gentlemen, City Burgesses and ministers of the gospel and commoners of all sorts in the Kingdoms of England, Scotland and Ireland, by the Providence of God being of one Reformed Religion... calling to mind treacherous bloody plots, conspiracies against true religion, after mature deliberation resolved and determined... [pledged themselves, their estates and their lives] 'to extirpate Popery, Prelacy superstition and

prophaneness,' and to proclaim their own repentence for their sins.[398]

The Scots, of course, naturally demanded their expenses for the good work. In October a Parliamentary committee was raising £40,000 'for the speedy bringing in of our brethren of Scotland into this realm for our assistance in this great war', and in November they sent forty chests of silver by sea — on account of £200,000 promised. Money was borrowed right and left, in a hand-to-mouth operation— £3,000 for example, in pieces of eight at 4s 4d each to be repaid in four or six weeks. In the spring of 1644 another instalment of £30,000 was paid out of the revenues of sequestered Royalist estates, which was as well, for the Scots were getting 8 per cent on the balance unpaid.

Thus on 25 September, five days after 'first Newbury' when the Covenant was taken at Westminster, a new and preponderant force had entered the war. Scots zeal for religion and depredation had combined with the superior financial resources that the Parliament had mobilized to change the balance of potential military power. Pym had achieved his objective and finished any hope of compromise just in time. As Ranke puts it 'He had adopted the alliance

> ... as a great political necessity, and held to it firmly, although the English revolution was thus led far beyond its original aim. His views were directed not to the restoration of the equilibrium between the Crown and Parliament, but to the establishment of the completed preponderance of the Parliamentary power, and this implied the subjection of the spiritual element also... On his connection with London he based his audacious resolve to deprive royalty, in which the power of the conqueror was perpetuated, of the arms which constituted its splendour and greatness. In order to obtain

power to bring in to the field for the purpose a popular army... he adopted the decisive means of taxing the necessities of life: for he was a financier by profession, and was the first to bring excise to England'.[399]

It followed that

Already [as Hexter writes] by August 1643, Pym's great constructive work was done... The clash of arms at Marston Moor and Naseby, the thundering hoofbeats of the Ironside regiments, the clamorous prayer to the Lord of Hosts rising from the ranks of the New Model Army on the eve of battle, all drowned out one quiet little truth: the fact that the triumph of Parliament over the King, as distinguished from the manner and *élan* of it, owed less to Oliver Cromwell than to a pudgy little man whose last year was spent amid tidings of disaster at Westminster and whose body lay at rest in the Abbey long before Parliament plucked the first fruits of victory.[400]

On 8 December Pym died, when, as Heath puts it, 'the kingdom was in a flame which he had chiefly blown up, nor likely to be extinguished'.[401] After his body had been publicly exposed to refute his enemies' allegation that he had been devoured by lice, or like Herod, by worms, on 14 December he was 'buried with great ceremony: his body carried by six of the Lower House and four of the Lords. He is interred among the old Kings of England. The Scots,' added the Italian observer, 'are still in their own country, waiting for spring and more money.'

17: THE SCOTS INTERVENE

THE SCOTS, NOW, in Digby's phrase 'the predominant evil' for the Royalists, did not in the event wait so long. On 19 January 1644 they crossed the Tweed to link up with Manchester and the Fairfaxes. The momentum of the war had increased: in that bitter winter neither side went to ground, and in London a Committee of Both Kingdoms (of seven peers, fourteen commoners and four Scots) was formed to coordinate strategy. Parliament now levied regular taxation in the King's name and used it to destroy him, while on 2 February they ordered all men over eighteen to take the Covenant, a decision enforced by the local Parliamentarian committees.

Ministers of religion had to 'read it distinctly and clearly in the pulpit, and during the reading thereof the whole congregation to be uncovered, and at the end of his reading thereof all to take it standing, lifting up their right hands bare, and then afterwards to subscribe it severally by writing their names (or their marks, to which their names were to be added) in a parchment roll or a book, wherein the Covenant was to be inserted, purposely provided for that end, and kept as a record in the parish'.[402] If taken seriously, the Covenant was a radical commitment; utterly to abolish the whole Anglican hierarchy and, save for an ambiguous escape clause 'according to the Word of God and the example of the best reformed Churches', to impose on England the complex and authoritarian hierarchy of the Presbyterian Kirk. Moreover the Parliament's order was accompanied by officially sponsored iconoclasm in the churches, when fine sculptures were now more systematically defaced, elaborate and splendid windows smashed, rood lofts, screens and roofs destroyed. A greater fanaticism had come into the war, following the Parliament's alliance with their brethren of Scotland.

Charles again wintered in Oxford, much concerned with raising any help he could get from abroad. In October 1643 the King's representatives had done a massive deal with a Captain van Haesdonck, who had ten ships in the trade, to deliver 4,000 muskets with bandoliers at 24s each, 1,200 pairs of pistols with holsters and spanners at 56s a pair, 600 carbines with bolts and swivels, 20 tons of match and 400 barrels of powder, all at Weymouth and had paid him £14,000.[403] In a private way, in November, Rupert had agreed that van Haesdonck should raise two hundred foreign soldiers, to be brigaded with the same number of Englishmen. Both were to be paid at the usual English rates to which were added all booty and ransom money, half to be assigned to those who actually took it, the commanders getting a double share. The Prince was to have a quarter of all takings, at 5s in the £1; van Haesdonck at 2s 6d and the sergeant major at 1s. For Rupert war was, among other things, a business. The foreign troops were to be brought over to Weymouth, where a fast mail service to Cherbourg was now being organized with better relays of horses to connect it with Oxford.

In the fields of high diplomacy the King again indicated that he hoped the Prince of Wales might marry the daughter of the Prince of Orange and he also sounded out the French and the Portuguese. But the Dutch would still not commit themselves; the French, following Richelieu's death in December 1642 now ruled by Mazarin, were wary of making enemies of the Parliament; and Charles's uncle, the martial Christian IV of Denmark, needed all the ships he had for a war with the Swedes. And over Ireland the King, no more than anyone else, could not put a foot right. If he accepted the support of the native confederate Catholic Irish, he alienated the loyal Anglo-Irish Protestants, and when Irish Protestant troops came over through Chester the fury of the local English against any Irish was indiscriminate. Charles had now made Montrose, still in Oxford, Lieutenant General of any Royalist forces that might be raised in Scotland, but his prospects there seemed dim.

On the main front the King took a personally distasteful decision when he summoned what he later termed a 'mongrel' Parliament to Oxford. Thirty Royalist peers and over a hundred Members of the Commons attended: Oxford was under deep snow and they assembled in the great Hall of Christ Church, the log fires blazing, the light, reflected from the snow, pale through the high windows. In Royalist eyes the clique at Westminster or 'perpetual parliament' had betrayed England to the Scots; but Charles proclaimed a pardon for all members who came in to Oxford — 'that all the world may see how willing and desirous we are to forget the injuries and indignities offered to us, and by a union of English hearts to prevent the lasting miseries which foreign invasion must bring upon this Kingdom'. Constitutionally, since it included the King, the Oxford Parliament could claim to supersede the one at Westminster; they voted that the Scots incursion had been a *de facto* declaration of war, so that anyone who supported it was a traitor; they also, imitating Pym, voted an excise — easier to vote than to collect. But by 16 April 1644, in the face of a military threat to Oxford and a food shortage, Charles prorogued them.

He also tried a gambit he would use again in a more dangerous context — playing off the Independent sectaries against the intolerant Presbyterians; both, by Anglican standards, equally in error. The Independent Dr Philip Nye, for example, preaching to the Lords and Commons at Westminster on the day the Covenant had been taken, had argued that 'the word of God and the example of the best reformed Churches' did not imply accepting the Presbyterian Kirk. So Charles, as part of a complicated intrigue, offered to make him one of his chaplains, though Nye had peculiar ideas about ritual, holding that the preacher should keep his hat on while the congregation sat bareheaded, but that at communion they should each do the opposite. This stalking horse never started, but the idea of an alliance with the Independents in return for toleration remained in the King's mind.

The Queen was now expecting her eighth child, but by the spring Essex's army was again advancing on Oxford, and the city had become too dangerous for her confinement. So on 17 April Charles and the two princes escorted her to Abingdon on her way to Bath and Exeter. After an agonizing parting she wrote, 'Farewell my dear Heart, I cannot write more than that I am absolutely yours', and Charles wrote urgently to Sir Theodore Mayerne in London, 'Mayerne, for the love of God go to my wife.'[404] The famous physician was allowed to travel by coach to Exeter, and to the Queen's remark, 'Mayerne, I'm afraid I shall go mad some day', is said to have replied, 'Your Majesty need not fear going mad, you have been so for some time'; but he attended her to good effect. On 16 June Princess Henriette, afterwards Duchess of Orleans, was born, and soon the King could write, 'I must again rejoice with thee in thy happy delivery. As to the christening of my younger, and, as they say, my prettiest daughter, I heartily thank thee that, being so far, thou wouldst stay for my direction.' She should be baptized, he directed, by Anglican rites in Exeter Cathedral.

But Essex's army was now close to the city and the Queen asked him to allow her to take the waters at Bath; whereat he impolitely replied 'that it was his intention to escort Her Majesty to London, where her presence was required to answer to the Parliament for having levied war on England'. So, only a fortnight after her daughter's birth, the Queen left Exeter in disguise, with only two attendants and her confessor, and after hiding in a hut under 'litter' while Parliamentarian soldiers plodded past, on 29 June she reached Pendennis Castle at Falmouth. Here she at once went aboard a Dutch boat, and Warwick's blockading squadron being dispersed off Torbay, Salcombe and Dartmouth, she got to sea. A Parliamentarian warship then gave chase and fired on her, whereupon the Queen commanded the captain to blow up his ship rather than be taken. But French vessels intervened and the English sheered off; then the ship ran before a heavy storm round the dangerous Breton coast to Chastel, a cove near Brest, where the Queen and her following clambered over the rocks and took refuge in some fishermen's huts. Alerted of the visitor, the Breton gentry soon arrived, and the Queen was eventually rehabilitated and given apartments in the Louvre and a house at St German-en-Laye. She was thought much changed — shrunk to a shadow, though her eyes were as brilliant as ever; her wit and vivacity, and her bad political judgement, unimpaired. Charles would never see her again.

The year 1644 had not begun well for the King. In spite of the disaster at Roundway Down, Waller remained a hero to the London populace, and Parliament had put him in command of troops raised in Kent, Sussex, Surrey and Hampshire. In a brisk winter campaign he had taken Alton and Arundel Castle, and on 29 March had defeated the Earl of Forth, still the senior Royalist commander, at Cheriton, east of Winchester. Though his London troops as usual demanded to go home,

Waller had poised a threat to Oxford itself.

The King had to look to his defences, and on 9 April he himself rode out of Oxford and next day inspected nine thousand troops in the beautiful arena of Aldbourne Chase, spent the night at the Seymours' mansion at Marlborough and returned next day by Wantage to Oxford. He had to muster an adequate field army, yet keep the towns guarding Oxford garrisoned; so, to set men free for a mobile force, Reading and even Abingdon were abandoned.

Essex, working in collaboration with Waller, was already at Henley and at once occupied Reading; he then advanced as far as Islip, and by 1 June Waller was in Abingdon. Oxford was in jeopardy; the King himself might be captured. So saying he 'would be dead first', Charles with a substantial force escaped between the two armies over Port Meadow to Burford, and thence to Worcester.

Essex then played into his hands. After a meeting with Waller (whom he detested) at Chipping Norton in the Cotswolds, he sent Waller 'a King-chasing' and he insisted on dividing their armies; Essex himself moving down to the south-west to relieve Lyme Regis and Plymouth and threaten Exeter. By a complex manoeuvre Charles managed to double back across to Buckingham, then turned to face Waller near Banbury. On 29 June, the day of the Queen's escape from Falmouth, at Cropredy Bridge over the Cherwell, with Charles himself in command, the Royalists routed Waller's army, taking eleven guns and several colours. Waller in his own words had been 'extremely plagued by the mutinies of the City Brigade, who are grown to that height of disorder that I have no helpe to retain them, being come to their old song of "home! home!"'[405] Oxford had been saved.

Having dealt with Waller, Charles now determined to save Exeter and followed up Essex at once. By 15 July he was in Bath; by the twenty-sixth in Exeter itself — though too late to rejoin the Queen. But before he had turned west he had received dire news: on 2 July the admired Rupert and the trusted Newcastle had been totally defeated at Marston Moor outside York by a Scots-Parliamentarian army. All England north of the Humber was now in effect lost to the King; and in spite of his own personal victories in the west and the subsequent exploits of Montrose in Scotland, it was a blow from which the Royalists never recovered.

In the spring of 1644 Rupert had cut right across the Midlands to take Newark-on-Trent, commanding the routes from London to the north and from the north into East Anglia. But by April the weight of the Scots advance had begun to tell, and Newcastle had shut himself up, besieged in York against massive allied assaults. So early in May Rupert had begun a swift campaign to relieve him; starting from Shrewsbury he had swept up to Lancashire, taken Stockport, sacked Puritan Bolton, taken Liverpool and Preston. By mid-June, with 1,400 men, he was marching on York over the Pennines, and by 30 June, the day after Cropredy Bridge, he was at Knaresborough, only fourteen miles west of the city. Leven, Fairfax and Manchester were forced to raise the siege and draw out towards him across the Ouse on to Long Marston Moor, commanding the Knaresborough road. But Rupert outmanoeuvred them and relieved York from the north, and with 'York siege raised and their boat bridge gained over the Ouse',[406] the defenders joined in plundering the besiegers' camp. By a characteristically swift campaign Rupert had obtained his main objective.

But now, in part through his uncle's commands, in part through Newcastle's, he overreached himself. On 14 June, after his narrow escape from Oxford, hunted about in Worcestershire by Waller and not yet aware that Essex was moving off, Charles had written an unwontedly emotional letter to his nephew:

> But by now I must give you the true state of my affairs which… is such as enforces me to give you more peremptory commands than I would willingly do. If York be lost, I shall esteem my crown little less [lost]; unless supported by your sudden march to me; and a miraculous conquest of the south before the effects of their northern power be felt here. But if York be relieved, and you beat the rebel army of both kingdoms, which are before it; then [but not otherwise] I may possibly make a shift [upon the defensive] to spin out time until you come to assist me. Whereupon I command and conjure you, by the duty and affection which I know you bear me, that all new enterprises laid aside, you immediately march according to your first intention with all your forces to the relief of York.

Eager enough by temperament to attack, Rupert had accepted this instruction, not only to relieve York but to beat the rebel army of both kingdoms, as a command. He might well have succeeded had he kept up the momentum of his campaign, but Newcastle and his methodical Scots second-in-command, James King, Lord Eythin (a veteran of the battle of Lemgo where Rupert's rashness had led to defeat and capture) were slow to move. Exhausted by the siege and jealous of his own dignity, Newcastle had resented coming under Rupert's orders, though in a letter of courtly flattery he had given the Prince the opposite impression, concluding, 'I am made of nothing but thankfulness and obedience to your Highness's commands.'

When therefore Rupert, who had not had time even to enter York, turned back south-west in the dawn of 2 July and advanced on the enemy, now moving off towards Tadcaster, Newcastle and his men had not appeared. Newcastle was against fighting that day at all and did not himself arrive until nine o'clock, and his troops not until much later. Rupert thus lost the initiative and the chance to attack while the enemy was on the move or reforming, and the allies now turned to give battle — twenty-eight thousand and thirty or forty guns against Rupert's seventeen or eighteen thousand, and much inferior artillery.

Facing north, the Scots Parliamentarians, who were superior in cavalry, also had the advantage of position — as Sir Thomas Fairfax wrote of Marston 'Fields', part of the larger Hesson Moor: 'The enemy was drawn up in a battallia on the moor a little below us.' Cromwell was on the left; Sir Thomas Fairfax on the right, flanking the Scots and English infantry.

As the July day of rain and sunshine wore on, it seemed that there would be no immediate action. But in fact, though it was now late afternoon, the experienced Scots commander Leven had resolved to attack, for the Royalists had committed the same error that Harold had at Hastings: to stand, with an inferior force, immobile and within striking distance of a superior and dynamic enemy. For no sooner had Rupert dismounted for supper and Newcastle retired to his coach, at about seven o'clock, in a heavy rain storm, than the allied centre moved rapidly down into the attack. The brief battle was hotly contested: 'Our right wing,' recorded Fairfax, 'failed because of the furzes and ditches we had to pass over'; once the Royalist cavalry cut through the allied centre and Fairfax himself was cut off — 'so taking the signal out of my hat I past through them, as one of their own commanders, and got to my Lord of Manchester's horse,... only with a cut on my cheek'.[407]

Thinking all lost, Leven and Lord Fairfax, Sir Thomas's father, both fled the field. But Cromwell's East Anglian Ironsides, intact on the left, now charged the unprotected Royalist flank and turned defeat into victory. The Yorkshire Whitecoats, in the tradition of their Anglo-Danish ancestors, fell nearly to a man in a 'ring' as they stood. Newcastle in humiliation and disgust retired to York, then took ship for Hamburg. Rupert, who had escaped through a beanfield, rallied substantial remnants of his army and made off to Richmond, then over the Pennines to Chester.[408] Under the July full moon, according to Fairfax, four thousand Royalist dead lay upon the field. Cromwell, writing to his brother-in-law Colonel Walton, announced victory and bereavement:

> Truly England, and the Church of God hath had a great favour from the Lord in the great victorie given unto us, such as the like never was since the War begunn... we never charged but wee routed the enimie... God made them as stubble to our swords. Sir, God hath taken away your eldest son by a cannon shott. It brake his legge wee were necessitated to have itt cutt off whereof hee died.

Such was the first result of the Scots-Parliamentarian alliance and it was decisive.

But away in Cornwall, the King was still to win his own personal victory. After parting from Waller at Chipping Norton, Essex had been instructed to mop up the entire west, but at Blandford in Dorset his instructions had been countermanded. On 14 July he had written to the Committee of Both Kingdoms protesting at their amateur interference.

> In yours of 30th you desire me to send such a force to the West as might be able not only to restore Lyme Regis but to recover the whole of the West again. I therefore resolved to march away with my whole army westward, a strength little enough in my judgement to effect what you desire. Now you direct me to make a stand and send only a considerable body of horse to the relief of Lyme Regis — a town of narrow passages which could not possibly be relieved by cavalry.

His foot, he continued, were now 'quite disheartened', though if some long-expected pay came down with the ammunition we do not despair of deserving it'.[409]

Essex had proceeded to Dorchester and on 24 June the Royalists in Weymouth 'condescended to yield upon quarter' and with leave for the officers to march out with their horses and swords, the common soldiers with sticks and with no tax imposed for delinquency. But in Wareham the Royalists had counter-attacked — marched very far into the country both with horse and foot, till the Governor of Weymouth 'fell upon them at the turn pike of Dorchester and killed and captured about 1,500 of them and marched on Wareham'.[410] Soon, with the help of Warwick and his ships, Lyme had been relieved, and by mid-July even £20,000 of pay had arrived. Then, having failed to catch the Queen in Exeter, Essex had moved further west to Tavistock and relieved Plymouth, reckoning that Waller in the Midlands would have contained the King. But he had miscalculated, Charles was after him and on the twenty-sixth, the day when Charles, coming from Bath by Ilchester and Chard, entered Exeter, he rashly moved into Cornwall, rather than turn and fight, intent on capturing the tin mines and underestimating the Cornish detestation of foreigners. Charles had him trapped.

Ironically, after the turning-point in the war had in fact come at Marston Moor, the King now personally conducted his ablest campaign. With Essex at Bodmin, Charles with sixteen thousand men advanced rapidly by Crediton and, skirting Dartmoor by Okehampton, came down to Launceston on 2 August, threatening Essex across Bodmin Moor. Whereat Essex, anxious to regain contact with Warwick's warships, turned into the well-wooded country of southern Cornwall by the Fowey valley to Lostwithiel and secured the port of Fowey. Charles stayed six nights at Liskeard, regrouped his army, personally sacked the insubordinate and now treasonous Wilmot, and put Lord Goring in charge of the cavalry and Hopton in charge of the artillery. He then advanced on Lostwithiel and made his headquarters at Boconnock on high ground four miles east of it. There with a wary professional skill he slowly closed the trap on the Parliamentarian army.

Gradually the outposts of resistance and the higher ground were captured and the troops widely enough dispersed to impose a sufficient blockade. By 30 August 1644 Essex's position was untenable: he had to break out. That night his cavalry under Sir William Balfour, who had saved the day at Edgehill, managed to escape; but the foot and the guns, attempting to get to Fowey in heavy rain, were bogged down. The Royalists occupied Lostwithiel, and Charles himself, with his Lifeguards, pursued the enemy through the steep south Cornish fields and luxuriant hedges. That day on horseback, in a lull in the battle, he knighted Sir Edward Brett for gallantry, and that night in gusty Atlantic weather, which prevented the Parliamentarian ships making Fowey, 'his Majestie lay in the field, his meat dressed by Mr. Hixts' and slept under a hedge. And that night, also, Essex was rowed out from Fowey to one of Warwick's ships and was soon on his way to Plymouth: no more than the other grandee, Newcastle, could he face the degradation of formal surrender — and indeed as a proclaimed traitor he may have been wise to make off.

The day of 1 September 1644 dawned relatively calm. Skippon, one of the abler Parliamentarian generals, wanted to fight; but, overruled, he asked for a parley; six thousand men surrendered, marching out 'pressed all in a heap like sheep though not so innocent'.[411] The Royalists captured forty guns, quantities of ammunition, stacks of weapons. And the victory had been due to the King himself: 'He had been generalissimo in practice as well as in name — From his headquarters at Boconnock he controlled the whole wide-flung front... the more deeply one examines this little studied campaign the clearer stands out the firm grip on the situation that Charles had possessed. In short the campaign of Lostwithiel was a triumph for the King and the most striking success obtained by the royalists in the whole of the war.'[412] But Charles was too great a gentleman to gain the full advantages of victory. For 'here his Majesty's clemency was most eminent: when having all the infantry at his mercy, he not only pardoned the soldiers in general, but admitted the chief officers to kiss his hand; only refused that favour to Major General Skippon, as being too great an enemy to his majesty's honour and safety'.[413] Many of these pardoned, officers and soldiers, whose trade had become war, reorganized under the Parliamentarian colours and fought that October at second Newbury.

By 10 September the news of Essex's disaster had reached Waller who was now at Salisbury. He was trying, generally in vain, to solve the perennial problems of raising horses. 'The ordinance for raising horses,' he wrote, 'will not prevail in this country. One of us is going to Poole to encourage the sea towns, then to Blandford to endeavour the gathering of the Dorset and Wiltshire horse into a body.' He demanded £5,000 and moved west to Shaftesbury. That autumn Secretary Nicholas's father wrote from Wiltshire: 'I have been plundered of all my horses by special warrant from the Chief Commander of the Parliament forces.' He had also been 'set back by £500 his property with continual payments and billeting of soldiers and such like', so that his house had been 'in worse case than an Inne'.

In spite of his victory the King too was still living from hand to mouth. In the previous winter he had been reduced to a scheme for paying his troops only a quarter in money and the rest in kind. Once a year they would have a new suit and a long cloak, a new montero hat with steel cap, and a new saddle and bridle, a pair of boots and stockings — with more boots and stockings thrown in every four months — and sufficient keep for a man and horse. This scheme, if it was ever tried, would hardly have been popular.

Meanwhile, the Scots still occupied the north and the Parliament dominated East Anglia, most of the home counties and the east Midlands, but in late August, having raised what troops he could around Shrewsbury and from Wales, Rupert had returned to Bristol, the greatest Royalist stronghold and economic asset in the west; but Parliamentarian Plymouth had not yet been reduced and Prince Maurice had to be left to contain it. Charles however was determined to relieve the Royalist garrison at Basing House, and full of confidence, he moved east through the autumn countryside. At the end of September he halted for a week at Honiton; by 1 October he was at Maiden Newton in Dorset, then he moved on to Digby's mansion at Sherborne and to Sturminster Newton. On 10 October, with the trees in autumnal splendour, he stayed four days at Bryanston, on the Stour, then proceeded to Lord Salisbury's manor at Cranborne, whence he occupied Salisbury and remained there three days.

Waller had hastily withdrawn to Andover, but the King's cavalry under Goring, making for Basing House, caught and beat him out of it. Essex meanwhile had reorganized 'the same bands that his Majesty had disarmed and shown mercy to at Lostwithiel' (many transferred back to Southampton and Portsmouth) and Manchester had moved down from Reading; reinforced by Skippon's cavalry, they soon made the relief of Basing impracticable. So Charles turned north to Newbury to the Royalist strongholds, Donnington Castle and Shaw House, both north of the Kennet and commanding the London Road. In contrast to the position before first Newbury the Parliamentarians at second Newbury were now east of the town at Thatcham; yet though Charles now had only nine thousand men on 26 October 1644 he was tactically better placed. But as luck would have it for him Essex was ill, of flux and vomiting, and out of action at Reading, and although Manchester was notoriously indecisive, Waller, Cromwell and Skippon — a formidable trio — forced a bold move. On Sunday, October 27 they made an encircling march north with their main strength through the open country round Chieveley, then down to Boxford, where, crossing the Lambourn, they 'fell with horse and foot' on the Royalist rear at Speen, while Manchester from the East made a feint attack on Shaw House. They failed to close the trap, for Manchester did not synchronize his later and main attack, but the Parliamentarians held the field. Charles himself, leaving his stores and artillery at Donnington, escaped through a narrow gap, and riding all night and most of Monday for fifty miles, met Rupert at Bath, while his army retreated by Wallingford to Oxford intact.

At first Newbury the Royalists had missed a big chance; at second Newbury their enemies missed another. By the thirtieth the indefatigable King was off again with Rupert and three thousand horse by Cirencester and Oxford to reinforce his army. Then on Monday, 6 November, he held a great rendezvous and dinner at Bullingdon; and that night, with festive acclamation, Rupert was declared lieutenant general under the King and — nominally — under the Prince of Wales; old Lord Forth and Brentford, wounded at Newbury and past active command, being superseded. Then marching out by East Ilsley over the downs the enlarged Royalist army descended on Donnington, retrieved its guns and invited attack — a provocation declined. So they made off to Lambourn and Marlborough whence, after eight nights, Charles moved over to the Bear at Hungerford to mask another succouring of Basing House, in fact now relieved. So, with his outpost fortresses secured, the King returned to Oxford for the winter by Wantage and Faringdon.

Though the intervention of the Scots and the loss of the north had in fact been irretrievable, his campaign of 1644 in the south had been pretty successful and the one in which he had himself done most. After two years of campaigning the royal aesthete had shown his mettle, and a horsy leathery life in all weathers probably proved more congenial to one who had always loved field sports than the tedious days of political intrigue, gossip and argument among his own courtiers in Oxford, or than the boring delegations from Westminster, much though Charles, as a Scot, enjoyed an argument.

It was just the King's comparative success that at last forced the Parliament to reform their armies. On the day that Charles returned to Oxford the Committee of Both Kingdoms began to consider how to do so. Hitherto commanded, as by a kind of natural right, by half-hearted aristocrats such as Essex and Manchester — increasingly concerned at the continuing war and anxious to come to terms with the King — the armies had been raised, under the general but ineffective command of Essex, in a piecemeal and local manner. When sufficiently frightened, the Londoners had decisively intervened, and from the Eastern Association in East Anglia Cromwell had personally raised the Ironsides, who, imbued with their leader's own fanaticism and well disciplined, had won the greatest reputation.

A new professionalism was emerging: but it was not yet organized. As Waller pointed out, to finish the war the Parliament needed a large, regularly paid standing army, under tried professional command, and, unlike locally raised forces, ready to go anywhere, storm the regional centres of resistance that kept the war going, seek out the enemy and destroy him. In collaboration with the Scots such an army would be overwhelming: indeed the war had not ended that year only through the ill co-ordination of the Parliament's armies. Hence in the January of 1645 the Parliament resolved to create a big 'new Modell'd Army' of twenty-two thousand men and they accepted the political manoeuvre of a 'Self-Denying Ordinance' whereby no member of the Parliament was to hold command — a polite way of getting rid of Manchester and Essex — thus clearing the way for the steady and popular Sir Thomas Fairfax and, by means of commands of limited duration, for his dynamic cavalry commander — Oliver Cromwell.

18: THE DEFEAT OF THE ROYALISTS

AT THE BEGINNING of 1645, a year of the war that proved disastrous to him, Charles held unshaken to his original position. 'The settling of religion and the militia,' he wrote to the Queen of negotiations with the Parliament, 'are first to be treated on; and be confident, that I will neither quit episcopacy nor the sword which God hath given into my hands.'[414] Although his military position had worsened, his political prospects seemed better, while the exploits of Montrose in Scotland over the winter had opened new prospects for the summer campaign. Apart from the natural friction between the Scots and English Presbyterians, a deeper rift was now opening among the King's adversaries. Where both wished to maintain a hierarchy and a monarchy, most of the more radical Independent sectaries, of whom Cromwell was the most forceful and cunning both as soldier and politician, wanted not, of course, democratic majority government, but toleration of a fairly broad range of religious belief, and rule by 'Saints' whose success in battle signified that they were a predestinate elect of God by His free Grace.

Such claims threatened any religious hierarchy, Presbyterian as much as Anglican, and the Scots understood this: 'You ken very well,' wrote one of them after second Newbury, 'that Lt. General Cromwell is no friend of ours and no well-wilier to his Excellence [Essex]', but rather a potential incendiary between the two nations; they should examine 'whilke way wud be best to take to proceed against him... and that will clepe his wings.' Though at the crunch, when the real army radicals attacked property and military discipline, Cromwell rounded on them, put them down and emerged as a military saviour of a shaken but basically intact establishment; new men of obscure origins were coming up in the army under his wing, and republican ideas, neo-classical and sectarian, were getting about. That continental realist Cardinal Mazarin, watching 'the English tumults', wanted to retain an adapted monarchy and prevent the British Isles going the way of the Dutch. So his envoys now pressed Charles to conciliate the Scots, who were at least not republican, and no less but not much more heretical to a Catholic than the Anglicans. Two themes thus dominate the first half of the year 1645: Charles's attempt to link up with Montrose, his failure to do so and his final irretrievable defeat on 14 June at the fatal battle of Naseby, 'wherein the King and his partie were in a woeful manner worsted',[415] and the halfhearted attempt to come to terms with his Scottish subjects, continuing until he went over to them at Southwell in Northamptonshire on 5 May 1646 and lost his liberty.

After the English Parliament at Westminster had taken the Covenant in a close religious and political alliance with the Scots, they stepped up religious persecution by way of showing good will. And who more conveniently placed as their victim than Archbishop Laud? In the autumn of 1644 they had set about impeaching him. Charles had been deeply concerned: although Laud was a subject, he had become the King's close confidant after the death of Buckingham; in spite of his plebeian bustle and irascibility, a 'father in God'. Now shut up for years in the Tower, he had been cumulatively persecuted. He had early rejected the chance to escape, though the amiable and eminent Grotius, who had himself in his day escaped from captivity and in the guise of a mixed cargo of washing and Arminian theology, suitably ventilated, had urged him through his protégé Edward Pocock, the scholar in Arabic, to do so as well. But Laud had replied that he was almost seventy, and why should he 'go about to prolong a miserable life by the trouble and shame of flying'? And where, he had asked, could he go? If he went to a Catholic country, his alleged Popery would be confirmed; if to Holland, he would be 'baited' by Anabaptists.

Gradually numerous enemies had closed in; he had early resigned from the Chancellorship of Oxford University, which had replied 'as long as the arts are studied and letters are both honoured and honourable, your Chancellorship will always be felt by the present and remembered by the future generations'.[416] Now his library was confiscated and sold and he had to petition the House of Lords for maintenance since all his income had been sequestered. But he clung to the remnants of his jurisdiction, and in May 1643 the egregious Prynne, now chairman of the committee for his prosecution, had searched his room with ten musketeers and confiscated his papers, and what was worse, his intimate diary. Through that year and the next the heavy-footed processes of the law had dragged on.[417] It was impossible to prove treason, so the lawyers argued that enough accumulated misdemeanours amounted to it; whereat one of Laud's counsel replied, 1 never understood before this time that two hundred couple of black rabbits would make a black horse.'

But by now Marston Moor had been fought; the Scots were even more important and Prynne's culminating revenge proved deadly: he edited, distorted and published Laud's diary, and had copies of it distributed to the few peers trying the impeachment. In the autumn of 1644 the preachers had roused the mob to demand the Archbishop's execution, and in January 1645 the Lords, in fear of violence, admitted that though he was not guilty of treason, he could be convicted by an ordinance of Parliament. A pardon from the King was of course brushed aside, and so vindictive were the Commons that they rejected Laud's petition to be spared the obscene agony of being hanged, drawn and quartered. But on 10 January he was, in fact, accorded a relatively clean death, beheaded at one stroke on Tower Hill.

At Oxford Charles had long expected the event: it was none the less sinister, another ugly portent[418] that further hardened his determination not to take the pending treaty of Uxbridge with the Parliament as anything but a way to spin out time.

For Charles had been encouraged to think that time was on his side by news from Scotland. In the often ill-conducted and clumsy campaigns of the Civil War, the military genius of James Graham, Marquis of Montrose, flashes like a blazing and ephemeral comet in the superb setting of the Scottish Highlands. Initially discouraged by the King, in February 1644 he had been appointed lieutenant general in Scotland; and that August, in disguise, he had returned to his country and begun a brilliant campaign. For in July about eleven hundred Catholic Irish (an instalment of a Royalist army of ten thousand promised by the Earl of Antrim) led by Alaster McColl Keitach — known to the English, more compendiously, as Alexander MacDonald — had landed on the grand peninsula of Ardnamurchan on the west coast. Like their leader, many had brought over their women and children, and they were hereditary enemies of the Campbells of Argyll. Montrose, then at Carlisle and unable after Marston Moor to obtain help from Rupert, had therefore at once re-entered Scotland disguised as a groom, and in the nick of time joined the Irish, who had advanced rapidly to Blair Atholl in the central Highlands, where the river Garry runs south-east to the pass of Killiecrankie and to Pitlochry. Here he had met and won over the Scots clansmen sent to attack the invaders, and raised the royal standard over the combined force. He had then advanced past Scone on Perth, the strategic key to the south, and although his Covenanting opponents had fought with the slogan 'Jesus and no quarter', he had routed them at Tippermuir and captured the important city.

The Royalists in Scotland had again taken heart, and Montrose in a lightning campaign had now swept down to Dundee on the Firth of Tay, then up to Aberdeen, which the Irish and the Highlanders with great enjoyment had taken and sacked. Unable to garrison it, Montrose had turned to guerrilla tactics, disappearing into the central Highlands and, drawing his pursuers after him, exhausting them until the winter and the northern darkness closed in. The prospect of victory and plunder had now roused other Royalist clans, and many Scots MacDonalds had joined Montrose, eager to attack their hereditary enemies. So that dark December of 1644 Montrose made west for Loch Awe, south of Ben Cruachan and east of Oban, and struck south to Inverary, the heart of the Campbell power. While Charles had been fighting second Newbury and its aftermath and playing for time from Oxford, Montrose had proved himself a guerrilla leader of a winter war who could have held his own in the Balkans or Afghanistan.

By January 1645 he was making north-west to the fastnesses of Loch-aber with more of the clans coming in — Stuarts of Appin, MacDonalds of Glencoe, Keppochs, Camerons, McCleans; then, in deep snow, he turned on Argyll himself, and attacking at dawn destroyed his army at Inverlochy, at the head of Loch Linnhe near modern Fort William, while Argyll made off in his galley down the loch.

Well might Montrose write to the King, now spinning out the negotiations at Uxbridge:

> Forgive me, sacred sovereign, to tell your majesty that in my poor opinion it is unworthy of a King to treat with rebel subjects while they have a sword in their hands... Through God's blessing I am in the fairest hopes of reducing this Kingdom to your Majesty's obedience, and, if the measures I have concerted with your other subjects fail me not... I doubt not before the end of the summer I shall be able to come to your majesty's assistance with a brave army.[419]

Gathering further support from Grants, Seaforths and Mackenzies, Montrose now marched up the Great Glen to Morayshire, then in April, descending again by Pitlochry and Dunkeld, raided Dundee and again escaped into the hills. Then at the end of June, at Alford in Aberdeen, he defeated another Covenanting army, and striking south in mid-August, routed another at Kilsyth between Glasgow and Falkirk. Montrose had briefly won Scotland for the King: on 18 August 1645 he entered Glasgow, and as lieutenant governor of the realm convened a new Parliament and knighted Alaster McColl Keitach.

Although Rupert, with a realistic appraisal of the overall military facts, now urged Charles to compromise, both Laud's tragedy and Montrose's success confirmed the King in rejecting the treaty of Uxbridge, saying that he 'disdained to reign, if it might be so named, the slave of Parliament with the sacrifice of his cause and his friends'. But since Marston Moor and the loss of the north the original strategy of a three-pronged attack on London had perforce changed to the more limited one of giving battle where best the King could. Newcastle and Shrewsbury had fallen, but the Royalists still controlled most of Wessex, Devon and Cornwall; they retained Bristol and could recruit in Wales. In Wiltshire, for example, although in December 1644 Ludlow had briefly captured Salisbury, fortified the Close and the belfry and raided the King's 'horse quarters' at Upavon, he had soon been driven out over Harnham bridge and up Harnham hill over the snow to Odstock, and escaped to Southampton.[420]

Meanwhile the New Model was being formed. Contrary to much popular myth, it was no volunteer army of 'saints': eight thousand men were conscripts and between February and June 1645 Parliament had issued five ordinances to press them, so that on 12 May the Venetian ambassador commented that 'the violence and force used by Parliament to compel men to serve in the war' was 'cooling off' the 'fervour of the common people'.[421] Conscripted through the county committees, the men were sometimes seized openly in the streets. But the City of London alone had raised £80,000 and the new army would reach its target of twenty-two thousand men. Though the Cavaliers called it the 'new raw army' it was not rooted in any one region and could be ordered anywhere; above all it had a more professional command, capable of more clear-cut initiative.

For Charles, Montrose's campaign and the friction between the Scots, the Parliament and the Independents, made the Scots army in northern England a promising, if rather distant, target for attack. On 5 March he sent the Prince of Wales, who was now fourteen and whom he never saw again, to hold a separate Court at Bristol. This was the boy's first independent if nominal command, and his satisfaction is evident in the portrait painted of him that year.

Although in April Cromwell, advancing on Oxford, tried to cut the Royalist communications with the Cotswolds and the Severn valley and took Islip, the garrison at Faringdon defied him, and he drew off to Newbury to concert plans with Fairfax for an attack on the west, the remaining reservoir of Royalist power. In May 1645 Charles could thus hold a grand rendezvous at Stow-on-the-Wold to launch his summer campaign,[422] and though the Parliamentarians under Fairfax, pursuing his western design, again threatened Oxford, Newark-on-Trent still held, and the King, to draw Fairfax off from besieging Oxford, after marching west and recruiting on the Welsh border, struck right across the East Midlands into an area vital to Parliament. Charles had abandoned the attempt on the Scots army in the north and on 31 May the Royalists stormed and sacked Leicester, to the delight of the recruits from Wales. Near Daventry, in good hunting country, Charles now briefly took some respite, but Sir Thomas Fairfax had decided to seek him out. Raising the siege of Oxford and marching rapidly east by Newport Pagnell on 14 June he caught him at Naseby Field in Northamptonshire, between Rugby and Market Harborough. Had the Royalists taken Rupert's advice, they would have refused battle and retired on Newark through Harborough; but Charles, again ill-advised by civilian courtiers and set to return to Oxford in triumph, offered Fairfax just the battle he sought. Cromwell had now arrived, and together they outnumbered the Royalists by about two to one — 15,000 to about 7,500 — though they had less advantage in horse.

For in the dawn of 14 June 1645 the King took a risky decision. He turned back and faced the enemy from a strong position, good for cavalry, with his guard and standards making a splendid spectacle in the last battle fought by a reigning monarch on English soil. Fairfax had occupied Naseby village and had now advanced north from it, with Skippon commanding the infantry, Cromwell the right, Ireton the left. 'Both sides,' wrote an eyewitness, 'with mighty shouts exprest a hearty desire of fighting.' As usual Rupert on the Royalist right carried all before him, but as usual his horse went for the Roundhead baggage train. The Royalist infantry also attacked; Skippon was badly wounded, Ireton though wounded and captured, afterwards escaped. The King's gamble had nearly come off. But now Cromwell and his Ironsides took charge — he routed the Royalist cavalry on their left but, unlike Rupert, he had held back a substantial reserve, and ordered that anyone dismounting to plunder would be shot. He now launched the reserve on the flank of the Royalist foot. Charles himself, seeing the rout of his left wing, made to charge their pursuers with his Lifeguards, but according to Clarendon, the Scots Sir Robert Dalyell, Earl of Carnwath, described by Baillie as a monster of profanity, and, as Clarendon puts it, 'swearing three or four foul Scottish oaths', seized the bridle of the monarch's horse, shouting, 'Will ye goo upon your death in an instant?' — an intervention that a Gustav Adolf or a Henry V would surely have disregarded. The King's mount was checked; then, someone shouting 'to the right!', the entire royal cavalcade bolted for five hundred yards — the wrong way. The Royalist cavalry reserves had by now been deflected and dislocated; Fairfax himself, now known as 'Fiery Tom', captured the standard of the Lifeguard itself. Rupert, returning with what men he had retrieved, found most of the Royalist foot in the act of surrender.

Writing to speaker Lenthall in terse sentences, Cromwell summed up the battle:

> Wee after three howers fight, very doubtfull, at last routed his armie, killed and took about five thousand... very many officers, but of what qualitye wee yet know not. We took alsoe about two hundred carriages, all hce had, and all his gunnes being twelve in number, whereof two were demie

> cannon, two demi culverings and [I think] the rest sacers...
> Sir, this is none other but the hand of God...

The battle had not been a triumph for the New Model, but it had been for the Ironsides, who had saved the day. In fact the casualties had been relatively light — probably about five hundred Royalist dead and three hundred horses, though the victors massacred three or four hundred camp followers, probably Welsh women and children, under the mistaken impression that they were Irish Catholics.

The disaster was total: when Marston Moor had lost the north, 'Naezby wher the fight was this Satterday' lost the Midlands. The Banner Royal was captured, most of the regimental colours, the King's own coach ('the King's wagon'), the cabinet with his private papers, including letters to the Queen, which, suitably edited and at once printed, proved his political duplicity.

> All the ordnance, ammunition, the King's stuff, household carriages, and all the baggage of the army were totally lost... the King himself in person being necessitated, with his own troop only, to charge through their body to escape. From Leicester we marched (North West) to Ashby-de-la-Zouche, in the night (twenty-eight miles) and came thither about break of day and halted there.[423]

Fairfax referred to the 'abundant goodness of God' — the 'whole body of the enemy taken and slain'. In terms of war it was the end. From now on Charles was a hunted man; soon after, he wrote to the Prince of Wales that, should he himself be captured, the Prince was never to submit to any dishonourable condition even to save his father's life.

Having accounted for the Midlands, Fairfax now turned to deal with the last region of Royalist strength. He moved fast across the Midlands into Wessex, to mop up Dorset, relieve Taunton, take Bristol and subdue the entire west, where the last considerable Royalist army under Goring was still in being. By 30 June he was at Marlborough and marching for Amesbury, though since it was Fair day at Marlborough some laggards had afterwards to be rounded up by an officer from Devizes. Then, after a rendezvous at Stonehenge, where Hugh Peters, the fanatical army chaplain, demanded the destruction of the 'heathenish temple', a major task for which there was happily not the time, the army cut south-west by Bowerchalke in the Ebble valley up to the road to Blandford and Dorchester.

It was now that Fairfax encountered the 'Club Men'. They were part of a spontaneous movement widespread in the Severn Valley, around Worcester, Clun and Bishop's Castle, and round Stokesey Castle in Shropshire; they flourished also in Berkshire, Hampshire, Surrey and Sussex, but remained strongest in Wiltshire, Dorset and Somerset. They were 'neither for King nor Parliament, but [stood] upon their own ground for the preservation of their lives and fortunes' or as at Worcester because 'their wives and daughters had been exposed to utter ruin by the soldiers', so that they had 'associated themselves in a mutual league for each others defence'. They were mainly peasants and subsistence farmers, led by local gentry and clergy who had turned out to defend their homes, parishes and livestock from the depredations of both sides. The main leaders in Wiltshire were fairly substantial men: Thomas Bennet, JP, of Pyt House, worth £600 a year, who alleged afterwards that he had been forced to join them to protect his property, John Penruddock of Compton Chamberlayne, who was to lead the Penruddock rebellion of 1655, and Thomas Hollis, gentleman, of the Close at Salisbury.

Other leaders were less effective; as, typically, Parson Waterman of Wootton Rivers, who led his parishioners to a muster near Marlborough, while other parsons 'vapored' up and down the county.

Since they were conservative, and when not infuriated by Royalist garrisons, potentially for the King, as well as being relatively inarticulate, they have received less attention than the far less representative and numerous Levellers and Diggers, whose leaders were articulate, pamphleteering intellectuals. Had Charles been less encased in the frigid aloofness of his royalty, more adaptable, less circumscribed by the arrogant Court, he might have made more of their potential support, for they were already very strong, able by their numbers and knowledge of the country to paralyse the communications and supply of the armies. Ludlow says that they would assemble to the ringing of church bells, wearing white ribbons for peace: 'they met with drums, flying colours, for arms they had muskets, following pikes, halbards, great clubs, and suchlike'. They wanted to stop the disruption of their farming and their markets but were not above 'coming to the horse quarters and stealing the horses'.

Some of Fairfax's men first met them at Salisbury, where Sprigg says they 'appeared absolute mentors',[424] and Ludlow remarks that they 'would not suffer the contending armies to fight, but make them drink together and so made them depart to their several garrisons'. They were here indeed very strong, and on 6 June their leaders met three or four thousand of the West Wiltshire peasantry at Grovely, who agreed to articles of organization; rendezvous were held at Warminster and Upavon, while following an alarm of plunderers, the Club Men in Salisbury itself 'went out roaring up and down the country, hooping and bellowing'.

As the army moved south, they came on the Dorset Club Men, whose leaders petitioned for passes to lay their 'articles' before both King and Parliament. Fairfax, perforce, had to speak them fair, and late in June John St. Loe, Esquire, of Fontmell Parva (who was to come out in Penruddock's Rising) took a petition to Charles, while one was taken to Parliament by Thomas Trenchard, Esquire, Robert Culliford of Encombe, and the Rector of Durweston near Blandford. The petitioners asked for an immediate local cessation of the war, to pay off the garrison towns at a substantial rate until King and Parliament agreed to dispose of them, the authority of the Justices of the Peace to be restored to them and their officers, and pressed men allowed to return freely without penalty, and that farming or trade be again properly carried on to provide essential supplies; in sum, the restoration of normal life. Though Sprigge thought they were 'definitely evil against Parliament', Heath believed their demands 'reasonable'.

Fairfax had to get on with the war. A seasoned political general, he made rings round them in negotiation, while playing for time: he quoted from the King's letters taken at Naseby, raised the bogey of French and Irish invasion — so how could Weymouth or Lyme (vital defensive ports) possibly be neutralized? But he promised to enforce strict discipline in the camps and to stop the plundering and requisitioning that had provoked the grievance. Having parried their demands, the general sought out Goring, who was besieging Taunton; he marched to Beaminster and Crewkerne, and when Goring raised the siege, and turned to face him at Langport on the Yeo, on 10 July 1645, Fairfax routed him. The last Royalist army was finished. It remained to reduce Bristol and with it all the west including Cornwall; but to capture Bristol was a major undertaking, and the Parliamentarians would take their time.

But the Club Men remained a menace, and Cromwell dealt more faithfully with them than had Fairfax. On 1 August Fleetwood caught and imprisoned fifty of their leaders in Shaftesbury; and on the third, 'Lord's Day', Cromwell dispersed about ten thousand of them who had assembled to 'fetch them away'. Then, moving south, he found another four thousand at the Iron Age fort of Hambledon Hill above Shroton on the Stour. This 'Club Army' defied him and when his men 'fell on', they 'shot from the old work' — killed one or two soldiers and some horses. But skirting round the oval camp and attacking up the steep bank, Desborough distracted the defenders from guarding the entrance, where Cromwell's own troops now broke in. Many Club Men were cut down or wounded, while 'the rest slid and tumbled down the great steep hill at the hazard of their necks'. Thus Oliver Cromwell taught the men of Dorset not to meddle in high politics.[425]

It was the end of them as a military threat, though not as a political resistance. 'No doubt,' writes Heath, '... they had some design for the King, as was guessed from the general affection of these parts formerly and constantly to his cause: but whatever it was, it was now defeated; and the club-folks had Club-law.'[426] Their protest had been spontaneous, justified and widespread; unlike the Diggers, they knew how important it was that farming should be properly carried on. They continued to contribute to a popular underswell of resentment, more articulate by June 1648 in the *Declaration of the County of Dorset* against the 'arbitrary power' of the local Parliamentarian committees consisting generally of the 'tail of the gentry' and their 'smirking' hangers-on. This conservative underswell, directed in part at centralizing government as such, particularly if in military guise, contributed, as would the Penruddock rebellion, to make the Cromwellian sword government ephemeral, and thus to the Restoration.

While Fairfax had been dealing with the west, Charles had retreated to Hereford, intending to raise troops in Wales and in the hope of more substantial aid for the old Irish Catholics, with whom he had long been negotiating. All through August 1645 he never slept more than two nights in one place, and though he got back to Oxford on the twenty-eighth, on the thirtieth he was off again to Moreton-in-Marsh and on the thirty-first, the day of Montrose's victory at Kilsyth, he was at Worcester, with 'no dinner', after a 'cruel day'. Leaving Raglan on the Welsh border on 18 September, he marched and countermarched from six in the morning till midnight, and the next day for many miles over the Welsh mountains; diary entries of 'prand: in camp'; 'dinner in the field', or even 'no dinner', became more frequent. By 24 September he was in Chester but a sortie by his cavalry was defeated at Rowton Heath. Moreover, even Montrose had now come to disaster. His power had been ephemeral, for like others based on the Highlands he had never mastered the Lowlands, the only lasting power-base in Scotland. Disappointed when forbidden to plunder Glasgow, half the Irish had gone off to plunder Galloway in the southwest instead, and when on 5 September Montrose had marched south to the border with a diminished force, he had been caught at Philiphaugh west of Selkirk, before he could double back into the southern uplands, and overwhelmed. The remnant of the Irish, though they had surrendered, were massacred along with their camp followers; Montrose however got back to the Highlands at Blair Atholl, where he still made empty threats of guerrilla warfare.

At Hereford Charles had received crushing news. On 11 September Fairfax had stormed Bristol, and Rupert, with only fifteen hundred men to defend it, had capitulated, to save useless slaughter. After this 'prodigious surrender', wrote Digby, 'all was in danger of being lost — and we were put to wander again and trye our fortunes anewe'. The surrender of the strategically essential city and port of Bristol hit Charles hard. Beneath his apparent confidence, the facts were sinking in, and he lost his contrived poise. Rupert was a close royal kinsman, and Charles felt the surrender as a personal betrayal; even, at the instigation of Digby, as the culmination of treachery. For he had never quite forgiven the Prince for his professional opinion in the spring that, when negotiations at Uxbridge were going on, the war being lost, a negotiated peace was necessary; and since August 1644 Rupert's elder brother, the Elector Charles Louis, had been in London, a pensioner of the Parliament and a potential claimant to the throne. So on 14 September, from Hereford, Charles had written in anger:

> Nephew, Though the loss of Bristol be a great blow to me, yet your surrendering it as you did, is of so much affliction to me that it makes me not only forget the consideration of that place, but is likewise the greatest trial of my constancy that has yet befallen me; for what is to be done after one that is so near me as you are, submits himself to so mean an action? (I give it the easiest term). I have so much to say that I will say no more of it.

Only in August Rupert had assured him he could hold the city for four months.

> Did you keep [he asked] it four days? was there anything like a mutiny? Many questions could be asked — but now, I confess to little purpose. My conclusion is, to desire you to seek your subsistence [a particularly cutting phrase] until it shall please God to determine of my condition, somewhere beyond seas;

to which I send you herewith a pass; and I pray God I make you sensible of your present condition, and give you means to redeem what you have lost; for I shall have no greater joy in a victory, than a just occasion without blushing to assure you of my being, Your loving uncle and most faithful friend CR.[427]

Having, in his anger, thrown out his best general, the King had even revoked the Prince's commission, sent Nicholas a warrant for the arrest of Colonel Legge (the able Governor of Oxford) as one of the Prince's closest colleagues, and even one for the arrest of the Prince himself should he prove recalcitrant. After the 'inexcusable deliverye upp' of Bristol, he told Nicholas, he could do no less: 'In my care for the preservation of my sonne [York], of you my faithful servants there' and of 'that important place my Citty of Oxford'. It would be best, he had considered, to secure Legge first. And he had added a postscript, 'Tell my sone that I shall lesse greeve to heere that he is knocked on the heade, then that he should doe so meane an Acte as in the rendring of Bristoll Castell and Fort upon the termes it was C.R.'[428]

By 20 September, under better control, Charles had written to Prince Maurice that he considered that 'this great error' had in 'no waise proceeded from Rupert's change of affection to me or my cause, but meerly by having his judgement seduced by some rotten-hearted villains, making pretentions to him'; and promised that when it pleased God to 'enable him to look upon his friends like a King, Rupert would be thankful for the pains he had spent on his armies': the Prince's defection, he insisted, had in no way 'staggered' him from his good opinion of Maurice.

Rupert, still at Oxford, was not the man to take his uncle's letters or the intrigues long conducted by Digby and other civilian courtiers against him, lying down. Following

Montrose's defeat, Charles had abandoned an advance north of Chester and crossed the Midlands to Welbeck Abbey, near Newark; and when the Prince, in defiance of orders, was reported to be arriving hot foot, Digby, hastily given a contrived appointment, was dispatched on a rumour that Montrose was still in the field as lieutenant-general north of the Trent, an empty position from which after successive disasters he took refuge in the Isle of Man and then in Ireland. On 16 October Rupert arrived at Newark, and brusquely thrusting into the royal presence demanded to put his case for the surrender of Bristol. Charles refused to speak to him; although the Prince was twice vindicated by the Council of War. Perhaps because on 8 October Parliament had settled £8,000 a year on Charles Louis, out of delinquents' estates and the King's own revenues, Charles maintained an icy disfavour, emphasized when he relieved Sir Richard Willis, a friend of the Prince, of the governorship of Newark. There followed something like a mutiny — as the King put it: 'I shall not Christen it, but it looks very like' — and Rupert and his supporters were informed that they could make their own dispositions for disbandment.

By 5 November by devious and dangerous ways the now almost fugitive monarch returned to Oxford and here in December, since the Prince had refused the Parliament's demand that he should swear never to fight for the King again as the price of a pass to go abroad, formal civilities were resumed; but Rupert was never again given even minor responsibility. Charles, with the resentment — even fear — that he felt for dominant men, such as Strafford, and with the pride and aloof ingratitude of his royal temperament, had deprived himself of his best commander.

In the south too the campaign was now in effect finished. Gradually the Royalist strongholds caved in; on 18 December Hereford fell to a night attack through snow; then on 3 February 1646 Chester, and with it any hope of a base for an Irish army. Worcester still held out, but in January, down in the West Country, Fairfax took Dartmouth, offering the garrison half a crown a head to go home or three shillings to join the supposedly dedicated New Model;[429] and in mid-February he stormed Torrington, where the Royalists blew up the church roof in denying their ammunition to the enemy. On 13 March their remnant surrendered at Truro.

Three days earlier the Prince of Wales had escaped from Penzance to the Scilly Isles. Here the weather was appalling. 'The castle contained some half dozen barely habitable rooms and there was no fuel to warm them... the islanders, scraping a living from the soil, seldom ventured out to fish, and showed not the faintest interest in Prince Charles, or indeed in anything that was happening on the mainland... so he was often soaked and always hungry, but he did not complain.'[430] In December Fairfax had made an insidious offer that the Prince should disband his troops, present himself to Parliament and in effect collaborate in deposing his father. But young Charles rejected it with contempt: 'Rogues and Rebels — are they not content to be rebels themselves but they must have me of their number?' Even in the Scillies he was not safe, and on 14 April — the day after the fall of Exeter and the capture of his infant sister, the Princess Henrietta Anne, by the Parliament — a Roundhead squadron was off the islands, to be dispersed by a storm. The Prince and the council at once left for Jersey in the *Proud Black Eagle*, a Royalist pirate ship that brought him to the plenty and relative security of the island — a very narrow escape.

King Charles meanwhile, reduced to defending Oxford, had summoned Sir Jacob, now Lord Astley, from Worcester; but in the cold dawn of 21 March, at Stow-on-the-Wold, intercepted and defeated, he had made his oft-quoted and historic remark, seated on a drumhead: 'You have done your work, boys. You may go play, unless you fall out among yourselves.'

In fateful succession the King's hopes had been cut off. Ever since the fall of Bristol, Charles had been obviously rattled, his diplomacy becoming more wild and contradictory. He feared that if the Prince were captured by Parliament or forced into compromise, he would himself be exiled or even murdered, his struggle in principle defeated. Hence the King's letter to the Prince not long after Naseby.

> Charles, it is very fit for me now to prepare for the worst. Wherefore know that my pleasure is, whensoever you find yourself in apparent danger of falling into the rebel's hands, that you convey yourself into France, and there be under your mother's care: who is to have the absolute power of your education in all things, except religion; in that not to meddle at all.

The King now required instant obedience, 'without grumbling'.[431] Hence also his instructions — as far back as November — that the Prince must not go to Scotland or Ireland — better to Denmark.

Charles's other concerns were less realistic: how to keep the support of the Irish Protestants, yet gain that of the old Irish Catholics? Of course the problem baffled him. His viceroy Ormonde's position became impossible: for Charles was negotiating through an English Catholic, Lord Glamorgan, direct with the old Catholic confederates, rebels in Ormonde's eyes; and in October 1645 the papal nuncio Rinuccini had arrived in Kerry well equipped, in addition to his religious authority, with money and arms. Whereat Glamorgan had made a secret treaty to concede all the Catholic demands in return for the longed-for Irish army to invade England. But among the papers of the belligerent Catholic Archbishop of Tuam, killed in battle near Sligo in October, had been a copy of the treaty, and by January 1646 it had arrived at Westminster. Ormonde, earlier informed, had already arrested Glamorgan and Charles had repudiated the treaty. But the King's credibility had been even further undermined: nothing could have panicked and infuriated Parliament, the army and the vast majority of the English and Scots more than the prospect of a Catholic Irish army launched on them by their own King. So that hope was dashed. So were chimerical hopes of aid from the Pope, or of direct aid from Mazarin.

That spring Charles's own proposal to come in person to London and meet the Parliament — climb down though it was — was brushed aside. While negotiating with the Irish Catholics he had characteristically also approached the Independent generals in the army — showing how impartially he would try to manipulate anyone; they were all, he felt, his subjects. Nor had he shrunk from a wild project by the Queen of a mercenary invading force from the Continent, to be landed at Hastings, once so successful as a base for invasion.

In this predicament Charles's natural illusion was to count on the loyalty of his Scots realm. After all he was King of Scotland born; and since January Mazarin's envoy, Jean de Montreuil, following the traditional French policy of playing off the old Scots alliance against the English, and anxious to back the more authoritarian and monarchist of the two regimes against a possible republic, had been persuading him to come to terms with the Scots. The mounting disagreements over religion between the rigid authoritarian Kirk and the Erastian English Presbyterians encouraged Montreuil; he even, vainly, imagined that the Covenanters would rescind their fierce hostility to Montrose, whose followers and collaborators they were then in fact executing when they could catch them.

Charles had at first objected on the ground that Presbyterianism was incompatible with monarchy, but as the rift between the Scots and the Parliament widened and, in the spring of 1646, Fairfax's army, having pacified the West Country, began to march on Oxford, and even staunch Royalists were giving in and compounding their estates, he again thought that the Scots would prove the least repellent of his enemies. In spite of Montreuil's last-minute warning that they regarded him as far gone in 'sin' and would accept nothing but the full Presbyterian hierarchy, which Charles had in private repeatedly refused ever to accept, he decided that they were his best option. For the Scots, he wrote to the Queen in March, 'I promise thee to employ all possible pain to agree with them, so that the price be not giving up the Church of England, with which I will not part on any condition whatsoever.' But Charles concurrently wrote privately to Ireton, perhaps to lay a false trail, offering to disband his armies on condition of his keeping the throne; but as he had no significant armies to disband, the offer was not taken seriously — merely referred to Cromwell, who at once, to show his own honesty and the King's duplicity, laid the message before Parliament. All bolt holes save the one to the Scots now seemed stopped.

It was now full spring and Fairfax's army was nearing Oxford; even Woodstock and Faringdon might become untenable, and the terms of surrender offered were generous

— with low rates of compounding for those with estates. And Montreuil, now with the Scots outside Newark, wrote that they would certainly treat the King with respect. So on the evening of Sunday 26 April 1646 Charles held his last Council in Oxford. He intended, he said, to go to London, but that if they heard nothing from him after three weeks, they were to surrender the city on the best obtainable terms. During the night Charles then suffered his first personal degradation, as he had his beautifully trimmed hair, once depicted by Rubens and Van Dyck, hacked off by 'Jack' Ashburnham, his groom of the bedchamber, and his elegant beard disfigured (Ashburnham, a kinsman of Buckingham, MP for Hastings and treasurer and paymaster to the armies). Charles's only other companion was one of his chaplains, Dr Michael Hudson, a Fellow of Queen's College, Oxford, who as 'Scoutmaster General' knew the lie of the land and the intricacies of the roads.[432] At three in the spring morning, as the Oxford bells struck the hour, the King of Great Britain and Ireland, in the guise of a servant and riding behind his supposed masters, well-to-do gentlemen armed with passes to London where they were supposedly going to compound, was let out of the East Gate at Oxford over Magdalen bridge; the governor, who had strict orders to prevent anyone entering or leaving the town for five days, calling out to his sovereign, 'Farewell, Harry!'

Even as he set out, it is not certain if Charles's mind had been made up. He may have thought to make for King's Lynn and take ship to Montrose, but the town was now in the hands of Parliament and his chances of a ship would have been slight. He may have thought to make for London, go to ground there and so escape abroad; or even to present himself to Parliament or the City — hardly a hopeful course. Suffice it that he did not make straight for the Scots at their headquarters between

Nottingham and Royalist-held Newark, but rode by Dorchester-on-Thames and Nettlebed in the Chilterns to Maidenhead and so to Hillingdon. The bluff worked. Well-tipped guards at Dorchester-on-Thames let them pass. But one of Ireton's troopers rode with them after Nettlebed and asked the supposed servant who his masters were, too respectful to question them after the fine air with which they produced their pass. Was his master, he asked, one of the House of Lords? Merely of the Commons, 'Harry' replied.

At Hillingdon, north of modern Heathrow, no message, if one had been expected, came from London; and they turned off to the north-east to Harrow and then north to St Albans, where they thought themselves pursued: but the galloping horseman who overtook them turned out to be merely a drunk. That night, having covered a lot of ground, they slept at Wheathampstead. And here it seems Charles came to a decision; if he could get tolerable terms, he would go to the Scots; if not, to Lynn. So Dr Hudson was sent on to Southwell, near Newark, to contact Montreuil, and the King and Ashburnham proceeded to Downham Market in Norfolk.[433] After a night in an ordinary inn near Newmarket — a place the scene of better days — on 29 April the King and Ashburnham crossed the fenland and arrived at the White Swan at Downham Market, about ten miles due south of King's Lynn. From Downham, having (they feared) roused suspicion when the local barber commented that 'their hairs had been cut with a knife', they moved south-east to Mundford on the Brandon-Swaffam road where Hudson rejoined them. He brought news that the Scots had verbally agreed to 'secure the King in his person and honour', not press him to do anything against conscience, declare for the King if Parliament remained obdurate, and to protect Ashburnham and the chaplain.

So Charles made his fateful decision. Abandoning the project of taking ship at King's Lynn, they rode east to Crimplesham, where Charles, lately disguised as a clergyman, now changed clothes again; then turning south crossed the Ouse at Sunthery Ferry and rode west through the spring weather under great fenland skies past Ely, with its historic cathedral dominating the landscape, and on to Erith and Huntingdon. Having traversed the fenland by the less-frequented southern route rather than more directly to Peterborough, held by the Parliament, they turned north, and after the long ride Charles rested for the third time at Little Gidding, soon to be wrecked by Puritan soldiers. He dared not stay, but pushed on to a tiny inn at Coppingford, whence, riding through the night, they came to Montreuil's lodgings at Southwell early in the morning of 5 May.

It had been a long and exacting journey, and save for a brief interlude between Hampton Court and the Isle of Wight, the last one the King would make on his own. Soon the Scots Commission arrived, hot foot and argumentative, from their camp near Newark, and they plainly meant business. They had not done badly in the shifting power balance between the Parliament, the defeated but numerous Royalists, the army Independents and themselves, and they now held what looked like a trump card.

# BOOK IV: THE PRISONER

19: SCOTS, PARLIAMENT AND ARMY

THE SCOTS LOST little time in removing their prisoner from the clutches of Parliament, though not to Scotland, and none at all in subjecting him to intense theological argument; they had intervened mainly to prevent the English, either Anglican or sectarian, from contaminating their own form of Calvinist discipline. For the first time Charles found himself deprived of the elaborate respect that even his now dilapidated Court had accorded him. His coming had surprised his captors, whose negotiations with Montreuil had been inconclusive; but the Royalist stronghold of Newark-on-Trent having surrendered at the King's command on 9 May, the Scots began to march back to Newcastle-on-Tyne, their ministers arguing with and preaching at him as occasion served. They pressed him to repudiate Montrose, whom on 19 May he ordered to disband his army and leave Scotland, and they planned to hand over Ashburnham and Dr Hudson to the Parliament.

But their main and reiterated demand was that Charles sign the Covenant. He was now in effect a prisoner; although he soon had some personal attendants, his spaniel Rogue and his greyhound Gypsy. 'I never knew what it was to be barbarously baited before,' he wrote to the Queen, out of the fog of theological argument. To gain time and 'bring good out of it' he went on arguing, while in June he wrote to the English Parliament offering again to negotiate.

On 9 June 1646 at Marston, north of Oxford, the Parliamentarian army leaders held a Council of War. Cromwell, Skippon and Ireton were unanimous that Oxford should not be taken by storm. With three to four thousand troops in the garrison under Sir Thomas Glenham, a particularly belligerent new governor, the place was protected by rivers and by 'meadows overflowed' on all sides save the north, and the colleges themselves were potential fortresses. The generals had to keep the army intact, for they were 'well assured that they dealt with an enemy who had lost neither wit, friends, activity or resolution to play his game once more if he knew at which card to begin'.[434] So they had to gain the city by treaty. Charles had already ordered Newark to surrender, and by 25 June he had consented to the surrender of Oxford. The terms were favourable, particularly for Cavaliers with estates who were willing to compound; the garrison marched out with drums beating, colours flying and the full honours of war, as did those of the outlying garrisons of Faringdon and Woodstock, who got the same terms, while the four-year-old clutter of officials, courtiers, yeomen of the buttery and the bakehouse and the rest dispersed along with their dependents as best they could.

The university was in a bad way.

> When Oxford was surrendered [writes Aubrey] the first thing General Fairfax did was to set a good guard of soldiers to preserve the Bodleian library. 'Tis said there was more hurt done by the Cavaliers (during their garrison) by way of embezilling and cutting off chaines of books, than there was since. He was a lover of learning, and had he not taken this special care, that noble library had been utterly destroyed, for there were ignorant senators enough who would have been contented to have it so.[435]

The town on the other hand had done pretty well out of the war:

> Many inhabitants [Wood records] had gained great store of wealth from the Court and royalists that had for several years

continued among them; [though many young men of the town, as of the university, he adds censoriously, had become] debauch'd by bearing armes and doing the duties belonging to soldiers, as watching, warding, and sitting in tippling houses for whole nights together.[436]

The young Duke of York had now been taken to London, where along with the Princess Elizabeth and the Duke of Gloucester he was kept a kind of hostage in St James's Palace. The sixteen-year-old Prince of Wales, however, after an agreeable stay in Jersey when he had developed his passion for sailing, had on 26 June landed at Saint-Malo on his way to the Court of France. This move, made at the urgent command of both his parents, but against the advice of Hyde and Culpepper, had at least put him out of range of the Parliamentarian fleet.

The King now found it hard to get news of his wife, and it was not until 12 August that he even realized that the infant Henrietta Anne had arrived in France. 'Though I was so ignorant,' he wrote to her mother, 'that but for you I knew not that she was gone out of England. Yes, I fully approve her journey.' But the Queen, reckoning one lot of provincial heretics no worse than another, and convinced of the value of the 'Auld' French alliance with the Scots, now urged him to take the Covenant; to which he roundly replied that the Scots would never declare themselves for him unless he should make such concessions for the destruction of monarchy, which by the Grace of God he would never do. He had now, he concluded, 'very little hope of any strong visible force (which he believed must begin abroad) arriving in time to save him'.

The Scots, the Queen, the English Calvinist oligarchy and the French all wanted the King to underwrite an authoritarian Presbyterian settlement, as against the Independent sectaries in the army and outside it, some of whom were republicans. But again, at the end of August 1646, Charles reiterated that his giving way to such Presbyterian government as would content the Scots would be the 'absolute destruction of Monarchy,… if episcopacy must be totally abolished and the depending of the Church torn from the Crowne. I hope,' he concluded desperately, 'you will not deny [this] for if you doe I shall leave off thinking of anything but how to dye.'

Already a year before, though with little chance of success, for they were cutting across the time-honoured and tenacious establishment of the manor, squire, JP and parson, Parliament had ordained that all 'parishes and places whatsoever (as well as private places exempt of jurisdiction classical, provincial and or others)' be brought under the government of congregational national assemblies; though to the disgust of the theocratic Scots Kirk they had also provided that the national supreme authority should meet 'only when… summoned by Parliament and continue as Parliament ordered and not otherwise'.[437] They had also laid down in the *Rules at the Lord's Supper*, firmly and unequivocally for the benefit of all concerned, including any sectaries with odd ideas, 'that the soules of the faithfull, after death, doe immediately live with Christ in blessedness, and that the soules of the wicked doe immediately goe into Hell's torments'. 'There shall be,' they had concluded firmly, 'a Resurrection of the Body.'

By the end of June Parliament had drafted the Propositions of Newcastle to submit to the King. They were as stringent as those of Uxbridge: the King must take the Covenant, though the English form of Presbyterianism was left imprecise; and Parliament was to control the armed forces of 'militia' for as long as twenty years. Charles could only prevaricate and again play for time.

But his obstinate tenacity had its effect. The Scots did not know what to do with him, and by September Parliament decided to get the Scots army out of England and get hold of the King. After prolonged bargaining £400,000 had been agreed as the price of the Scots campaign and occupation, and in October Parliament put the lands of the archbishoprics and bishoprics in England and Wales in the hands of trustees, who were to sell them off to raise money to pay off the Scots. All the great historic titles — Canterbury, York, Winchester, Salisbury, Durham — had been 'abolished and taken away'. The trustees were mainly London aldermen, speculators and surveyors, who would have their profits.

By the end of September Charles, who could haggle with the best of them, was attempting compromise, always with the proviso in his own mind that it would be temporary. A Presbyterian hierarchy was to be established, but only for three years — not a very practical idea — while a Grand Assembly of sixty divines — far too many — should be convened, one-third Presbyterian, another Independent and the last, presumably Anglican, chosen by himself. This Assembly was to consult at length with a Committee of both Houses of Parliament and finally, taking their advice into account, King and Parliament would decide the future. Charles hoped so much from this device that he conceded the control of the armed forces to Parliament for ten years, after which they would revert to the Crown. Not surprisingly, the Scots turned his offer down.

Trapped and lonely, bored by uncouth divines, Charles was now thinking of escape. 'I command you,' he wrote to the Queen, 'to give me your opinion freely — which is less hurt to my crown and posterity, that I bee a prisoner, within my own dominions or at liberty elsewhere? For be confident that this must be my case shortly.'

As the winter drew in in the north, the King became more melancholy. He had not expected to be kept out of his own native realm and his capital, Edinburgh, where he would have attracted loyalty and intrigue; but Argyll insisted on his exclusion. Nor could the Covenanters understand why, if he had never meant to agree with them, he had ever come. No wonder that Charles, though he solaced himself with books, chess and golf, appeared 'sullen'.

On 12 December he wrote to the Queen with unwonted forthrightness: 'This damned covenant is the product of Rebellion and breeds nothing but treason';[438] he was 'much bound in conscience,' he reiterated, 'to do no act to the destruction of monarchy'. Further, now that the Prince of Wales was in France, he had another fear. If, under his mother's influence, he offered more to the Scots than his father, what would become of the King? 'In what security do you think I can be when it shall be believed that my son will grant what I deny? I will only conjure you, as you are Christian no more thus to torture me.' On 20 December Charles again asked Parliament to let him come to London for a settlement; but on 28 December the financial deal that paid off the Scots was concluded.

By 2 January 1647, in sheer despair, having tried and failed to escape at Christmas, he wrote:

> Dear Heart, I must tell thee that now I am declared what I have really been ever since I came to this army, which is a Prisoner, the difference being only that heretofore my escape was easy enough, but now is more difficult, if not impossible. Having showed thee this sad truth (which to me is neither

new nor strange) I shall need to say no more for I know thy love will omit nothing that is possible for my freedom.

Determined to escape the Scots and having no illusions that the French would declare for him, he was now contemplating 'a voluntary imprisonment by the English'. The Scots had after all refused to let him into Scotland: and he could hardly go to the Highlands — he would there be 'infallibly lost'; as for Ireland or Jersey, he would not say they were impossible, but in England he thought he might be 'better used'.

On 2 January 1647 the Parliamentarian Commissioners, the great peers Northumberland and Pembroke — now turncoats both in the King's eyes — arrived in Newcastle. They invited Charles to accompany them to one of his own properties, the large and elegant Elizabethan mansion of Holdenby or Holmby House in Northamptonshire, originally built for Sir Christopher Hatton, where Charles had sometimes lived as a child. On 28 January, amid the insults and catcalls of the inhabitants, the Scots army marched out of Newcastle and the Parliamentarians under Skippon marched in. Two days later, after they had crossed the Tyne, £100,000 was paid up, and on 3 February the second instalment, leaving £200,000 outstanding. In fact these sums were for arrears of pay, but the timing had been clumsy: it got about that the monarch had been 'sold'. And, indeed, had he not been handed over, the Scots would probably not then have got their money.

The King was now assigned two new attendants. One was James Harrington, the political theorist, a pioneer of the economic interpretation of history, with whom, says Aubrey, Charles 'disputed about Government'. The King came to love his company 'but he would not endure to hear of a Commonwealth' — Harrington's obsession. The other was

Thomas Herbert, who had travelled in India and Persia and written a vivid and racy account of the Court and habits of Shah Abbas the Great of Iran; the King rightly considered him a spy but tolerated him and came to like him. His account of the imprisonment and trial is often valuable.

As Charles proceeded south through the winter weather by Durham, Richmond and Wakefield, the gentry flocked to attend him, and the country people came in such numbers to be touched for the King's Evil that proclamations were issued limiting their access. Church bells pealed, salutes were fired; the King was welcomed back with a real but politically deceptive enthusiasm and relief.

The aftermath of the long war had been wretched: the expensive army was still mobilized — 'the costly ever-present soldiers'[439] capable of gross indiscipline, riot and drunkenness — hardly the 'saints in Arms' sentimentally depicted — while the jumped-up local Parliamentarian committees and Presbyterian congregational assemblies were overriding the normal authority of the justices of the peace and the established clergy. Disbanded officers had turned highwaymen — indeed the eighteenth-century 'gentlemen of the road' had their origin in the Civil War. England had always been a monarchy, and most people felt that the Crown stood for an order and security that was threatening to collapse. Already in 1643 Lord Thomas Savile had summed up moderate opinion: 'I love religion so well that I would not have it put to the hazard of a battle. I love liberty so much that I would not trust it to the hand of a conqueror'; and speaking for most men of property great and small, 'I would not have the King trample on Parliament nor the Parliament lessen him so much as to make way for the people to rule us all.'

Charles had a case when he assumed that none of the contending parties could do without him. The social fabric, deep-rooted since Anglo-Saxon times, was still very strong. The feeling that ordinary life must be sustained was evident among the people, who obstinately carried on with their agriculture and markets and industry in spite of the dislocation — how else could the wars have been financed? — while many in ruling circles, close-knit by their formal, if amateurish, classical education, retained a solidarity of interest and outlook in spite of doctrinal and political differences.

In 1645 for example, Parliament had found time to order that 'whereas for diverse years there hath not been any election in the College of Eaton, and this year, by reason there was no Provost settled in King's College in Cambridge, the times for election have lapsed... the Lords and Commons order that there shall be an election of scholars in the manner heretofore accustomed'. All rents and revenues, too, were to be received and disbursed to the immediate use of the college, freed and discharged from all taxes and charges.[440] And in Oxford, when Royalist dons were threatened with sequestration, Parliament could order that since the seizure and sales of their 'books, etc.' would be a great discouragement to learning and undo their ancient and famous university, no sales need then actually be made, though their owners had to make inventories of their subjects for the sequestrators. Nor was poaching left unchecked. Parliament ordained that 'by reason of the great liberty that several idle and loose persons at this time take unto themselves, by guns, tracing hares in the snow, setting dogs and other unlawful means to kill and destroy game of all kinds through the Kingdom, in contempt of Law and authority, which, if not timely prevented, will prove a destruction to the said game in all parts', the justices of the peace were to enforce the statutes against such depredations.

Down in Wiltshire, in the autumn of 1646, Ludlow recorded from 'the Devizes' that after they had waded through depths and difficulties with the blessing of God, and he was disbanding Royalist troops 'whose brigade had received their six weeks pay,… there we found civilities and quiet behaviour, and we conceive the leaving of the soldiers free to dispose of a horse hath much conduced [to this]'. That December, while the King was still with the Scots, Parliament too saw to it that God was propitiated for the entire nation's 'great neglect and prophanation of morality' by a 'Monthly Fast', in which the whole people were deeply humiliated before the Lord, and which was enforced by mayor, bailiffs and constables, specially exempted from any charge of assault and battery if they had to coerce recalcitrants in the course of duty. And this was followed up in February 1647 by a 'Day of Public Humiliation before the Lord' — 'lest we partake in other men's sins and thereby be in danger of their plagues'.

In this state of public anxiety, with the majority looking for a stable settlement, though with formidable minorities, as usual in revolutionary situations, out for power, Charles again hoped to restore the hierarchy and to come into his own. His prestige was still inescapable; a prisoner, he could yet command a radiating and incalculable influence. And he was by instinct a devious, if ineffective, intriguer. Perhaps he hoped to overreach the more obviously forceful and talented men with whom he seldom felt at ease. But he miscalculated: the overwhelming fact, overshadowing the country, was now a larger, more expensive and better organized army than England had ever had. It was something new: a standing army, politically dangerous, and the civilian politicians, magnates, landowners, merchants and office holders in Parliament, for whom it had won the war, now wanted to get rid of it. The obvious solution was to disband most of the regiments with a generous settlement, with arrears of pay included and an indemnity for acts of violence committed in the war. But the Parliament had just paid out £200,000 to the Scots: they had not the money. So the obvious thing was to use part of the army in Ireland, where the original rising, which had so much contributed to the outbreak of the Civil War, had still not been put down. A solution was all the more urgent, since many senior officers had risen, in accordance with Cromwell's policy for the New Model, from obscure origins, and some were careerists who held radical political and religious views, propagated among their men.

The shabby treatment of the army, to whom the politicians owed their victory, though intelligible in the economic and social stress of the time, would prove extremely unwise. As for Charles, as he rode south, he was looking for his own potential advantage, and the conflict of the Presbyterian oligarchy in Parliament with the Independents in the Commons and in the army seemed to give it to him.

Reporting to Mr Speaker Lenthall on the victory at Naseby, Lieutenant General Cromwell had concluded his letter with a hint of menace. 'Honest men served you faithfully in this action. Sir, they are trusty. I beseech you in the name of God not to discourage them. I wish this action may begett thankfulnesse and humilitye in all that are concerned in itt. Hee that venters his life for the libertye of his countrie, I wish hee trust God for the libertye of his conscience and you for the libertye hee fights for.' This liberty the Independents now feared they would be denied; moreover the political radicals in the army feared that if the King now came to terms with the wealthy Presbyterian interest in Parliament, the cohesion of the old establishment would be restored, then, with the old civilian distrust of a standing army, disband it, and with it their own power and livelihood, even safety. Charles was experienced enough a *politique* to see his chance of playing hard to get with both sides. Meanwhile at Holdenby — his own property and a house and estate he and the Queen had always enjoyed — he resumed, after long months, some of the respect, formality and luxury of his old routine, though he was not allowed an Anglican chaplain.

By February 1647 the tensions between Parliament and army had increased. Following Ormonde's handing over of Dublin and the territories he still controlled to the Parliament, the victorious Catholic confederates under the papal nuncio were determined to establish the rest of Ireland as a Catholic kingdom. Anxious already to cut down the standing army in England, Parliament was thus resolved to repudiate any 'cessation' of the war and to launch a massive reconquest: 4,200 horse and 8,400 foot were to be launched on Ireland, while only 6,600 horse and essential garrison troops were to be maintained at home. And not only that: apart from a lord general, there were now to be no officers above the rank of colonel and no member of the House of Commons could retain his commission. As Ranke puts it, 'It is known from the German wars what a tendency to independence prevailed among the generals in the armies of that age.'[441] All ranks, Independents or not, had to take the Covenant.

Sound in principle as it was to reassert civilian control of the armed forces, a more provocative policy could hardly have been devised, and nothing was conceded about arrears of pay. So when some hopeful politicians came down from Westminster to encourage recruitment for the army for

Ireland, they were met with demands for liberty of conscience and payment of cash. On 21 March 1647 at a conference of officers convened by Fairfax, no one would volunteer; then, true seventeenth-century Englishmen, they drew up a petition. At once, more disturbingly, the other ranks drew up one as well: and a revolutionary threat had now arisen. The troopers of the cavalry regiments appointed 'agitators' — agents — two for each regiment — who combined in a protest addressed to the generals, and soon the foot followed their example. Representatively and in common the 'agitators' dilated on the just grievances of the army. Characteristically the politicians climbed half-way down: Cromwell, whose commission as Lieutenant General had lapsed, Skippon, Fleetwood — who had outmanoeuvred the Club Men at Hambledon Hill — and Ireton were all members of Parliament and as such they now got better terms for the troops — but not good ones: payment of only part of their arrears of pay, and debentures on the state — for what they were worth — for the balance.

Alarmed at this insubordination by the military, the Presbyterians at Westminster now colleagued more closely with the Scots, and on 20 May Charles was gratified to receive an invitation from the House of Lords to come down to Oatlands near London to discuss the proposals he had suggested in September. Events, as he had expected, seemed to be playing into his hands. None of the contending factions, it seemed, could do without him.

In the late evening of 3 June — Charles had been over to Althorp that afternoon — the routine of the great house at Holdenby was disturbed by the arrival of a large troop of horse. Their commander, George Joyce,[442] was only a cornet (the subaltern officer who carried the colours), and his instructions, probably unofficial, derived from the agitators and certain officers including Ireton on the Army Council, who was indirectly backed by Cromwell who had not yet resumed his commission. Joyce had first made sure of the captured Royalist artillery at Oxford, which Parliament had ordered up to the Tower, and then proceeded without reference to his own commander-in-chief, Fairfax, the Lord General, to make sure of the King. The Parliamentary Commissioners having fled, Joyce took charge and early on 5 June Charles inspected five hundred horse drawn up before Holdenby House. 'And now,' he asked Cornet Joyce, 'tell me where your Commission is? Have you anything in writing from Sir Thomas Fairfax?... Pray deal ingenuously with me, where is your Commission?' In his brief historic moment Joyce said the right thing. Pointing to the well-ordered ranks, 'Here,' he replied, 'is my commission.' 'Indeed,' answered the King with a flash of Stuart charm, 'it is one I can read without spelling. It is as fair a commission and as well written as I have seen in my life — as handsome and proper a company of gentlemen as I have seen this many a day.' And reckoning that he was now better placed — with Parliament and the army competing for him — he politely acquiesced, as he obviously had to, asking with ironic gaiety, 'Where next, Mr. Joyce?' They settled for Newmarket.

Apprised of this coup, Fairfax at Bury St Edmunds at once dispatched Colonel Whalley with two regiments of horse to interrupt the cavalcade en route for Huntingdon. But the King refused to return to Holdenby; and even when Fairfax himself met him near Cambridge he remained obdurate. 'Sir,' he said with a sublime miscalculation, 'I have as good an interest in the army as you'; 'by which,' comments Fairfax himself, their own Lord General, 'I plainly saw the broken reed he leaned on'.[443] It was a natural miscalculation. The army had the power and were under apparent control. They had spontaneously organized a council of officers and a council of 'agitators' elected by regimental committees, and these councils had become merged in the Grand Council of the Army. Ireton, a tiger for constitution making, might well find a more realistic way out than the mean and bigoted Presbyterian who now dominated Parliament.

During June and early July at Royston and Hatfield Charles was treated with full ceremony, and appeared on affable terms with the great men of the Army. He now first met Cromwell, who was impressed by him and perhaps interested in the rewards he could still offer. But as Charles and the grandees conferred, the army on which their power depended was getting impatient. With arrears still unpaid the men were demanding to march on London. Hastily on 1 August Ireton produced a new basis of settlement. Under the 'Heads of Proposals', modified by a fortnight's intense discussion by the Army Council and with the King, the terms were far more favourable to Charles than the Propositions of Newcastle. He had to allow the Parliament to nominate the great officers of state for ten years and after that nominate three of them; he had to surrender the militia for ten years; but the bishops, and much of their property, were restored, shorn only of the legal jurisdiction of the old ecclesiastical courts. The fines of delinquent Royalists were much diminished, and good terms offered to any who would join the army for Ireland. And, remarkable innovation, Parliament was to be biennial, and elected through a constitution that redistributed seats in proportion to population and importance. There was to be a much-needed Council of State existing in its own right. Such was the army's price for a deal with the King against the Presbyterians, against London, where the numerous trained bands had been removed for the army's control, and against any renewed incursions from the Scots.

During these promising negotiations Charles had at last been allowed to see James, Duke of York, whom he had not met since he had left Oxford, and also the Princess Elizabeth and the Duke of Gloucester, whom he had not seen for five years. He met them at Maidenhead and brought them back to Caversham; and while in residence at Hampton Court he continued to see them. For the last time the King's prospects looked hopeful. He had, after all, lost the war; and his prerogative power had been limited, but he had kept the bishops and he would in time regain the militia.

But Charles and the generals had miscalculated the shifts of power. Early in June Fairfax had been compelled to sanction a general rendezvous of the army, and Cromwell, when he knew that Joyce's coup had come off, had rejoined the army, under a threat that if he did not they would go their own way without him. Then on 14 June they had made more radical claims. In the *Declaration of the Army* they insisted that they were representative of the people (which they were not), demanded an immediate dissolution of Parliament, and toleration for the Independent sects. Moreover, since the rigged by-elections of 1645-6, many of their leading officers had entered Parliament, including Ireton, Fleetwood, Blake and the radical Rainsborough, who, unlike the others, had taken up with the Levellers, whose leaders were John Wildman and John Lilburne. Contrary to much received opinion, the Levellers were in modern terms radical liberal individualists, not social-democrats; they looked for free trade, the destruction of monopolies, the rationalization of the law and administration and the redistribution of Parliamentary seats according to population, as well as biennial Parliaments. They did not advocate anything like universal suffrage, but wished to exclude apprentices, servants and all in receipt of parish relief, and, of course, beggars. Their radical doctrines tended to individualistic anarchy and the subversion of the existing order by free enterprise. Nor were they republican, but were quite ready to deal with the king, whether it was Charles I or Charles II. What they had in common with Cromwell and the Independents was hatred of bishops and Presbyterian discipline, and a determination to maintain freedom of conscience in religion. They were now exploiting the discontent in the army, where they won a brief but limited following. The Presbyterian oligarchs in the House had reacted with fury, alarmed at the army's demands, and had called out the London trained bands while their preachers had whipped up a London mob. On 26 July it got out of hand and invading Parliament forced it to rescind even the compromise settlement of the fundamental grievance — the army's claim to arrears. In the ensuing tumult the Speakers of Lords and Commons, Manchester and Lenthall, along with eight peers and fifty-seven of the Commons, betook themselves to the army on Hounslow Heath.

So on 6 August Fairfax had to order the occupation of London, which was done efficiently and economically by an encircling movement to Tilbury on the north and Gravesend on the south of the Thames estuary. The Tower and Westminster were also occupied; army headquarters were now established at Putney and the King installed at Hampton Court. Charles must still have thought that he had done well to conciliate the generals, though in fact they were being carried on a tide that would sweep them away from him. For when in a rehabilitated Parliament, anxious to conciliate the Scots and the Presbyterians, the Propositions of Newcastle were again submitted to him, the King, after some show of consideration recommended the army's proposals and reiterated his desire for a personal treaty with himself. A settlement sponsored by the generals still seemed in the offing, akin, as it now appears retrospectively, to that of 1688, with Cromwell in the role of General Monck.

The Presbyterian conservatives in Parliament killed the proposals out of hand. Cromwell and Ireton could not manage the Parliament for whom the army had won the war and whom they had now rescued from the London mob. The proposal to restore the bishops had created fanatical opposition. Moreover all the military offers had not, of course, really affected the King's intransigence. He had always regarded Cromwell and his colleagues coldly as 'rogues', and even while negotiating with them, had never recognized the army's claim to represent the people. Indeed, while on apparently close terms with the generals, Charles in his devious and dangerous way had again been negotiating with the Scots, who had now modified their demands about the Covenant, for he hoped that the Presbyterians in Parliament, the Londoners, the resurgent Royalists and a Scots army might give him even better conditions than the English generals.[444] So, as might be expected, Ireton's constructive compromise failed. Charles had been let down by the generals; Cromwell had been roundly snubbed by Parliament, and having strained his credit with the radicals in the army by colloguing with the King and — worse — by failing to obtain their arrears of pay, he had endangered his whole basis of power and even his personal safety. Always a realist, he put his power-base first; Cromwell abandoned the King.

For the army was seething with discontent, and for the first time in English history really radical demands were being made with substantial power behind them. The peasant's revolt of 1381 had been effective but brief and savagely put down; other peasant risings had been even less successful; now, when more people could read and the printing presses poured out pamphlets, the first formidable but short-lived attempt at social revolution took place.

The most influential but not the most extreme political propagandist was John Lilburne, whose *Jonah's cry from the Whale's Belly* and other sensational pamphlets, holding forth on supposed Anglo-Saxon liberties filched by 'Norman colonels', were written in the Tower, where he had previously done time for a breach of privilege against the House of Lords. They had a wide if ephemeral influence. The more extreme Levellers — the term meant originally people who threw down fences of enclosures, not those who wanted to 'level' all wealth — derived a good deal from the medieval tradition of the Lollards. Lilburne was a compulsive exhibitionist and demagogue, Wildman a lawyer on the make; but Walwyn, for example, was deeply religious, preaching brotherly love and rational Christianity, while Overton, a radical sceptic who still clung to salvation by faith, was a robuster pamphleteer and wrote, among other works, the *Nativity of Sir John Presbyter calculated by Scale Sky, Mathematician in Chief to the Assembly of Divines*.

The rank and file of the army were no more deeply imbued with religious ideas than the personnel of most armies, for the chaplains, attached to the staff, had far less influence than was once supposed; many conscripts probably shared the objectives of *The Good Soldier Schweik*, and regiments under military discipline were obviously not organized on the lines of an independent congregation or they would not have won their battles. But the clash of religious disputation created an explosive mixture on the surface of demographically deeper tides of discontent over pay and conditions. The men were captive audiences to the ranting of fanatical preachers and the propaganda of the agitators, who in Fairfax's, their own Lord General's, opinion had decisive influence. 'The power of the army,' he wrote afterwards, 'I once had was usurped by the agitators [the word's original meaning was neutral — it meant simply agents, those appointed to act], the forerunners of confusion and anarchy...' And he adds, most pertinently, 'at that time the pay was withheld from the army which increased their distempers... which gave these factious agitators occasion to carry on their design of raising their own fortunes upon the public ruin'.

This contemporary view of the more articulate representatives of the army reflects the alarm of most men of position and property when, briefly, the rift in the establishment opened careers to men hitherto outside it, and disclosed a strange world of popular discontent and aspiration. Hence, in the autumn of 1647, a real threat to the discipline and so the power of the army: the men had long been demanding their pay and indemnity for unlawful acts committed in the war — though 'many who had cried out "Indepmnity, Indepmnity!" afterwards asked what it was'.[445] Now on 18 October in *The Case of the Army Truely Stated* the radical minority made the revolutionary demand for manhood suffrage, along with biennial Parliaments, declared that all authority derived from the people, and ignored the King and the House of Lords. From 26 to 28 October and again early in November, in the since-famous debates in Putney Church between the Generals and the radicals, they attacked property itself. Cromwell and Ireton let them talk, argued with them, called prayer meetings;[446] but the rift in the establishment would be closed, discipline restored. It was plain however that Fairfax's and Cromwell's first task was to keep the army together, which they did. In November, having had a ringleader shot for incitement to mutiny on parade, Cromwell imposed a formal engagement on the army to obey its general officers and their General Council. The King was now a liability and a problem, to be got rid of. How, Providence would doubtless show.

At Hampton Court that autumn Charles began to feel the wind of disfavour. The guards were more numerous and less polite; the army leaders were no longer attentive. As the November fogs in the Thames valley crept round the rambling brick Tudor palace, he still hoped for a Parliamentarian-Royalist coalition in league with the Scots, whose Commissioners were already urging him to flight. Now it happened that the officer commanding at Hampton Court was Colonel Whalley, a cousin of Cromwell, who now conveniently discovered that the Levellers were plotting to assassinate the King — an unlikely contingency, as they were not republican.

On 11 November Charles received a warning, purporting to come from a witness, probably false, of a Leveller meeting where it had been 'decided and resolved for the good of the Kingdom to take [his] life away' — a message well calculated to make the King bolt; for Charles, though a brave man, always feared assassination. So that night, again accompanied by Jack Ashburnham and joined by Colonel Legge and Sir John Berkeley, former governors of Oxford and Exeter respectively, he stole away from Hampton Court. As when he had left Oxford, he had not yet entirely decided where to go, but rode south through the November night into Hampshire until he got next day to Titchfield Abbey, the mansion of the Earl of Southampton between Fareham and the Hamble river close to the sea.

He had a mind, if necessary, to go to France, and a vessel had been ordered to stand by. Ashburnham however had previously met and liked the Governor of Carisbrooke Castle in the Isle of Wight, young Colonel Robert Hammond, a cousin of Cromwell and son-in-law of Hampden, who, after killing a man in a duel and a successful fighting career, had applied for the sinecure post 'because he found the army was going to break all its promises with the King, and he would have nothing to do with such perfidious actions'.[447] The King therefore sent Berkeley and Ashburnham to sound him out. They rode to Lymington, where, stormbound, they spent the night, then crossed to Yarmouth and so to Carisbrooke and Newport, where they found Hammond, who appeared horrified at taking responsibility for the King — having retired to the island for a quiet life — and 'fell into passionate and distracted expressions'. They had made his position impossible, he said 'by bringing the King into the island, if at least you have brought him, and if you have not, pray him not to come'.[448] Though Berkeley advised against it, Ashburnham decided to bring Hammond to the King, so they all three went to Cowes and so across back to Titchfield.

Charles was not pleased. 'What!' he exclaimed, 'have you brought Hammond with you? Then you have undone me, for I am by this means made fast from stirring.' If he mistrusted the Governor, suggested Ashburnham, he would himself 'secure' Hammond: 'No,' replied the King, 'it is too late now to think of anything but going through the way you have forced upon me, and to leave the issue to God.' And Charles, having received Hammond cheerfully, then proceeded in his company to Carisbrooke.

20: CLOSING IN

BEFORE LEAVING HAMPTON Court Charles had written to the House of Lords: 'I appeal to all indifferent [impartial] men, if I have not just cause to free myself from the hands of those that change their principles with their condition, and who are not ashamed openly to intend the destruction of the nobility, by taking away the negative voice; and with whom the Levellers' doctrine is rather countenanced than punished.' He had pledged himself to 'endeavour the settling of a safe and well grounded peace', and once more complained that he had been repeatedly refused a hearing by his own Parliament.

At first he enjoyed ample liberty on the island. There were only twelve old men in the castle garrison; furniture from Cranborne was shipped across the Solent and the amenities of Carisbrooke improved — the inventory of the furniture is sumptuous: one bed worth £160, another worth £210, Turkey carpets, etc. Charles still had many of his favourite books, and the local gentry and populace welcomed him. He could ride and hunt in Parkhurst Forest, well stocked with deer, and enjoyed his last days of relative ease and comfort. But his busy, devious mind was following the usual incompatible objectives: the Parliament had not responded to his request to the Lords, or to a detailed compromise offer that had followed it up; they still demanded a settlement roughly in terms of the Propositions of Newcastle, now passed by the Commons into four Bills for Charles to take or leave. He rejected them, and the Parliament resolved to boycott the King by voting not to make more 'addresses' to him or receive any messages from him. Then on 24 December, after a fruitless appeal to the leaders of the army from whom he had escaped to mediate between him and Parliament, he made a fateful decision. He signed an Engagement with the Scots Commissioners with whom he had long been negotiating. It was very favourable to them: the Covenant to be imposed by statute — a major concession; a Presbyterian hierarchy for three years pending a final religious settlement by King and Parliament; no toleration — the sects to be put down; the army to be disbanded. And if this impracticable scheme were opposed — as it obviously would be — the Scots would again intervene in arms.

It surely took some nerve for the King, still in fact at the mercy of the army, to sign such an Engagement; but the formidable line-up of Scots, well-to-do Presbyterian conservative Parliamentarians, London and the Royalists was just what the Queen and the French wanted, and reflected powerful interests in the country. Implacably determined to regain what he considered his full divinely ordained rights, and again confident of his personal safety, Charles was ready to start another war.

He was also set on making another escape, and during the spring devised a series of ineffective attempts to do so, either to Scotland or to France. On 20 January Manchester wrote to Hammond warning him that the King 'had constant intelligence given him in all things which he received by the hands of a woman who brings it to him when she brings him his clean linen'.[449] Charles kept up a cheerful front — 'H.M. is as merry as formerly... after morning prayer takes usually before dinner some six or eight circuits about the castle wall and the like in the afternoon, if fair'. He spent much time each day in private and 'speakes most to us at dinner' of the affairs of Ireland, Scotland and London. His relations with Hammond were 'quiet and fair', and when messages came from London he would ask how his children did. His 'table' was costing the large sum of £10 per day — Hammond's own allowance as governor was 30s.⁴⁵⁰ But Hammond, who was a bachelor, had sent for his mother to help him keep house, and he had been assigned a gratuity of £1,000 and £500 a year for himself and his heirs.

Early in February 1648 Charles first tried to break out. Already suspicious, Hammond had posted four gentlemen to take turns to watch outside his door. A plot was therefore devised by Richard Firebrace,⁴⁵¹ his Page of the Bedchamber and Yeoman of the Robes, in conjunction with servants and local gentry, for breaking out of the bedchamber through the ceiling and so passing through the rooms above to a part of the castle unguarded by the sentries. Naturally the Committees of both Houses of Parliament — the effective government — got wind of it. 'The King's escape,' it was reported, 'is designed in this manner thus, by one Napier and a servant of David Murray's, whom we take to be the King's Tailor.'⁴⁵²

So the plot was prevented; the King's freedom curtailed. Later in February the King demanded of the governor, 'Why do you use me thus? Where are your orders for it? Did you not engage your honour you would take no advantage for them against me?... You are an equivocating gentleman. Will you allow me my chaplains? You pretend to liberty of conscience — shall I have none?' Whereat the exasperated Hammond replied, 'I'll speak to you when you are in a better temper.'

Charles was now more straightly confined, though the 'Barbican' or 'parade ground' of the castle was converted into a bowling green and a summerhouse put up. Five hundred men were brought over from Poole, and early in March Hammond arrived in the royal apartments to search for papers, at which, according to one account, Charles boxed his ears and thrust the papers into the fire. Nor was his incursion unjustified, for the King was in fact again planning to escape.

This time, on the evening of 20 March, alerted by pebbles thrown up to his window, he was to squeeze through a casement overlooking the inner court (where no sentry was posted), negotiate the castle wall by a rope and be met by his rescuers with horses; they would then convey him to a 'lusty boat'. Firebrace was convinced that the King could not squeeze through the 'upright bar between the casement windows'; Charles believed he could and shrank from filing through the metal plate that held it. 'I have been considering the Bar of my window,' he wrote 'and fynde that I must cut it in two places: for that place where I must cut it above I can hide it… but there is nothing that can hide the lower part.' The noise, he feared, perhaps rightly, would give him away. And at the critical moment Firebrace proved right. The King got stuck and was with difficulty eased back into the room. 'While he stuck,' Firebrace recollected, 'I heard him groan.'[453] But he could not come to help him. The horses and the lusty boat had waited that night in vain. Which non-event, from the Royalist point of view, was a pity, for as Gardiner writes, 'There can be no doubt that if the King had been really at large, a welcome would have been accorded him before which even the army would have found it difficult to stand.'[454] And even the republican Marten then admitted, 'We had better have this King back to oblige him, than to have him obtruded on us by the Scots.' Feeling was now high for the King, even in London.

But after the attempt of 20 March Charles was removed from his rooms in Hammond's quarters of the castle to a gable-fronted Elizabethan building in the quarters of the chief officer, considered easier to guard. This move prevented another amateurish escape plot at the end of March, to be effected by bribing a sentry, who gave it away.

In fact the only member of the royal family to escape was the Duke of York. On 20 April, under cover of a game of hide and seek in the garden of St James's, James, now aged fourteen, had slipped through a gate and been smuggled down to the Thames. Disguised as a girl in a gown of 'mixed mohair colour and black' and wearing a scarlet petticoat, the Duke had reached Middelburg on Walcheren, and so the Hague and the Court of his sister, the Princess of Orange. The King was delighted at the news.[455]

The accumulated tensions that the King's diplomacy had increased had now broken out, and the second Civil War, brief, but bitterer than the first, had begun. It had started in South Wales then spread to the north. On 23 March the Parliamentarian commander of Pembroke Castle had declared for the King, and by the end of April the Royalists had captured the key border towns of Berwick-on-Tweed and Carlisle. Charles had hoped to benefit by the war he had fomented, but the army was now furious against him. On 29 April the Army Council, though it no longer included the regimental agitators, held an emotional prayer meeting at Windsor and resolved that it was their duty to call Charles Stuart, 'that Man of Blood', to account 'for the blood he had shed and the mischief he had done to his utmost against the Lord's Cause and the people of these poor nations'. And as they prepared to deal with their adversaries in Wales, Scotland, the English counties and the City registered the revolutionary vote that 'neither this King nor any other of his posterity should ever reign King of England'.

At some risk to themselves, the generals had tried to do a deal with Charles: but Parliament had blocked it and it had never been popular with the rank and file. Thrown back on the army, the source of their power, they now had to stay with it — literally 'to live and die' with it — for they now knew they could not count on the King. They had always disliked the radical policies canvassed by the Levellers and others further to the left, as the Diggers and Fifth Monarchy Men; doctrines that the grandees of the army considered anarchic and impracticable at a time when 'the attitude of the poor to their lot seems often to have been one of careless stoicism... When starvation threatened, the poor were capable of using violence to secure food for themselves, but they made little contribution to the political radicalism of the time and showed no interest in attempting to change the structure of the society in which they found themselves'.[456] Moreover the generals had reasserted discipline, and still the common interest of the army in securing pay and indemnity for acts of war made it far the strongest of the contending factions to which the unnecessary conflict had reduced a hitherto comparatively thriving nation.

This fact of the army's solidarity Charles had not understood: he had hoped that the radicals would drive the generals into his own camp; but he was right to think that London and the major towns and the counties in general wanted a settlement. Unprecedented taxation and continuing uncertainty were bad for trade, at home and abroad, and the established gentry in the counties were determined to regain their old authority as justices of the peace against local Parliamentarian committees. Indeed the original resentment against his own relatively mild centralizing innovations had now been transferred to the much more onerous and efficient innovations of the Parliament. Many men of property now wanted the 'militia' nominally back under the King — in effect, as before, in their own hands — and feared that the army, 'had a design of taking away monarchical government and making themselves high and mighty'. The scene was thus set for a collision between the army and the rest, and in the event the oligarchic Parliament's victory would be their own ruin. The military power was confirmed, the Royalists quelled, the Scots routed, the men of property overridden, the feelings of all sides embittered, and the King, who had fomented the troubles, left helpless, the obvious victim and scapegoat of the army's revenge.

By May 1648 the Royalist revolts were widespread in England. On 20 May a bogus Prince of Wales appeared at Sandwich, but as his hair was flaxen and his complexion fair 'though somewhat tanned', and the real Prince was 'very black', he was evidently an impostor. On 21 May the Royalists rose in Kent and soon seized Rochester and Dartford, and on 27 May — a very important event — the fleet in the Downs mutinied against the plebeian and fanatical Leveller Rainsborough who had ousted Vice Admiral William Batten. They turned Rainsborough ashore and demanded that Batten be reinstated: even Warwick could do nothing with them, and nine ships and their crews, including Batten, who was knighted on arrival, went over to the real Prince of Wales. There were disturbances in London, Leicestershire, Nottinghamshire and the West Country and the threat of more.

Charles, watching from the Isle of Wight, was now more sanguine, particularly as the Scots were demanding — now of all times — that the New Model be disbanded and were preparing to intervene. But the generalship, mobility and interior lines of the army proved decisive. Cromwell went down to Wales; on 1 June Fairfax drove the Kent Royalists out of Maidstone and when they crossed the Thames to join the

Royalist rising under Sir Charles Lucas at Colchester, he pursued them by way of Tilbury and by 14 June attacked Lucas in the town; Ireton in the meantime put down further resistance in Kent. But the Roman walls and the castle of Colchester, resolutely defended by Lucas and Sir George Lisle, defied him. On 20 June Parliament ordained that all who took part in the war were guilty of high treason; but Cromwell was immobilized at Pembroke Castle, Fairfax besieging Colchester. Now, Charles hoped, was the opportunity for the Scots.

They failed to take it. Gone were the days of Covenanting fervour under the blessing of the Kirk; the commander-in-chief this time was the Royalist Duke of Hamilton, not the most resolute or efficient of men, and since the Kirk disapproved of the expedition, recruits had been slow to come in. It was not until 6 July that they even crossed the border, and then only with three thousand horse and six thousand foot, and without artillery. They lingered in Carlisle for a week, but by 11 July Cromwell had taken Pembroke Castle and by the end of the month he was himself marching north, having instructed Lambert to delay the Scots and keep them west of the Pennines, out of Yorkshire, where the local Royalists were stronger. Hamilton's army, now seventeen thousand strong, but deficient in ammunition and supplies, advanced through a series of Lancashire downpours, by Lancaster and Garstang to Preston near the mouth of the Ribble, while his forward troops got down as far as Wigan.

Cromwell, with only nine thousand men, running a major risk, then took this overextended army in flank. He crossed the Pennines to Clitheroe and advanced west down the north bank of the Ribble, and on 17-18 August 1648, after heavy fighting in enclosed country in vile weather, routed the main body of the Scots. Hamilton fled south from Cheshire to surrender at

Uttoxeter, Staffordshire, later to be executed for treason. Over three thousand foot surrendered. By a bold, swift stroke Cromwell had decided the war. He went on into Scotland, reinstated the Covenanting Argyll, reclaimed Berwick and Carlisle. On 28 August Colchester at last surrendered 'at mercy'; Lucas and Lisle were shot the same day.[457]

The second Civil War was over, but not its aftermath. During a wet and boisterous summer, Charles had remained cooped up in Carisbrooke while his hopes of rescue receded. The fleet under the Prince of Wales proved more interested in doing battle with the ships still loyal to Parliament than with taking off the King from the Isle of Wight, and Charles was reduced to spinning out negotiations in the hope that the victory of the army would make them the more detested by the Parliament. And here he calculated correctly. The news from Scotland came very ill to the Westminster Calvinist oligarchy, and despite their vote of 'No Addresses' passed in December, refusing to have any further truck with the King (that February they had 5,600 copies of it printed), they now approached him again.

   They had not lately been making themselves any more popular: that February all stage players and players of interludes and common players had been 'heartily declared to be and are taken to be rogues and punishable, notwithstanding any licence from the King or anyone'. All stages, galleries, seats and boxes were to be pulled down, and any players taken up after this ordinance were to be whipped or gaoled. When sports were repressed — partly to keep order as well as to put down pleasure — the mass of the people were probably more concerned. In London in April, on the verge of renewed war, Cromwell himself had been called in to quell a riot because a game of 'tip cat' had been suppressed on the 'Lord's Day'; at Bath the people were so fond of bull baiting that in defiance of the authorities they had carried on with it outside the city, beating a drum; at Warminster there had been food riots. Deserters from the New Model, such as John Sheppherd at Kilton who for a whole summer 'lay in the furze' living by robbery, terrorized the villagers in Somerset. After the bad harvest of 1647 wheat in Wiltshire reached the fantastic price by contemporary values of 64s a quarter; up and down the country in an always precarious and relatively underdeveloped economy, there was hunger, unemployment, discontent. And during that vile summer 'from May to Mid-September [there were] scarce three dry days together'.[458] To propitiate the Almighty and strike at the Independent sects Parliament ordained, brutally and comprehensively, that heresy and blasphemy were capital crimes.

In these unpropitious circumstances the more conservative Parliamentarians had hastened to renew negotiations with the King, who for his part was ready to make apparent concessions — which he intended afterwards to repudiate. So on 24 August both Houses repealed the vote of 'No Addresses'; Cromwell was still in Scotland or on the border, and on 18 September an elaborate conference began at Newport, Isle of Wight, at the head of the Medina river close to Carisbrooke. While the militants in the army were coining republican slogans, and the more religious-minded taking their victories as a confirmation of God's grace, the conservative men of property headed by Pembroke, who had done nicely out of the war, by Salisbury and by representative Commoners, refurbished the old proposals for another discussion.

Charles had spent much time on the island in reading and contemplation, and at Newport he handed over the manuscript of his reflections (revised at Hampton Court and Carisbrooke) which, transmogrified and expanded by Dr Gauden into the mannered pages of the *Eikon Basilike* or *The Pourtraicture of his Sacred Majestic in his Solitudes and sufferings*, in 1649 became a bestseller and a triumph of Royalist propaganda.[459]

Indeed the King's learning and introspective piety made him pretty self-sufficient. He was a scholar, who understood authors in the original — whether Greek, Latin, French, Spanish or Italian — and 'none was better read in history of all Sorts'. He also enjoyed theological disputations with young Mr Troughton, Hammond's chaplain, from whom he always 'parted merrily'. He particularly missed having his own chaplains, and civilly declined the offer of others of the Presbyterian persuasion — preferring to be 'Chaplain to himself'. Though he did not write *Eikon Basilike*, he provided much material and he annotated his Bible, which he handed to Juxon on the night before his execution with strict injunctions that it should be conveyed to Charles II, with exhortations to read it. He also read Andrewes's *Sermons* and Hooker on *Ecclesiastical Polity* and translations of Tasso and Ariosto and, for recreation, Spenser's *Fairie Queene*. He himself translated Sanderson's *de Juramentis* (On Oaths), and wrote in his own copy of the works of Shakespeare, '*Dum Spiro Spero*', 'while I live I hope'. 'Which,' says Herbert, putting a political gloss on it, 'he wrote frequently as the emblem of his hopes as well as endeavours for a happy agreement with the Parliament.'[460] He made up or cited a Latin verse:

> It is easy in adversity to despair of life:
> he does more bravely who knows how to face misery.

When the negotiations had failed, he wrote in November to the Prince of Wales: 'We know not but this may be the last time we may speak to you and the world publicly. We are sensible in to what hands we are fallen; and yet (we bless God) we have these inner refreshments the malice of our enemies cannot perturb: we have learned to busy ourself in retiring into ourself...'[461]

The negotiations at Newport were a last effort to close the rift in the establishment made by the rich civilian oligarchy that, after attaining its main purpose — for 'most of the lasting achievements of the English Revolution [had come] during the first two hundred days of the Long Parliament...'[462] — had pressed its advantage too far, and was losing power to the army and a King who was basically incapable of compromise. The danger from the radicals and their following, now articulate and organized in the army and inspired with iconoclastic zeal against established Church and monarchical State, was now patent; Given the authoritarian Presbyterian outlook, the prospect of toleration, so attractive to those brought up on modern liberal, rationalist principles, then appeared to the Parliament extremely dangerous. The sects, since so much cried up by historians, in fact included a broad lunatic fringe; and the orthodox Presbyterian Calvinists, having done away with transubstantiation, the essential mystery of the Catholic faith, were now threatened with an attack even on the idea of 'Providence', whereby they had retained a coherent world view. 'By 1645 the reaction against formal prayer had gone so far that an Essex Anabaptist could declare that "no one but witches and sorcerers use to say the Lord's Prayer". Extreme sectarians regarded the very idea of a professional clergyman as magical.'[463] Threatened by this kind of collapse of authority, on 29 August the Parliament directed that the election of elders throughout the whole newly imposed Presbyterian hierarchy should proceed — a measure embarrassing for some of the less learned Anglican brethren who had conformed to the Covenant, since it included stiff tests in Greek, Latin and even Hebrew.

These measures was bound to enrage the sectaries in the army: the Parliament men realized that it was the more urgent to settle with the King; but they had miscalculated. Charles never took them seriously, and power had already passed to the military. Yet the Committee of both Houses were still determined to reassert themselves: on 5 September, for example, a Lieutenant Colonel Kelsey, in command of the Oxfordshire Horse, had disputed Parliament's order to suppress dissident forces without the command of Fairfax. 'You are to know', they had written 'that this Committee has power to give orders to the Lord General to command all the forces of the Kingdom for preserving the peace. We are wholly dissatisfied with this deportment of yours.'[464] Two days later Parliament had been informed that the pay of the Horse Guards who protected the House was exhausted; unless it was renewed 'the guards would cease'. That problem at least had been promptly solved. Meanwhile there was urgent concern about the security of the Yarmouth fisheries, and indeed of the communications with Scotland against a threat from the Royalist fleet, while the Royalists in the Scilly Isles, in their strategic position to interfere with trade, were still in revolt, and pirates were making the Channel dangerous as far east as Weymouth.

When on 18 September the strong Parliamentary delegation from both Houses arrived on the island, Charles, with his attendants the Duke of Richmond, the Marquis of Hertford, the second Earl of Lindsey and the Earl of Southampton, was installed, under parole not to make off, in Sir William Hodge's house in Newport, where the King was 'to have his liberty, be treated with honour' and his personal safety guaranteed. John Crewe, one of the delegates, even hoped that, if after forty days both sides could come to an agreement sanctioned by Parliament, 'his Majesty [would] come to London or to some of his courts near London, for if all shall be agreed and signed, all jealousies then are ended and vanished'.

Charles merely deployed the old arguments. He again objected that he had given his oath to maintain the bishops, thought it sacrilege to alienate Church lands, argued that 'episcopacy had been exercised by the Apostles'; but he made major concessions over the militia, government appointments and the temporal power of bishops, though he stuck at refusing pardon for Rupert, Maurice, Newcastle, Bristol and other Royalists. 'What will be the conclusion,' wrote Crewe, 'I am doubtful.' If this proved 'but a fyght off shore' it would make 'the ensuing rough ocean the more terrible'; and by 6 November he was writing: 'a break is like to hazard the Navy and lose Ireland… and no man knows what will become of religion and the Parliament without a Peace'.[465]

His fear was justified. Charles had not meant the concessions seriously. Even on 7 October, while the so-called treaty of Newport was being negotiated, he had written: 'notwithstanding my too great concessions already made, I know that, unless I shall make yet others which will make me no King, I shall be but a perpetual prisoner… To deal freely with you, the great concessions I made this day — the Church, the militia, and Ireland — were made merely in order for my escape which, if I had not hoped, I would not have done.' Not surprisingly, when, on 27 October negotiations on the treaty were concluded, the Parliament rejected the terms, though without breaking off negotiations, and on 30 October the King was writing: 'Believe me I shall speedily be put to my shifts or couped up again.' He hoped to get away to the Royalist fleet, soon to be gratified by the news that Rainsborough had been shot at Doncaster by Royalists still holding out at Pontefract. On 12 November the King's followers were reported as enquiring about the tides, hoping to get him to Gosport, whereat Ireton instructed Hammond: 'You should see to the securing of that person from escape.' As a last resort Fairfax and the Army Council again sent Charles the *Heads of Proposals*, whereat the King temporized, offered to come to London and consider them in consultation with Parliament. He evidently still felt that he had a strong hand, and might settle with Parliament at the army's expense; and if Parliament had then brought him to London he might have done so.

This the army leaders were determined to prevent. So on 24 November at army headquarters at Windsor it was decided that the King's person must again be secured. Hammond was superseded by a Colonel Ewer, a tough customer who had been a 'serving man', whose orders were to take him to Hurst Castle on the Solent. When Hammond refused to hand over the command, both men left the island to appeal to headquarters. The resulting hiatus of authority was the King's last, most urgent, and most favourable chance to get away. Again he failed.

On 15 November Hammond had again been warned that 'the design holds for the King's escape' and 'to escape without exciting your suspicions he intends to walk out on foot a mile or two as usually in the daytime, and then horses are laid in the Isle to carry him to a boat'. The plan had come to nothing, but now it was even more urgent to escape. For the army was now on Charles's track. On 18 November the Council of Officers, though they had brought the Leveller indiscipline under control, accepted a *Remonstrance of the Army*, devised by the republican-minded Ireton, the 'theoretician' of the revolution, which demanded that 'the capital and grand author of our troubles, the person of the King,... may be speedily brought to justice for the treason, blood and mischiefs he's therein guilty of. Two days later the *Remonstrance* was submitted to Parliament, backed by a covering letter from Fairfax to the Speaker asking him to lay it before them immediately. Parliament, continuing the negotiations, ignored the *Remonstrance* — the King called it 'The Thundering Declaration of the Army' — for a week; but plainly the army leaders were now more openly determined both to conciliate their radical rank and file and thwart any misunderstanding between King and Parliament. At any minute now they might seize the King. And on 28 November when the negotiations at Newport publicly ended, Charles's formal farewell to the Commissioners was full of foreboding.

> My lords, you are come to take your leave of me, and I believe we shall scarce ever see each other again; but God's will be done. I thank God I have made my peace with him, and shall without fear, undergo what he shall be pleased to suffer men to do unto me. My Lords, you cannot but know that, in my fall and ruin, you see your own, and that also near to you. I pray God send you better friends than I have found. I am fully informed of the whole carriage of the plot against me and mine. [Nothing, he concluded, afflicted him more than the miseries he foresaw for his three kingdoms] drawn upon them by those who, upon pretence of public good, violently pursue their own interests and ends.[466]

On 29 November, a stormy day, a Colonel Cobbett arrived in Newport with troops from Windsor. The King was to be forcibly removed: that evening the guards were doubled, with musketeers, their matches burning, posted at the door of the King's bedroom itself. Richmond now urged Charles to escape: he had himself got the password and donning an officer's coat he and Captain Edward Cooke walked out past the sentries and returned. Cooke had horses and a boat waiting: he begged Charles to take the chance; in the darkness and confusion it might well have come off.

But the King made difficulties. He had given his parole, he said, he would not break it. The parole, they argued, had been to Parliament, not the army. But Charles was obdurate. Perhaps he was past caring.

Early on 1 December Charles, still not knowing his destination, was taken to Freshwater harbour a little beyond Yarmouth, and made the short crossing of the Solent — it took three hours — to Hurst Castle (or, as Herbert calls it scornfully, 'Blockhouse') at the end of the long spit of shingle beach that juts out between Lymington and Christchurch. At Newport the lieutenant colonel in charge, a rough soldier, tried to get into the royal coach, whereat the King for once lost his temper. 'It has not come to that yet,' he said, 'get you out.' He insisted that only his gentlemen, Herbert and Harrington, should accompany him; the lieutenant colonel had to ride. The King had been, for once, openly moved at parting from his entourage of the four great peers.

Hurst is one of the castles built by Henry VIII from Calshot westward to Portland and St Mawes, and today it is little changed. A compact, miniature and in its day formidable example of Tudor military architecture, it commands a magnificent view of the western entrance of the Solent, with the Needles to the south-west and the little town of Yarmouth opposite. There is still much coming and going of shipping, and in Charles's time the prospect must have been busy. But a shingle beach does not make easy walking, and the little King's habitual brisk exercise must have been slowed down. An operational fort, its immensely thick walls were pierced only by narrow apertures; so that 'his room was neither large nor lightsome; at Noonday (in the winter season) requiring candles and at night he had his wax lamp set as formerly in a silver bason which illuminated his bedchamber'. The cry of gulls and the smell of seaweed, the occasional flash of sunlight on breaking waves, may have relieved its grimness, but in the long December nights the tramp of sentries and the isolation made it sinister.

And the King's reception had been disconcerting: the local commandant, a Captain Eyre, appeared uncouth — 'ready to receive the King with small observance,' writes Herbert — 'his look was stern, his hair and large beard were black and bushy, he held a Partizan [a halberd] in his hand, and (Switz-like) had a great Basket hilt sword by his side; hardly could one see a man of more grim aspect and no less robust and rude was his behaviour'. But after some 'admonishing', this bear became 'mild and calm', even co-operative, and Charles was not without attendants who kept up an attempt at state, while the country people flocked to the narrow doorway to watch him dine.

After nearly three weeks of this monotonous routine the King had lost his habitual poise, for when the flamboyant and fanatical General Thomas Harrison, the son of a butcher at Newcastle-under-Lyne, who had volunteered for Essex's Lifeguard, won rapid promotion and at the least provocation would 'discourse very fluently and pour himself out in the extolling of free grace', and had denounced the King as a man of blood, arrived at Hurst Castle during the night, Charles, startled by the rattle of the drawbridge, rang his silver bell before dawn, asked who it was and remarked 'that is the man that meant to kill me... This is a fit place'. In fact, they did not meet: Harrison had come to arrange his transfer; and on 17 December, reassured, Charles left Hurst for Windsor Castle, 'leaving', he said, 'the worst for the best Castle in England'. He rode up with an escort of cavalry by way of Ringwood, then through the forest by Romsey to Winchester where he was made heartily welcome by the mayor, aldermen, clergy and people, and so to Alton. Near Farnham he actually encountered Harrison, in a velvet cap, new buff coat and a crimson sash richly fringed, who gave the King a bow 'all *a soldado*'; but when before dinner in his quarters in the town Charles took him aside and, taxing him with threats, tried to make something of him, all he got was an equivocal answer. 'It is not true sir. What I did say I will say again. The Law is equally bound to great and small and justice has no respect of persons.'[467] The King, says Herbert, 'found this spoken to no good end and left further communication with him'.[468] At Bagshot a last feeble attempt was made to exchange the King's supposedly lame horse for a swift hunter belonging to Lord Newburgh, but the amateurish plot was detected and anticipated and a more sober animal substituted. He would of course have been caught quite soon anyway.

At Windsor, 'a place he had ever delighted in', Charles was given his usual bedchamber towards the end of the castle ward and accorded much of his old state: he was served, with fanfares, on bended knee, and allowed to walk on the long terrace and 'enjoy the grand prospect of the Thames towards the fair college of Eton' and the woods beyond. But none of the nobility or gentry were allowed to pay their respects. In fact he was doomed.

On 2 December, the day after the King had been safely secured at Hurst Castle, the army had seized power. Judging by results, their leaders were now convinced that providence was clearly on their side, and they made a radical move, declared for the dissolution of the Long Parliament and new elections. Fairfax also demanded £40,000 from the City for arrears of army pay and seized £28,000 in cash from the Parliamentary Committee for the Advancement of Monies. Parliament had defied them, and unfortunately for Charles, their defiance had involved the King. The Presbyterian Members of Parliament had voted, justly enough, that he had been removed to Hurst Castle without their consent, and that, in spite of the breakdown of negotiations at Newport, the King's replies had after all provided a basis for a settlement.

The defiance had proved their ruin. On their own authority the Army Council — Fairfax, as so often, appears to have abdicated his political responsibility as Commander-in-Chief — Ireton and his colleagues had decided to purge the House of Commons — a better alternative, they thought, than a dissolution and an election that might return a more hostile Parliament. So on the early morning of 6 December 1648 soldiers were posted at the entrance to the House in a coup known as Pride's Purge. Identified by Lord Grey of Groby, forty-seven members were arrested, and ninety-six had been turned away. Of the remaining seventy-eight, about twenty refused to sit until their imprisoned colleagues were released; the remainder were entirely dependent on the army. Parliament had forfeited what constitutional authority they still possessed.[469]

After 6 December there was thus no power in England but the sword. Two days later, Oliver Cromwell, who had declared that 'he had not been acquainted with the design, yet since it was done he was glad of it and would endorse and maintain it', took his seat, to be formally thanked for his victories over the Scots. Having disposed of the Long Parliament, save for a subservient remnant aptly afterwards termed the 'Rump', the army now had to decide what they were to do with the King.

21: THE FRAME-UP

PRIDE'S PURGE[470] HAD marked a hardening in army policy — a *coup d'état*, mainly by a republican-minded minority. But it had been reluctantly connived at by the military 'grandees', as the Levellers called them, who were all in the same boat, determined to save their own careers — and perhaps their lives — by preventing a settlement between King and Parliament. For that was still on the cards, with the House of Commons voting by 129 to 83 that the King's final proposals were a basis for negotiation, though they had made the crucial mistake of not at once bringing the King to London. Harrison, who had much to lose, had put the interests of the senior officers with brutal frankness: at the conclusion of such a treaty, he declared, 'we shall be commanded by King and Parliament to disband, the which if we do we are unavoidably destroyed... and if we do not disband, they will by Act of Parliament proclaim us traitors and declare us to be the only hindrance of settling peace in the nation'. And traitors met a traitor's death: it might be the King's life or theirs. Further, in the cloudy turbulence of his introspection, Cromwell was brooding on the evidence that God by punishing the King had sanctioned his own mission. But although 'impaled between the dictates of Providence and gentry constitutionalism',[471] his instinctive and ruthless opportunism showed him a way out.

On a more primitive level, many of the soldiers were demanding a scapegoat for the bloodshed of the wars, and indeed a blood sacrifice might well appease an incalculable Almighty, who must be extremely annoyed with His Englishmen considering the catastrophes He had lately been inflicting on them. Add to this the politically astute idea 'that the price of heading off the radicals was the King's death', and the case for victimizing the 'grand Delinquent' was formidable. And if God had witnessed against the King, the sins of Parliament were also blatant: 'I verily think that God will break that great Idol the Parliament,' said one enthusiast, 'and that old jog-trot form of government of King, Lords and Commons.'

In the drizzle and darkness early in an English December — on Sunday the tenth it began to snow and in parts of the country there were threats of famine — the political decisions were made. The Presbyterian preachers in London were now rabid against the army; but the public appeared indifferent to the purge of the Commons, having little love for politicians. Though in a mood of 'glum and resentful endurance',[472] the Londoners and probably the rest of the country seemed cowed: and 'from the removal of the King from Newport until his death on the scaffold not one of the King's subjects risked their lives to save him'[473] — as one Royalist paper put it, 'to the perpetuall Dishonour of the English Nation', 'who could stand still and see their sovereign murthered only for maintaining their liberties'.[474]

At Windsor Charles kept his last Christmas forlornly enough. At Newport, in anticipation of going up to London, he had ordered fine new clothes of velvet with gold embroidery and a satin-lined cloak, which may have accorded with the hollow ceremonial with which he was still surrounded. In the castle, that stronghold of royalty, the routine carried on of its own momentum, and after Christmas the Army Council had to send down a special order that it be discontinued. The King, whose long-contrived impassivity in public remained unshaken, now merely dined in private, selecting what few dishes he wanted to be sent in. The predominantly loyal populace at Windsor, who had gathered to cheer him on his arrival in the rain, were excluded from witnessing the formal meals hitherto served at the English Court with the strictest protocol in Europe. The officer in charge, Colonel Matthew Thomlinson, was relatively humane, and continued in charge of the King until the day of his execution, but Charles is alleged to have been subjected to systematic insult. 'Whilst he was at Windsor,' said one Royalist paper, 'they let the very rascallity of the souldiery revile him… "You with a pox on you" (said one soldier) "must have fifteen pounds a day allow'd you for your table, but we poor soldiers that stand in the cold must not have isd. to releeve us with. Well Stroaker… we shall be quit of you ere long."'[475] To such a pass had come the monarchy of Henry VIII and Elizabeth I.

Charles still had Thomas Herbert with him, but James Harrington, having refused to spy on attempts at rescue, had been dismissed. At Newport the King's major courtiers had been set aside and he now had no confidant, for Herbert, who exculpates himself in his *Memoirs* and did his best, was not his man but a watchdog. His enemies were closing in for the kill, and the leaders of them, now Oliver Cromwell and his son-in-law Ireton, were the most powerful men in the kingdom. From wanting to save the King's life — why kill captive Charles I to make free Charles II king? — Cromwell had now come round to believe that Providence through manifest signs had predestined the King's death, and that he must be the instrument of it. He was prepared now even to root out monarchy, for he must have known — as did Napoleon when he had the Duc d'Enghien shot — that there could afterwards be no reconciliation between himself and the dynasty. But as he had kept clear of Pride's Purge, which he would have preferred to have been made by expulsion from within, he now wanted to kill the King with all the threadbare appearance of legality and consent that he could muster — and kill him soon. For he well knew the diamond-hard determination and obstinacy that in the last resort the devious King could command: he could not reckon on frightening him by the mounting threats into accepting a dogeship. Under the usual smokescreen of cant and prayer, Cromwell now meant business.

The Army Council and its creation, the Rump, had now consolidated their position: the Levellers and radicals had been allowed to blow off steam in much ill-ordered debate, and on 18 December the remnant of the Commons, with shrewd timing, had at last granted John Lilburne the £3,000 compensation he had been awarded for persecution under the King's regime, and that high-minded and eloquent man had at once made off to County Durham to collect it from the Royalists on whose estates it had been charged. In the City too, a Royalist lord mayor, elected when the treaty of Newport looked promising, had been shackled when General Skippon, still commanding the trained bands, had packed the Common Council with adherents of the army and the Commons.

The lawyers had been less pliable, and the fellow-travelling intellectuals shocked. The Chief Justices withdrew from the proceedings: Bulstrode Whitelock, who, it will be recalled, had refused to prosecute Laud, and although a Parliamentarian had been a friend of Edward Hyde and consistently worked for compromise, now deliberately left London for the country; while the intellectual Algernon Sidney protested volubly to Cromwell, who replied in exasperation, 'We will cut off the King's head with the crown upon it.' The clerk of the House of Commons also resigned. Leaving no stone unturned, on 29

December the Army Council listened to the revelation of Elizabeth Poole of Abingdon, for 'during the Civil War period it became common for prophets to lobby the King or the Army leaders with accounts of the visions in which God had declared his political preferences',[476] but she proved too incoherent to be politically serviceable.[477]

It had now been determined that the King should be brought to trial: on 2 January 1649, the day that Lord Denbigh, sometime ambassador to Venice and Turin in the 1630s who had collected works of art for Charles and since fought for the Parliament, was sent to him with specious offers, but the Rump House of Commons, having prejudged the question, sent up an ordinance to the remnant of the Lords creating a special tribunal to try the King for treason, at the same time resolving that he had committed it 'by levying war against Parliament and Kingdom'. The ordinance was of course rejected by the remnant of the Lords (twelve of them, including Northumberland, Pembroke, Manchester and Denbigh). So on 6 January 1649 the Rump House of Commons made a revolutionary claim. 'The people under God,' they asserted, were 'the original of all power'; and 'the Commons of England in Parliament assembled, being chosen by and representing the People, [had] the supreme power of this nation.' Further, they claimed that whatever they enacted or declared had the force of law, even without the consent of the monarch or the Upper House. On the same day they followed up their ordinance by asserting the entirely unconstitutional right to promulgate a 'High Court of Justice' of 135 commissioners, specifically empowered to sit for forty days to try their sovereign. So not only the relatively new-fangled Tudor style prerogative but the ancient hierarchy of the medieval *communitas regni* with its balance of estates was swept aside. Their action led to a short-lived Republican Commonwealth and Protectorate, resoundingly proclaimed to the world by Cromwell's determination to kill the King with the fullest publicity, as a quasi-legal deliberate act of state.

Apprised of these illegal and ominous proceedings, for 'the Long Parliament had shrunk to an unauthorized assembly, meeting by permission of the soldiers to do what the soldiers told them',[478] Charles remained calm. He had been playing with hopes of rescue by an army from Ireland or from the Continent, though he now knew he would be deposed. But he was not yet convinced that he would be murdered: 'It is true,' Herbert reports his saying, 'my grandmother, the Queen of Scots, suffered under Queen Elizabeth but she was no sovereign, but subject to law. Indeed some Kings of England have been lamentably murdered by Ruffians in a clandestine way, old Chronicles inform us, but the facts were neither known nor approved of by any King.' He expected to be confined to the Tower, while the Prince of Wales or perhaps the young Duke of Gloucester — a child young enough to be conditioned for a dogeship — nominally succeeded him. His mood was impassive, resigned. When informed on 7 January that he was to be removed to Whitehall, he had merely remarked, 'God is everywhere alike in wisdom, power and goodness.' Though only forty-eight, he now looked old, his hair and beard grey, pouches under his eyes, though he held himself with his old dignity and was physically fit, so that the physicians afterwards thought he could have lived to a ripe old age. He left Windsor in his coach between ranks of musketeers and pikemen of the guard, then, accompanied by the inevitable Harrison and a party of horse, he was taken through bitter weather to the Palace of St James's.

Here again the momentum of royal service carried on; Charles again dined publicly in state in the presence chamber, with the old formality. Then the Army Council caught up with what was going on and they 'brought his meat up by soldiers, the dishes uncovered',[479] which was 'an uncouth sight to the King'. So again he took his meals in private.

On 19 January he was hustled by sedan chair to his usual rooms in Whitehall across the park; security precautions were increased: musketeers with their matches smouldering and stinking were stationed at the door. Next day, even more heavily guarded by musketeers and pikemen under the command of the appropriately named Colonels Hacker, Huncks and Axtell, Charles was moved by curtained barge to Sir Richard Cotton's large house up river but nearer Westminster Hall, where the trial was to take place. The last days of the royal aesthete were pervaded by the stamp of sentries, the bark of military command, the smell of leather and sweat and of the tobacco that, like his father, he had always particularly disliked. The army and the Commons had stumbled upon a technique later elaborated in our own day — the trial of a 'war criminal', with some of the niceties of psychological preparation.

Westminster Hall, the scene of Strafford's trial and attainder, had been hastily prepared for an even more important event. The Norman walls and elaborate roof put up for Richard II, another fated royalty with artistic taste, had been echoing to the hammers of workmen putting up crude screens, galleries and boxes for another sinister, exciting and profitable occasion. In similar haste the remnant of the Commons, which the excluded but still indefatigable Prynne terms the 'present unparliamentary junto' (and the Royalists 'Noll Cromwell's journeymen') had nominated the 135 notables, of whom they hoped to implicate about half, to try the King. In fact some could not have reached London in time in the depth of a bitter winter, and though the quorum, cautiously put at twenty, was always exceeded, forty-seven of those nominated to the tribunal never turned up and eight more cut after the first session. Only 59 out of 135 signed the death warrant.

Appointed by the Rump of the Commons, which had no claim to be representative even of the politically conscious nation, merely of a political and military faction, the tribunal had no shred of legality itself; but the essential of revolution was there: a resolute clique under ruthless leaders. The revolutionary republicans even in the purged Commons were a small minority: they tended to be older than the others — veterans of Jacobean and early Caroline political struggles, many of them born 'younger sons'; not very many had been to the universities or Inns of Court, and those that the army had secluded or imprisoned tended to be the ones who had. Some of the most fervent radicals came, not surprisingly, from the north — from 'beyond Humber' as the Anglo-Saxons would have said. None of them came from the oligarchic group that had originally coalesced round Pym, nor was it just a revolution of Independent sectaries against Presbyterians: 'it was a revolution against moderates of all political colours'.[480] Moreover, since most of them, rich or poor — and most were poor — were in debt and creditors of the state, they wanted no compromise with the Royalists; 'the statistics show very clearly that the Revolutionaries were more likely than any other group to obtain financial benefit from the Revolution'.[481] About two-thirds of them had bought confiscated Royalist land and 'were keenest on the drive for official place'. Add to these perennial human motives the dogmatic neo-classical republicanism of

Ireton — the intellectual force behind his father-in-law — the fierce and representative fanaticism of Hugh Peters, the army chaplain, who wanted a blood sacrifice to appease the Almighty, and the fear of the higher officers for their own careers and even lives in the quarrelsome litigious world of seventeenth-century England, and a 'sadistic authoritarian behaviour pattern' becomes intelligible.

As the hastily improvised but elaborate frame-up took shape, more men of moderate and responsible opinion drew back. Only one lord, and that Lord Grey of Groby, so called by a courtesy title as the son of the Earl of Stamford, signed the death warrant. Of the four baronets, three, as sometimes happens, were considered disreputable; the tribunal was not, as the Cavaliers alleged, 'a court of brewers draymen, but it was not a court of the gentlemen of England'.[482] Nor was it one of the people. The Army Council certainly did not represent the Levellers and radicals whom they were circumventing and would soon put down — indeed Lilburne hated the 'grandees' so much that he said he would prefer a king. As for the soldiers, 'although most of the cavalry could read... the infantry were nearly all illiterate',[483] most of them were conscripts and many turncoats; their political motives were hazy and fickle — mainly they wanted pay and continuing employment. Fairfax was perhaps lulled, says Wood (as puzzled as most commentators by the conduct of this extremely able soldier but incapable politician) by the crisis into 'a kind of stupidity'; he says himself that he only remained in command to keep the men in hand. At free quarters in the occupied City they were extremely unpopular, and behaved brutishly at the King's trial. No more than the 'Rump' did they represent the nation: the Club Men of Dorset and Wiltshire were probably far more representative of the farmers and peasants who then formed the great majority of the Englishmen. It was just because the army was so much detested that at the Restoration, after a decade of 'sword government', the old civilian regime of King, Lords and Commons was restored, for the army had wrecked Parliament and overridden the rule of law, the most tenacious of all the political traditions of England.

While Charles was still at Windsor, the tribunal — or 'High Court of Justice' — met for the first time. Only fifty-three of its members had mustered in the Painted Chamber, originally decorated for Henry III. The newly appointed attorney general had pleaded illness, and the main prosecution fell to Isaac Dorislaus,[484] a Dutch immigrant, and John Cook,[485] a fanatic and vindictive personality, solicitor general and principal counsel for the prosecution. They drew up a resounding proclamation that the court would sit on 10 January, and on the ninth 'Serjeant Dendy rid into Westminster Hall, with the mace belonging to the House of Commons on his shoulder, and some officers attending him all bare [headed]: and, the guard of horse and foot being in both palaces, six trumpeteers sounded on horseback in the middle of Westminster Hall and in the meantime the drums did beat in the Palace Yard, after which proclamation was made'.[486] It was again made in the City, before the Exchange and in Cheapside. The Act of State was not to be done in a corner.

It remained to find someone ready to be President of the Court. Reluctantly, John Bradshaw, an undistinguished barrister and a younger son of Cheshire gentry, shouldered the appointment. He had been put into the tribunal as a substitute for the judges who had refused to join it, and, elected president in his absence, he had accepted the next day. He was assigned the spacious deanery of Westminster as his residence and laid in 'a high crowned beaver hat lined with plated steel to ward off blows' — still to be seen in the Ashmolean Museum at Oxford.[487] By the eleventh the court had a Lord President and the charges against the King had now to be formulated. They gave rise to a long, learned and acrimonious discussion lasting more than a week while the King was at St James's.

On Saturday 20 January 1649 Charles was brought from Cotton House into Westminster Hall. Here, in face of the court, the serjeant-at-arms received him and conducted him to a crimson chair placed opposite the Lord President and the tribunal, who occupied the south end of the building. The King was thus disadvantageously placed with his back to most of the public and to many of those who had paid high prices for boxes and places in the galleries. By modern standards security arrangements, as at Strafford's trial, were rudimentary, but he was strongly guarded by halberdiers and musketeers. While the King was being sent for, the tribunal had answered a roll call, and when Fairfax's name was called, a masked lady, later known to be Lady Fairfax, called out not very audibly, 'He has more sense than to be here.'

Charles preserved a regal calm; he wore black relieved by the blue of the garter ribbon of the George and the big silver star of the Order on his cloak:

> After a stern looking upon the Court, and the people in the galleries on each side of him, he places himself in the chair, not at all moving his hat, or otherwise showing the least respect to the court. He then riseth up again, and turns about, looking downwards upon the guards placed on the left side and on the multitude of spectators on the right side of the great hall; the guard attending him in the mean time dividing themselves on each side of the court, and his own servants,

following him to the bar, stood on the left side of the prisoner.[488]

'Charles Stuart, King of England,' began the Lord President, from his own crimson chair and canopy of state, 'the commoners of England assembled in Parliament [a euphemism for the Rump] being sensible of the great calamities that have been brought upon the nation... and according to the duty they owe to God, to the nation and to themselves, have constituted the High Court of Justice before which you are now brought, and you are to hear your charge, upon which the Court will proceed.'[489] Cook followed this up: 'My lord, on behalf of the Commons of England and of all the people thereof, I do accuse Charles Stuart, here present, of high treason, and high misdemeanour.' 'Hold a little,' said the King, and when Cook, who was by him, took no notice, he rapped him on the arm, whereat, with an ill omen, the silver head of the King's cane rolled to the floor.

No one retrieved it — Herbert says he was on the other side — and Charles eventually stooped and retrieved it himself. But the Solicitor General was not to be denied: the Clerk of the Court read out the charge. Its essence was the old medieval accusation that he had ruled like a tyrant by will, not by the laws, and that he had levied war upon his own people. The charge then descended to particulars — rehearsing landmarks of the conflict, 'by which cruel and unnatural wars, much innocent blood of the free people of the nation have been spilt, damage incurred, parts of the land spoiled — some of them even to desolation'.

Charles remained impassive, merely smiling in contempt at the words tyrant, traitor, murderer and public enemy of the commonwealth. The court then demanded his reply. He gave none. He merely denied its jurisdiction. In the stress of the event, 'his deportment was very majestic and steady'; his stammer had left him; he spoke with lucidity and force. From this denial, impeccable in law, he never moved.

> I would know [he asked, pertinently] by what power I am called hither... Now I would know by what authority, I mean, lawful (there are many unlawful authorities in the world, thieves and robbers on the high-ways) but I would know by what authority I was brought from thence [the Isle of Wight] and carried from place to place (and I know not what) and when I know what lawful authority I shall answer. Remember I am your King, your lawful King, and what sins you bring upon your heads, and the judgement of God upon this land: think well upon it! I say, think well upon it before you go from one sin to a greater... I have had a trust committed to me by God, by old and lawful descent; I will not betray it, to answer a new, unlawful authority.

Overriding Bradshaw, he drove home the argument: 'England was never an Elective Kingdom; but an hereditary Kingdom for near these thousand years: therefore let me know by what authority I am called hither. I do stand more for the liberty of my people than any here whatsoever.' But Charles pressed his advantage with authority. 'Let me tell you; it is not a slight thing you are about... you shall do well to satisfy first God and then the country, by what authority you do it... There is a God in heaven, that will call you, and all that gave you power, to account.' Lamely, the Lord President replied, 'We are satisfied with our authority... it's upon God's authority and the Kingdoms.' Not to be deflected, Charles countered, 'For answer, let me tell you, you have shown no lawful authority to satisfy any reasonable man.' He would stand, 'as much for the privilege of the House of Commons, rightly understood, as any man'. Bradshaw again replied that the tribunal was satisfied with its own authority, and adjourned the session.

As he rose from his chair, Charles glanced at the sword and mace on the table before the Lord President: 'I do not fear that,' he said. To shouts of 'Justice! Justice!', and also to some of 'God Save the King', he left the hall for Cotton House. There he had so little privacy, with soldiers even in his bedroom, that he refused to undress or go to bed.

Sunday, or Lord's Day as the Puritans called it, intervened, and Charles spent most of the day at his devotions in company with the amiable and now aged Juxon who, it will be recalled, in his younger days had been a popular Bishop of London and a less popular administrator during the personal rule. The tribunal, meeting in the Painted Chamber, decided that if the King refused to recognize the court, he would be told that his guilt would be assumed.

On Monday 22 January it was Charles who attacked. Cook, conferring with the learned Dutchman, was slow to begin, so the King, using the other end of his cane, poked him into action.[490] But Charles kept the initiative. It was not, he said, his own case alone that concerned him: 'it is the freedom and liberty of the people of England; and, do you pretend what you will, I stand more for their liberties. For if power without law may make lawes, may alter the fundamental lawes of the Kingdom, I do not know what subject he is in England who can be sure of his life, or anything that he calls his owne'; 'What you do,' Bradshaw interrupted, 'is not agreeable to the proceedings of any Court of Justice'; but the King, 'though no lawyer professed,' repeated that 'he knew as much law as any gentleman in England... and therefore (under favour) I do plead for the liberties of the people of England more than you doe'. The Lord President then warned him he would be held in contempt of court, but Charles replied that he did not know how a King could be a delinquent. And he again denied the tribunal's authority. 'You ought not to interrupt,' said Bradshaw, 'when the Court is speaking to you.'

The Clerk of the Court then reiterated the charge: 'Charles Stuart, King of England, you have been accused on behalf of the people of England of high treason and other crimes: the Court has determined that you ought to answer the same.' All this Charles knew already. Doggedly he stuck to his argument. He also required time to elaborate it. 'Sir, tis not for prisoners to require.' 'Prisoners! I am not an ordinary prisoner.' The King again demanded proof that the House of Commons had the jurisdiction claimed: his case in law was unanswerable. Exasperated, Bradshaw commanded, 'Sergeant, take away the prisoner.' But as Charles left the hall the clamour was worse: the soldiers, writes Herbert, 'made a hideous cry for "Justice! Justice!"', a noise so 'uncouth' that the King was taken aback. 'Did you hear the soldiers cry for Justice?', he asked Herbert. 'I did and marvelled thereat.' 'So did I, the officers ordered it.' On his return to Cotton House a soldier said 'God bless you' and Charles thanked him, whereat an officer struck the man with his cane on the head, and the King remarked drily that the punishment exceeded the offence.

On Tuesday 23 January Charles was still intransigent, 'for the charge,' he said, 'I value it not a rush; it is the liberty of the people of England that I stand for. For me to acknowledge a new court that I never heard of before, I that am your King that should be an example... for to uphold justice, to maintain the old lawes, indeed I do not know how to do it... By your favour, you ought not to interrupt me. How I came here I know not. There's no law for it to make your King your prisoner...' Again Bradshaw fell back on the clerk: 'Clerk, do your duty.' The King: 'Duty, Sir!' And again he refused to answer the court, and the clerk 'recorded the default'. When again told that he was before a court of justice, the King remarked shortly, 'I see that I am before a Power.' The court then adjourned again to the Painted Chamber. For the time table of the frame-up had been upset: 'The situation was grave. The progress of the trial was little short of disastrous.'[491] Protests were pouring in, waverers were multiplying; Fairfax had boycotted the court.

Envoys had now arrived from the Dutch Estates appealing that the crisis should be settled by arbitration. The four great courtiers, Richmond, Hertford, Lindsey and Southampton, pledged their lives and estates to guarantee any terms that would restore the King. But Cromwell and Ireton, the republican Marten, Harrison and the 'grim Colonels', who had won the wars, knew the realities of power. There was no one in the islands or on the Continent who could intervene: they had the King by the throat and intended to finish him off.

So on Saturday 27 January the Lord President wore a scarlet judge's robe as 'befitting the business of the day', and including him sixty-eight members of the tribunal were present. As the King came in the deep-throated concerted shout again went up, 'Justice, Justice, Execution!', while in seventeenth-century confusion, Colonel Axtell was 'laughingly entertaining the soldiers, and scoffing aloud'. Silence being procured, Bradshaw again cited the charge of treason 'exhibited in the name of the people of England', whereat the 'malignant lady', afterwards known again to have been Lady Fairfax, cried out from the gallery, 'Not half the people, it is false; where are they or their consents? Oliver Cromwell is a traitor.' Axtell shouted, 'Down with the whores, shoot them', the musketeers raised their pieces and the 'woman was hustled out'. As already obvious, sentence had been decided, but Bradshaw conceded that before it the King might speak.

Charles, having declared that 'all things had been taken from him save conscience and honour', then played his last battered card. He again demanded to be heard before the Lords and Commons in the Painted Chamber: 'I do conjure you,' he said, 'as you love the liberty of the subjects and the peace of the Kingdom, that you grant me a hearing before sentence is passed.' Carried away by his own argument, he knew he had won a verbal victory: but, again, as a tactician he was unpractical; he had left it too late. What chance could there be, with the House of Lords virtually dispersed and in abeyance and the Commons a purged remnant, of any fairer hearing than the court had given him? It was widely thought afterwards that what he termed 'the propounding of somewhat to the Lords and Commons... for the peace of the Kingdom', might have been an offer to abdicate in favour of the Prince of Wales, but there is no proof of it, and his inflexibility makes it unlikely. He remained determined not to recognize the jurisdiction of the court. But his reasonable proposal had apparently shaken John Downes, auditor of the Duchy of Cornwall since 1635 and MP for Arundel, who made a scene and was silenced by Cromwell: 'What ails thee, art thou mad?'[492] Bradshaw withdrew the court to consider the King's request.

It did not take long. 'After the Lord President had cited many things in relation to the power of Kings' and to their being called to 'account for breach of trust', and after more concerted soldierly shouts of 'Justice, Justice, Execution!', the clerk read out the sentence. Whereas the Commons of England had appointed the Court and the accused had refused to answer the charge of high treason, the Court had adjudged that for all these treasons and crimes he, the said Charles

Stuart, as a tyrant, traitor, murtherer, and a public enemy, shall be put to death, by the severing of his head from his body.'

With a rustle of robes and cloaks the whole tribunal rose to their feet. The King still tried to argue, 'Will you hear me a word, Sir?'

'Sir, you are not to be heard after the sentence.'

'No, sir?'

'No, sir,' said the Lord President, 'by your favour sir. Guard withdraw your prisoner.'

'I may speak after the sentence,' the King countered. 'By your favour sir, I may speak after the sentence ever. By your favour [hold] the sentence. Sir, I say, Sir, I do…'. Then recovering from his renewed stammer, 'I am not suffered for to speak, expect what justice other people will have.'

According to Herbert, on 27 January as Charles was hustled from the hall after sentence and passed down the stairs, the soldiers scoffed at him, 'casting the smoke of their tobacco upon his face, one more insolent than the rest spitting in his face'. Charles merely took out his handkerchief and wiped off the offence, saying, 'Well, Sir, God hath justice in store both for you and me.' By one account he was then conveyed to Whitehall in a 'common Sedan chair, carried by two common porters', who had removed their hats, until the soldiers, who shared the current obsession with punctilio about headgear, made them resume them, while the people cried out, 'Why do you carry the King in a common Sedan? as they do such as have the plague [a sidelight on why it spread]. God deliver your Majesty.' But Herbert says he was taken to Cotton House and to Whitehall again by water. On Sunday afternoon Charles was again moved back to St James's. He had less than three days to live. The frame-up had achieved its purpose.

22: THE KILL

IN THE PALACE of St James's, still not much altered since that day, though diminished by modern buildings, Charles took stock of his condition. During his 'trial' he had reached the height of his powers, and in spite of his political and strategic failures won a personal and moral ascendancy which, confirmed by what the Royalists considered his political martyrdom, would make him a legend. It greatly contributed to the restoration of the monarchy. His range was limited: as G.M. Young puts it, 'If he could have made the deeper part of his mind move and kept the surface quiet, all would have been well. But his intellect was all eddy and no tide.'[493] He was no statesman; he had little sense of the politically possible and an erratic judgement of situations and men: he could not conceive being any other kind of king than he was or any society other than the conservative hierarchy of which the Crown was the apex. But in this he was representative of most of his subjects. Now, incapable of compromise, he could only face the end, in the conviction of his God-given duty and the serenity of an unquestioning faith. His was not an original mind; he had always accepted the ideas inculcated by his upbringing. For Charles and most of his contemporaries believed — with the same conviction that most of us now believe the proved certainties of science — that he would go straight from the scaffold to the presence of God.

On Sunday 28 January, in the light of this imminent experience, he made his dispositions, clearly, sensibly and in order. He had already had his dogs removed — they now only distracted him. He refused to see his most faithful and closest courtiers, in part perhaps because the treacherous and grasping Elector Palatine had come with them, but mainly because he had always been a family man. The Rump Parliament had permitted him to see his daughter Elizabeth, aged thirteen, and his son, Henry of Gloucester, aged eight. So in order to give them what remnant of jewellery he possessed he dispatched Herbert with a diamond and emerald ring to a Lady Wheeler in Westminster, who in exchange gave him a sealed casket containing all the jewels he still had left, mainly broken collars from the Order of the Garter. That day, too, he was allowed through the good offices of Colonel Thomlinson, who afterwards made a military career in Ireland, but was exempted from vengeance at the Restoration for his civility to the King, to receive Henry Seymour, a messenger from the Prince of Wales. By him the King sent his last message to the Prince and his last letter to the Queen, waiting in helpless anxiety in the Louvre in Paris and unable to persuade a French government preoccupied with acute political strife to useful action — which indeed was beyond their power.

The Scots had long been vigorously protesting against the trial and sentencing of a King of Scotland by the English, but the Spaniards were naturally concerned to keep in with the winning side. The only continental government to make an official protest remained the Dutch. Since the Prince of Wales was in the country and was the brother of their Stadthouder's wife, they could hardly do less. But the story that the Prince sent a blank paper signed and sealed on which the then rulers of England could write what agreement they liked in return for the King's life is probably false.[494] There was now no hope, and the King knew it.

That evening Juxon was at last allowed to attend him. He found Charles brisk, cheerful and businesslike, and when he condoled with him, the King cut him short:

> Leave off this my lord, we have not time for it: let us think of our great work and prepare to meet that great God, to whom ere long, I am to give an account of myself, and I hope I shall do it with peace and that you will assist me therein. We will not talk of these rogues in whose hands I am: they thirst after my blood and they will have it, and God's will be done. I thank God I heartily forgive them and we will talk of them no more.

The Bishop remained with him for three hours in relative privacy, though soldiers looked in at the door every quarter of an hour to see that the King was still there. Some Presbyterian ministers offered to pray with him — an irrelevant distraction. Charles answered, 'Thank them from me for the tender of themselves; but tell them plainly that they have so often and so constantly prayed against me, that they shall never pray with me in this agony.' So, in that dark bitter winter the fires still blazed in the warm rooms and the King, still vigorous and alert, used what time was left to him with dignity and presence of mind. But outside this transient human scene lay black annihilation and icy death.

On Monday afternoon they brought in the children, who knelt before their father. Elizabeth was a serious child, intelligent enough to fear the full implication of the agony; the little boy, fated to die at twenty in the year of the Restoration, was already spirited. Concerned above all for the succession, Charles commanded his daughter to tell James, Duke of York, who had some boyish rivalry with his elder brother, that he must now look on Charles not as his brother, but as his sovereign. 'Sweetheart,' he said, 'you will forget this.' 'No,' replied Elizabeth, 'I will never forget it while I live.' In tears, she promised 'to write down the particulars'. He told her he would die a martyr and that he doubted not but that the Lord would settle the throne upon his son, 'so that we should all be happier than we could have expected to have been, if he had lived. With many other things,' she wrote pathetically, 'which at present I cannot Remember.' He told her to tell the Queen that his love would be the same to the end. Then taking Gloucester on his knee he said '"Sweetheart they now will cut off thy Father's Head". Whereat the little boy looked intently at him. "Mark, Child, what I say. They will Cut off my Head and perhaps make thee a king. But — mark what I say — you must not be a King so long as your brothers Charles and James do live, for they will cut off your Brothers' Heads (when they can catch them) and Cut thy Head off too at last... I charge you do not be made a king by them".' At which, writes Heath, 'the child sighing said, "I will be torn in pieces first", which falling unexpectedly from one so young made the King rejoice exceedingly'.[495] Their father then gave the children all the jewels save his George, which was made of a single onyx, and after a final embrace and blessing they were taken away, Elizabeth to die in captivity at Carisbrooke a year after.

Charles now had less than twenty-four hours to live. Indeed, he expected to die the next morning. Brought up as a royalty always on show, he instinctively did all he could to make his end dignified and memorable. He arranged that the relatively humane Colonel Thomlinson, not the inarticulate Colonel Hacker,[496] who had wanted to place two musketeers in the King's bedroom during his last night, but had been dissuaded by the Bishop and Herbert, would attend him, and presented

Thomlinson with his gold toothpick case as a token of trust and pardon. He then conferred again with Juxon, but spent his last evening reading and praying alone nearly till midnight. He then slept soundly, his room lit by a great cake of wax set in his silver basin, in his curtained bed until about half past five of the morning of Tuesday, 30 January. After further prayers, he asked Herbert, who had spent the night on a pallet bed in the room, to help him dress, and when in agitation Herbert seemed careless about combing his hair, he said, 'Prithee, though it be not too long to stand upon my shoulders, take the same pains with it as you were wont to do: I am to be a bridegroom today, and must be trimmed.'[497]

With detailed foresight — for he had always had a sense of theatre — Charles had a nightcap provided under which on the scaffold they could stow his hair, and he put on an extra shirt in case he should shiver. 'Let me have a shirt on more than ordinary,' he asked Herbert, 'by reason the season is so sharp as probably may make me shake, which some observers may imagine proceeds from fear. I fear not death. It is not terrible to me. I bless my God I am prepared.' Juxon now arrived, and Charles gave him his remaining books — his Bible, carefully annotated, for the Prince of Wales, and for the Duke of York his elaborate silver-figured ring, which, properly manipulated, could be both a sundial and a calculator. His gold watch was for the Duchess of Richmond, a daughter of Buckingham, and wife of the cousin who had attended him through all vicissitudes and who would arrange his funeral. The King then took the sacrament, and by the Anglican calendar, not as he had supposed by the Bishop's choice, the lesson described the passion of Christ. Rather diffidently Colonel Hacker knocked; but only at a second peremptory summons did the King give the command, 'Open the door, Hacker hath given us a second warning.'

Outside it was a bitter day, the ground iron-bound with frost, rime on the grass. With Juxon on his right, and Thomlinson, his hat doffed, on his left, Charles stepped out across the park. As for a routine military execution, the loud 'ill-tuned' drums beat a slow march 'as on a solemn and sad occasion',[498] but Charles, like his eldest son, always walked fast. He demanded a brisker pace.

So the King came to Whitehall, and here, with a clumsy but not a calculated refinement of cruelty, he was kept waiting from about half past ten to nearly two o'clock. He had expected, as he marched briskly across the park, to suffer almost at once. So there, probably in the green chamber next to his own bedroom, the King, who had fasted after his communion, had to wait. He had to because the remnant of the House of Commons had met in emergency session, for they had forgotten that the moment Charles I was dead, Charles II would be king. It was urgent to pass a Bill making it illegal to proclaim the fact. So, early that morning, they had read the Bill twice; but it had to be formally engrossed before the third reading, and doubtless, unlike their sovereign, who had only reluctantly been persuaded to take some bread and a glass of wine in case he should faint on the scaffold, they needed refection; so it was not until after one o'clock that they met to give the Bill a third reading, and not until nearly two that it was passed.

Meanwhile, not far off in Westminster School, the redoubtable Dr Busby was leading the King's Scholars in the usual Latin prayers for the sovereign. Charles spent the ghastly time in silence or in conversation with Juxon and Herbert, to whom the tensions must also have been severe. Then, for the third time, Colonel Hacker knocked on the door.[499]

Juxon and Herbert fell to their knees and kissed hands, but Charles told Hacker to lead on. Through the old palace, past close ranks of guards, they emerged into the scene of former luxury and splendour — the finely proportioned banqueting hall, so revolutionary in style in Jacobean England. It was now desolate, some windows boarded up, the atmosphere that of a guard room.

The decision to kill the King in Whitehall had been taken for better security, and to avoid taking him through the sullen and uneasy populace to the Tower, for here the relatively wide streets gave room for a substantial force of cavalry, pikemen, and halberdiers to have been drawn up and if necessary to charge. To improvise a scaffold had been no problem, with no disputes between government departments or workmen over who should put it up. In those simpler times it had been erected in under three days, and suitably draped in black.

Through one of the elegant windows, enlarged for the occasion, Charles stepped out into the cold. Juxon went with him; Thomlinson, according to the King's request, was there as well as Hacker, and — an innovation since Tudor times — a couple of shorthand writers as well as the guards.

The executioner was masked and macabre. He was the usual professional, known as 'Young Gregory' Brandon, having succeeded his father of that name in his calling, and he had plenty of experience, having accounted among others for Strafford, Laud and the Hothams.[500] But he was disguised, as was his assistant, with false hair and a beard. The King would have expected this, but not the abnormally low block, a mere eight inches high, with staples fixed on either side in front of it to tie him down if he struggled — a precaution devised with a grotesque misreading of his character and which he marked with a disdainful smile. But he now 'looked very earnestly upon the block and asked if it could be no higher'. It could not, replied Colonel Hacker firmly.

Charles had made notes for the speech, then expected under these circumstances, but seeing that he would have no considerable audience, since the cavalry and the guards blocked him off from his subjects, and those who had clambered on the roofs of the hall and the neighbouring houses were equally inaccessible, he spoke mainly to Thomlinson and the journalists. There were only a dozen people on the small scaffold.

What he said was not new: he eloquently reiterated his speeches at the trial, adding only one thing, his private obsession, that his fate was God's judgement on him for his betrayal of Strafford: 'an unjust sentence that I suffered to take effect is punished by an unjust sentence on me'. He appeared entirely collected, but showed his fear when someone brushed against the axe — saying quickly, 'Take heed of the Axe — pray take heed of the axe' — or perhaps, 'Hurt not the axe, that may hurt me.' In conclusion he summed up the philosophy of government for which he was to die.

> I must tell you that [the] liberty and freedom [of the people] consists in having a government, those laws by which their life and their goods may be most their own. It is not for having a share in government, Sir, that is nothing pertaining to them. A subject and a sovereign are clear different things... Sir, it was for this that now I am come here. If I would have given way to an arbitrary way, to have all changed according to the power of the sword, I need not have come here; and therefore I tell you (and I pray God it be not laid to your charge) that I am the Martyr of the people.

Prompted by the Bishop, he added, 'I die a Christian according to the profession of the Church of England as I found it left by my father… I have a good cause and a gracious God, I will say no more.'

Then turning to Juxon, and taking off his George, he handed it to him for the Prince of Wales, with one word, 'Remember'.[501] He also said to Hacker, 'Take care that they do not put me in pain.'[502] Then, taking off his doublet, he resumed his cloak, for though the sky was now brilliantly clear,[503] the day was bitterly cold; Juxon and the executioner then helped him to push his abundant greying hair under the tall satin nightcap. There was but one stage more, said Juxon, to the crown of glory. 'I go from a corruptible to an incorruptible crown,' replied the King, adding almost with a touch of relief after the years of stress, 'where no disturbance can be, no disturbance at all.'

Then, looking at the horrid little block, 'Is it fast?' 'It is fast, sir.' 'Strike,' he told 'young Gregory', 'when I put my arms out this way' and stretched them out. Then 'after that having said two or three words (as he stood) to himself, with heart and eyes lift up, immediately stooping down, he laid his head on the block'. Some of his hair had again come loose, and the executioner, determined to do a perfect job, put it back again, whereat Charles, thinking he was going to strike, said, 'Stay for the sign.' He received a memorably English answer. 'Yes I will, an it please your Majesty.'

Somehow, lying nearly prone, Charles made the signal: the bright axe, professionally handled, flashed in the winter sunshine and sheared through his neck at one annihilating stroke. The tragedy was done.[504]

As Dr Philip Henry, then a seventeen-year-old Student of Christ Church, Oxford, and formerly the favourite pupil of Dr

Busby at Westminster,'[505] included in one of Busby's portraits, long after narrated as an eyewitness, 'at the instant when the blow was given there was such a dismal groan among the thousands of people that were within sight of it (as it were WITH ONE CONSENT) as he had never *heard before*; and desired he might never hear the like again, nor see such a cause for it'. He also remembered that 'immediately after the stroke was struck... according to order, one troop [went] marching from Charing Cross towards King Street, purposely to disperse and scatter the people, and to divert the dismal thoughts that they could not but be filled with by driving them to shift everyone for his own safety'.[506] Thus with military precision Oliver Cromwell and his generals inaugurated the rule of the sword, masked until 1653 by the Rump Parliament of the Commonwealth, but under the Protectorate undisguised. An unnecessary war had been concluded with a crime that was a political blunder. As that sober historian J. R. Tanner points out, 'By the deed militarism, in the moment of triumph, began to preface the way for the Restoration.'[507]

The typically seventeenth-century sequel reflects ill upon the army's discipline. The people, in the old Tudor fashion, crowded round, under, and up the scaffold to 'dip their handkerchiefs' or other things in the King's blood, and they were 'admitted for moneys'; others bought blood-soaked pieces of board, the soldiers charging the high rates of a shilling or a half crown, 'more or less, according to the quality of the persons that sought them'. And after the King's body had been carried off and embalmed at Whitehall, the public were admitted for payment to see the coffined monarch at St James's, 'by which means the soldiers got store of moneys, insomuch as one was heard to say "I would we could have two or three such Majesties to behead, if we could but make such use of them.'"[508]

Cromwell and Ireton were too busy to attend to such things. They had managed to detain Fairfax with prayer or discussion, in apparent ignorance of what was afoot, during the King's execution. Short of starting another civil war, there was not much that Lord General Fairfax could do. They were all concerned for their lives and to hold together the army, the basis of their power. They had need to. Ormonde in Ireland at once proclaimed Charles II. In Scotland he was at once proclaimed in Edinburgh.

There remained to arrange to give the King a decent burial: even when murdering their King the English liked to seem respectable. For a week he lay at St James's (where it is most unlikely that Cromwell appeared, a muffled figure, gazed upon him and left murmuring 'cruel necessity'[509]). Since Westminster Abbey would obviously attract Royalist demonstration and a cult, it was ordered that he should be interred in St George's Chapel at Windsor. Parliament assigned £500 for expenses and put the Duke of Richmond in charge. So on the night of 7 February the King's coach, hung with black velvet, left St James's drawn by six horses, followed by four other carriages, conveying Herbert and the major courtiers, dressed all in deep mourning. Guided through the winter night by torches, the procession came to Windsor on the eighth, when Richmond, Hertford, Lindsey and Southampton, who had all attended the King at Newport, arrived to inspect the chapel. They objected to the shallow grave already prepared in the chancel, and insisted that the King be buried in the royal vault, where, they discovered, lay the enormous coffin of Henry VIII and the smaller one of Jane Seymour. Charles, it was decided, should occupy the space left for Catherine Parr, who, having married again, had not been placed there.

In the afternoon of 9 February the King's coffin, borne by soldiers and with the four peers carrying the ends of the pall, was brought out from St George's Hall. The sky had been clear but now, silently 'the snow began to fall so fast, as by the time they came to the west end of the Chapel Royal the black velvet pall was all white'. Charles had worn white at his coronation. And 'so went the white King to his grave, in the forty eighth year of his age, and the twenty second of his reign'. Inside the cold chapel there was also silence: the military governor had refused to allow the Anglican service of committal to be read and Juxon refused to read the Presbyterian rubrick. So the King was lowered into the dark vault, and there, under the inscription 'King Charles 1648' (by the old reckoning), in incongruous proximity to Henry VIII, he lies to this day.

AUTHOR'S NOTE

No system of notation can answer every reader's needs. I have sought to preserve essential information for the reader at the foot of the relevant page, and have consigned points of reference to the back of the book. But the reader may seek a reference both in the footnotes and in the reference notes.

ABBREVIATIONS

CCSP: Calendar of the Clarendon State Papers
CSP: Clarendon State Papers
CSPD: Calendar of State Papers Domestic
CSPV: Calendar of State Papers Venetian

A NOTE TO THE READER

If you have enjoyed this book enough to leave a review on **Amazon** and **Goodreads**, then we would be truly grateful.

The Estate of John Bowle

Sapere Books is an exciting new publisher of brilliant fiction and popular history.

To find out more about our latest releases and our monthly bargain books visit our website:
saperebooks.com

1. J. S. Morrill, *Cheshire 1630-1660. County, Government and Society during the English Revolution* (Oxford 1973), p. 26.
2. See B.H.G. Wormaid, *Clarendon, Politics, History and Religion* (Cambridge 1951).
3. Sir John Harington, *Nugae Antiquae*, ed. the Rev. Henry Harington (1779), 1, p. 4.
4. *Maseres Tracts, Several Observations upon the Life and Death of Charles 1st, late King of England* (1815), p. 138.
5. I am grateful for this information to Professor J. H. Elliott of the Institute of Advanced Studies at Princeton.
6. The Rt Rev. Robert Keith, *The History of the Affairs of Church and State in Scotland from the Beginning to the Reformation in the Year 1368*, ed. J.P. Lawson (London 1844), II, p. 508.
7. Antonia Fraser, *Mary Queen of Scots* (London 1969), p. 224.
8. Keith, *op. cit.*, p. 403.
9. Fraser, *op. cit.*, p. 282.
10. At their worst in the censorious article in the *DNB*: 'It is clear that Darnley's intellectual gifts were quite below the average. [He was] mentally and morally weak... with *strong animal passions*. The theory has been formed that this brilliant and beautiful widow of twenty-two fell violently in love with the girl-faced youth of nineteen. If so, *the fact would be little to her credit*' (my italics).
11. *The Memoirs of Robert Carey*, ed. F.H. Mares (*Series of Studies in Tudor and Stuart Literature*, F. H. Mares and A. T. Brissnende, Adelaide) (Oxford 1972), p. 59.
12. *Ibid.*, p. 63.
13. *Ibid.*, p. 69.
14. It was published in revised and final form in 1603. James was a fluent writer. He had begun to write doggerel verse at fifteen and three years later in 1591 published *Essays of a Prentice in the Divine Art: his Poetical Exercises*. He surrounded himself with a convivial clique of other *literateurs* and continued to write verses for the rest of his life, beside his heavyweight works on political theory, such as his *The True Law of Free Monarchies* (1598), and pamphlets on current matters of public and social importance.
15. D. Harris Willson, *James I and VI* (London 1956), p. 33.
16. Sir Anthony Weldon, *The Court and Character of King James by Sir A. W.: being an eye and eare witnesse. Qui nescit dissimulare nescit regnare*, published by Authority (London 1650). This small book, though it appears to

be fair to James, is slanted heavily against the Stuarts and is bitterly hostile to Buckingham. Published in the year after Charles I's death, it concludes: 'I take the boldness to advise all that are faithfull to this land to take heed how they side with this bloody House.'

[17] He was not, as often supposed, regularly inebriated, 'though Buckingham's jovial suppers... made him sometimes overtaken, which he would the very next day remember and repent with tears. It is true, he drank very often, which was rather out of custom than any delight, and his drinkes of that kind of strength, a Frontinak Canary, High Canary wine, Trent wine and Scottish ale, that had he not had a very strong braine he might daily have been overtaken, although he seldom drank at any time above four spoonfuls, many times not above two' (*ibid.*, p. 179).

[18] D. Harris Willson, *James I and VI* (London 1956), p. 184.

[19] *CSPD*, 1603-10, p. 128.

[20] Henry Ellis, *Original Letters. Illustrative of English History* (1824), III, p. 92.

[21] *Ibid.*, III, p. 94.

[22] *Ibid.*, p. 95.

[23] *CSPD*, 1611-18, p. 67.

[24] Ellis, *op. cit.*, III, p. 72.

[25] *CSPD*, 1603-10, p. 246.

[26] The petitioners were more extreme than is often realized. Some wished to abolish kneeling at communion, since the gesture was common to idolaters, and bread and wine as well, as having been dedicated by pagans to Ceres and Bacchus. One of the Fellows of Trinity, Cambridge, confuted this argument: 'Though the gesture of Kneeling has been abused to Idolatrous Service, yet it is not necessary to be abolished [and Bread and Wine] though inuented by Man and prophaned to Idolatrye may be restored to the Service of God... The simple doing of a thing before abused is not a Show of Evil' (*Lambeth MSS 447*, pp.182-204).

[27] *Truth Brought to Light and Discovered by Time, a Discourse and historic Narrative of the first XIIII years of King James's Reign* (London 1651). *Somers Tracts, a collection of scarce and valuable tracts, chiefly as relating to the History of these Kingdoms*, ed. Walter Scott (London 1809-15), n, pp. 262-363.

Carr was a younger son of Sir Thomas Carr of Ferniehurst in Scotland. He had been thrown from his horse when in attendance at, though not taking part in, a tilting match and had broken his leg. From that moment James had taken charge, lodging Carr in Court, bestowing on him Ralegh's fine property at Sherborne, and even making him a Knight of the Garter.

[28] Agnes Strickland, *The Queens of England* (1845), VIII, pp. 102-3.

[29] It was in 1611 that James raised money to pay the troops in Ireland, where Scots Protestants had been encouraged to settle in Ulster, by selling hereditary baronetcies to anyone worth more than £1,000 a year, if they would pay £1,080 in three annual instalments. It was expected that two hundred would be sold; but response was slow, and only about a hundred applications came in the early years, which raised £90,000. But the institution took root and over the centuries fostered some eccentric, even endearing, characters.

[30] F. Braudel, *The Mediterranean in the Time of Philip II* (London 1973), 1, p. 451.

[31] *Ibid.*, p. 521, citing Lescabot, *Histoire de la Nouvelle France*.

[32] *A discourse on the Most Illustrious Prince Henry, late Prince of Wales, written anno 1626 by Sir Charles Cornwallis, Knt. (Somers Tracts)*, 11 (London 1641), pp. 217ff.

[33] Sir Roger Coke, *A Detection of the Court of England during the last four Reigns and during the Interregnum* (London 1694), 1, pp. 60-1.

[34] *Ibid.*, p. 221.

[35] The question has been cleared up by Norman (afterwards Sir Norman) Moore, historian of St Bartholomew's Hospital, in *The Illness and Death of Henry, Prince of Wales, in 1612. A historical case of Typhoid Fever* (London 1882). There is absolutely no need to postulate porphyria without sufficient evidence.

[36] Sir Theodore Turquet Mayeme MD (1573-1655) was born at Mayerne near Geneva of a Piedmontese family. He studied at Heidelberg and Montpellier and by 1600 had settled in Paris, where his relatively modern methods incurred the hostility of the College of Physicians. But he became a fashionable doctor at the French Court, and in 1611 came to London as First Physician to the King. James entirely trusted him, and knighted him in 1624. He remained Principal Physician to Charles I, left many volumes of recorded cases he had attended, and did much research on chemicals, including research on cosmetics for Queen Henriette Marie.

[37] Cited in Moore, *op. cit.*, as translated from *Relation Veritable de la maladie, mort, et overture du corps du tres Hault et tres Illustre Henri Prince de Valles, decide a St. James les Londres le vi Novembre 1612*.

[38] John Nichols, *The Progresses, Processions and Magnificent Festivities of King*

James the First, the Royal Consort, Family and Court (London 1828), II, p. 483.
39 *Ibid.*, II, p. 490.
40 *Ibid.*, II, p. 485.
41 Moore, *loc. cit.*
42 Nichols, *op. cit.*, II, p. 463. 'The magnificent marriage of the two great Princes, Frederick Count Palatine and the Lady Elizabeth, daughter to the Imperial Majesty of King James and Queen Anne, to the comfort of all Great Britain.'
43 Arthur Wilson, *A History of Great Britain, Being the Life and Reign of James I* (London 1653), p. 64. Wilson (1595-1652), a native of Yarmouth, had been a dependant of Essex, who had taken him with his household for rescuing a woman servant from drowning at Chartley. He wrote an autobiography, *Observations of God's Providence in the Tract of my Life*, and various plays, such as *The Inconstant Lady* and *The Corporall*. His *History*, like Weldon's, is very hostile to the Stuarts.
44 Arthur Wilson, *A History of Great Britain, Being the Life and Reign of James I* (London 1653), p. 65.
45 Thomas L. Moir, *The Addled Parliament, 1614* (Oxford 1958), p. 48.
46 *Ibid.*, p. 134.
47 D. Harris Willson, *The Privy Councillors in the House of Commons* (Minneapolis 1940), p. 4.
48 The family, which had originated at Evreux in Normandy, claimed to have come over with the Conqueror, and early acquired large estates on the Welsh Marches, augmented by marriage to the heiress of Lord Ferrers of Chartley in Staffordshire. In 1550 the boy's grandfather had been created Viscount Hereford, and in 1572 Earl of Essex. Robert, born Lord Hereford, had been sent to Eton, where Sir Henry Savile, the translator of Tacitus, was provost, and then to Merton College, Oxford, where Savile had retained the wardenship. After his formal marriage Essex travelled in France and the Low Countries. He thus went through the elaborate education of his class and time; but he was no 'intellectual' or cosmopolitan, preferred sport and country life and was never an intimate of Charles's Court, though officially part of it.
49 Scabrous details were made public. 'He and I,' testified the Countess, 'have lain together in naked bed all night, but *non potuit* — he could not.' Her husband alleged that the fault was hers. She had employed the notorious Dr Forman, astrologer and quack, to 'use all his subtlety and devise really to imbecillitate the Earl'; and she had rinsed

his linen in camphor to 'lessen and debilitate' him. It was alleged in reply that the Countess had obtained 'an artifice too immodest to be expressed' that would have hindered consummation and 'so tormented him'.

50 Nichols, *op. cit.*, II, pp. 721-3.
51 *Ibid.*, III, p. 48.
52 *Ibid.*, III, p. 66.
53 The university authorities issued careful regulations to keep the undergraduates from thronging the King and the Prince, who were in Trinity, and to moderate dress, 'considering the fearfull enormities and excesse of apparel seen in all degrees, as namely strange pekadivelas, vast bands, huge cuffs, shoe roses, tuffs, locks, and tops of hare unbeseeming that modesty and carriage of students in so renowned an universitie'. Fines and even imprisonment were threatened, presumably with some effect.
54 C. V. Wedgwood, *Strafford, 1593-1641* (London 1935), p. 32.
55 Nichols, *op. cit.*, III, pp. 80-1.
56 *Ibid.*, III, p. 101.
57 Willson, *James I and VI*, p. 353.
58 Weldon, *op. cit.*, p. 130.
59 James Howell, *Epistolae Ho-Elianae, Familiar Letters Domestic and Foreign upon emergent occasions*, 8th edn (London 1713), p. 3.
60 *CSPD*, 1611-18, p. 333.
61 Willson, *James I and VI*, p. 98.
62 Nichols, *op. cit.*, III, p. 225.
63 *Ibid.*, III, pp. 208ff. 'The Illustrious Hope of Great Britain. The High and Mighty Prince Charles... The Ample Order and Solemnity of Prince Charles his Creation.'
64 The ringers were not paid much: 5s for ringing when the King came to Whitehall, and for the performance as well; in our money about £5.
65 Willson, *James I and VI*, p. 92.
66 Weldon, *op. cit.*, p. 136.
67 Prince Henry had obtained Ralegh's confiscated estate at Sherborne, allotted to Somerset, for a compensation of £20,000, intending to restore it to Ralegh. After Prince Henry's death, it was bought by Sir John Digby, afterwards Earl of Bristol.
68 Howell, *op. cit.*, p. 6.
69 *CSPD*, 1617-21, p. 512.
70 Ellis, *op. cit.*, III, pp. 103-4.

71 Howell, *op. cit.*, p. 15.
72 *Ibid.*, p. 17. In fact they fell on a dungheap and crawled away with minor injuries.
73 The rival candidate, John George, Elector of Saxony, was not only, as Howell observed, a Lutheran and so repugnant to the Calvinists, especially the Dutch, but 'spending his days in the hunting field, and his evenings in deep carouses, from which he seldom retired sober, he had neither time nor inclination for intellectual culture' (S. R. Gardiner, *History of England, from the Accession of James I to the Outbreak of the Civil War* [London 1883-4, 111, p.275]).
74 Ellis, *op. cit.*, III, pp. 112-13.
75 Willson, *James I and VI*, p. 161.
76 *CSP*, 1621-3, p. 185.
77 Confabulations that inspired the Puritan divine and caricaturist Samuel Ward, town preacher of Ipswich, to depict the destruction of the Armada and the discovery of the Gunpowder Plot, flanking the Pope and Cardinals colloguing with the King of Spain and the Devil — a cartoon that occasioned official protest from the ambassador, who saw it as an insult to his master (see D. George, *English Political Caricature* [Oxford 1959], 1, plate 3).
78 See John Aubrey, *Brief Lives*, ed. O. Lawson Dick (London 1950), pp. 8-16, for a famous account.
79 Born in 1584 at Bathampton, son of Thomas Mompesson and Honor Eastcourt of Salisbury, he married Catherine, daughter of Sir John St John of Lydiard Tregooze near Swindon, whose sister had married one of Buckingham's half-brothers, and became MP for Great Bedwyn in 1614. He later obtained from the favourite the commissionership for the licensing of inns. He was still well enough off in 1643 to lend Sir Edward Hyde, afterwards first Earl of Clarendon, £104, and to pay £561 9s 0d as a Royalist to the Sequestrators.
80 He retired to live obscurely in his lodgings in Gray's Inn and 'had the unhappiness after the heights of plenitude to be denied Beer to quench his thirst for he did not relish the Beer of the House'. He survived into the reign of Charles I, dying in 1626, leaving an intellectual legacy that dwarfs the politicians and lawyers who were so important in his day (CSPD, 1623-5, p.74).
81 John Williams was born in 1582 of minor Welsh gentry of Conway, and educated at Ruthin and at St John's College, Cambridge, where he became a Fellow and to which he left a substantial endowment for

the library. By 1610-12 the old Welshman was already a proctor for the university. Appointed chaplain to Lord Chancellor Ellesmere in 1610, he obtained prebends at Hereford, Lincoln and Peterborough, and by 1617 he was a chaplain to the King, who enjoyed his ornate sermons. He also had Buckingham's favour, and in 1619 became Dean of Salisbury, one of the richer deaneries, where, unlike his successor, he avoided embroilment with the Chapter. Appointed in 1621 Dean of Westminster, he now became the Duke's principal adviser.

[82] *CSP*, 1618-23, p. 278. The King set up a commission of enquiry of five bishops and three lawyers who found by a majority in favour of Abbot, the saintly Launcelot Andrewes of Winchester dissenting. James formally pardoned the Archbishop, but when some of the new bishops refused to be consecrated by him, Abbot commissioned three others to do his office. He also settled £20 a year on the keeper's widow, which, says Oldys the antiquary, 'soon procured her another husband' (*DNIB*).

[83] John Aubrey, *Brief Lives*, ed. O. Lawson Dick (London 1950), p. 729.

[84] G. W.Prothero, *Select Statutes and other Constitutional Documents. 1558-1625* (London 1906), p. 310.

[85] *Ibid.*, p. 314.

[86] Ellis, *op. cit.*, 111, pp. 116-17. Joseph Meade, Fellow of Christ's College, Cambridge, to his kinsman, Sir Martin Stuteville of Dalham, Suffolk.

[87] The Jesuits in Antwerp, Howell reported, had put on a play in derision, 'feigning a post to come puffing upon the stage, and being asked "what news?", he answer'd how the Palsgrave was like soon to have shortly a huge formidable Army, for the King of Denmark was to send him a hundred thousand, the Hollanders a hundred thousand, and the King of Great Britain a hundred thousand; but being asked "hundreds of what?" he replied that the first would send 100,000 *red herrings*, the second 100,000 *cheeses* and the last 100,000 ambassadors to deal with "these German broils"' (Howell, *op. cit.*, p. 89).

[88] *Somers Tracts*, 1, pp. 471-2.

[89] John Digby, first Earl of Bristol (1580-1653), came of Warwickshire gentry and had studied at Magdalen College, Oxford. He had first attracted the King's favour by reporting on the conspiracy to seize Princess Elizabeth during the Gunpowder Plot, and been made a Gentleman of the Privy Chamber and knighted. In 1607 and 1611 he

had already been sent to Madrid to sound out the project for a marriage between Prince Henry and the elder Infanta, Donna Anna, who in fact married Louis XIII, and had discovered which of the English politicians were in Spanish pay. High in the royal favour, in 1616 he had again been sent to Madrid for the preliminary negotiations for the marriage of Prince Charles to the Infanta Donna Maria; and on his return he had been granted the great estate of Sherborne, forfeited by Ralegh and now by Somerset. In 1618 he had been created Lord Digby. Now as Earl of Bristol, he got no good of his embassy, for Charles and Buckingham made him the scapegoat for their failure.

[90] The King, though not in premature senility, but often still very shrewd, observant and obstinate, was getting more difficult and more exasperated. In 1622 the Buckingham women had tried to divert him by dressing up a pig as an infant and the old Countess as a midwife and baptizing it. But James, 'hearing the ceremonies of baptism read and the squeaking noise of the Brute he most abhorred', was furious and cried out, 'Away, for shame.' He had also kicked one of his oldest attendants for losing some papers, saying, 'Fare you well, sir, I will never see your face more.' Soon repentant, he had sent for the man, apologized and, it was rumoured, asked his pardon on his knees.

[91] *Reliquiae Wottonianae* (The Life and Death of the Duke of Buckingham) (London 1651), p. 81. Cited in Ellis, *op. cit.*, III, p. 123.

[92] Endymion Porter (1597-1649) became one of Charles's closer confidants. Brought up in Spain, but mainly of English origin, he had been a page to Olivares, and on Charles's accession remained a Groom of the Bedchamber. He became a collector of fines for the Star Chamber, made money in trade with the East Indies, and became a patron of the dramatist Davenant and the poet Herrick, as well as being one of the King's principal agents in collecting pictures. In 1641 he became MP for Droitwich. He was ruined and exiled in the Civil War.

[93] *Somers Tracts*, 1, pp. 525ff.

[94] *Ibid.*, 1, p. 530.

[95] *Ibid.*, 1, p. 540.

[96] Most of the descendants of Charles V, including Philip IV, had a Flemish look as well as the underlip 'incident to the race'. Only Don Fernando, Cardinal Archbishop of Toledo, the younger brother to the King, had a swarthy appearance, which made him much more

popular among the people.
[97] Ellis, *op. cit.*, III, pp. 139-40.
[98] James Hay, first Earl of Carlisle, was one of James I'S earliest and least deleterious favourites. He had been brought from Scotland, already a Gentleman of the Bedchamber, heavily endowed, richly married, and in 1610 created Lord Hay. He was always wildly extravagant, but proved a shrewd diplomat as envoy in Paris, Brussels and Heidelberg. In 1618 he was created Viscount Doncaster and in 1622 an Earl, before being sent again to Paris to smoothe over the consequences of Prince Charles's expedition to Madrid. He was regarded as a model diplomat — hence Buckingham's appeal.
[99] Ellis, *op. cit.*, III, pp. 145-8.
[100] *Ibid.*, III, pp. 153-4.
[101] See *CCSP*, 1, item 275.
[102] *Ibid.*, item 226.
[103] Howell, *op. cit.*, p. 147.
[104] *A Relation of the Royal Festivities and Jeugo de Cannas, composed by Don Juan Antonia de la Penna... translated out of the Spanish* (London 1623), *Somers Tracts*, 1.
[105] *Ibid.*, p. 546.
[106] *Somers Tracts*, vi, p. 550.
[107] *The Chamberlain Letters*, ed. Elizabeth McClure Thomson, with a preface by A. L. Rowse (London 1965), p. 313.
[108] *CCSP*, 1, item 230.
[109] Ellis, *op. cit.*, III, pp. 159-60.
[110] *CCSP*, p. 172.
[111] Against all this the Countess d'Olivares's present to the Prince, which arrived in March, was '48 gammons of bacon, diverse vessels of great olives, as many of olives without stones; a great quantity of capers and caperons, many froils or tapnets of special figs, many sweet lemons and 300 weight of dried or candied melocotons, great quantity of other suckets or sweetmeats, besides 48 melons, all which in three carts was conveyed into the riding place or house of St. James'. The gift was substantial, but much less stylish, and Charles never vouchsafed to set eyes on it.
[112] Cited in Willson, *James I and VI*, p. 428.
[113] Thomson, *op. cit.*, p. 325.
[114] Ellis, *op. cit.*, III, pp. 167-8.
[115] He had begun life as a handsome and industrious apprentice, married his master's daughter and became a well-to-do merchant in

his own right. By 1605 Receiver of Customs for Dorset and Somerset, in 1614 he had become MP for Hythe. Two years later he was Master of Requests and by 1619 Master of the Court of Wards and Chief Commissioner for the Navy. He had married (*en secondes noces*) one of Buckingham's relatives, and in 1622 he had been created Baron Cranfield. He wrote a fine, bold Renaissance hand.

[116] Harris Willson, *op. cit.*, p. 163.

[117] Keith Feiling, *A History of England* (London 1963), p. 450.

[118] He lived on in retirement, was restored his seat in the House of Lords only in 1640, did his best to stay neutral in the Civil War, and died in 1645.

[119] A bastard of the Prince von Mansfeld, governor of Luxembourg, he had been legitimatized by Rudolf II but denied any estates; so he took service against the Habsburgs and even turned Protestant. After the victories of Spinola and Wallenstein in 1625 and 1626, he died in the service of the Venetians at Sarajevo.

[120] Ellis, *op. cit.*, III, p. 180.

[121] For originals see *CSP*, 97; and *CCSP*, 1, Appendix II, for full text and translation.

[122] Quoted in Willson, *James I and VI*, p. 433.

[123] *Ibid.*, p. 438.

[124] Two years after a Select Committee of Parliament examined the evidence, but could find nothing proved against the Duke beyond 'transcendent presumption'.

[125] Nichols, *op. cit.*, IV, p. 1,000.

[126] Willson, *James I and VI*, pp. 446-7.

[127] Ellis, *op. cit.*, III, p. 183.

[128] *Basilikon Doron*, p. 262.

[129] Sir Dudley Carleton, Viscount Dorchester (1573-1632), came of Oxfordshire gentry, and was educated at Westminster School and Christ Church, Oxford, then travelled for five years abroad. In 1604 he became MP for St Mawes, in 1610 he was appointed ambassador in Venice and knighted, then in 1616 ambassador at The Hague. In 1625, through Buckingham's favour, he became Vice-Chamberlain to the Royal Household and a privy councillor, and next year Lord Carleton. In 1628 he was created Viscount Dorchester, and after Buckingham's death, at which he was present, Chief Secretary of State. He was twice married, but none of his children survived, and he was succeeded by his nephew, another Dudley Carleton. He was a skilled and successful diplomatist, and his correspondence is a rich

source of information on his times.
[130] *CSPD, 1625-6*, p. 10.
[131] *Ibid.*, p. 32.
[132] Ellis, *op. cit.*, III, p. 189.
[133] *Ibid.*, III, p. 190.
[134] *Ibid.*, III, p. 198.
[135] *Ibid.*, III, p. 197.
[136] John Rushworth, *Historical Collections of Private Passages of State, weighty matters in Law, and remarkable proceedings in five Parliaments, beginning in the sixteenth year of King James anno 1618, and ending the fifth year of King Charles anno 1629* (1721 edn), 1, p. 171.
[137] Willson, *Privy Councillors*, p. 169.
[138] *CSPV*, 1625-6, p. 143.
[139] *Ibid.*, p. 146.
[140] *Ibid.*, p. 147.
[141] *CSPD, 1625-6*, p. 21.
[142] In which office he had been succeeded by Sir Thomas Coventry, who held it until 1640.
[143] Pembroke, nephew of Sir Philip Sidney through his mother, and a great patron of learned men, had been Chancellor of Oxford University since 1617, and in 1624 Broadgates Hall was renamed Pembroke College after him. He also presented valuable manuscripts to the Bodleian Library. His fine statue stands in the main courtyard of the library.
[144] Security arrangements were not efficient. Sir Simonds D'Ewes, on whose eyewitness account this description is based, 'spying a doore guarded by one and thronged at by few', found an easy entrance, 'the good genius of the guard man guiding his gentler thoughts' so that, 'being in, the narrator instantly settled [himself] on the stage on which stood the roiall seate' (Ellis, *op. cit.* III, pp. 216-17).
[145] 1578-1640, son of Sir Thomas Coventry, a Fellow of Balliol and barrister of the Inner Temple, who had become Lord Chief Justice of the Common Pleas, and bought an estate at Croome in Worcestershire. Thomas had also studied at Balliol and at the Inner Temple and in 1617 through the influence of Coke had become Solicitor-General. He was an able and respected lawyer who tried to diminish the constitutional conflicts between King and Parliament, one of the few assets of the King's government until his death in 1640.
[146] Rushworth, *op. cit.*, 1, p. 618.

¹⁴⁷ *CSPV*, xx, pp. 68-9.
¹⁴⁸ *Ibid.*, p. 175.
¹⁴⁹ *Somers Tracts*, IV, pp. 108-13.
¹⁵⁰ By 108 votes to 103 — a result achieved after a contest that demands the pen of C. P. Snow as deployed in *The Masters*. Some of the dons tried to delay the election: but the Heads of Houses were for Buckingham. So 'we of the Body', wrote Meade, 'run one unto another to complain', and set up a rival candidate, the Earl of Berkshire. But the Heads of Houses 'belaboured' their Fellows, and the Master of Trinity 'sent for his, one by one, to persuade them, some twice over'. When the Duke was elected, the Master of Clare 'made the College exceed that night etc.'. As the members of Parliament for Cambridge had voted for the impeachment, 'the Commons were wonderfully exasperated', though Charles wrote to the University to tell them that they partook of his royal affections, and the Duke wrote them a letter of stifling urbanity.
¹⁵¹ *Somers Tracts*, IV, pp. 88-9.
¹⁵² See Strickland, *op. cit.*, VIII, pp. 168-9.
¹⁵³ *Ibid.*, VIII, p. 102.
¹⁵⁴ Sir Thomas Darnell Bt, a substantial landowner in Lincolnshire, had been committed to the Fleet prison, where he applied for a writ of *Habeas Corpus*. It was denied him since he had been imprisoned *per speciale mandatum domini regis*. His fellow-victims were all substantial landowners, one of them in Shropshire, another in Norfolk.
¹⁵⁵ John Selden (1584-1654) was the son of a Sussex yeoman, who, according to Aubrey (*Brief Lives*, p. 271), 'played well on the violin' and married an heiress from Kent. He was educated at Chichester Free School and Hart Hall, Oxford, and read Law at the Inner Temple. He was a friend of Camden, the antiquary, and of Ben Jonson, and the scope of his erudition was vast; as in *England's Eponomis* (1610) on the laws of the Britons, Anglo-Saxons and Vikings; *The Duello*, or *Single Combat*, on duelling; and his *Titles of Honour* (1614), and the controversial *History of Tythes* (1617) from Abraham to his own day. In 1623 he had been MP for Lancaster, in 1626 for Great Bedwyn, Wilts, and by now sat for Ludgershall in that county. Following Coke, he became the greatest intellectual force behind the opposition, and Charles Imprisoned him in 1629-31, though in 1636 he regained favour by arguing against Grotius, against the freedom of the seas, in his *Mare Clausum*, which maintained that Great Britain had entire jurisdiction over all surrounding seas. In the

Long Parliament of 1640 he sat for Oxford. He was also famous as an Orientalist, having early published a treatise on the gods of Syria, and could thus mock the Assembly men about their 'little gilt Bibles', and would baffle them sadly; 'seyd he "I do consider the original;" for he was able to run them all down with his Greeke and Antiquities' (*op. cit.*, p. 272). Selden is now most widely known for his *Table Talk* recorded by his secretary Richard Milward and published in 1689.

[156] Rushworth, *op. cit.*, 1, p. 504.

[157] *Ibid.*, 1, p. 631.

[158] See *Reliquae Wottonianae*, pp. 112ff., for this eyewitness account. Cited in Ellis, *op. cit.*, III, pp. 254-6.

[159] Dudley, Lord Carleton's account to the Queen (Ellis, *op. cit.*, III, pp. 257ff).

[160] *Reliquae Wottonianae*, *loc. cit.*

[161] Felton was not tortured, as he would have been in Tudor times, but by the judges' decision merely hanged. Both Felton and the King wanted his right hand to be cut off first, but the judges said there was only one penalty for murder. Felton 'much magnified the King's mercy at so easy a death and died repentent of "that great sin"... He took his death very stoutly and patiently. He was very long a dying' (Ellis, *op. cit.*, III, p. 281).

[162] *CSPD*, 1628, p. 268.

[163] 'Prince Charles was borne, a little before one of the clock in the afternoon: the bishop of London had the honour to see him before he was an hour old. At his birth there appeared a star visible a very long time of the 'day, when the King rode to St Paul's Church to give thanks to God... but this star then appearing some say was the planet Venus... (Rushworth, *op. cit.*, [1680 cdn], II.

[164] S.R. Gardiner, *The Personal Rule of Charles I. 1628-57* (London 1875), 1, p.2.

[165] Rushworth, *op. cit.*, 1, p. 627.

[166] *Ibid.*, 1, p. 644.

[167] Born in 1560 at Oudewater in Holland, he had been educated at Utrecht and at Leiden, studied at Basel and Geneva and visited Rome. In 1603 he had become Professor of Theology at Leiden.

[168] Cited from Tanner, *English Constitutional Conflicts* (Cambridge, 1928), p. 69; in Wallace Notestein, *Commons Debates for 1629* (Minneapolis, 1921), p. 103.

[169] Rushworth, *op. cit.*, 1, p. 562 (italics mine).

[170] R. Zaller, *The Parliament of 1621. A Study in Constitutional Conflict*

(Berkeley 1971), p. 1.

[171] *Ibid.*, p. 186.

[172] *CSPD*, 1628-9, p.52.

[173] David Underdown, *Pride's Purge. Politics in the Puritan Revolution* (Oxford 1971), p. 24.

[174] Sir Thomas Wentworth, Bart, Viscount Wentworth, afterwards first Earl of Strafford, had been born in 1593, son of Sir William Wentworth of the great estate of Wentworth Woodhouse, Yorkshire. He had been educated at St John's College, Cambridge, studied at the Inner Temple, and travelled on the Continent. He had represented Yorkshire in the Addled Parliament, and again in that of 1621, and his first wife having died in 1622, in 1625 married Arabella Holles, daughter of Lord Clare and sister of Denzil Holles. In the Parliament of 1625 he again sat for Yorkshire and opposed Buckingham's foreign policy, though not the prerogative of the King. In the Parliament of 1628 he became one of the most forceful critics of the government, and in the year before had been briefly imprisoned for refusing to pay a forced loan; but he had already in 1627 applied for the presidency of the Council of the North and attempted to come to terms with the King. In 1631, Wentworth's second wife died, the mother of his children, and in the following year he married Elizabeth, daughter of Sir Godfrey Rodes.

[175] He came of a family of successful lawyers, well established at Roxwell in Essex, the son of Sir Richard Weston, with a strong Catholic tradition. He had studied at the Inner Temple, and been employed on important but unsuccessful embassies to Brussels in 1620 on behalf of the Elector Palatine. He had done his best to cope with Buckingham's impossible demands for the expedition to the Ile de Re and was a relatively able administrator. His policy was pacific and pro-Spanish but became hostile to the French. In February 1633 Charles created him Earl of Portland. He was unpopular, both as an exacting Lord Treasurer and a crypto-Catholic.

[176] *CSPD*, 1631-2, p. 433.

[177] C.V. Wedgwood, *The King's Peace, 1637-1641* (London 1955), p. 151.

[178] Brian P. Levack, *The Civil Lawyers in England. 1630-41* (Oxford 1973), p. 3.

[179] *Ibid.*, p. 50.

[180] As Dr Duck — the reputed relative of the Stephen Duck, Thresher Poet of Wiltshire ('By civil law the Ducks first got a name') who left £20,000 and provoked the rhyme:

We hope the Parliament his feathers will pluck,
For being so busy, Dr. Duck

Levack, *op cit.t* p. 195.

[181] Wedgwood, *The King's Peace*, p. 155.

[182] Charles Wilson, *England's Apprenticeship. 1603-1763* (London 1965), p. 13.

[183] *CSPD*, 1628-9, p. 578 (italics mine).

[184] See Keith Thomas, *Religion and the Decline of Magic* (London 1971), for a masterpiece of original research in this field.

[185] R. Lennard (ed.), *The English Sunday. Englishmen at Rest and Play*, 1558-1714 (Oxford 1931), p. 98.

[186] Thomas, *op. cit.*, p. 94.

[187] Wedgwood, *The King's Peace*, p. 92.

[188] *Somers Tracts*, III, p. 56.

[189] See Cobbett, *State Trials*, III, pp. 402-25.

[190] '*Vi et armis in quendam Florence Fitz-Patrick, yeoman, insult' facit, et cum eodem... diabolice, felonice, et contra naturem rem veneream habuit, peccatumque abominandum... inter Christianos non nominandum*', etc. The lawyers investigated Athelstan's laws on rape, though on the other charge they had to declare that 'of the *crimen sodomiticum* our law had no knowledge before Henry VIII': before that such lapses had been left to the jurisdiction of the canon law, whose tariff on penances, devised during the Dark Ages, had been milder.

[191] See also *The Arraignment and Conviction of Mervin Touchet, Earl of Castlehaven, with portrait as frontispiece* (London 1642). This portrait is reproduced in Sir Richard Colt Hoare's *History of Modern Wiltshire (Hundred of Dunworth)* (London 1829). On p. 16, Colt Hoare writes 'I shall not offend the delicacy of my readers by stating the cause of this trial' and of 'his untimely end'; and records that 'Anne, the wife of the profligate Mervyn, obtained a complete pardon for all his atrocious acts which she (perforce) was obliged to endure.'

[192] Sir Ellis Waterhouse, *Painting in Britain*, 1530-1790 (Harmondsworth, 1969), p. 46.

[193] 'He was a learned man, of immense reading, but is much blamed for unfaithfull quotions. His manner of Studie was thus: he wore a Long quilt cap, which came 2 or 3, at least, inches over his eies, which served him as an Umbrella to defend his Eies from the light. About every three houres his man was to bring him a roll and a pott of ale to refocillate his wasted spirits: so he studied and dranke and munched some bread; and this maintained him till night, and then, he

made a good Supper' (Aubrey, *op. cit.*, pp. 250-1).
[194] *CSPD*, 1633-4, p. 13.
[195] Rushworth, *op. cit.*, II, p. 178.
[196] Gardiner, *op. cit.*, 1, p. 358.
[197] *Ibid.*, 1, p. 361.
[198] In the original, '*Legatus est vir bonus peregressus ad inentiendum Reipublicae causî*'. Wotton (1568-1639), born at Boughton Hall, Kent, son of Sir Thomas Wotton and Eleanor Fince, had been educated at Winchester, New College and Queen's College, Oxford, where he had become a friend of John Donne. He had travelled on the Continent and written a survey, posthumously published, of the *State of Christendom*. He had served Essex as an intelligence agent, and been sent to Scotland by the Grand Duke of Tuscany to warn James VI of a plot to kill him. On James's accession, Wotton had been rewarded by being sent as ambassador to Venice, a position he had held intermittently from 1602-24. He had also been employed on missions to the Hague and Vienna, and bought pictures and works of art in Venice for Buckingham. But the diplomatic career then carried no certainty or pension, and Wotton had been thankful to be made Provost of Eton in 1624, though this salary was only £100 a year and maintenance.

In 1627 Charles I came to his rescue with a pension of £200, raised in 1630 to £600, to enable Wotton to write a history of England, which he never wrote. A charming dilettante, with wide worldly experience, he was a very successful Provost, and 'a constant cherisher', as Isaak Walton wrote in his *Life*, 'of those youths in the school in whom he found either a constant diligence or a genius that prompted them to learning', one or more 'hopeful youths' being taken or boarded in his own house. He was an intimate of Walton, and described in a poem the pleasure of angling as he 'sat quietly on a summer evening on a bank a-fishing at Eton'. He is best known for his poem on Elizabeth of Bohemia,

You meaner beauties of the night
and for his:
How happy is he born and taught,
That serveth not another's will.
The best account of him is by Logan Pearsall Smith, *Life and Letters of Sir Henry Wotton*, 2 vols (Oxford 1907).
[199] Charles Wilson, *op. cit.*, p. 98.
[200] *Ibid.*, p. 100.

[201] H. R. Trevor-Roper, *William Laud* (London 1940), p. 221.

[202] A prestige ship sanctioned by Charles himself, although the experts concerned with pirates using vessels of sixty tons, 'Dunkirk built' and 'rare goers' with six guns, would have preferred a swifter and more manoeuvrable vessel.

[203] Not his namesake (1568-1637) the prolific author, playwright and pioneer of improved horse breeding, who is credited with importing the first Arab horses into England, and who wrote the account of the last fight of the *Revenge* (*The Honorable Tragedie of Sir Richard Grinville Knight*) echoed by Tennyson, and is best remembered for his *Discourse on Horsemanship* (*How to Chuse, Ride, Traine and Diet both Hunting and Running Horses*), the *Complete Farrier*, and the *Young Sportsman's Instruction*.

[204] *CSPD*, 1635-6, p. 224.

[205] *Maseres Tracts*, p. 145.

[206] Born in 1582 the son of the receiver general to the see of Chichester, he had been educated at Merchant Taylor's and St John's College, Oxford, where he had succeeded Laud as President and won reputation as a preacher when vicar of St Giles, and as an administrator when vice-chancellor (1626-7). He became Dean of Worcester and in 1632 Bishop of Hereford before being translated to London.

[207] For a vivid and detailed account see Trevor-Roper, *op. cit.*, pp. 287-94.

[208] *Ibid.*, p. 188, citing *Verney Papers* (Camden Society 1853).

[209] *Ibid.*, p. 293, citing Crosfield's Diary (3 September 1636).

[210] Rushworth, *op. cit.*, II, pp. 50-1.

[211] *Ibid.*, II, p. 74.

[212] Trevor-Roper, *op. cit.*, p. 279.

[213] So as not to interfere with the classical curriculum he had to lecture at 8 a.m. once a week during Lent and during the vacations, and — a typical Laudian touch — all bachelors of arts were required to attend or be fined. Doubtless to widespread relief, in 1637 Pococke returned to the Levant, where he collected more manuscripts, and did not return until 1641, to find his patron in the Tower. Laud however had secured the income of the lectureship by settled lands for its maintenance in Bray, in Buckinghamshire, so well that even the Parliamentarian sequestrators failed to plunder them.

[214] *CSPD*, 1633-4, p. 284.

[215] *Laud's Works* (Oxford 1852), V, p. 349.

²¹⁶ Rushworth, *op. cit.*, II, p. 55.
²¹⁷ Where it is largely evident, by diverse arguments, by the concurring authority and resolution of Sundry texts of scripture that popular stage plays (the very Pomps of the Divell)... are sinful, heathenish, lewde, ungodly spectacles and most pernicious corruption condemned in all ages. Dedicated to the Master of Lincoln's Inn' (1633).
²¹⁸ *Ibid.*, p. 208.
²¹⁹ Trevor-Roper, *op. cit.*, p. 164, quoting from D'Ewes, *Autobiography*, II, p. 105.
²²⁰ Francis, Lord Cottington (1578-1652) came of Somerset gentry with connections at Court, from Godmanston near Bruton. He had early visited Spain and become consul at Seville, and Clarendon writes of him: 'It is true that he was illiterate as to the grammar of any language, or the principles of any science; but by his perfectly understanding the Spanish (which he spoke as a Spaniard), the French and Italian languages, and having read much in all, he could not be said to be ignorant in any branch of learning, divinity only excepted. He had a very fine and extraordinary understanding of the nature of beasts and birds and above all in all kinds of husbandry' (*History, op. cit.*, pp. 753-4). In 1613 he had become a Clerk of the Council, but had returned to Spain, and in 1622 become Secretary to the Prince Charles, whom, as already recorded, he had accompanied there in the following year. He had quarrelled with Buckingham, but after his death had become ambassador to Madrid. In 1629 he had been appointed Chancellor of the Exchequer, which office he would retain until 1642, when he was succeeded by Edward Hyde. In 1631 he was created Lord Cottington and in 1635 became Master of the Court of Wards. Clarendon says that he 'lived very nobly; had a better stable of horses, better provision for sports (especially of hawks, in which he took great delight)'. He was an ironically witty and disillusioned man of the world, regarded by Wentworth and Laud as dilatory and corrupt.
²²¹ Sir Francis Windebank (1582-1646) came of a Lincolnshire family and had risen through the patronage of the Cecils, his father having accompanied Lord Burghley's son Thomas, afterwards first Marquis of Exeter, on his travels abroad. He had been educated at St John's College, Oxford and studied Law at the Middle Temple, then travelled widely until 1608, when he had entered the Office of the Signet, of which he had in 1624 become Clerk. He was made

Secretary of State through Weston's influence, despite the superior claims of the diplomat Sir Thomas Roe. He became MP for Oxford in the Short Parliament of 1640 and for Corfe Castle in the Long one, but that December fled to France and died in Paris.

[222] Trevor-Roper, *op. cit.*, pp. 310-11.

[223] Condemned to prison, Ward fled briefly to Holland on release, but returned to Ipswich where after his death in 1640 his loyal congregation extended his salary of £100 to his widow and eldest son for their lifetimes.

[224] This at Salisbury in 1625. See Paul Slack, 'Poverty and Politics in Salisbury, 1597-1666', in *Crisis and Order in English Towns, 1500-1700*, ed. Peter Clark and Paul Slack (London 1972), pp. 164-203, on which admirable study this account is based.

[225] See J. U. Nef, *The Industrial Revolution in France and England. 1340-1640*.

[226] See Trevor-Roper, 'The General Crisis of the Seventeenth Century' in *Crisis in Europe*, ed. T. Ashton (London 1965), p. 27.

[227] Trevor-Roper, *op. cit.*, p. 93.

[228] Clarendon, *History of the Great Rebellion*, VIII, p. 82.

[229] Born in 1594, son of William Hampden of Great Hampden, Buckinghamshire, he had early come into his inheritance; his mother had been a daughter of Sir Henry Cromwell of Hinchingbroke, so he was a cousin of Oliver. Educated at the local grammar school at Thame and at Magdalen College, Oxford, he had read law at the Inner Temple and in spite of his mother's ambitions had not sought the peerage which his wealth could probably have obtained him at the Jacobean Court. He had refused the forced loan of 1626 and as a member of Parliament for Wendover, Buckinghamshire, had supported Sir John Eliot in the impeachment of Buckingham. He was an assiduous committee man and intensely legal-minded; a friend of Coke and Selden, he had looked after the interests of the Eliot family when Eliot had been imprisoned in the Tower.

[230] Sir John Finch, Baron Finch of Fordwich (1584-1660), already mentioned when held down as Speaker in the Chair, came of a distinguished family of Eastwell, Kent, related to Heneage Finch, second Earl of Winchelsea, who in 1661-9 was ambassador at Constantinople, and wrote an entertaining account of his mission. Sir Henry, his father, had been a successful lawyer who had written *Law, or a Discourse thereof in Four Books* (1627) which in various titles remained authoritative until superseded by Blackstone; he had also

written *The World's Great Restauration at the Calling of the Jews*, in which he envisaged that, converted to Christianity, they would attain world empire, a *jeu d'esprit* for which James I briefly had him imprisoned. John Finch read Law at Gray's Inn, became MP and recorder for Canterbury (1620 and 1625) and for Winchelsea in 1624. In 1626 he became recorder to the Queen, and was elected Speaker in 1628. In 1634 he became Chief Justice of the Common Pleas, and in January 1640 he would become Lord Keeper in succession to Sir Thomas Coventry. Impeached in 1641, he fled that December to Holland.

[231] Rushworth, *op. cit.*, III, Appendix, pp. 220ff.

[232] Cobbett, *op. cit.*, 1, p. 843.

[233] In our terms, 'Nonconformist'.

[234] *DNB*.

[235] G.E. Aylmer, *The State's Servants, The Civil Service of the English Republic 1644-1660* (London 1973), p. 321.

[236] Trevor-Roper, *Laud*, p. 323.

[237] *CSPD*, 1638, p. 474.

[238] Cobbett, *op. cit.*, *Proceedings against the Bishop of Lincoln for scandalizing the Government*, III, pp. 803 ff.

[239] Osbaldeston, himself an old Westminster, was the son of a London haberdasher. Elected to Christ Church, he had proceeded to Gray's Inn, before being made joint Head Master of Westminster in 1621, then Head Master in 1625. As a prebendary of the Abbey he made friends with Williams, who added to his office a prebend at Lincoln, and the rectory of Wheathamsted, Hertfordshire. He was restored to his benefices by the Long Parliament, though afterwards sequestered by them, and died in retirement in 1659.

[240] *CSPD*, 1638, p. 285.

[241] *Ibid.*, p. 568.

[242] Davenant had been born in Oxford in 1606 to the wife of John Davenant, proprietor of the Crown Tavern and in 1621 Mayor of Oxford. According to Aubrey, she was a' very beautiful woman of very great witt'. 'Mr. William Shakespeare,' Aubrey continues, 'was wont to goe into Warwickshire once a yeare, and did commonly in his journey lye at this house in Oxon... Now Sir William would sometimes, when he was pleasant over a glass of wine with his most intimate friends — e.g. Sam Butler, author of *Hudibras*, etc. say, that it seemed to him that he writt with the very spirit that did Shakespeare, and seemed contented enough to be thought his Son' (Aubrey op. cit., p. 85). Be that as it may, Davenant fought for the King during

the Civil War.
[243] List of pictures painted by Sir Antonio Van Dyck (*CSPD*, 1638-9, p. 196).
[244] *CSPD*, Addenda, 1625-49, p. 573.
[245] *The King's Arcadia: Inigo Jones and the Stuart Court*, eds John Harris, Stephen Orgel and Roy Strong (London: Arts Council 1973).
[246] *CSPV*, 1637-9, xxiv, p. 296.
[247] *Ibid.*, p. 300.
[248] Trevor-Roper, 'General Crisis', p. 116.
[249] James Heath, *A Chronicle of the Late Intestine War in the Three Kingdoms... in Four Parts, viz. the Commons war, Democratic, Protectorate, Restitution*, 2nd edn (London 1676), p. 3.
[250] *Memoirs of the Life of Colonel Hutchinson, with a fragment of autobiography by Mrs. Hutchinson*, ed. James Sutherland (Oxford 1973), p. 48.
[251] See J. P. Cooper, 'The Fortune of Thomas Wentworth, Earl of Strafford', *Econ. Hist. Review*, 2nd series, XI (1958).
[252] C.V. Wedgwood, *Thomas Wentworth. First Earl of Strafford. 1593-1641. A Revaluation* (London 1961), p. 137.
[253] And one of Thomas Hobbes's most eloquent and entertaining adversaries: in his *Catching of the Leviathan* (1658). See my *Hobbes and his Critics* (London 1951), pp. 114-33.
[254] Heath, *op. cit.*, p. 5.
[255] *CSPV*, *op. cit.*, xxiv, p. 426.
[256] Rushworth, *op. cit.*, II, p. 734.
[257] Ellis, *op. cit.*, III, pp. 285-7.
[258] *Ibid.*, pp. 285-7.
[259] *CSPD*, 1638-9, p. viii.
[260] *CSPV*, xxiv, p. 56.
[261] *CSPD*, 1638-9, p. 595.
[262] Wedgwood, *Strafford*, p. 269.
[263] *CSPD*, 1638-9, p. 548.
[264] John Pym (1584-1643), son of Alexander Pym of Brymore, near Bridgwater, had been educated at Broadgates Hall, now Pembroke College, Oxford, and studied law at the Middle Temple. He had represented Caine, Wiltshire, in the Parliaments of 1614, 1621 and 1624, and early tried to mobilize opinion against Catholics as such. In 1625 and in 1626 and 1628 he was member for Tavistock, Devon, and took a prominent part in the impeachment of Buckingham. He had thus won reputation in handling religious and financial policy; hence his treasurership of the Providence Company. In the Short

Parliament Pym ably summed up the grievances against the King's government, supported the Scots in their rebellion and showed his talent as a political organizer and committee man. In the Long Parliament he again sat for Tavistock, and soon established his ascendancy in the Commons and in committees as an indefatigable organizer and tactician.

[265] *CSPD*, 1639, p. 21.

[266] Heath, *op. cit.*, p. 18

[267] Sir Henry Vane (1589-1655), came of a substantial family of Hadlow, Kent, and had been educated at Brasenose College, Oxford and at Gray's Inn. He bought various court and legal offices including that of Cofferer to Prince Charles, and in 1629 became Comptroller of the Royal Household. He had sat in Parliament since 1614 and been employed as a diplomat in negotiations in Holland and Germany to recover the Palatinate. In the Short and Long Parliaments he represented Wilton. In 1641, convinced of his treachery, the King dismissed him from all his offices and he went over to Parliament.

[268] Sir Harry Vane, 'the younger' (1613-62), had been educated under Osbaldeston at Westminster School, at Magdalen Hall, Oxford and at Leiden and Geneva. He developed fanatical Calvinist religious opinions and from 1635-7 emigrated to Boston, Massachusetts. Appointed in 1639 Joint Treasurer of the Navy, he became MP for Hull in the Short Parliament. Following his father's dismissal, he lost office and went over to Parliament where he became the most formidable civilian leader next to Pym. He was violently against the bishops and identified himself with the extremist republican interest. He believed that all political power came from the people and his defiance after the Restoration made Charles II consider him too dangerous to live. He was excepted from pardon and executed.

[269] Hume, *The History of Great Britain* (London, 1970 edn), p. 434.

[270] See S.R. Smith, 'London Apprentices as Seventeenth Century Adolescents', *Past and Present*, 61 (February 1974).

[271] Trevor-Roper, *Laud*, pp. 388-9.

[272] Spalding, *History of the Troubles and Memorable Transactions in Scotland 1624-45*, ed. W. Skene (Aberdeen 1829), 1, p. 321.

[273] Cited by Wedgwood, *Strafford*, p. 296.

[274] Rushworth, *op. cit.*, III, p. 1,335.

[275] *Ibid.*, III, p. 1,336.

[276] *The Journal of Sir Simonds D'Ewes. From the Beginning of the Long*

Parliament to the opening of the trial of the Earl of Strafford, ed. Wallace Notestein (New Haven 1923), p. 6.

277 Leopold von Ranke, *A History of England. Principally in the Seventeenth Century* (Oxford 1875), II, p. 339.

278 Lucius Cary, second Viscount Falkland (1610-43) came of ancient Somerset and Devonshire stock. His father had been Lord Deputy in Ireland, and his mother was the only daughter of Sir Lawrence Tanfield, Chief Baron of the Exchequer, with whom the boy lived as a child and who, excluding his mother probably as a Catholic, made him his heir. He thus inherited the estate at Great Tew and substantial property in Burford. Aubrey alleges that in his youth he was 'wild' and 'apt to stab', but soon 'took to be serious' and 'grew to be a hard student' (*op. cit.*, p. 56). In 1633 he succeeded his father and settled permanently at Great Tew which he made a centre for poets, wits and scholars; he was himself a poet and dabbled in theology, inclining to Socinian (proto-Unitarian) opinions. He volunteered for service against the Scots and sat for Newport, Isle of Wight in the Short and Long Parliaments. A moderate Royalist, like his friend Edward Hyde, first Earl of Clarendon, he was reluctantly involved in politics and detested the war, ingeminating 'Peace, Peace', at the crucial siege of Gloucester, when the soldiers wanted to take the city by storm.

279 Wedgwood, *Strafford*, p. 306.

280 *The Letters and Journals of Robert Baillie, A.M., Principal of the University of Glasgow. 1637-1662*, ed. David Laing, 3 vols (Edinburgh 1841), 1, p. 316. Many of his letters are addressed to his colleague William Spang at the Scots merchants' house, still extant, at Veere on Walcheren. Though his handwriting was appalling ('Even in regard to his own name Baillie seems at no period of his life to have had a fixed mode of writing it' [p. vii]), he doubled (copied) his letters, and included many documents, so that his long and fluent writings are particularly illuminating. As a Presbyterian he detested the Independents more than he did the Court party, for he equated a Presbyterian regime with monarchy.

281 Wedgwood, *Strafford*, p. 316.

282 George Goring, Lord Goring (1608-57) was the son of Sir George Goring, first Earl of Norwich, who had made his way at the Jacobean Court as a gentleman of the Privy Chamber, a buffoon and a wit, and had won applause at a feast for Prince Charles's eighteenth birthday by producing 'four huge brown pigs piping hot and bitted and

harnessed with ropes of sausages all tied to a monstrous bag pudding' (*Dictionary of National Biography*). He had become Master of Horse to the Queen, Commissioner for the export of butter and shared in the tobacco and other monopolies. These happy days were ended in 1640 by the Long Parliament, and Norwich gave all he had to the King's cause. George the Younger had early been reputed a jovial lad' and had married a daughter of the wealthy Earl of Cork, but by 1633 had been £8,000 in debt, so Cork had bought him a colonelcy in the Dutch service when he had been lamed for life at the siege of Breda. Like his father he was in favour with the Queen and in 1639 had been appointed governor of Portsmouth. In view of his betrayal of the Royalist plot, Parliament wanted him to be second in command to Essex, but in August 1642 Goring declared for the King. After a chequered career in the Civil War he fled to the Netherlands, then took service in Spain, where he died in poverty in Madrid.

[283] This distinction between the person and the position of king was not, as often supposed, new. It had been made about Edward II: 'Homage and oath of allegiance relates more to the Crown than to the person of the King, and is more tied to it than to the individual' (The Lords Ordainers to the King, 1311).

[284] Robert Baillie, *Letters and Journals*, 3 vols, ed. D. Lang (1841-2), 1, p. 353.

[285] Wedgwood, *Strafford*, p. 389.

[286] Rushworth, *op. cit.*, III, p. 1,365.

[287] Trevor-Roper, *Laud*, p. 406.

[288] *Ibid.*, citing Baillie, *op. cit.*, 1, p. 309.

[289] *The Memoirs of Edmund Ludlow (1625-1672)*, ed. C.H. Firth, 2 vols (Oxford 1894), 1, p. 23.

[290] Thomas Hobbes, *Behemoth, or the Long Parliament* (written *c.* 1668 and also called *Dialogue of the Civil Wars in England*), ed. F. Tonnies, 2nd edn ed. M.M. Goldsmith (Cass 1969).

[291] *Ibid.*, p. 136.

[292] Mary was probably the most attractive of the King's daughters, but, brought up at the Frenchified English Court, she did not take to the Dutch, whose language she never bothered to learn. She proved quite able in contending with the Dutch political factions, and a staunch ally of her brothers in exile. The early death of Prince William brought her heavy responsibilities, and in 1657 she became regent for her son. Ironically, it was the restoration of Charles II that brought her to London and which ended her life, for she caught smallpox and

died there in 1660.

²⁹³ John Nalson LL.D, *An Impartial Collection of the Great Affairs of State from the Beginning of the Scotch Rebellions in the year MDCXXXIX to the murther of King Charles I, wherein the first occasion and the whole sea of the late troubles in England, Scotland and Ireland are faithfully represented. Taken from authenticall Records and Methodically Digested* (London 1682), 1; (1683), in, p. 736. These collections are in the Royalist interest, designed to counteract the alleged Parliamentarian bias of Rushworth and publicized under Charles II by royal command. The frontispiece of the first volume depicts a weeping Britannia, in a bad way, with a battle going on behind, crown, sceptre and mitre scattered at her feet.

See the World's glory once, here sits forlorn.

Exposed to Foreign and Domestic Scorn.

The frontispiece of the second volume depicts a ship labouring in a hurricane with the crew casting a crowned figure overboard with a milling and fighting crowd in the foreground.

When Royal Sovereign, weather beaten lay

On the proud billows of the popular sea.

A land like Canaan heretofore

Till by mad zeal into confusion hurl'd

'Twas made the scorn and byword of the world.

²⁹⁴ Meaning that a Parliament should be summoned after a lapse of three years without one.

²⁹⁵ Nalson, *op. cit.*, III, p. 776.

²⁹⁶ Ranke, *op. cit.*, II, p. 274.

²⁹⁷ In the Civil War he became a captain of a foot company from Leicester and though captured by the Royalists, continued to wield his pen with its usual vigour, for example *A Dedication demonstrating… that all malignants, whether they be prelates, etc. are enemies to God and the Church*. He then turned against the Independents and enjoyed a brisk controversy with John Lilburne, the Leveller.

²⁹⁸ Ranke, *op. cit.*, II, p. 270.

²⁹⁹ John Atherton, born 1598, sone of the rector of Bawdsdripp, Somerset, had studied at Gloucester Hall (now Worcester College) and Lincoln College, Oxford, then entered into holy orders and became rector of Huishcombe Flower in that county. His moral failings had been a godsend for Strafford's political opponents, as to the Irish Catholics, delighted to see a bishop of the English establishment in such a case; they taunted him on the very gallows and even interrupted his edifying valedictory speech.

The Penitent Death of a Woefull Sinner, or *The Penitent Death of John Atherton, late Bishop of Waterford, in Ireland*, by Nicholas Barnard, Dean of Ardagh (Dublin 1641, London 1642), was written to assuage the scandal and is illuminating for seventeenth-century psychology. Following a regimen devised by the Dean of Ardagh, Atherton put aside rich clothing, darkened his room, ate by himself or fasted, had his coffin by him, and made out an indictment against himself. Yet somehow he could not really repent, though he repented of having read 'naughty books', of attending plays and of general high living. He recalled 'gripings of conscience' but also how 'after some reformation' he had returned again, to his sins *like the Dogge to his Vomite or like the Hogge washed in Myre*.

Gradually, aided by the good Dean, he began to feel really penitent; naturally not one for tears, he now wept. He also looked through Foxe's *Book of Martyrs*, and 'the examples of good men's deaths did much to animate him', and he wrote pious letters of farewell to his wife and children. On the fatal morning he asked only for a 'little salt butter and brown bread, cheerfully hoping to be invited to the supper of the lamb in the next world'. His speech on the scaffold was elaborately eloquent and he died by hanging with as much dignity as he could.

300 William Seymour, first Marquis and second Earl of Hertford and second Duke of Somerset (1588-1666) was directly descended from the Seymours of Wolf Hall near Wootten Rivers in Wiltshire through Protector Somerset, brother-in-law to Henry VIII, and from Lady Catherine Grey, who had a claim on the throne through her descent from Henry VIII's sister, Mary, Dowager of France and Duchess of Suffolk. After the escapade of his secret marriage with Lady Arabella Stuart, he had been allowed to return to England and married Essex's sister Frances. In 1621 he had been created Earl of Hertford. He had immense estates in the West Country, originally accumulated by Protector Somerset. After the war, in which he fought for the King, he was allowed to compound for his estates and was created Duke of Somerset at the Restoration.

301 Author of *Microcosmographie*, or *A Peece of the World discovered in Essays and Characters* (1628), an entertaining work, for the characters, if rather cynically drawn, are representative and illuminating of the time. It went on selling for many years and was edited by Bliss in 1811. Earle accompanied Charles II into exile and, appointed Dean of Westminster at the Restoration, tried to moderate the persecution of

the Nonconformists. He was then translated first to the bishopric of Worcester, then in 1663 to Salisbury. He died in Oxford two years later, and there is a monument to him in Merton Chapel. Amid political prelates and fanatics of both sides, he appears to have been a kindly and attractive person.

[302] See Wedgwood, *The King's Peace*, p. 448.

[303] David Mathew, *Scotland under Charles I* (London 1955), p. 275.

[304] *Ibid.*, p. 279.

[305] 'There came out of Germany from the Wars home to Scotland one gentleman of base birth, born in Balveny, who had served long and fortunately in the German wars, who was called... his Excellence... inferior to none but the King of Sweden under whom he served among all the cavalry' (Spalding, 1, p. 130, quoted by Mathew, *op. cit.*, p. 275).

[306] Sir Edward Nicholas (1593-1669) son of John Nicholas of Winterborne Earles in the Bourne valley near Salisbury, Wiltshire, and Elizabeth Hunton of East Knoyle in that county, was educated at Salisbury, briefly at Winchester, then at Queen's College, Oxford. In 1612 he entered the Inner Temple, and by 1618 became secretary to Lord Zouch, Lord Warden of the Cinque Ports. He was MP for Winchelsea in 1620-1 and 1623-4, in became Secretary for the Admiralty under Buckingham, and in 1627-8 MP for Dover. After Buckingham's death Charles retained him at the Admiralty and made him Clerk of the Council, and in November 1641 he became Principal Secretary of State, an office he held in Oxford through the war with Falkland and the second Lord Digby as his successive colleagues. In 1646 he took refuge in Jersey and then in France, and remained with Charles II through his worst vicissitudes. After the Restoration, in 1662 he retired to East Horsley in Surrey.

[307] *The Nicholas Papers. 1641-52*, ed. G.F. Warner (Camden Society 1886), 1; (new series) XL, p. 41.

[308] *Ibid.*, 1, p. 58.

[309] *Memoirs and illustrations of the life and writings of John Evelyn, F.R.S., in which is subjoined the Private Correspondence between Charles I and his Secretary of State, Sir Edward Nicholas*, ed. W. Bray (London 1819), n, p. 56. Connolly, an Anglicized Irishman, was awarded £500 by Parliament and recommended to the King for a pension of £200 a year, probably never paid.

[310] Nalson, *op. cit.*, II, p. 899.

[311] Ranke, *op. cit.*, II, p. 290.

312 Sir Edward Dering, cited in Wedgwood, *The Kings Peace*, p. 483.
313 John Evelyn, *Memoirs*, p. 65.
314 Already on 6 November Nicholas had warned of a resolution that Parliament 'here finds that all Councills have been the cause of all the troubles in Ireland, and that unless your majesty will be pleased to discharge yr ill councellors that are about you, and to take such as ye Kingdoms can confide in, the Parliament doth hold itself absolved from giving assistance for ye business of Ireland' (Evelyn, *op. cit.*, II, p. 62). The resolution had been postponed, but had shown the way of the wind.
315 Clarendon, *History of the Rebellion*, IV, pp. 49-58.
316 During the King's absence they had spied upon the Queen's household at Oatlands, making enquiry about the Prince of Wales's servants and his frequenting Oatlands. The Queen had replied that he had come to celebrate his sister's birthday (Evelyn, *op. cit.*, II, P. 57).
317 Clarendon, *History of the Rebellion*, 1, p. 322.
318 *Somers Tracts*, IV, pp. 141ff.
319 Hobbes, *Behemoth*, p. 2.
320 Sir Thomas Lunsford (1610-53?), one of the most ferocious of the Cavaliers, came of impoverished Sussex gentry, and was early charged with poaching deer in the park of Sir Thomas Pelham, whom in 1633 he had physically attacked. Confined to Newgate, he had escaped. Outlawed, he had retired to France, but in 1640, he was pardoned by Charles and commanded a regiment in the Second Bishops' War. Compensated for his dismissal from the Tower by a knighthood, he escorted the King and Queen to Hampton Court. In 1649 he emigrated to Virginia, where he died, leaving families by his three successive wives. He was a red-headed man with a limp and a reputation for cannibalism because a libeller had written that he was fierce enough to eat children. "'The Colonell,' said Sir Philip Stapleton, Pym's colleague… "could not so content himself, but imitating the water toade, seeing the shaddows of a horse bigger than itself, sweld, to compare with the same and so burst'" (*Somers Tracts*, iv, p. 358).
321 Son of Sir Thomas Haselrig of Noseley, Leicestershire, he had married a sister of Robert Greville, 2nd Lord Brooke, a member of the Providence Company. In 1640, as MP for the county, he had bitterly opposed Laud, promoted the attack on the bishops and the attainder of Strafford. He became a bold though rash cavalry commander during the Civil Wars, and in 1647 went over to the

Independents. He fought again in the second Civil War and took part in Cromwell's campaign in 1650 against the Scots. He did very well out of the wars and bought up huge estates from the confiscated lands of the bishopric of Durham, but he became deeply detested by the Royalists and in 1660 was committed to the Tower, where he died in the following year.

[322] Edward Montague (1602-71), eldest son of Sir Henry Montague, first Earl of Manchester, and Catherine, daughter of Sir John Spencer of Yarnton Manor, Oxford. After attending Sidney Sussex College, Cambridge, and becoming MP for Huntingdon, he had accompanied Prince Charles to Spain, and in 1626 been created Baron Kimbolton through the influence of Buckingham. He had negotiated with the Scots at York and been in constant consultation with the opposition in the Commons. In November 1642 he succeeded his father as Earl of Manchester and became one of the principal commanders in the Parliamentary armies, though not one of the more successful. He strongly opposed the 'trial' of the King and became one of the architects of the Restoration.

[323] *The Journal of Sir Simonds D'Ewes, Bart., from the First recess of the Long Parliament to the withdrawal of the King from London*, ed. W.H. Coates (New Haven 1952), P.379.

[324] Not, as alleged, by the satirist Marston, said to have 'found out the plan from the Jesuits', since Marston had died in 1636.

[325] D'Ewes, *op. cit.*, p. 393.

[326] *Somers Tracts*, IV, p. 345.

[327] Rushworth, *op. cit.*, IV, p. 477. William Lenthall was an Oxfordshire gentleman who had prospered by the law, at which he had made £2,500 a year. He had bought Besselsleigh, near Cumnor, and Burford Priory from Lord Falkland, and in 1640 became MP for Woodstock. At first ineffective as Speaker, and disliking the long sessions, he had thought in December 1641 to return to the law, but his conduct on 5 January induced the Commons to vote him £6,000, so he changed his mind. In 1643 he became Master of the Rolls, a Commissioner of the Great Seal, and in 1647, Chancellor of the Duchy of Lancaster. Scared of mob violence during the conflict between Parliament and the army, he threw in his lot with Fairfax, but returned to the Speakership following the agreement between Fairfax and the Parliament. He acquiesced in the trial and execution of the King, became a kind of head of state under the commonwealth, and connived both at Cromwell's elevation to be

Protector and with Monk at the Restoration. He sent £3,000 to Charles II at Breda, so escaped Royalist vengeance, and in 1660 returned to Burford Priory, where he died in 1662.

[328] *Somers Tracts*, IV, p. 389.
[329] *Ibid.*, IV, p. 390.
[330] *Ibid.*, IV, p. 348.
[331] Ranke, *op. cit.*, II, p. 325.
[332] *CSPD*, 1641-3, pp. 3-6.
[333] *Ibid.*, p. 252.
[334] Hutchinson, *op. cit.*, pp. 62-3. This remarkable biography of a Nottinghamshire squire who defended Nottingham Castle from June 1643 to 1646, by his highly intelligent and well-educated wife, was written in 1664 and published in 1806. It depicts some of the more attractive aspects of the Puritan character.
[335] J. H. Hexter, *The Reign of King Pym* (Harvard 1941), p. 200.
[336] J. H. Hexter, *The Reign of King Pym* (Harvard 1941), P.4. This trenchant American study is still the best account of Pym.
[337] Wormaid, *op. cit.*, p. 27.
[338] Heath, *op. cit.*, p. 30.
[339] *Ibid.*, p. 45.
[340] Sir P. Warwick, *Memoirs*, pp. 196-8, cited in *Somers Tracts*, IV, p. 367.
[341] For the best appreciation of this important document see Corinne Comstock Weston, *English Constitutional Theory and House of Lords, 1556-1832* (London 1965), p. 6 and Appendix 1, pp. 263-5.
[342] *CSPD*, 1641-3, p. 336.
[343] *A True and Exact relation of the Manner of His Majesties setting up his standard at Nottingham on Monday the 22 August 1642. Somers Tracts*, iv, pp. 471-5.
[344] *CSPD*, 1641-3, p. 382.
[345] Clarendon, *Selection from the History of the Rebellion and Civil Wars, and his Life by Himself*, ed. G. Huehns (Oxford 1953), p. 208.
[346] *Ibid.*, p. 210.
[347] Slack, *op. cit.*, p. 25.
[348] The parishioners of St Dioni's Back Church in London petitioned the Commons against John Warner, Bishop of Rochester, who, undaunted, had kept up his Laudian principles. They complained that he had set the communion table altar wise, with three ascents of black and white marble, and a new font, been 'very contentious about tithes', denounced Puritanical knaves and compared lecturers to ballad singers at market.

³⁴⁹ *CSPD*, 1641-3, p. 391.

³⁵⁰ Sir Jacob (by 1645, Baron) Astley was a Norfolk gentleman, who had served in the Netherlands and under Gustav Adolf, and also as Governor of Plymouth.

³⁵¹ And indeed his second wife decamped to the King's garrison at Oxford, where she bore a son to one of the Cavaliers, and Essex died with no direct heir.

³⁵² Robert Bertie, first Earl of Lindsey KG, born in 1582, the eldest son of Peregrine Bertie, Lord Willoughby de Eresby, was a highly educated aristocrat, descended through his mother from the de Vere earls of Oxford; he had travelled much abroad and developed his estates in Lincolnshire by draining the fenland. He had also fought in the Low Countries and succeeded Buckingham as Admiral of the Fleet against La Rochelle. In 1626 Charles had created him Earl of Lindsey.

³⁵³ *CSPD*, 1641-3, p. 395.

³⁵⁴ *Ibid.*, p. 399.

³⁵⁵ *Somers Tracts*, IV, pp. 476-7.

³⁵⁶ Ellis, *op. cit.*, III, p. 291.

³⁵⁷ Wedgwood, *The King's War*, p. 121.

³⁵⁸ At the beginning of the war musketeers — skilled men — got 6s a week, though the cavalry got 17s 6d. Later in the New Model Army the pay was more regular: the soldiers had 9d a day and the cavalrymen 12s 6d. The officers were always far better paid — a Royalist captain of foot had £2 12 6d a week, with top Royalist generals receiving £10 a day. See Brigadier Peter Young and Richard Holmes, *The English Civil War. A Military History of the Three Civil Wars 1642-51* (London 1974), p. 51.

³⁵⁹ Young and Holmes, *op. cit.*, p. 42.

³⁶⁰ *Ibid.*, p. 35.

³⁶¹ *Ibid.*, pp. 38-42.

³⁶² *Ibid.*, p. 72.

³⁶³ 'When the King wanted to regale ministers and officers of the adverse party, in order to extract secrets from them in their more cheerful hours, he made Ruthven field-marshal of the bottle and glasses, and he could drink immeasurably' (*DNB*, citing Harte, *Life of Gustavus Adolphus*).

³⁶⁴ Heath, *op. cit.*, p. 40.

³⁶⁵ *Three speeches made by the King's most excellent Majesty: the first to divers Lords and Colonels, in his Majestie's Tent; the second to his soldiers in the Field;*

the third to his whole army immediately before the late of Batell of Keinton near Banbury (Somers Tracts, pp. 478-9).

[366] The widespread popular impression that the Cavaliers charged wildly down the *escarpment itself* is naturally quite wrong.

[367] Heath, *op. cit.*, p. 41.

[368] *CSPV*, 1641-2, p. 191.

[369] Clarendon, *op. cit.*, p. 281.

[370] Such is the modern estimate, though Heath gives it at six thousand 'as by this count it was judged who had the burying of them' (Heath, *op. cit.t* p. 41).

[371] A monument in Radway Church remains poignant. It is to: Henry Kingsmill, Esq. second son of Sir Henry Kingsmill of Sidmonton in ye county of Southampton. Kt. whoe serving as a Captain of foot under his Matie Charles the First of Blessed Memory was at the Battell of Edgehill as he was manfully fighting in behalf of his King and country unhappily slaine by a cannon bullett, in memory of whom his mother, the Lady Bridget Kingsmill, did in the fortieth year of her widdowhood in the year of our Lord 1670 erect this monument.

I have fought the good fight. I have
finished my course. Henceforth is layd up
for me a Crown of Righteousness.

The effigy, though slightly mutilated, is particularly revealing of the details of contemporary dress.

[372] The Parliament was long pursued by complaints by civilian wagoners who had lost their horses and vehicles in the battle. As a petition in January 1643 of Francis Parr of Shoreditch, who complains that he had two servants and four horses employed by the Parliament in which service one of his men was killed 'by those barbarous cavaliers, and the other never heard of since', and also his four horses taken away. In March, surprisingly, he got £24 compensation for the horses. Robert Bennett, a carter of Exeter, whose wagon laden with Devonshire cloth had been pressed into the artillery train and all lost, obtained £82.

[373] *The Life and Times of Anthony Wood*, abridged from Andrew Clark's edn with an introduction by Llewelyn Powys (London 1932), p. 17.

[374] *Ibid.*, pp. 15-16. Wood's elder brother, for example, then at Christ Church and aged eighteen, 'left his gown at the town end' and having done good service at Edgehill was taken into the Royalist army. He became 'boisterous' and martial, and later took service under

Cromwell, but in 1651 died of the flux at Drogheda in Ireland.
[375] Heath, *op. cit.*, p. 41.
[376] Marlborough was an obvious place to raid by the Royalist cavalry, probably bored with detention in Oxford, since it could be approached rapidly over the Berkshire downs by Wantage, Lambourne, Baydon and Aldbourne. Wilmot and Digby with four thousand men, after a desultory and inaccurate bombardment from the common — from which the target cannot be seen — managed to infiltrate the town, apparently by the passage to the yard of the present Castle and Ball Hotel, though they failed to take the Mound, now part of the College. A hundred and twenty prisoners were marched off over the bleak downs to Oxford, where they suffered severe hardship in the dungeons of the Norman castle. It was impossible to hold the town; but it had been badly damaged as a base for Parliamentarian attack on the roads to Bath and the west. One Cavalier song runs:
God damn me, ram me, sink me down to hell
If ever in Marlborough do any Roundheads dwell!
[377] Heath, *op. cit.*, p. 186.
[378] The inhabitants were fined £4,000 and told to raise £3,000 to pay for a Royalist garrison.
[379] Deprived of his Fellowship by the Parliament in 1646, he lived by his wits abroad and in Oxford until the Restoration, when in 1661 he was knighted and made DCL of Oxford and FRS, though he failed to stay the course as MP for Wilton; Aubrey says he was 'exceedingly bold confident and witty, not very grateful to his benefactors; would He damnably' (Aubrey, *op. cit.*, pp. 23-4).
[380] Aubrey, *op. cit.*, p. 186.
[381] Sir William Waller (1597-1668), was the son of Sir Thomas Waller, lieutenant of Dover, and Margaret, daughter of Lord Dacre. He went to Oxford, then travelled abroad, fought for the Venetians and in the wars in Germany, then studied the law at Gray's Inn. He married a Devonshire heiress and in 1640 was elected MP for Andover. Of Puritan opinions, he early joined the Parliament as a colonel of horse, making his first reputation by the capture of Portsmouth in September 1642. After a chequered but sensational military career, he was retired in 1645 under the Self-Denying Ordinance that forbade MPs to hold military commissions, and threw himself into politics on the side of the Scots and the Presbyterians. But he incurred the hostility of the Independents and the army, and in August 1647 he

left for France. Returning next year, he was arrested by the army and imprisoned for three years in North Wales. He remained on bad terms with Cromwell, but was elected a member of the Council of State, which brought about the Convention Parliament of the Restoration.

[382] David Underdown, *Somerset in the Civil War and Interregnum* (Newton Abbot 1973), p. 117.

[383] *Ibid.*, p. 86.

[384] Ellis, *op. cit.*, III, pp. 293, 295-6.

[385] He had succeeded his father Lord Fairfax of Cameron in 1640, and inherited estates at Denton in Yorkshire, which country he represented in the Long Parliament, where he supported the Parliamentarian side. As the commander of their forces in Yorkshire, he had signed a treaty of neutrality with the Royalists, at once annulled by Parliament. He proved an indifferent commander and was superseded when the Self-Denying Ordinance of 1645 disqualified members from command. He died in 1648. His son Thomas, third Lord Fairfax, on the other hand, proved a highly successful commander-in-chief. Educated at St John's College, Cambridge, he then fought in the Low Countries. In 1642 he became second-in-command to his father in Yorkshire, and after his capture of Leeds in 1643, won a growing reputation. His military ability has been overshadowed by the dominating personality of Cromwell, technically his subordinate during the Civil War, but politically in a different class. Fairfax had few ambitions and was content to go into retirement in 1650, though only thirty-eight. For a perceptive view of him, see Maurice Ashley, *Cromwell's Generals*, (London 1954).

[386] *The King's Cabinet Opened*, 13 February 1643, from *A Selection from the Harleian Miscellany* (London 1793), p. 356.

[387] 'The Journal of Prince Rupert's Marches, 5 Sept. 1642-4 July 1646', *EHR*, XIII (1898), pp. 729-41.

[388] During the eighteenth century rumours got about that Hampden had perished through the explosion of his own pistol, an idea reinforced when Lord Nugent, his first biographer (1831), dug up what he thought to be his body and amputated both arms. But since Nugent afterwards considered he had disinterred the wrong body, the evidence is hardly admissible. Contemporary accounts concur that the squire of Stoke Mandeville was shot by the enemy and died, probably in the Greyhound Inn, at the Parliamentarian headquarters at Thame. There is no evidence that his last words were 'O Lord,

save my country' — an obvious eighteenth-century accretion.

[389] Heath, *op. cit.*, p. 46.

[390] See Young and Holmes, *op. cit.*, p. 132, for an admirable account of one of the most interesting battles of the entire war.

[391] See Hutchins, *History of Dorset*, 1. The spirited Lady Bankes again defied the Parliamentarians in April 1646, when the King's cause was hopeless, and held out for eight days until betrayed by treachery. The castle was then 'slighted' and became the imposing ruin familiar today. Lady Bankes, impoverished by sequestrations, survived to see the Restoration.

[392] *Iter Carolinum, being a succinct relation of the necessitated marches... of His Majesty Charles I, Somers Tracts*, v, pp. 263 ff.

[393] Heath, *op. cit.*, p. 47.

[394] Falkland as a high-minded character has been accorded a similar moral prestige to Hampden; he was deeply depressed by the war and the extremist courses then prevalent on both sides, so that he may have deliberately sought to end his life. But Aubrey maintains that 'At the fight of Newbury my Lord Falkland being there, and having nothing to doe to charge; as the two armies were engaging, rode like a madman (as he was) between them; and was (as he needs must be) shott. Some that were your superfine discoursing politicians and fine gentlemen, would needs have the reason of this mad action of throwing away his life so, to be his discontent for the unfortunate advice given to his master as aforesaid (he had advised the King to besiege Gloucester); but, I have been well enformed, by those who best knew him, and know intrigues behind the curtaine (as they say) that it was his griefe of the death of Mris Moray, a handsome Lady at court, who was his mistress, and whom he loved above all creatures, was the true cause of his being so madly guilty of his own Death, as aforementioned' (Aubrey, *op. cit.*, pp. 56-7).
There is an obelisk to Falkland and the Cavaliers at the first turning to the right off the Andover road out of Newbury; it has Greek and Latin inscriptions as well as English and is made of dun-coloured stone or granite: not very appropriate to the neighbourhood.

[395] Aubrey, *op. cit.*, p. 193.

[396] *Ibid.*, pp. 59-60.

[397] The makers of tobacco pipes, now taxed, petitioned that they were now reduced to beggary; only a fifth of the pipes usually in demand were now made, 'foul pipes being oftener burnt than formerly'.

[398] Rushworth, *op. cit.*, 111: ii, pp. 478 ff. The actual oath ran: 'I, A.B., in

Humility and reverence of the Divine Majesty, declare my hearty sorrows for my own sins and the sins of the nation which have deserved the calamities and judgements that now lie upon it.' The participant pledged himself not to consent to the laying down of arms for so long as the Papists, now in open war against the Parliament, 'shall by force of arms be protected from the justice thereof'; and to assist the forces raised by both Houses of Parliament, against the forces raised by the King without their consent. 'And this vow,' he concluded, 'I make in the presence of All Mighty God.'

399 Ranke, *op. cit.*, 1, p. 393.
400 Hexter, *op. cit.*, p. 136.
401 Heath, *op. cit.*, p. 56.
402 Edward Husband (ed.), *A Collection of all the Public Orders, Ordinances and Declarations of both Houses of Parliament, 1646*, p. 420.
403 *CCSP*, 1, item 1729.
404 Strickland, *op. cit.*, 8, p. 111.
405 *CSPD*, 1644, p. 301, cited in Young and Holmes, *op. cit.*, p. 189.
406 'Journal of Prince Rupert's Marches', p. 736.
407 *A Short Memorial of Thomas, Lord Fairfax, written by himself* (London 1699), in *Somers Tracts*, v, p. 374ff.
408 Here also, wrote a Roundhead, was slain 'the accursed cur', Rupert's dog Boye, allowed in the confusion to follow him into battle. During his captivity at Linz the Prince had acquired a beautiful white dog 'of a breed so famous' that the Grand Turk wanted 'to obtain a puppy thereof'. Boye was alleged to be a familiar spirit, 'not perhaps a downright divell' but perhaps a Lapland witch 'now by art a handsome white dogge'. He is generally described as a 'poodle' but only on the slender evidence that his mother had been called Puddle. Since the Grand Turk had heard of him, he may well have been an animal of larger and more spectacular breed. See Warburton, *Memoirs of Prince Rupert and the Cavaliers* (citing *Observations on Prince Rupert's Dogge called Boye*) (London 1842), 1, p. 99.
409 *CSPD*, 1644, pp. 233-4.
410 *Ibid.*, p. 352.
411 Cited in Wedgwood, *The King's War*, p. 339.
412 Young and Holmes, *op. cit.*, p. 212.
413 *Iter Carolinum*, p. 268.
414 *The Kings Cabinet Opened*, p. 342.
415 Anthony a Wood, *Life and Times*, abridged by Llewellyn Powys (London 1932), p. 29.

[416] Cited by Trevor-Roper, *Laud*, p. 413.
[417] See Trevor-Roper, *Laud*, pp. 418-26, for these transactions and their sequel. Relieved when his old pupil, the lawyer, Bulstrode Whitelocke, refused to appear against him, telling the House of Commons that the Archbishop 'did me the favour to take a special care of my breeding at St. John's College in Oxford, and that it would be disingenuous and ungrateful for me to be personally instrumental to take away his life, who was so instrumental in the bettering of mine' (Whitelocke, *Memoirs*, p. 75, cited in Trevor-Roper, *op. cit.*, p. 421).
[418] Pathetically, Laud had willed £800 to St Paul's: X1*000 to the King and £2,000 'forgiven': £500 and plate to St John's College, Oxford. 'I forbear to name, who has the money,' he wrote, 'lest the same storm should fall on them which have driven me out of all I had considerable in my own possession.' The usual hack rhymster turned the tragedy to farce:

Can Britain's Patriarchal Peer Expire
And Bid the world, goodnight without a choir?
How sweetly wentst thou hence, thy fluent tongue
Warbling they own swanlike expedicum.

[419] Cited by Wedgwood, *The King's War*, p. 392 — a vivid narrative on which this brief account is based. See also Wedgwood, *Montrose* (London, 1966), for a full account.
[420] See *Ludlow's Memoirs*, pp. 109-12, for a vivid account.
[421] Leo F. Solt, *Saints in Arms. Puritanism and Democracy in Cromwell9s Army* (Stanford 1959), p.15.
[422] That month, to encourage morale, he had commanded Garter King of Arms to grant 'to such loyal subjects as distinguished themselves against the rebels such argumentation of arms as would fitly express their merits'.
[423] *Iter Carolinum*, v, p. 273.
[424] For a detailed and fascinating account of them and the campaign see Joshua Sprigg, *Anglia Rediviva: England's Recovery, being the history of the motions, actions, and successes of the Army under the immediate conduct of His Excellency Sir Thomas Fairfax Knt* (1647), 1854 edn, p. 61. The compiler — he compiled it, he says, 'for the public good' — was the son of a steward of New College, an Independent preacher and a member of Fairfax's household. In 1649 he was rewarded by the appointment of Fellow and Senior Bursar of All Souls, where, Wood says of him, 'he was of civil conversation, but far gone in enthusiasm and blamed

much by some of the Fellows there for having the history of our Saviour's ascension, curiously carved over that college gate, to be defaced, after it had remained there from the foundation of the house' (*Athenae Oxonienses*, iv, p. 137, cited in *DNB*). His book gives a detailed and well-written account of Fairfax's campaigns, though it is self-righteously favourable to the Roundheads. It is dedicated 'To all Englishmen' 'My dear countrymen, for to you I direct this story, for it is yours, in your land were these battles fought, these actions done for your sake, etc.'

[425] According to Sprigg (*pp. cit.*, p. 89) four hundred, of whom half were wounded, were locked up in Shroton Church, among them a few local clergy. Cromwell addressed them, gave them their liberty, promised to stop the army plundering and to hang any Club Men who assembled again. See also A. R. Bayley, *The Great Civil War in Dorset* (Taunton 1910).

[426] Heath, *op. cit.*, p. 83.

[427] Ellis, *op. cit.*, III, p. 312.

[428] *Ibid.*, III, p. 315.

[429] Wedgwood, *The King's War*, p. 405.

[430] See Hester W. Chapman, *The Tragedy of Charles II* (London 1964), p. 79, for an admirable account of the Prince's adventures.

[431] J. Bruce (ed.), *Charles I in 1646* (London 1856), p. 1.

[432] After the journey this martial cleric, arrested at Sandwich trying to escape to France, soon evaded his captors, but early in 1647 he was re-arrested at Hull and incarcerated in the Tower. But in 1648 he again escaped, disguised as an apple vendor, and during the Civil War raised a troop for the King. Defending Woodcroft House, Northamptonshire, he was flung over the battlements, but clung to a spout until his hands were cut off, whereat he fell into the moat. He managed to ask to be allowed to die on land, but was knocked on the head with a musket, and his tongue cut out and exhibited as a trophy. Such were the amenities of the time.

[433] See R. W. Ketton-Cremer, *Norfolk in the Civil War* (London 1969), pp. 310-25.

[434] Sprigg, pp. 283-6.

[435] Aubrey, *op. cit.*, p. 104.

[436] Wood, *Life and Times, op. cit.*, p. 31.

[437] *Acts and Ordinances of the Interregnum 1642-1660*, 1 (1642-9), p. 749. In August 1645 an ordinance for 'taking away of the book of Common Prayer and for the establishment and putting in execution of the

Directory for the public worship of God' had ordained that the knights and burgesses of the several counties 'shall send printed books of the said Divinity fairly bound up in leather, unto the committees of Parliament in the counties who shall deliver it to the officers of the parishes 'to be paid for by the Inhabitants'. The constables were to deliver it to the minister who was to read it, instead of the book of Common Prayer, on pain of a fine of £5 for the first offence, £10 for the second and a year in prison for the third. If he preached against it he could be fined up to £50.

438 *CSP*, II, p. 63.
439 Underdown, *Pride's Purge*, p. 77.
440 *Acts and Ordinances*, p. 758.
441 Ranke, *op. cit.*, p. 482.
442 Though not technically a regicide, Joyce helped to bring the King to trial, became a colonel, then governor of Portland. But he conspired against Cromwell and in 1653 was cashiered. Employed on counter-espionage, after the Restoration, he fled to Holland and died abroad. See *A True Important Narrative concerning the Army's Preservation of the King* (Rushworth, *op. cit.* vi, pp. 513ff.).
443 *Somers Tracts*, VI, p. 394.
444 Warned of this gambit, according to G. M. Young, Cromwell and Ireton may have intercepted one of the King's letters to the Queen sewn into a saddle, in which he reassured her that far from thinking of the Garter and the Viceroyalty of Ireland for Cromwell, 'he should know in time how to deal with the rogues, who instead of a silken garter should be fitted with a hempen cord... "and then," said Cromwell, "we resolved his ruin"'. Young thinks the evidence for this story quite good enough to make it in a general sense admissible, but that the details and the date are doubtful (*Charles I and Cromwell* [London 1935], p. 856).
445 See Joseph Frank, *The Levellers, The History of the Writings of three seventeenth century social democrats, John Lilburne, Richard Overton, William Walwyn* (Harvard 1956).
446 See *Clarke Papers*, ed. C.H. Firth (London 1891), 1, pp. 66ff.
447 *DNB*. It is just possible that, given Hammond's close ties with Cromwell, the latter's unexplained visit to the Isle of Wight early in September and Ashburnham's present dependence on Cromwell, Carisbrooke Castle was deliberately designed as another place of imprisonment for the King, who was manoeuvred into going there.
448 *The Memoirs of Sir John Berkeley* (London 1699), p. 378.

449 *CSPD*, 1648, p. 6.
450 *Ibid.*, p. 30.
451 Firebrace (1619-91) attended the King with devotion throughout his vicissitudes and on the eve of his execution Charles urged Juxon to recommend him to the Prince of Wales. In 1660 Firebrace was again taken on in the royal household, though this time in the less intimate, if more lucrative, positions of Chief Clerk of the Kitchen, Clerk Comptroller Supernumerary of the Household and Assistant to the Officers of the Green Cloth. His eldest son become a Fellow of Trinity, Cambridge, the other Sheriff of London and a baronet.
452 See Sir Thomas Herbert, groom of the Chamber to His Majesty (ed.), *Memoirs of the last Two years of the Reign of Charles I* (London 1813). Experienced in describing life in India and Persia, Herbert often depicts places with singular accuracy, as Carisbrooke, Hurst Castle and Windsor.
453 George Hillier, *A Narrative of the attempted escapes of Charles the 1st from Carisbrooke Castle* (London 1853).
454 *History of the Great Civil War*, IV, p. 94.
455 He missed his children, and a local boy became a great favourite with him. One day, seeing him with a child's sword, Charles asked him what he meant to do with it, and when the child replied 'to defend you with it against your enemies', gave him a signet ring off his finger, long preserved in the boy's family.
456 Thomas, *op. cit.*, p. 17.
457 Both were veterans of Dutch campaigns and had fought through the civil wars. Lucas was a native of Colchester, educated at Christ's College, Cambridge; Lisle, son of a courtier, Sir Lawrence Lisle, a connection of Buckingham's who had obtained the monopoly of collecting the tobacco imposts. He had been governor of Faringdon at the surrender in June 1646. Both died with defiant courage.
458 *CSPD*, 1648, p. 73.
459 John Gauden, Bishop of Worcester 1605-62, is now considered to be its main author, as the style, if not the occasional elevation, often resembles that of his other writings, and he was amply rewarded after the Restoration with the bishopric of Exeter, and, that not sufficing, briefly of Worcester. A Suffolk man, educated at St John's College, Cambridge, and at Wadham, he had been in Warwick's entourage, taken the Covenant and held Presbyterian livings. But he denounced the *Taking and Destroying of our Sovereign Lord the King* in a work dedicated to Fairfax, and though he kept his preferments, attacked

Cromwell (see H. R. Trevor-Roper, *The Eikon Basilike. The Problem of the King's Book. Historical Essays* [London 1957]).

[460] Herbert, *op. cit.*, p. 64.

[461] *CSP*, II, pp. 44, 453, cited by Wedgwood in *The Trial of Charles I* (London 1964), p. 30.

[462] Christopher Hill, *God's Englishmen* (London 1970), p. 55.

[463] Thomas, *op. cit.*, p. 69.

[464] *CSPD*, 1648-9, p. 271.

[465] *Ibid.*, p. 319.

[466] Cited by Wedgwood, *The Trial of Charles I*, p. 33.

[467] Harrison was not a man to go back on his beliefs. At the Restoration he remained in England, when he could have escaped, and died defiantly, reaffirming his principles. His more deluded followers expected his Resurrection.

[468] Herbert, *op. cit.*, p. 123.

[469] For the first six months of 1649 the largest attendance at a division was only seventy seven... as a rule fifty was considered a good house. See Tanner, *English Constitutional Conflicts of the Seventeenth Century, 1603-89* (London 1928), p. 152.

[470] Thomas Pride, though said to have derived his name from St Bride's foundling hospital in London, probably came from Somerset, and he began life as a brewer's drayman. In the army he had won rapid promotion, done well at Naseby and at the storming of Bristol, and had championed the grievances of the soldiers over arrears of pay. In the second Civil War he had commanded a regiment in Wales and at Preston, and he was one of the Commissioners for the King's trial and signed his death warrant. He afterwards commanded a brigade at Worcester and Dunbar, and was granted an estate of £500 a year in Scotland out of 'delinquents" lands. He then made a fortune as a contractor victualling the fleet, bought the royal palace of Nonesuch and was knighted by Cromwell. Though he resisted the Protector's project to make himself king, he became a member of his House of Lords. He was a Puritan who put down cockfighting and betting on it, and also purged the bear garden by having all bears put down. He died in 1658, so all that the Royalists could do to him was to dig him up, hang him and bury him at Tyburn, and confiscate Nonesuch, which was restored to the Crown.

[471] Underdown, *Pride's Purge*, p. 337.

[472] Wedgwood, *The Trial of Charles I*, p. 47.

[473] *Ibid.*, pp. 47-8.

⁴⁷⁴ *Mercurius Elencticus*, no. 1, cited in J.B. Williams, *A History of English Journalism to the Foundation of the Gazette* (London 1908), p. 201.
⁴⁷⁵ *Ibid.*, p. 203.
⁴⁷⁶ Thomas, *op. cit.*, pp. 138-9.
⁴⁷⁷ See *Clarke Papers*, II, pp. 150-4.
⁴⁷⁸ Young, *Charles I and Cromwell*, p. 138.
⁴⁷⁹ Herbert, *op. cit.*, p. 158.
⁴⁸⁰ Underdown, *op. cit.*, p. 233.
⁴⁸¹ *Ibid.*, p. 246.
⁴⁸² *Ibid.*, p. 189.
⁴⁸³ Wedgwood, *The Trial of Charles I*, p. 56.
⁴⁸⁴ Isaac Dorislaus (1595-1649) came from Alkmaar in Holland, read law at Leiden, emigrated to England and was appointed Lecturer in History at Cambridge, where his interpretation of Tacitus in a republican sense led to his lectures being discontinued following the protests of the vice-chancellor. He had become a judge advocate in Essex's army and then a judge in the Court of Admiralty. Dispatched in May 1649, after the King's death, to negotiate an alliance with the Dutch, the learned man was clubbed to death by English Royalists at The Hague.
⁴⁸⁵ John Cook, a lawyer of obscure extraction, had been employed by Strafford in Ireland and travelled extensively on the Continent. After the trial he was rewarded by being made Chief Justice of Munster in Ireland, where he did swift justice on the defeated Irish, was assigned property in Waterford and County Cork, and promoted to the Irish Court of Upper Bench. But his legal career was interrupted, for in 1659 he was arrested by Royalists, shipped back to England and hanged as a regicide in October 1660.
⁴⁸⁶ *Somers Tracts*, V, p. 192.
⁴⁸⁷ Born in 1602 at Wibersley Hall, near Stockport, he had read law at Gray's Inn. By 1643, he had been elected judge of the Sheriff's Court in London and in 1646 Chief Justice in Cheshire and in 1648 Mayor of Chester. After the King's trial, he was made President of the Council of State, given a gratuity of £1,000 and an income of £2,000 a year and made Chancellor of the Duchy of Lancaster. He stood up to Cromwell when he dissolved the Rump of the Long Parliament in 1653 ('no power under heaven can dissolve them but themselves, therefore take you notice of it') and later accused the Protector of having 'committed the most horrid treason that ever was heard of'; but he died in 1659 at the deanery, having declared that if he had to

try and condemn the King again he would do it. In 1660 he was retrospectively attainted, exhumed, and hung up at Tyburn, his head being exhibited in Westminster Hall.

[488] *State Trials*, 1, p. 1,017.

[489] This description is based on the contemporary and fullest account founded on shorthand notes taken at the time and edited and sanctioned by Gilbert Mabbot, the censor: *A perfect narrative of the Whole Proceedings of the High Court of Justice, in the trial of the King, in Westminster Hall on Saturday the 20th and Monday 22nd of this instant January; with the several speeches of the King, Lord President and Solicitor General. Published by authority, to prevent false and impertinent relations. To these proceedings of the tryal of the King I say Imprimatur. Gilbert Mabbot. Printed January 23rd 1648* (9 by modern reckoning). This, together with the collection of *State Trials*, gives the best evidence available. It is printed in *Somers Tracts*, v, pp. 197-214.

[490] By refusing to recognize the court, Charles spared himself and others the harangue that Cook had prepared 'if the King had pleaded to the charge, and put himself upon a fair trial'. He had meant to call Charles 'the Original of all Injustice and the Principal author of more miseries to the Freeborn people of this nation than the best Arithmetician can well enumerate', and to allege that he had connived with Buckingham to poison his father, 'being wholly given up to the counsels of the Jesuitical party that they [might] cast their net into our troubled waters and thus catch more fish'. If, he would have continued, the pilot is drunk and running his ship on the rocks, the passengers may throw him into the sea, and if, as he believed, the King had had a hand in the Irish Massacre, he should die. For good measure, he would have denounced the King for patronizing the stage and reading Shakespeare's plays (see *Somers Tracts*, iv, pp. 170ff.).

[491] Wedgwood, *The Trial of Charles I*, p. 146.

[492] Downes, a creature of Cromwell's, had done well out of buying up bishops' lands at Petworth and Chichester and in 1649 sold his auditorship for £3,000. He was afterwards appointed to the Committee of State. By the Restoration he was a rich man but, though condemned as a regicide, he escaped execution by an exaggerated account of his protest, and died in penury in prison.

[493] Young, *op. cit.*, p. 14.

[494] See Wedgwood, *The Trial of Charles I*, p. 170.

[495] 'What the King said to me 29 of January last, being the last time I

had the happiness to see him in? Cited by Heath, *op. cit.*, p. 216.

[496] Colonel Francis Hacker came of a Nottinghamshire family, who, save for him, were all Royalists. He fought well in the wars and was said to have given away his share of plunder to the Parliament and his soldiers. He supported Cromwell's regime, but was no politician, 'all who have known me', he said at his trial in 1660, 'in my best estate have not known me to be a man of oratory and God hath not given me the gift of utterance as to others'. He might have escaped at the Restoration, but Mrs Hacker, thinking to help her husband, was foolish enough to produce the warrant of the King's execution, when the Lords wanted evidence against regicides, instead of destroying it. So Hacker was hanged, but in consideration of his Royalist family not drawn and quartered, and so decently interred.

[497] *Memoirs of Sir Philip Warwick*, pp. 340-6.

[498] Heath, *op. cit.*, p. 217.

[499] Huncks had refused to sign the warrant to the executioner.

[500] There is not sufficient evidence for the rumours that anyone, let alone Joyce or even Cromwell, had taken his place — typical *canards* of popular imagination.

[501] The Parliament forbade this transaction, and a 'cabinet' which the King had given Juxon was searched for papers.

[502] *Ibid.*, p. 220.

[503] Young, *op. cit.*, p. 172.

[504] Modern doctors consider that the King can have felt nothing; the cut was too swift for the reaction to the blow to reach the brain.

[505] He became a rather tiresome Nonconformist divine, but wrote capacious and illuminating diaries, published in 1882.

[506] Ellis, *op. cit.*, III, p. 323.

[507] Tanner, *op. cit.*, p. 154.

[508] *Mercurius Elencticus*, in Williams, *op. cit.*, p. 205.

[509] 'The incident is just possible, but it sounds much more like one of the inventions which seem to spring up naturally to supply something missing in the story' (Wedgwood, *The Trial of Charles I*, p. 202).

www.ingramcontent.com/pod-product-compliance
Lightning Source LLC
Chambersburg PA
CBHW070524090426
42735CB00013B/2860